Ghosts of the Glory Trail

*"The Foundations of States are laid upon
the Graves of Pioneers."*

Ghosts of the Glory Trail

〚 Intimate glimpses into the past and
present of 275 Western Ghosttowns 〛

By NELL MURBARGER

Cover design by Roy Purcell

NEVADA PUBLICATIONS
4135 Badger Circle,
Reno, Nevada 89519

Printed in the United States of America
ISBN: 0-913814-59-8

Published by Stanley W. Paher
NEVADA PUBLICATIONS
4135 Badger Circle,
Reno, Nevada 89519
775-747-0800
spaher@sbcglobal.net

DEDICATED to my Father and Mother who taught me to love the out-of-doors, to respect old things and old people, to find peace in aloneness, and beauty everywhere.

THE AUTHOR

BORN AND REARED in the historic Black Hills country, made famous a generation earlier by Wild Bill Hickock, Calamity Jane, and other frontier notables, Nell Murbarger, as a child, was so fascinated by Western American history that she determined to make its researching and recording her life career. As a result of that decision, her travels in the territory west of the Rocky Mountains have extended over an estimated 250,000 miles in the past 30 years. She has recorded millions of words of notes, and has written about this fascinating Western region more than 1000 articles which have seen publication in 125 different periodicals. In recognition of this prodigious effort and the consistently high quality of her work, she is among the few American authors who have received the coveted Award of Merit conferred by American Association for State and Local History, in Washington, D.C. Additional top honors gave been accorded her material by California Association of Press Women, and National Federation of Press Women.

FOREWORD

E MPTY STREETS, wrapped in sage and silence, weary old buildings, drowsing in the sun; crumbling walls, and nameless graves, and a lone wind whispering through the night—this is a ghosttown, a mining camp that has had its day, has sung its song.

Looking on silent mills and cold chimneys, on streets undisturbed by the wheels of commerce, men find it easy to condemn such abandoned settlements as symbols of defeat or, even worse, as symbols of man's greed and perfidy; but this is wrong.

To stigmatize the western American ghosttown is to repudiate the pioneers responsible for its building—those men and women who traveled the Glory Trail into earth's dim corners, who wrested gold and silver and copper from lonely hills, and remained to fill lonely graves. That many of the towns they founded were destined to oblivion, is not important; it is only important that not even the smallest of those transitory camps was born wholly in vain.

However brief its hour of glory, each helped to break down the West's great barriers of Time and Distance.

However spectral its remaining ruins, each served as a stepping stone on the long, rough road to permanency and stability. . .

When the last man to have lived in these towns has staked his last claim on earth, still these Ghosts of the Glory Trail must stand symbolic of that shining, Never-to-Come-Again era, when giants strode through the land with man's greatest dream cradled in their hearts.

That this book may lead to better understanding of the frontier boom camp, and the period that sired it, is the hope of its author. . .

And now, credit where credit is due. . .

To everyone, everywhere, who has made available to my use old journals, diaries, ledgers, newspapers, unpublished manuscripts, clippings, correspondence, or other historic material; or who has given personal information, or otherwise assisted in supplying the material contained in this book, I extend my limitless gratitude.

In addition, I wish to thank especially Nevada State Historical Society, Reno; Nevada State Library, Carson City; and Utah State Historical Society, Salt Lake City, for unlimited use of historic archives and research facilities; and the county recorders of every Nevada county for the always cheerful manner in which they have borne my protracted researching through old newspaper files in their vault rooms.

Organizations and individuals who have permitted my use of treasured and historic photographs, include: Nevada State Historical Society, Reno,

Plates 23, 34, 35, 44, 45, 52, 53; Nevada State Highway Department, Plate 14; Douglas Robinson, Bishop, Calif., Plates 26, 28; Frank A. Goodale (deceased) Los Angeles, Plates 33, 40, 41 (from photos made originally by the pioneer Rawhide photographer, Ned E. Johnson); Elsie Fay Jumper, San Diego, Plate 47; J. L. Vandiver, Wells, Nev., Plate 54; Ed Green, Lovelock, Nev., Plate 51; Marye L. Moss, Bakersfield, Calif., Plate 16; Harry Wiley, (deceased) Gold Point, Nev., Plate 29. Map engravings of ghosttown areas, prepared by Norton Allen and published originally in *Desert Magazine,* have been made available to my use through the generosity of Randall Henderson, editor of *Desert Magazine.*

For permission to include in this book certain of my material originally used and copyrighted by them, I am indebted to the publishers of *Desert Magazine, Salt Lake Tribune, Sunset, True West, Popular Publications, Nevada State Journal, Scenic Southwest, Western Sportsman,* and *Long Beach Press Telegram.*

—And to my typist, LaRene Prowse, who often went beyond the call of duty in devoting midnight hours to tedious transcription of smudged notes and dim old records, and to typing and retyping this manuscript, I shall be forever grateful.

Without the aid of these wonderful folks—and all others who gave help and encouragement—this book could not have gone to press.

—NELL MURBARGER

Somewhere-in-the-Great Basin,
July 15, 1956.

CONTENTS

Illustrations

Maps

I

Ghost Country

BETWEEN THE Wasatch Mountains, of Utah, and the crest of California's Sierra Nevada, lies the Great Basin of the Intermountain West—a high, wide, wonderful land of few people, and far horizons, and cold, bright stars, and limitless sky.

It is also a land of ghosts—the Ghosts of the Glory Trail.

Every land on earth, every period of time, has known its deserted villages, but only the Western United States has propagated them in wholesale quantities. Sired by hope and suckled on honest labor, they were cities that flourished for a day, and faded, and were forgotten.

How many such ghosttowns there are in the West, or even in the Great Basin area, is impossible to say, but their number is far greater than is generally realized. Since I became interested in these old camps, about 30 years ago, I have visited and photographed more than 400 of them, and have collected historical material on nearly three times that many; yet, scarcely a week passes that I do not learn of other ghosttowns previously unknown to me.

That nearly every one of these towns began life as a mining camp, might seem to be an indictment of the mining industry and mining methods, but the blame lies elsewhere.

It lies in the cold, hard, inescapable truth that once mineral has been taken from the ground, there is nothing man can do to effect its replacement. Therefore, it follows that the states richest in mineral wealth must become, in turn, the states richest in ghosttowns—and that means The Great Basin.

If you've ever given any thought to these former boom camps, you may have wondered how they came into being, and what sort of folks lived in them, and why they were started, at all, if only to be abandoned in the end.

It's really very simple.

The pattern for the first Western American ghosttown was cut in California, as an aftermath of the Goldrush, of 1849. For every Argonaut made wealthy by that mad stampede, many others failed to connect with pay-dirt, and by the middle 1850s, hordes of disappointed gold-seekers were turning away from California's overcrowded diggings. Still trailing the Golden Fleece, they forged north into the Oregon wilderness, and south to Mexico. They crossed the Colorado river, into what is now Arizona; and they poured back over the Sierra Nevada into the Great Basin—the Great Unmapped.

As a group of prospecting partners made their way across mountains or desert—using their burros' tails for a compass, as the saying goes—they never lost sight of the fact that their quest was for precious metal. Along with pitting their wits against hostile Indians and daring heat and cold and thirst and starvation, they took time to pan the gravel of every stream, and to sample quartz ledges; and if they found "color," they staked claims and tested the ground until dwindling food stocks or depleted ammunition forced their return to the nearest settlement—a term that embraced a lot of territory in the Intermountain West of 1850 to 1880! A new mining strike might be made 100 miles from the nearest grocery store, 200 miles from a postoffice—a journey that involved many days of weary plodding over parched desert flats, and across stream beds where no water flowed.

Once back in what passed for civilization, our partners exhibited their ore samples and boasted. The "close-mouthed miner" is largely an imaginary product of 20th century fiction. The old timer was as garrulous as he was generous. When he had found a good thing, he wanted the whole wide world to know about it!

"Hell's fire, pardner—there's enough gold in that mountain for every man in Washoe! Come on—grab yourself a claim!"

It wasn't necessary to twist anyone's arm—they came!

If the ore proved to be rich and fairly plentiful, and a few glowing reports percolated to the outside world, there might even be a "rush" to the new strike.

We mid-20th-centurians, diddling around with our Geiger counters, and black lights, and "strategic minerals" that look more like road building material than anything else, can have little idea of the feverish excitement that attended every major mining stampede of 75 to 100 years ago.

Into remote lands, that for untold centuries had known only sagebrush and jackrabbits, suddenly would be flooding a tidal wave of seething humanity—prospectors, mining engineers, surveyors, opportunists, longline skinners, faro dealers, tradesmen, painted women of the night, bullwhackers, saloonkeepers, assayists, Chinese, Indians, Cousin Jacks, Yankees, Chileans, Mexicans—a roaring deluge drawn from every mining camp between Sonora and British Columbia and all bound for the same destination—the same Poor Man's Paradise! Jostling, shoving, boasting, quarreling, cursing, exhibiting ore samples and assay certificates, buying and selling "mines" without ever laying eyes on the property, fighting to purchase flour at $75 a sack and bacon at $3 a pound—fighting for a chance to pay a dollar a night for a pair of dirty blankets and space on the ground to roll them.

That was your mining stampede—a typically Western extravaganza, repeated over and over again, for a period of more than 60 years.

Nobody knew, of course, whether this newly-discovered district would be washed-up in two months, or would go on producing for two years or two centuries. The only possible manner in which the extent or value of an ore deposit might be determined, was to dig the ore out of the ground, mill it and sell the bullion, and count the money.

While that digging and milling was being accomplished, the miners and mill hands couldn't be expected to knock off work and travel 100 or 150 miles across country, every time one of them ran low on plug-cut or blasting powder. Furthermore, our frontier miner was distressingly human. He wanted to belly up to a bar, now and then, and h'ist a few. He wanted to break the killing grind of his labor with an occasional fling at faro or blackjack, and he had a strange hankering for naughty, painted women— maybe because they reminded him of nice, *unpainted* women he had left behind in Kansas and Ohio. What was more important, our miner had hard money in his jeans—likely more money than he had ever known— and he was willing to pay double what his "state-side" brother would have given for the same stock in trade.

The only practical solution to these sundry problems was to start a new town at the scene of discovery.

It was easily done. Pitching his tent, the purveyor of wet goods turned a wagon box on its side to serve as a bar, and installed as stock and equipment a barrel of rot-gut whiskey and half a dozen tin cups. Assayists and Chinese laundrymen hung out their shingles. Someone began serving meals; someone started a livery stable.

Many such towns never progressed beyond the tent stage—"Rag Towns" they were called. But if the district held up encouragingly, the tents would be succeeded by wooden buildings; eventually, by brick and stone. The population of the camp would come to embrace several thousand persons—women and children, as well as men. Hotels and banks would be built. Newspapers and volunteer fire companies would be founded, lodges chartered, schools and churches organized.

Everything would zip along handsomely for two years, ten years, maybe for even 30 years. But at last, would come a day when astute citizens of the camp would begin to realize that the old town was losing her bounce. Some of her ledges were petering out, mills were no longer working at capacity, more passengers were riding the outbound stages than were arriving.

When the handwriting appeared on the wall, the wise ones got out— and soon!

Some camps died slowly, painfully, surrendering one at a time their courthouse, their schools, their railroad service, newspapers, prestige. Other camps went "Pouf!" like a candle flame in the wind.

Regardless of how they died, grief that attended their passing was not prolonged.

So the old camp was through? So, what the hell! Over on the Reese River, up in the Rubies, down in the Pintwater range, Somebody knew Somebody Else who had found gold nuggets big as cabbage heads and seams of native silver half as wide as the Humboldt river!

Sure, she'd been a good camp! But this new strike, pardner—this new strike'll beat her forty ways from Sunday!

The king was dead—long live the king!

After the major mines and mills of a district had closed, and the bulk of a camp's population had streamed away, business houses were abandoned—heavier merchandise still on their shelves. Fancy pianos and solid oak furniture—brought in by ox-team or mule back—were left behind as being unworthy of high freighting costs. Pack rats set up shop in grocery stores, birds began nesting in mahogany bars and crystal chandeliers, and greasewood and sage crept back into streets where gunplay and ribaldry had echoed. Peace, like a wooley blanket, settled over the town; and a lonely wind came to whisper around broken windows, and run its gaunt fingers over cold chimneys, and silent graves.

Another ghosttown had been born—another ghosttown for me to prowl.

They call me The Roving Reporter of the Desert. It's a good life. I'm my own boss. I'm not tied to a desk in a stuffy office; I'm seldom required to meet a deadline, and I haven't punched a timeclock in more than 20 years. Most of my work is done in the back country—the big empty spaces on the map, where the roads are thin, spidery lines, marked "Unimproved." Most writers, I presume, find such places a little too remote for their liking, so I have the field pretty well to myself.

I travel alone. My transportation, as well as my "office" and haven in time of storm, is provided by a ten-year-old Mercury sedan. Loaded with my bedroll and mess box, a five-gallon can of water, a few desert clothes, and my typewriter and cameras, it carries me an average of 15,000 miles each year—much of that distance over rocky roads and steep, dim trails that would scare the wheels off any of their shiny new models! It's a good car—as faithful as a burro. It takes me where I want to go and brings me back; and if it is no longer an important looking car it doesn't matter, because I don't claim to be an important writer.

I don't go out for "spot news." Now and then, by accident, I stumble over some "big" story and, of course, I cover it. But, given any choice in the matter, I prefer to leave the banner-line stuff to ambitious young men who can go without sleep for a week and still dash around aggressively, with vigilant gleams in their eyes and press cards stuck in their hat bands. They're welcome to the glory and glamour—along with the aspirin and bicarb; and while they're burning up the wires to hit the "early" edition, I'll go rolling merrily along my unambitious and unimportant way, writing unimportant stories about the little people in little towns 200 miles from any place known to the New York *Times*—the *Little People,* whose hearts and souls are as big as the wide land in which they live.

Cooking my meals on a campfire, sleeping under the stars wherever night overtakes me—pausing, now and then, to do a little prospecting or fishing—I ramble over the Intermountain country, visiting with sheepherders and fossil hunters, and turquoise miners, and cattlemen. I interview "oldest inhabitants" and the descendants of early pioneers, and dig out stories about desert folks who have gotten into trouble, or out of trouble, or have discovered a bigger or better Something, or an older Something Else.

Most especially, I write about the Ghosts of the Glory Trail, the boom camps that have shriveled into ghosttowns, and about the men and women I find living in these loneliest of lonely places. I write about ghosttowns because they fascinate me and I like to visit them; and because editors and their subscribers like to read about them—possibly because they seem to symbolize every stirring frontier episode since the storied days of Forty-Nine. Here, in the reality of splintered boards and crumbled stone is The Spot Where It Happened—where guns blazed, and men died, and life was rugged, and history was made.

Whenever I learn of an old camp I haven't visited, Conscience never stops nagging until I go there! Roads to such towns, in many cases, have lain unused for so many years that they've grown completely impassible to wheeled vehicles. In such circumstances I scout around for a packhorse or mule I can borrow, or I hang a knapsack and canteen on my back, and strike out afoot.

After scrambling over rocks and ruts and through desert brush for maybe half a day without seeing another person—I at last sight something definitely old and definitely man-made!

My introductory glimpse of the old town may be the tall silent chimney of a long-deserted mill; or it may be the crumbling walls of a big stone hotel, or the fallen headboards and fancy carved palings of an old cemetery plot.

Regardless of the form in which it comes, my first sight of a "new" ghosttown, invariably brings with it a quickening of the pulse, a tremor of excitement, and chilling thrill of anticipation that I wouldn't trade for any other thrill the world affords!

As soon as this initial excitement has spent itself, I get down to work.

Like a detective on the trail of a clue, I begin searching through the rubble—through the ruins of offices and banks and gambling halls that may have been standing deserted for more than half a century! I look for old letters and newspapers and pictures and canceled checks, and any other documents of historical worth; and before leaving the town, I photograph every structure of importance or interest, and make a complete record of every inscription appearing on grave markers. Later, as time permits, I will run down leads concerning former residents of the town, or their descendants, and spend days browsing through musty old newspaper files and other official records at the county seat.

Some of the more accessible ghosttowns still harbor a few inhabitants. Romanticists like to picture these last survivors as "die-hards" who have remained loyal to their respective camps because of a belief that the ore is still there and that someday the old town will stage a "come-back." Personally, I don't think many of these folks entertain such a hope. I think they simply stay on in the old towns for lack of anything better to do, and because they're old, themselves, and it's all the home they know. Many of them have a little mine back in the hills—a hungry little tunnel they've worked for a coon's age, and which still supplies them with beans and bacon and, once in a long while, with a new pair of boots and a few sticks of dynamite.

But even these "last survivors" are disappearing fast. Some camps have but a single resident; most of them have none.

I never met the last inhabitant of Candelaria, Nevada. As a matter of fact, I've never even learned his name—but I'm sure he would have been a nice fellow to know!

He had lived in a little shack below one of the mines and had contrived a simple irrigation system, using run-off water from the mine tunnel. At time of my first visit to Candelaria, in 1947, his canals and laterals were still faintly visible, but his water supply had failed long before and the bushes and trees in his yard were as dead as the old camp. Skeletons of apple trees, and peaches and apricots, stood brittle and dry —their naked, gray branches rattling in the hot desert wind. Over the tumbled down porch of the cabin climbed the thorny dead vines of what had been a rambler rose, and tall gaunt stems of dead hollyhocks stood in the parched yard, where even weeds had ceased to grow.

The old man evidently had lived there alone for many years after the mines and mills had closed and the camp had ceased to operate. It was evident, too, that he had been a methodical chap, for on the inside of his cabin door he had penciled in a cramped and palsied hand the dates and figures he considered memorable—when his first peaches and strawberries had ripened each year, how many pounds of plums he had harvested; the date his mockingbirds had hatched, and how many bouquets of flowers he had given to friends from Mina and Luning.

But now, the trees were dead, and the old man was dead. A lonely wind rattled the cabin door and tugged fretfully at the rusted stovepipe on the roof; and not even the old graveyard across the ravine was more pregnant with ghosts than this lifeless garden that had once bloomed in barren soil.

Sometimes, when I'm sitting alone beside my campfire in one of these old places, and the night is big and black, and frightfully still, it almost seems as if the Present is subordinated to the Past, and that the dead are closer and more real than the living. I have a strange feeling that the warmth of my campfire is being shared by all the misty, shadowy men who have peopled the Great Basin since history's beginning—Indians and fur trappers, Mormons, miners, good men and bad, slayers and slain — all those marching legions who have lived and loved and died, and gone to forgotten graves. All are an indivisible part of this rugged land, and I'm fiercely proud to be a part of it, too; a small and insignificant part, but a part.

I'm proud of The Basin, and its heritage. I'm proud of its terrifying immensity of broken mountains and purple gorges, of sage and sun and sky, and infinite space. Ranging my eyes over its vastness, I want to square my shoulders, and stand tall, and shout into the teeth of the wind, "This is my land!"

That it has been my privilege to salvage a few crumbs of that land's rich history, is one of the great satisfactions of my life.

2

"Richest Region on God's Footstool"

IN THE HIGH, remote mountains of northern Nevada, summer is one of the grandest experiences man can know. For a few fleeting weeks between the grudgingly-departed snows of June and the hurrying snows of September, all the gaunt hills are pulsing with promise, every canyon is fresh and Bible new—and the old village of Unionville is near to being a paradise on earth.

Scarcely more than a rifle shot west of town rise the dark, pine-forested peaks of the Humboldt range, their 9000-foot summits buried deeply in white. Born high in those trackless snowfields, Buena Vista creek takes its way through the heart of the settlement—chuckling around worn boulders, tossing its icy spray over watercress and wild roses, and washing the mossy roots of huge, old cottonwoods.

Late June finds the wild chokecherry thickets heavy with fragrance, and the pungent spiciness of sage and juniper drifting down from sun-warmed slopes. Ancient apple trees are white with bloom, and the soft dust of the old stageroad is patterned with tracks of quail and chukar partridges, and the pawprints of chipmunks and cottontails.

For more than two miles along Unionville's winding main street rise time-mellowed adobe walls, and old stone fireplaces. Wide verandas are wrapped in leafy bowers of Virginia creeper and honeysuckle, and lichen-grown fences are twined with thorny masses of old-fashion roses—Queen Bess and Cherokees, and Yellow Moss.

But the walls of Unionville are crumbled, her verandas are sagging, her chimneys cold. Gardens and pathways bear the stigma of neglect and deserted homes speak of long years passed since they were tended by loving hands.

All this because Unionville is a ghosttown. Her store buildings are empty of stores, her mine tunnels stand silent. The spooky black mill at the head of main street is draped in cobwebs and tenanted by bats; and where thousands of men once followed the lure of treasure, only five homes were occupied in July, 1953.

I had gone to Unionville to get a story from the Clarence Ernsts who were reopening the old *Arizona* silver mine as a scheelite producer. In the course of our conversation I learned that Mrs. Ernst was a native of

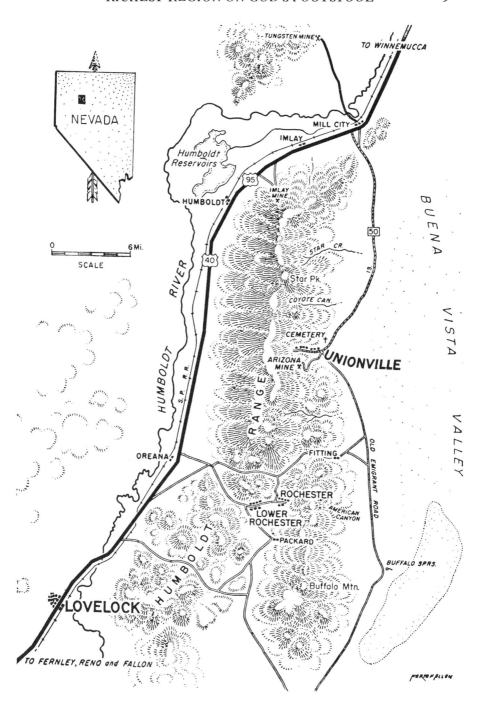

Unionville, and had lived there more than 60 years. When I began to question her about the early history of the place, however, she shook her head.

"I'm not the one to give you the story of Unionville," she laughed. "That will have to come from 'Grandma' Leonard. Grandma has lived here 85 years, and her parents and grandfather lived here before she was born. She can tell you anything you want to know about the town . . ."

The Leonard home was old—probably as old as most of the abandoned dwellings I had passed along the street—but it possessed a comfortable, lived-in look that the others lacked. There were checked curtains at the windows, tulips were blooming in the garden, and from the old chimney curled a friendly plume of wood smoke.

Martha Leonard, tiny and white-haired, listened alertly as I explained my interest in the town.

"Yes," she nodded, "it's true that I've lived in Unionville 85 years; yet, I'm afraid I can't help you a lot, because I was only a lass when the boom ended. But come in the house," the old lady added, with a bright, quick smile. "We'll have some milk and cookies, and I'll tell you what I can . . ."

For three hours I sat making notes at the oilcloth-covered table in the Leonard kitchen. All that while a robin was chirping in a tree by the open window, and a little clock on the wall was ticking away the time; but of these sounds I was only dimly aware. For the most part I was lost in the story being unfolded by this little "first lady" of Unionville. What did it matter that much of that story dealt with events not witnessed personally, but only heard from the lips of parents and grandparents? When one is groping back into history over more than half the life span of the United States of America, it is a rare privilege even to "shake the hand that shook the hand."

When rumors of rich silver deposits in the Humboldt range were brought to Virginia City in the spring of 1860, a dozen families took leave of that overcrowded district and set out for the new prospect, more than 100 miles to the north. Summer brought them to the mouth of a pleasant canyon in the north flank of the Humboldt range, and there, alongside a perpetual stream of clear, cold water, they founded the town of Humboldt City. A little way to the north flowed the Humboldt river—largest waterway in Nevada—and between the river and the new settlement lay the great East-West emigrant trail, then still traveled by endless queues of covered wagons and plodding ox teams. In the nearby hills grew adequate timber for building purposes, and wild game was abundant.

But Humboldt Canyon did not prove to be over-stocked with precious metals, and in the spring of 1861 there departed from that place a prospecting party composed of Capt. Hugo Pfersdorff, J. C. Hannan, four Paiute Indians and two burros. Gaining the crest of the mountains, the party looked down on a stream-watered canyon that broke away toward the east. It was a canyon so beautiful they gave it the Spanish name, Buena Vista—"Good View"; and when they found in those environs rich croppings of silver ore, the men hastened back to Humboldt City with news of their discovery.

By July 4 of that year, Buena Vista canyon had attracted settlers in sufficient number that an Independence Day celebration was held, and three days later the present site of Unionville was platted. As a means of awakening civic responsibility, a choice building site was offered, cost free, to every man who would contribute two days work on the public road, and on his assigned lot would make improvements to a value of $50.

At the time of Unionville's founding, the Comstock was shining as a star of first magnitude, but even in Virginia City were many who had failed to connect with a major bonanza. With all these lads spoiling for a second chance at the purse of Fortunatus, every rumor of a new discovery sent hopes zooming aloft and launched copywriters into stratospheric flights of fancy. By the magic potion of printers' ink, more than one mediocre strike had been transformed into a glittering Golconda that threatened to upset the economic balance of the world, and before the mines in Buena Vista canyon had produced even one wagonload of ore, the *Territorial Enterprise,* of Virginia City, had conferred upon the new district its benediction.

"I shall express an honest opinion based on a thorough examination," wrote the mining reporter of the *Enterprise.* "Humboldt county is the richest mineral region upon God's footstool! Each mountain range is gorged with precious ore! The other day an assay of mere croppings yielded $4000 to the ton! A week or two ago, an assay of just such surface development made a return of $7000 to the ton! Each day, and almost every hour, reveals new and startling evidence of the profuse and intensified wealth. . . . Have no fears of the mineral resources of Humboldt county. They are incalculable!"

And all the way from Salt Lake to San Francisco and Seattle, rang the clarion cry, "Ho! for the Humboldt!"

Among the first to answer that challenge were A. W. Oliver, newly-appointed probate judge for Humboldt county, and W. H. Clagget, attorney-at-law. Purchasing a team and wagon, the men set forth from Carson City in December, 1861. Accompanying them was Sam Clemens, a 26-year-old newspaper reporter, who would become more famous after adopting the pseudonym, Mark Twain.

"On the fifteenth day," according to Mark's account of the trip, as described in his volume, *Roughing It,* "we completed our march of two hundred miles and entered Unionville, Humboldt county, in the midst of a driving snow storm. Unionville consisted of eleven cabins and a liberty pole. . . . The rest of the landscape was made up of bleak mountain walls that rose so high into the sky from both sides of the canyon that the village was left, as it were, far down in the bottom of a crevice.

"We built a small, rude cabin in the side of the crevice and roofed it with canvas, leaving a corner open to serve as a chimney. It was very cold weather and fuel was scarce. . . ."

By the summer of 1863, there had been erected in the new camp more than 300 cabins, and new claim seekers were arriving at an average rate of 150 each week. Ground had been staked from the alkaline sink at the mouth of the canyon to the white crest of the Humboldts, and a mining recorder and seven deputies were busy recording claims.

Until permanent dwellings might be constructed, many of the emigrants erected brush shelters, or slept under their wagons and cooked their meals on open campfires. Extra stages and light rigs were pressed into service to accommodate those who could not obtain passage on regular stages; and before her second birthday, the new town had become a bustling frontier settlement with an assessed valuation of $187,763, and had been designated seat of newly-organized Humboldt county—then an empire nearly as large as all New England. Flanking the single narrow street that twisted for four miles through the canyon, were 18 stores, including general mercantiles, meat markets, pharmacies, and jewelry stores. There also were nine saloons and a brewery, two hotels, two express offices, four livery stables, a dentist, and a newspaper.

One of the next signs of urbanity to appear in the frontier settlement, was a schoolhouse. Built in August, 1863, of adobe brick the building was utilized for sundry purposes in addition to dissemination of the Three Rs.

Political conventions, dances, church services and sessions of the town board were held in it, as were meetings of the Masonic and Oddfellows lodges, and Sons of Temperance. Neither creed nor color, nor politics, constituted a barrier to the hall's usage. During Civil war years it provided a headquarters for both the strong Union League, and for Southern sympathizers who were soundly organized as Knights of the Golden Circle, and Sons of Liberty. When not otherwise occupied, the building served as drill ground and armory for the Unionville post of Buena Vista Guards—a smartly uniformed group of volunteer militiamen who lent their impressive presence to all patriotic celebrations and parades, and once in a while, even rode forth in pursuit of renegade Indians.

Although a Sunday School had been organized as early as 1862, and religious services were conducted more or less regularly, by visiting pastors, Unionville never had but one church. This was a creditable structure built under the stewardship of the Rev. L. Ewing, a reformed California gambler, and with the heavy financial support of J. C. Fall, Unionville's leading merchant and owner of the Arizona mine.

"But Mr. Ewing soon was called elsewhere," said Grandma Leonard. "After he left it wasn't long until the church building was sold and moved to Mill City where it was converted into a men's clubhouse and saloon. Sometime later, the 450-pound bell which had been bought by public subscription, was taken down to Star Ranch, where it was used for years to call the ranch hands to meals.

"I don't know just why, but Unionville never had another church . . ."

Even in view of this fact, Unionville was scarcely a city of the damned. She still had her good works and refining influences. She still had her Sons of Temperance.

Among the treasured heirlooms I was privileged to examine at the Ernst home were the old record books of this organization and a copy of its Constitution, Code of Laws and By-Laws—a set of regulations as grim as the ferries of Charon.

First two purchases noted in the treasurer's account embraced a total of $52 dispatched to San Francisco for "emblems, muslin &c for regalia." Numerous other expenses were incurred in the course of equipping the meeting hall; bills approved including $11.50 for stovepipe, plus additional appropriations covering tacks, whitewash, lime, alum, seats, curtains, lock for door, three pounds of candles, and 36 balls for balloting.

There were scoffers, naturally, who had the temerity to allege that not all the Sons of Temperance lived up to their code; but in view of the prices charged them for living commodities, it seems incredible that Unionville's citizens could afford to be anything other than temperate!

Milled lumber, for example, was almost prohibitive in price. Newspapers of the period quote dimension stock at $250 to $300 per M, but the Ernsts have records to show that lumber used in their two-story dwelling was ox-freighted to Unionville at a laid-down cost of one dollar per foot!

Roofing posed another great problem. A visitor to the Unionville courthouse found rain pouring unimpeded through the roof while the county clerk sat huddled with his records in one corner of his office.

"In that corner," wrote the visitor, "the rain didn't fall any thicker than it did outside."

Several months later, the county commissioners leased a former saloon with "concrete" roof as temporary location for the county offices. With beginning of the new rainy season it was found that the so-called "concrete" roof consisted of only a thin layer of lime and sand spread on canvas, the same providing about as much protection as muslin. Not until the practice of thatching was introduced by emigrant miners from Europe was the problem partially solved. Coarse wild rye grass from the bottom lands—the thatching material preferred by these artisans—was tied in bundles Old World fashion, laid butts-down on the roof, and bound in place with rawhide thongs. Properly assembled, such a roof was considered superior to shingles for excluding wind, snow, rain or dust.

But the annoyance of leaking roofs was not the No. 1 problem in Unionville. First rank in that regard was held by the bogie of transportation.

Beginning with the day and hour of her founding, Unionville had suffered from the malady of remoteness.

During fledgling years of the camp, practically all "outside" commodities were ox-freighted from Red Bluff, California, by way of Honey Lake—the summer of 1863 seeing ox-drawn freight wagons arriving in Unionville at the rate of a dozen or more daily. The Red Bluff *Independent,* in June of that year described the departure of 40 teams of oxen loaded with supplies for the Humboldt towns, and it was stated that a single flour mill at Red Bluff had shipped to Unionville 85 tons of flour! Freight rates varied from 7 to 14 cents per pound.

Nearest settlement larger than Unionville, herself, was Virginia City —35 hours distant by the fastest transportation available. Passenger fare between the two mining centers ran as high as $50 for one-way passage. Even mail service was costly. Under terms of a contract entered into with Wells, Fargo and company, in the winter of 1863, mail matter was carried between Unionville and Virginia City at a fee of 25 cents per pound. During the year following, mail transportation was expedited by the inauguration of a tri-weekly pony express between Idaho City, Idaho, and Virginia City, by way of the Humboldt towns. When the pony riders began delivering to Unionville the previous day's issue of Comstock newspapers, the isolated camp in Buena Vista canyon began to feel at last a oneness with civilization.

The year 1864 also brought the opening of telegraph service between Unionville and the outside world; and two years later, local communications were further facilitated when Lobenstein's Pony Express established a once-weekly service from Star City to Oreana, via Unionville, Limerick and Etna.

All this while, a bloody Civil War was raging in the East and partisanship was a sore issue in the canyon. With Loyalists living in "Upper Town" and Southern sympathizers in "Lower Town," (or "Dixie" as it was known) a buffer strip alluded to as "Centerville" stretched between the two hot-beds like a miniature Mason-Dixon line. A horse-drawn stage made hourly trips from one end of town to the other.

Possibly no event in the history of the town was acclaimed more heartily than was the birth of Humboldt county's first news medium, *The Humboldt Register.*

As the first ink-wet copies of the new journal were lifted from the press on the starry evening of May 3, 1863, a rifle brigade led by Unionville's silver cornet band formed ranks in front of the office and fired a rousing salvo of nine blasts. The Magnolia Saloon, at Carson City, had donated a case of champagne to brighten the festivities and by midnight the new publication had been toasted by innumerable rounds of fizz-water and 34 anvil salutes!

Even Editor W. J. Forbes considered this Unionville accolade one of the finest he had received in his entire career—and Editor Forbes' career had embraced a great many boom camps and many newspapers.

Just as there were boomers who responded to every new strike in the hope of annexing a bonanza, so there were other boomers who flocked to the new camps to deal faro and to shoe horses, to sling hash, and repair gunshot wounds—and some came to edit newspapers.

Editor Forbes was a newspaper boomer. Wherever a spectacular mining strike brought about the founding of a new town, Forbes—or one of his transitory brethren— appeared on the scene as miraculously as frogs after a rainstorm. With a battered Washington hand press and a couple of cases of type set up in a ragged tent or hillside dugout, the boom camp editor took a chew of tobacco or a slug of O Be Joyful, picked up his composing stick, and dedicated himself to filling "the long-felt need" of some shirttail camp a couple of months removed from bare desert.

In the opinion of Editor Forbes, the "long-felt need" of Unionville was culture. To that end, he set out to bring to the raw camp some of the finer things of life.

Early issues of the *Register,* (now preserved among the priceless archives of Nevada State Historical Society, at Reno) exhibit a front page wholly devoted to poems, essays, and gems from the classics. Were the subscriber interested in such uncouth affairs as murders, lynchings, fires, mining strikes, or other news of local origin, he might locate same on Page 3. National and state releases appeared on Page 2, and all advertisements were relegated to Page 4—the back page.

Forbes' make-up might be cock-eyed, his presswork mediocre and news sense atrocious—but in his piquant editorials, his star went into its ascendency. Writing under the *nom de plume, "Semblins,"* the frontier editor dipped his barbs in vitriolic wit and perfumed them with satire; and years before Mark Twain popularized the same style of writing, "Semblins Sayings" in the little *Humboldt Register,* of Unionville, Nevada Territory, were being copied and quoted by the metropolitan press from New York to San Francisco.

Lamenting the trials of building construction at Unionville, Forbes censored the policy of importing second quality lumber. "Half of it," he wrote, "is just what it is cracked up to be. The other half is knot . . ." Another time he attacked the matter of local firewood and hay, deploring his inability to distinguish between them. "Some of the firewood," he pointed out, "is so puny, and some of the hay so coarse . . ."

Editor Forbes also had his fun at the expense of the mining sharpsters. While numerous mines of the district were in legitimate production a great many others were no more than names on location notices and stock certificates in the pockets of promoters. Taking it upon himself to expose these frauds, the acrimonious editor expressed pretended fear of widespread hardship and multiple drownings when the rainy season got under way.

As basis for these fears, he pointed out that owners of certain speculative mining properties, who then had been "operating" in the canyon for two years, had not yet driven their tunnels in far enough to protect themselves from the rain!

In this connection, he proposed the adoption of a new state seal, suggesting it should show a mountain "with good croppings and float; in the mountainside an untaxable hole in the ground, six inches deep; nearby, a cedar tree; under its shade, two miners with a pack of cards, working assessments . . ."

After he had perused his weekly copy of *The Register*—had fully assimilated its cultural and social messages and laughed himself into a tizzy over Semblins' latest *bon mot*—the 90-years-ago citizen of Unionville could pick his choice of sundry amusements.

Practically any occasion from a new baby to a strike of highgrade was sufficient grounds for a parade, or a "Grand Ball."

Such balls were definitely blue-chip, the tickets generally selling from $5 up. One of the most brilliant celebrations in the life of the community was the Grand Military and Civic Ball which served as a kick-off for the Independence Day celebration of 1863. Starting at Unionville on the evening of July 3—with tickets at $8 each—the affair continued throughout the night. On the day following, all participants moved *en masse* to Star City, a few miles north of Unionville, and the celebration blazed onward with appropriate exercises, orations, feasting, rifle salutes, anvil salutes, and stirring martial selections by the silver cornet band. Climaxing the soiree was another all-night ball, in Star City.

With the nation's freedom and independence fittingly honored and democracy made safe for another year, the aching heads of Unionville trailed down Star Canyon and homeward as the sun was breaking over Buena Vista valley on the morning of July 5.

While celebrations of this magnitude transpired but once yearly, weekly dances were routine affairs, and nearly every issue of the *Register* carried announcements of band concerts, cake socials, literaries, foot races and jumping contests. Horse races were a popular event, as was a primitive sort of football played with a beef's bladder covered with buckskin. Whatever the issue, betting was active.

Fishing and duck hunting excursions (generally to Humboldt Lake) not only provided sport but fattened the larders of the populace. Small parties of three to six men, well fortified with what Editor Forbes called "well chosen spirits," would absent themselves from town for a few days and upon returning would bring back with them hundreds of fat ducks.

Whether due to the editor's cultural regimen or other reasons, Unionville was never an especially lawless camp. It had its killings, to be sure; but not in sufficient number that they became monotonous.

Due to lack of a jail in the earlier years of the camp, it was customary to remand prisoners to the custody of the sheriff. The sheriff, thereupon, pulled down a nice little bowl of gravy by feeding and guarding such lawbreakers at a cost to the county of $12 per day, per prisoner.

This custom, needless to say, had its critics. On one occasion the sheriff was charged with the safekeeping of a penny-ante burglar who had been shopping in Kraft's store one night after closing hours. There being no immediate prospect of a grand jury session, Editor Forbes suggested it would be better to let the prisoner go free than to hold him and further boost the county's indebtedness at the rate of $12 per diem. The prisoner, apparently concurring in this opinion, a few days later slipped his guard, stole a $250 horse, and blew town.

Even after Unionville progressed to the point of owning a bastille, its crackerbox-type construction was practically a guarantee that any prisoner who ran afoul of it would not be among those present when his day of judgment rolled around.

("Once when I was a small girl, a group of angry-looking men marched past our house with a prisoner they had taken from the jail," said Grandma Leonard. "They went on up the canyon . . . and when they came back, a few minutes later, the prisoner wasn't with them. Little girls, in those days, weren't supposed to know about such things, of course, but I remember folks whispering about a lynching . . .")

Time, meanwhile, had been marching on. The Civil war had ended, slavery had been abolished. The nation was mourning a martyred president, the Ku-Klux Klan had been organized, and the second Atlantic Cable laid. It was, in other words, 1866, and Unionville was five years old.

But Unionville—"the richest mineral region upon God's footstool"— was not happy. Elsewhere Progress might be swinging her mighty lantern, but Unionville still groped in the dark ages. For virtually every commodity she ate or drank, for every stitch of clothing on her back, for the powder and drill steel to blast her mountains and the machinery to operate her mills, Unionville still waited until plodding oxen—traveling at ten miles a day, and less—had dragged heavy freight wagons half way across California and a third of the distance across Nevada.

In 1864, the point of departure for the Humboldt towns began shifting from Red Bluff to Chico, 40 miles to the south, but any advantage in diminished time or cost was negligible. Freight rates continued high, and prices, as a consequence, were terrific. Unionville grocers, in 1866, were selling Sacramento Valley wheat flour at 12 cents a pound—nearly two-thirds of which price represented freight costs from California! Sugar was 40 to 45 cents a pound; honey, 75 cents. Kerosene—except for candles, the only means of lighting—was $4 a gallon. Candles were $8.50 a box.

Commodities produced locally, on the other hand, were fairly reasonable. Local eggs were bringing $1 a dozen—a ghastly figure by "back East" standards—but Unionville housewives considered such a price in the light of a bargain. They could remember, three years earlier, when the only hen-fruit available in local stores had been freighted from Honey Lake Valley, in California, and sold in the Humboldt towns at $2.50 a dozen! Locally grown potatoes, could be had at four cents a pound, and the best grade beef at 12 to 18 cents.

But man needs more than beef and eggs and potatoes to develop a new empire. He needs steel and copper and lumber, and blasting powder and boots, and a thousand-and-one other articles he cannot wrest from the bare hills. Almost since the day of her founding, Unionville's citizens had realized that their one escape from this beartrap of transportation lay in the acquiring of rail facilities, and with 1866, that long-awaited deliverance appeared to be near at hand!

The Central Pacific was building east from Sacramento toward a junction with the Union Pacific, then pushing west from the Missouri river. Although the exact route to be followed across Nevada by the new road had not been announced publicly, construction crews already were drilling tunnels in the vicinity of Donner Pass. Any school boy, with a five-cent footrule, could show that a straight line drawn from that point to Ogden, Utah, would pass but a few miles to the south of Unionville.

If love laughs at locksmiths, how equally true that hope laughs at logic; and how easy for the hopeful to bend that straight line only the barest trifle, so that these life-giving rails took their way through the broad Buena Vista valley, at the mouth of the canyon!

Certainly, it was an attractive card to draw to.

To occupy her time as she waited for the railroad, Unionville continued to hammer at her mountains. She toiled and sweated and grew callouses on her hands—but she didn't grow rich. This circumstance, in large measure, was due to the fact that freight tariffs and other contributing causes made ore milling in the Humboldt region terrifically expensive.

Under methods then employed, the milling of silver ore required great quantities of wood to generate the steam power whereby the stamps were operated. Advance predictions of the *Territorial Enterprise* notwithstanding, little of Unionville's ore was rich enough to enable paying $12.50 a cord for cedar or mountain mahogany with which to mill it.

Seeking an escape from this wood dilemma, J. C. Fall, owner of the *Arizona* mine, began in desperation to experiment with the use of sagebrush for fuel. Despite the tediousness of cutting and feeding the small, twisted limbs, Fall proved that the results from $4.50 expended in procuring sage were equal to, or better, than $12.50 spent for cordwood. With efficiency of the substitute fuel proven, other mills followed suit and within a few years, nearly every boiler in the area was being fired with sagebrush.

During seasons of heavy run-off, the water power available from Buena Vista creek also was used to supplement the steam power; but even with every expedient that could be employed, prevailing conditions made it impossible to cut milling charges below $50 to $60 per ton of ore. Unless he had a mine that was exceedingly rich, no man could afford to pay such a cost.

But all this, of course, would be changed—when the railroad came!

As he followed his veins and crushed his ore, and looked forward to a shining future, probably not a man in Unionville ever imagined that the camp's days were numbered. Or, if any had the intuition to realize that the end might be nearing, certainly they could not have foreseen the nature of the axe that would lay them low.

How could Unionville know that her prosperity was linked inseparably with the Concord coach and the ox-team and would pass, even as they passed? How could she know that her doom would be sealed by the very transportation progress for which she was striving?

First intimation of such development came on that black day when the canyon town learned that the Central Pacific had been routed to by-pass her! Instead of delivering the world to her waiting feet, its rails were being laid to follow the Humboldt river, on the far side of the mountain. To Unionville, this knowledge came as a blow almost beyond weathering; yet, it was only the first in a mounting series of losses.

The next blow came from a burgeoning settlement on the Humboldt, 50 miles to the north. If the town of Winnemucca had cherished any notions concerning the courthouse she had been wise enough to keep them to herself until 1869 when the new railroad neatly bisected her backyard. On the basis of this important development, the river town immediately launched a drive to acquire the Humboldt county seat.

It was a battle viciously fought. Each time the matter of moving the courthouse was brought to a vote, every man in Unionville rallied to defeat the issue. Convinced, at last, that she could not annex the county plum by means of the ballot box, Winnemucca carried the matter to the state legislature. Throwing everything she had into the fight, Unionville again defeated the attempt, but Winnemucca only girded her loins and had the bill reintroduced. This time, the issue was passed over Unionville's protests.

On the grounds that state interference in county politics was unconstitutional, Unionville filed an injunction to prevent the removal of county records to Winnemucca, but upon reaching the Supreme Court, in 1873, the suit was rejected, and the triumphant river town carried off the prize.

Already demoralized by the railroad's snub and a disastrous fire which had destroyed one entire block of her business district, this added loss was more than Unionville could weather. With exception of the *Arizona,* other mines of the district had not been notable for their yield. With scuttling of the silver market, even the great *Arizona* was forced to close, and Unionville began to die on the vine.

Among those not present for the deathbed scene was Editor Forbes.

With the keen perception necessarily possessed by chronic boomers, Forbes possibly had foreseen the impending retrogression. In any case, he had sold *The Register* in 1867, and had headed for a new strike across the mountains.

Moving restlessly from boomcamp to boomcamp, the old Fourth Estater eventually had found himself on the downgrade. Spiritually, physically, mentally and financially, he was slipping.

Groping desperately for any port in the gathering storm, Forbes had quit the publishing field to open a barroom.

"Out of twenty men," he had written on that occasion, "nineteen patronize the saloon for every one who reads a newspaper. I am going to follow the crowd . . ."

But, of course, it was useless to think that the creator of "Semblins" could stay away from printers' ink any more than a dyed-in-the-wool prospector can pass an outcrop without taking a sample. So, another year had found Forbes again drifting aimlessly from town to town. In the course of time he had reached Battle Mountain, and there had founded the *Measure for Measure*.

The new journal was not a success. Not only did it lose money from its first issue, but local regard for it never was especially high. In view of the trifling amount of advertising the sheet contained, it was an unending source of wonder that Forbes could manage to pay for even his ink and print paper, let alone buy enough food to sustain life in his emaciated frame.

And then came a morning in 1875 when it was realized that the old newspaper man had not been seen on the streets for several days.

Friends who investigated found his body slumped across his ragged bed in the cold, filthy hovel he had come to call home.

Old, hungry, ill, weary of life, and overwhelmed by the spectre of failure, W. J. Forbes had found the prospect of further living more terrifying than death by his own hand.

Or, possibly, this talented Nevada journalist never had entertained much fear of the Grim Reaper. Less than ten years earlier, he had written: "Death cannot be a matter of much moment to an editor; a local incident, a short, quick breath . . ."

Another five years and the mining camp in Buena Vista Canyon was breathing that same "quick breath."

In 1880, with the town's population shriveled from teeming thousands to a disheartened handful, J. C. Fall closed his big general store and moved away. In departing, he said he had spent at Unionville more than $3,000,000—most of which had come from the *Arizona* mine—and that he was unable to continue operations due to the government's ruinous discount on bullion.

The Fall Mercantile—now lying in ruins—was the last store to operate in the canyon.

"My parents and grandfather came to Unionville during the first years of the boom," said Martha Leonard. "With the time nearing for me to be born, Mother went back to Illinois so that I might arrive in 'civilized' surroundings; but in 1869, before I was six months old, she and I returned to Unionville. I attended school here, in the same building we still use for that purpose. It was built in 1871, at a cost of $2500, and school has been held there every term for 82 years.

"But now," she said sadly, "it looks as if there won't be another term in the old schoolhouse. There are only a few folks left in town— most of us old—and we've just naturally run out of children!"

Under Nevada law, a school may be maintained for three pupils, but she doubted if Unionville would be able to muster that many during the term ahead.

Turning to Mr. Leonard, who had come in from the garden and had been listening with interest, I asked at which point he had entered the Unionville picture.

"Me?" he said, with a twinkle. "Oh, I'm just a Johnny-come-lately! Just a poor tenderfoot schoolteacher from Wisconsin who came out West and got himself involved in matrimony!"

After beginning his teaching career in the Badger State, in 1882, Mr. Leonard later had emigrated to Nevada and secured a contract to teach the school at Dun Glen (a present day ghosttown, about 25 miles north-east of Unionville.) Still later he had obtained the job of teaching Unionville's school and had held that position 35 years, during which time he had brought the three R's to all the Leonard children, and many others.

One of the Leonard daughters—who later became Mrs. Orfa Hammersmark—had developed a desire to follow in her father's footsteps as an educator. With Mr. Leonard's retirement, Mrs. Hammersmark had stepped into his vacated post and, in 1953, had taught the small-fry of Unionville for 19 years, thereby making a father-daughter combination of nearly 70 years continuous teaching in what is now Pershing county. Another daughter of the Leonards—Mrs. Jane Davidson—had been then postmaster at Unionville for 45 years, and was still filling that position.*

"It was at Dun Glen I first met Mr. Leonard," put in Grandma. "I was only 16 at the time, but I knew he was everything I wanted in a husband—besides being *very* good looking!—and I didn't intend he should get away from me. We were married in September, 1885 . . ."

Leaving the Leonard home, I drove back down the winding street, past the time-mellowed ruins and deserted homes, to the old graveyard at the mouth of the canyon.

Walking through that place of silent sepulchres, I found my mind whirling through an endless compote of stories related by my Unionville

---

*At time of this writing, the fate of Unionville's postoffice is in doubt. In moving to discontinue service as of July 1, 1956, the Postoffice Department, in Washington, pointed out that cost of operating the office in 1955 was $1324, as against only $206.24 in receipts. First stamp sales were made at the office April 15, 1862.

hosts. Stories of the days when Mrs. Ernst's grandfather freighted from Sacramento to Unionville, and her grandmother operated the pony express station at Buffalo Springs, on the Idaho-Virginia City line; stories of later days when her daughter—Mrs. Ernst's mother—raised poultry and vegetables and hauled them by wagon to the Chinese city in American Canyon, a dozen miles down the range.

Stories, stories, stories without end; and yet, I knew that all the remembered tales of Unionville's youth were as nothing compared to the unrecorded history that had died with the men who made it . . . the unsung pioneers who sleep in these forgotten graves.

Leaving the cemetery to head down the long, lonesome road into Buena Vista valley, I turned for a last look at the fine old ruin in the canyon.

The evening was young, but the sun had disappeared behind the high, purple peaks of the Humboldt range. The air was growing chill, and dark shadows—like the relentless years—were stealing in to swallow the town.

3

Ophir, the Golden

*Then shalt thou lay up gold as dust, and the gold of Ophir
as the stones of the brooks*—Job 22:24.

W HEN SOLDIERS stationed in Rush Valley under Colonel Patrick
E. Connor first beheld the gleaming treasure contained in a remote
canyon of the Oquirrh mountains, in Tooele county, Utah, it is not surprising that their thoughts leaped back across the centuries to the famed
mines of King Solomon. Here, if they might believe their incredulous
eyes, lay a second Ophir.

While these soldier-miners had been given official permission to
indulge in prospecting "to open up the hidden treasure houses of nature,"
it was not any familiarity with geology or metallurgy which led them into
the Oquirrhs in the middle 1860s. Rather were they lured by the knowledge that Indians of the vicinity had for years been manufacturing lead
bullets, as well as crude ornaments of gold and silver, from ore mined
somewhere in the maze of canyons comprising that range. To amateur
prospectors, with more knowledge of parade grounds than gold pans,
such information can be wonderfully helpful.

Fastening upon the most promising canyon the name of Ophir,
Connor's men staked the St. Louis lode—thereby touching off a stampede
whose reverberations soon were echoing through the mining world. Born
overnight, the town of Ophir quickly filled the narrow canyon; her twisting
main street accommodating itself to the sinuous gorge, her painfully short
side streets climbing laborously up the vertical folds of the mountain.
Along earthen and plank sidewalks there sprang up a fantastic collection
of shacks, saloons, brothels and dance halls, and a frenzied rush of boomers
poured in from Nevada and California—miners to probe the Oquirrhs
with shaft and tunnel; sandpaper-tongued muleskinners to haul the ore
to mills; gamblers to pluck the rich harvest of the pasteboards and the
whirling ball.

Of the many exceptional jousts engaged in by Ophir's gambling
fraternity, one of the tales that will be recounted longest concerns a poker
game between Frank Payton and a chap remembered only as "Digger
Mike."

At the outset of what was to be the last hand, Digger had on the
table before him some $6000 in gold dust, coin and currency. Payton
had possibly $7000. As an opener, Digger tossed in a poke of gold.

Payton stayed and raised him $250. Digger "saw" the two-fifty and raised another $500 in dust, which Payton matched.

After the draw—with Payton taking one card and Digger standing pat—the betting mounted from hundreds into thousands. Eventually $12,000 in assorted collateral lay heaped in the center of the table. With the board in front of him cleaned, Digger called for a showdown.

Kibitzers pressed closer around the table. Tension mounted. Even the tinny piano momentarily fell silent.

Payton laid down a pair of fours.

As though drawn by a powerful magnet, the encircling eyes shifted to Digger.

But Digger, too, had been bluffing—on a pair of treys!

Payton scooped in the pot.

Several days later the winner's body was found in a nearby ravine, his skull bashed in and his money gone. The murderer was never caught.

With the Miners' Delight, Pocatello, Wild Delirium, Velocipede, and other of the earlier-located mines continuing to pour forth wealth in promising quantities, Mack Gisborn built a 20-mile toll road from Ophir to Stockton, where Colonel Connor had erected Utah's first large smelter in 1864. (Any connection between the Colonel's smelter and the fact he had encouraged the soldiers under him to go forth prospecting "to open up the hidden treasure houses of nature," is probably not coincidental.)

With completion of the Gisborn toll road, a stready stream of ore wagons soon was rumbling from the mountains to the smelter town in the valley. Not all stopped at Stockton. Some continued north to Lake Point, on Great Salt Lake, where Ophir's ore was loaded on barges for water transportation to the railroad at Corinne, northwest of Ogden.

As Walker brothers, Salt Lake banking concern, invariably kept a weather eye cocked for good investments, it was not long until they had entered the Ophir field. And when Marcus Daly was fired from the notorious Emma mine at Alta, Walkers immediately engaged him to manage their Ophir holdings.

Daly did all right by Walkers; and by staking the Zella claim in his own name, he also did all right by Daly. When Walkers later sent him to Butte, Montana, to seek promising investments for the firm, Daly used $30,000 derived from his mine at Ophir to purchase a speculative Butte mine known as the Anaconda. It was a purchase that ultimately would make him one of the world's two greatest copper kings.

Second of the great copper kings—Senator W. A. Clark of Montana —also claimed his cut from the Ophir jackpot. In addition to owning the rich Ophir Hill mine, he gave the town world accessibility through construction of a shortline railroad connecting with the Los Angeles and Salt Lake line near the present Tooele county town of St. John.

While Ophir's ore was a mixture of gold, silver, copper, zinc and lead, the role played by gold was relatively unimportant compared to the camp's spectacular output of the base metals and silver. A single stope at the Kearsarge mine is said to have yielded more than $1,000,000 worth of silver; while one of the largest silver nuggets ever mined in the United States was sent by Kearsarge to the St. Louis World's fair in 1904.

During the 30-year period from 1870 to 1900, total gold production of Ophir-Rush Valley mining district amounted to only $379,747. During that same period the district's production of silver and base metals rose to $13,143,086! Beginning with the turn of the century, Ophir's yield was reported separately from that of Rush Valley, and the years 1901-48 saw more than $28,000,000 in ore taken from Ophir's mines. Of this total, gold output represented but $212,801, while lead production soared to the staggering figure of 223,776,284 pounds, bringing $12,755,864. Also included in the total was close to $8,000,000 worth of silver, over $6,-000,000 in copper, and more than $2,500,000 in zinc.

As years went on, the percentage of the gross receipts which represented profit, grew steadily smaller. Caught between the three-way squeeze of rising production costs, low metal prices and diminishing ore bodies, one after another of Ophir's big mines ceased operation, and this town where 6000 persons had lived extravagantly, and fought and died gamely, started on the downgrade.

Even after all her large mines had closed, small operators continued to hammer at the stubborn ground and periodic strikes brought attempts to revive the old camp. None, thus far, has been crowned by spectacular success, and today finds mining in the canyon at a virtual standstill.

Even as a ghosttown, it would be difficult to imagine a more pleasant place than Ophir. Her remaining handful of dwellings are comfortable old homes shaded by immense boxelders and locusts. Edging the tumbled rock fences are hollyhocks and sunflowers, and a few cattle graze in pocket-sized meadows along a little stream.

When I visited Ophir in 1949, its postoffice was still serving a few families. A small general store, a Lilliputian hotel and a bar, comprised the business district. Most notable of the town's pioneer relics was the former city hall and fire station on Main street—an unpainted wooden frame building, with a square bell tower. Still housed in the old firehall were two high-wheeled, man-powered hose carts, their reels still equipped with webbing hoses.

Many a year had passed since a train whistle had cleft the air, or a wheel had turned on Ophir's shortline railroad, and rails, ties, even the old grade, had vanished from the canyon; yet, one decrepit passenger coach still stood in the ravine at the lower edge of town. Most of its ceiling had disappeared, weeds grew higher than its bed, and wild clematis had scrambled through the open windows and doorways and climbed over the broken top bows to fill the interior with a tangled cascade of white blossoms. Only this one old relic remained as a memento of Senator Clark's railroad whose long-ago arrival at Ophir had been greeted with jubilation and fanfare.

The present auto road, in its course through the canyon, winds past tumbled log cabins and barns, deserted apple orchards, abandoned mines and mills, and waste dumps without number. Varying in size from a dozen shovelsful of rock tossed out of a shallow prospect hole, to sprawling heaps where great mines operated over long periods of years, each of these dumps stands symbolic of man's sweat and strain and striving.

Many of those who toiled in the mines and pinned their faith on Ophir's largess, are sleeping today in a little cemetery high on the juniper-grown hillside. Drawn to this remote canyon for divers reasons—some good and some bad—they gained only six feet of rocky earth, the peaceful oblivion of a nameless mound, and a sunny spot in which to await Eternity.

Very possibly they would ask no more.

4

Saints and Sinners of Steptoe Slough

NEVADA'S BRASSY SUN had at last been swallowed by the pine-topped heights of the Egan range, and the blue shadows of evening were beginning to gather in the canyons and steal across the wide bareness of Steptoe Valley. It was supper time, and I was hungry and tired, and although I had covered more miles than I ordinarily drive in a day, a foolish sort of urge kept drawing me on.

I wanted to camp that night at old Fort Schellbourne.

Schellbourne has been a ghosttown for nearly 70 years, and throughout all the time I have known Nevada, it has been one of my favorite camping sites. Its cold spring water and shade would make it a desirable stopping place even without its great historical interest; and, of course, there is always a possibility of finding there my good friends, Ruth and G. C. Russell.

The Russells own the old town—lock, stock and barrel—as well as a lot of surrounding land. But because they also operate a full-time business at Tooele, Utah—nearly 200 miles distant, over unpaved roads —the time they are able to spend at the ranch is much less than they would prefer. With two years gone by since I had been at Schellbourne, I wondered who, if anyone, I would find there.

Forty-two miles north of Ely, in Nevada's White Pine county, the paved course of U.S. 50-93 is crossed by a graveled road—State Route 2. To the east, this road winds abruptly and sinuously to the summit of Schellbourne Pass, from which point it goes looping across the hills to the Goshute Indian country, and the Great Salt Desert, of western Utah.

With the good feeling of being "almost home," I turned my car into this easterly-trending road. Two miles and I had entered the lower fringe of foothills and was meeting the first scraggly vanguards of the junipers. At three miles I quit the main graveled thoroughfare for a narrow dirt side-road; and a couple of minutes later, I was entering upon the lonely main street of Fort Schellbourne.

My two years' absence had wrought no visible changes. The mountainous old willow trees and cottonwoods flanking either side of the street still met overhead in a green arch—their boughs interlacing until the road seemed to pass through a long, dark tunnel. Here were the same old stone-and-log buildings and pole corrals; and if the old brick stage station and postoffice was a trifle more frayed at the seams, it still appeared good for many a day. (Plate 9) As this rambling relic of Overland Mail days serves as the Russell's headquarters when they are at Schellbourne, I turned back past the building toward the kitchen door. One glance served to show that the station, itself, was unoccupied; but in its rear stood a battered old sheepwagon, its open door framing a yellow rectangle of lamplight.

Bounding from his lookout post under the wagon, a brown-and-white shepherd dog came racing to greet me.

"He grows lonely for people," said a soft voice. "We both do . . ."

Raising my eyes from the dog, I saw approaching me an old man, no taller than myself, and slight of build. Covering the lower portion of his face was a full beard, as soft and white as fine silk floss, and a rippling cascade of soft white hair fell to a point well below his shoulders. His shoes were broken, and the garments that hung loosely on his thin frame were patched and faded; yet, it seemed to me I had never known a more kindly and compassionate face, a more noble appearing soul. Here, I knew instinctively, was a man who would never be guilty of casting the first stone, and I found myself thinking that if Christ had attained to a great age, He would have looked much like this venerable patriarch of Fort Schellbourne.

Introducing myself, I inquired for the Russells—only to learn they were at Tooele. I remarked that Schellbourne seemed to be bearing up well under the passage of time. The old man shook his head.

"Oh, no!" he said. "It's going down fast . . . and it makes my heart bleed to see it! It didn't look much like this when I was teaming through here, 50 years ago . . ."

Remembering his role of host, he introduced himself as Tom Mulliner, current caretaker of the place, and offered to prepare supper for me. (Plate 11) When he learned of my plans to camp there, overnight, he insisted I should not stay outside, but should occupy the Russell's living quarters in the old stage station.

Preceding me into the huge, old kitchen, he lighted a kerosene lamp, kindled a fire in the cook stove, and set a teakettle of water over the flame. In only a few minutes the cheerful warmth of the pine-wood fire was driving the chill mustiness from the room, and the little teakettle began to sing—a thin, lonely song, befitting a ghosttown teakettle. Drawing on the Russell's well-stocked food supply, I cooked my supper and ate it, and washed the dishes and put them away. Afterward, as the fire crackled and the lamplight flickered on those 90-year-old walls, Tom and I sat in the shadows and talked of the days when Nevada and Utah were young.

His mother had come West as a baby, riding on top of the load in a handcart pushed across the plains by his Mormon grandmother, Tom said. He had, himself, been born at Lehi, Utah. As his father was en-

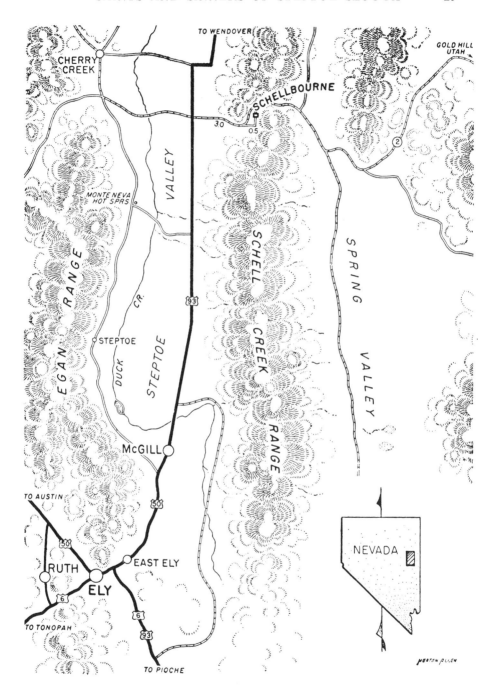

gaged in teaming to all the prominent Nevada mining camps of the 1860s, and 1870s, Tom grew up around horses, and soon as he was judged old enough to be entrusted with team and load, he followed in his father's footsteps, hauling supplies to the mining camps and ore to the mills. He teamed into Ophir and Mercur, Utah, and Cherry Creek, Nevada, when these present-day ghosttowns were seething with activity. He drove stage and drove freight wagons, and carried the United States mail on horseback from Gold Hill, Utah, to Cleveland, Nevada—a 50-mile route through heat and drought, and blizzards, and mountainous snow.

For 80 years this man had cast his lot in the bordering counties of Tooele and White Pine—most of that time around mining camps—yet, he had seldom engaged in mining.

"I tried it once—for about a week—but I couldn't stand it underground," said Tom Mulliner. "I had to get out in God's sunshine, again; out where I could see the sky and feel the wind . . . and be around horses."

As the old man continued to weave stories of pioneer days in the Steptoe country, the time slipped away, unnoticed by either of us, and the hour was late when my host refilled the depleted woodbox, wished me a pleasant good night, and returned to his sheep wagon home.

Spreading my bedroll on a bunk beside the stove, I blew out the flame in the lamp and laid down in the warm, soft darkness. It was very still and peaceful in the old station—even the ghosts seemed to have crept back in the walls and gone to sleep. After the fire had burned down to embers, a few red flickers still played on the water-stained ceiling; and as I lay there in the quiet dark, watching those changing light patterns, I found myself reviewing all the eras of history this old town had witnessed —history related that evening by Tom Mulliner, who had helped make it; history gleaned in the past from brittle emigrant diaries and yellowed newspaper files, and musty records kept by three generations of men . . .

Among the first white persons to look upon the Steptoe Valley and its sheltering ranges was Howard Egan, of Salt Lake City, an ex-major in the Nauvoo Legion. To prove his contention that a central route across Western Utah Territory would be shorter and otherwise preferable to the circuitous Humboldt River trail, Major Egan loaded himself and supplies on a mule, and in ten days—Sept. 19-29, 1855—rode from Salt Lake City, via the present site of Schellbourne, to Sacramento, a distance of 700 miles! Never before in history had such a feat of saddle endurance been known, nor has it been equalled since.

Major Egan had proven his point; and with inauguration of the first Overland Mail line, in 1858, the stages of W. G. Chorpenning were routed to follow the trail thus pioneered. Every 12 or 15 miles along this course were located relay points where spent horses might be exchanged for fresh teams; and one of those so established had been Schell Creek Station, later to be known as Schellbourne. The Pony Express and the first nation-spanning telegraph line later followed substantially the same route and utilized the same station facilities. With these vanguards of civilization, the first white settlers entered the region as station tenders and hostlers—and political troubles began brewing.

For untold centuries of time the grassy meadows fringing Steptoe Valley had been occupied by large Indian camps. With fish in the streams, pine nuts in the hills, and abundant wild game everywhere, the region constituted a desirable home and the redmen were not too willing to relinquish it to their white brothers—many of whom did not always behave in brotherly fashion. Although their smoldering resentment never ripened into large-scale battle, nuisance raids became a scourge on the land.

Pony Express riders, pounding through the mountains on their around-the-clock schedules, were shot from ambush; mail coaches were attacked, drivers and station tenders slain, corrals and barns burned, and horses stolen.

Out of such depredations grew some amazing endurance rides, greatest of which was that made by 20-year-old Billy Fisher. Leaving Ruby Valley, Nevada, July 3, 1860, Billy pounded east past one relay station after another—including Schell Creek—but due to Indian assaults, no relief riders were available. Before quitting the saddle, the young Expressman had ridden virtually non-stop to Salt Lake City, covering 271 miles in 35 hours. Six fresh horses and two mules had been supplied him en route.

Another episode, widely publicized at the time, was staged 12 miles west of Schell Creek, at Egan Canyon, one of the loneliest change stations on the entire route of the Pony Express.

Stationmaster Mike Holten and "Slim" Wilson, rider of the eastbound relay to Schell Creek, had a reasonably good idea of what was in store for them when they saw approaching the station one morning an Indian war party of about 80 mounted braves, nude but for loin cloths, and with their bodies greased, and faces streaked with paint. Any doubt concerning the visitors' intentions was answered conclusively when an arrow buried itself in the cabin wall close to Holten's head.

Using filled sacks of grain to barricade the station's only door and window, the beleaguered men began firing on the attackers, but so well were their adversaries concealed that few shots proved effective. With their ammunition supply at last nearly exhausted, the pair sought to gain fuller advantage of their few remaining rounds by making a stand in the open with their backs to the cabin wall.

No sooner had they burst through the door than they were engulfed in an onrush of Indians. Over the shrieks and gabble of the throng they could hear the old chief's shouted demand that his party be given food. Seizing upon this as a stay of execution, the Expressmen complied readily; but even after all the bacon, sugar and bread in the storehouse had been surrendered to him, the chief demanded still more. Pointing to the flour supply, he ordered, "Makum more bread!"

Throughout the remainder of that sweltering, soul-trying July day, the two Expressmen frantically applied themselves to the business of baking hot doughgods for that ravenous throng—the Indians, all the while taunting their victims and spurring them toward greater effort.

Meanwhile, as he had approached Egan Canyon from Ruby Valley, Express Rider Billy Dennis had spotted the war party in the station yard. Having passed a company of cavalry only a few miles before, he had whirled his mount and gone flying along the back trail for help.

Ordering 20 men to the mouth of the canyon to cut off the Indians' retreat, the officer in charge of the troops took 60 dragoons and set out for the station.

Uncle Sam's cavalry never made a better-timed arrival.

With the last of the flour baked and the bread consumed, the braves had closed for the kill. Overpowered and bound, the prisoners had been lashed to a wagon tongue planted in the station yard, tinder-dry sagebrush had been piled about their feet and ignited, and when the ringing hooves of the approaching cavalry sent the red tormenters fleeing for cover, the searing flames of the fire were curling about the boottops of Holten and Wilson.

Eighteen Indians and three soldiers were slain in the pitched battle that ensued; numerous men on both sides were wounded, and 60 Indian ponies were killed or captured. But the bulk of the war party made its escape into the hills.

Even after discontinuance of the Pony Express, mail stages continued to rumble through Schell Creek for a number of years, and Indian raids on these carriers became so flagrant that a company of cavalry was assigned to protect the station. With this development, the place was renamed Fort Schellbourne and soon afterward began taking on the dignified airs of a town.

Not all gory episodes in the early history of the place were attributable to Indians. There was, for example, the crime and execution of two young hoodlums from California.

Floated out of San Jose for some misdemeanor, the youths stole a packmule and started east. While crossing the Sierra they overtook three men who were trailherding to Salt Lake City 150 head of horses. As if the horses, alone, were not sufficiently alluring to men of few scruples, the owners foolishly let it be known they were carrying with them a small fortune in gold. The horses had been giving them considerable trouble, and upon the youths representing themselves as expert horse wranglers, they were hired.

The drive progressed smoothly as far as Schellbourne, where overnight camp was made. Next morning found the horses gone, as well as their owners and wranglers, and investigation revealed the hacked and battered bodies of the three horsemen. A quickly-formed posse hit the trail, and long before reaching Salt Lake, the youthful murderers were overtaken and captured.

Returned to Schellbourne for trial, the younger of the pair confessed that the men had been killed with a hatchet as they slept. Sentenced to death, the San Jose toughs were led to a plank scaffold, erected alongside the graves of their victims, and there were hanged.

("There are three unmarked graves in the cemetery," said Tom Mulliner. "I've always figured they might be the three horsemen . . . but where their murderers were buried, is anyone's guess.")

Those were grim days, hard days, when even humor was cut from a grim, hard pattern.

Between Schellbourne and the Egan range, to the west, lay Steptoe Slough which, during wet periods, became a soupy morass, almost impossible for loaded mail coaches to cross. Inasmuch as mail and express is scarcely in position to get out and walk, it was the passengers who were dispossessed.

Three choices were offered. The displaced ticket holder might remain at Schellbourne and pay the ghastly prices of that frontier camp until the slough dried in mid-summer; or, he might slog his way through three miles of bottomless mud; or, he might pay $40 to be carried across the bog on the back of a "tame" Indian.

As the hoop-skirted damsels of 85 years ago weren't suitably robed for playing piggy-back, the station agent at Schellbourne contrived a "sedan chair" fabricated of cottonwood poles and barley sacks. With the lady passenger seated fearfully within, or thereon, this crude litter was hoisted to the shoulders of four Indians who raced and stumbled through the muck to the other side of the bog—meanwhile exhibiting vast amusement at each terrified squeak and scream of their rider!

Regardless of the indignities forced upon passengers, Uncle Sam's mail had been transported faithfully across the slough for more than eleven years, but in the spring of 1869, with the great era of cross-country staging drawing to a close as track crews of the Pacific Railroad pushed nearer their point of rendezvous in northern Utah, morale of the Overland Mail line sank to an all-time low.

With no longer any incentive for maintaining their proud tradition of service, stage drivers began leaving newspapers and heavier mail at Schellbourne—ostensibly to be picked up "later"—and by April, 1869, there had accumulated at Schellbourne more than 400 sacks of mail, representing in excess of 20 *tons!* Twelve weeks, it was estimated, would be required to move it.

When the golden spike was driven at Promontory, less than three weeks later, and the last cross-country stage rolled through Schellbourne to the west, it is to be presumed that those 400 sacks of mail were still gathering dust in the company warehouse.

Meanwhile, silver ore had been discovered in the rocky ranges nearby, and Schellbourne had blossomed into one of the first mining camps in White Pine county. Additional dwellings and business houses sprang up, and three quartz mills were built.

Despite their spectacular beginning, Schellbourne's mines did not hold up well under intensive operation. By 1885 most of her frame buildings had been dragged across Steptoe Slough and up the mountain to Cherry Creek, and a majority of her citizens had removed to more promising fields.

With this development, Schellbourne became a ghosttown with "Uncle Billy" Burke, as its last loyal defender. Long after the glory of the town had departed, Uncle Billy and his family remained true to it; and when there was no longer any possibility of the place "coming back" as a mining camp, the Burkes acquired the townsite and adjacent valley as a ranch.

"The Burkes were still living here when I first made the acquaintance of Schellbourne, more than 50 years ago," Tom Mulliner had said.

Despite the generations of phantoms that must have been prowling these rooms—the restless spirits of teamsters and Indian fighters, and Express riders and miners—my sleep in the old stage station was quite undisturbed. Awakening, about sun-up, I had a strange feeling that my venerable host of the previous evening would not be anywhere around— that he had been only a gentle ghost with whom it had been my privilege to talk for a little while, and that the full light of day would find him vanished back into that shadowy realm where ghosts are presumed to live.

After I had prepared my breakfast and eaten it, and rolled my bedding and put it in the car, I began typing notes gathered the previous day, and about seven o'clock came a soft knock at the door. It was my venerable friend of the sheep wagon.

After we had talked for a bit, I said I wanted to get some pictures of the place, and asked if he would care to walk over to the old Wells Fargo bank building with me.

"Why, yes!" said the old man, with a twinkle. "I'll be proud to go with you; but I must warn you—you can't cash any checks there!"

With the old dog padding at our heels, and the soft dust rising in little puffs beneath our feet, we walked up the willow-shaded lane to the old bank. We examined the splendid stone masonry represented in its front wall, and speculated on why a bank should have had need for so many windows and doors—five pair of great, tall openings, each more than twice the height of a man, and each with heavy iron shutters, now green with age.

From the bank, we went across the ravine and up the slope to the cemetery—a small fenced plot in the midst of meadowland and wild flowers. Searching through the deep matting of grass, we found three graves with wooden crosses, but without identifying names or dates. Three other graves were marked with cut sections of iron wagon tire, hammered flat, and riveted together in the form of crosses. Into the three iron crosses had been chiseled three names—William, Eliza, and Marshal Burke —the family which had clung to Schellbourne for so many years after it had been forsaken by all others.

"You've seen our goldfish, I suppose?" asked the old man. Yes, I had seen them; but because it was a good morning for musing and dreaming, we wandered across the meadow slope to the big spring that waters all this valley; and in the clear pool, swimming lazily around the dark roots and dark rocks, I looked again upon the mysterious goldfish of Schellbourne.

No one knows for certain whence they came, nor how long they have been there. I've always rather supposed that some pioneer woman or girl had owned a cherished bowl of gold fish, and when she died or moved to some new location, her pets were turned into the pool to shift for themselves. However it happened, the fish have thrived and grown fat, and are big enough to fry—should one have an appetite for fried goldfish—and their numbers have multiplied until they fill even the stream that flows out of the spring and down the ravine.

We went on to prowl about other old buildings and corrals, including the log structure that legend has set apart as a one-time relay station of the Pony Express. Although the building looks old enough to have housed the Pony Express—or even the mythical winged horse, Pegasus—there is no proof that it ever served either of these purposes.

The old Army fort, too, has disappeared, along with the three quartz mills that sent their thunder through the canyon during those brief years when Schellbourne loomed as the white hope of Eastern Nevada's mining industry. All that remains of the town's ancient past are a few old log-and-stone buildings, five pairs of ponderous iron shutters, two rows of great old trees, a pond full of goldfish, and six old crosses in a graveyard.

With our circle of the townsite completed, Tom Mulliner and I returned to the stage station, and I said I must be going on my way to Wendover. My host expressed regret that I should leave without seeing the Russells; and while I was stowing my few belongings in the car, he collected a sackful of fresh eggs, a jar of cheese, and a bag of cookies, for my lunch.

"If Ruth had been here," he said in his soft voice, "she'd have fixed you a good meal. Ruth's right handy that way. But the old dog and me— we mean well, but we're not much good!"

As he dropped his work-knotted hand to the shepherd's head, the dog thumped his thin tail in answer and raised his brown eyes to the faded blue eyes of the old teamster.

They were still standing so as I left the yard and started down the long, green tunnel of willow trees, and back toward the highway.

5

Spanish Mines on the Colorado

FIRST TWO MINES in Nevada to be worked by white men are believed to have been the Techatticup and the Gettysburg, situated in El Dorado* canyon, between the present ghosttown of Nelson and the Colorado river. The Gettysburg further is said to have been the third mine patented in the United States,** and although date of the Techatticup's original discovery is not known, it is believed it was first located by a party of Spanish explorers in the late 1700s. After mapping their discovery and mining considerable gold, the expedition presumably returned to Mexico to procure more supplies and equipment.

These original discoverers, for some reason, never returned to work their rich vein, and nearly a century passed before there appeared in the canyon another group of Spanish-Mexicans who had in their possession the original old Spanish map of the area. Noted on the yellowed parchment were certain prominent landmarks which pointed conclusively to the Techatticup as the mine represented; but these later-comers had their long trek for nothing. The Techatticup had been rediscovered by Americans—probably by soldiers in the Fourth Regiment of Infantry, stationed down the river at Fort Mojave—and for several years had been pouring its treasure into the coffers of El Dorado Mining company. (Plate 6)

After discovery, or re-discovery of the district, about 1857, the town of El Dorado was founded and the Colorado Mining district organized in 1861. First shipments of ore went out that year to San Francisco, the material being carried down the Colorado river on paddlewheelers and barges, thence through the 800-mile length of the Gulf of California, and up the coast to the Bay City. First mill in the canyon—a 15-stamp affair—was built at the Techatticup mine in 1863***; and with the long and costly haul to San Francisco thus eliminated, the way was cleared for a boom.

---

*By modern makers of Nevada maps, the spelling of this name has been corrupted to "Eldorado." In old records of the canyon, however, it is written in the proper Spanish manner: El Dorado.

**Riggs, John L., The Reign of Violence in El Dorado Canyon, Third Annual Report Nevada Historical Society, 1911-12. Footnote by Clark Alvord.

***Lincoln, Francis, Church. Mining Districts and Mineral Resources of Nevada, 1921.

As time went on, other mines were opened nearby, additional mills were established; and about seven miles up the canyon from the original town of El Dorado, the new camp of Nelson came into being.

Nelson developed so rapidly that soon after close of the Civil War it was noted as the largest settlement in this isolated region which had functioned successively as New Mexico Territory (1850-63), Arizona Territory (1863-66), and finally, as the State of Nevada. The area now occupied by Clark county was then included in Lincoln county—giving Nelson and El Dorado the dubious distinction of being about as far from their county scat* as it was possible to be. As a crow might have flown— had any crow been able to exist in that parched land—the distance from those troubled camps to Pioche was roughly 160 miles. Via the circuitous route necessarily traveled by stagecoaches, however, the county seat lay nearly 300 miles distant, over the roughest sort of desert terrain, infested by outlaws and renegade Indians, and hazardous in the extreme.

As result of these conditions, Nelson and El Dorado became towns utterly without process of law. Before word might be carried from the canyon to Hiko or Pioche and response made by the sheriff's office, even a spectacular killing would be forgotten, the victim buried, witnesses scattered, and the killer lynched or lauded, as public opinion dictated.

Inasmuch as dozens of reports have been written and published concerning the spectacular rash of killings which attended and followed upon the "jumping" of George Hearst's Queen City mine property, near El Dorado, and also on the reign of terror kindled in that vicinity by the crazed Indian assassins, Ahvote, Mouse, and Queho, this writer believes that space available here can be put to better use than in retelling these more-than-twice-told tales.

We will, therefore, pass lightly over El Dorado's carnage, and consider, instead, the case of Ike Alcock.

Born in England, in 1856, Ike came to the United States as a child. After short periods of residence in Illinois, Nebraska, Utah, and Sterling, Nevada, he arrived in El Dorado Canyon in 1878, when he was a man of 22 years.

Ike Alcock continued to live in the canyon for three-quarters of a century; and in 1955, at the age of 99 years, was still living in Clark county. At that time he was an inmate of the county hospital, and for several years previously had been stone deaf; yet, even until his 97th year, his mind was clear and alert, and questions submitted to him in written form were answered almost as readily as when I first visited him at his home in Nelson, when he had been a gay young blade of only 90 summers. Even then, he had been quite deaf; but he still wore his original God-given teeth, he could read a newspaper without glasses, and his spare, rangy frame still towered more than six feet above the sod, and appeared as tough as a bull pine.

*Hiko. 1867-1871; Pioche, 1871-1909.

As a reckless young man who drank heavily, was handy with his dukes, and seldom passed a Saturday night without engaging in two or three fist-fights and shooting scrapes, young Ike Alcock had married an Indian girl who bore him five children and died when the youngest was but four months of age. Placing his children in the Stewart Ranch school, at the present site of Las Vegas, Ike returned to El Dorado where he worked for one mine after another, and gradually built up a name for all-around efficiency.

As one of the strangest experiences in his long mining career, he once recalled for me the time he was employed to "dive" for gold.

Believing the river silt contained a fabulous wealth of the yellow metal, an Eastern syndicate brought to El Dorado a vast amount of costly dredging equipment and a huge fuel barge to service it. Clad in regulation deep-sea diving gear and stationed at the intake pipe on the river bottom, it had been Ike's job to keep the silt flowing freely and the intake free of boulders which, otherwise, might jam the pump.

The operation had been fraught by virtually every sort of grief known to the mining industry. This, of course, had been many years before the stabilizing influence of Hoover Dam, and the water level in the Colorado was subject to abrupt rises and falls contingent upon upstream weather conditions. With one abrupt lowering of the waters, the immense barge was left stranded, high and dry, its mid-section resting on a ridge of rock. Due to the tremendous weight of the barge and the equipment it carried, the vessel soon split in two in the middle, and with the next rising of the mad river, the ship's disintegration was rapid.

After a sizable fortune had been lost in the effort, the ill-starred dredging project was abandoned.

(From the foregoing fiasco it should not be assumed that mining in the Nelson-El Dorado area was not a profitable operation when conducted in an orthodox manner. During years of its greatest activity, the district is believed to have produced close to $6,000,000 in gold and silver —the Techatticup mine, alone, being credited with a yield of $1,700,000.*)

Another unusual innovation in which Ike took part was the use of a 20-ton steam tractor (Plate 8) for transporting ore from the Techatticup mine to the mill on the river, about seven miles.

The tractor, originally, had been one of three purchased by the Pacific Coast Borax company with the idea of replacing mules used in drawing their world-famous "Twenty Mule Team" borax wagons, in Death Valley. When the first tractor placed in service on the Death Valley run exploded with a boom heard half-way across Nevada, the company hastened to sever its connections with the remaining two steel behemoths. It was one of these two that ultimately came to El Dorado.

---

*Ransome, F. L., Preliminary Account of the Goldfield, Bullfrog, and Other Mining Districts in Southern Nevada. U. S. Geological Survey Bulletin, 303. 1907.

After its arrival at Searchlight, by rail, the tractor remained in the station yard for ten days due to the fact that no one knew how to operate it. Having had some previous experience with steam engines, Ike finally volunteered to go to Searchlight and bring the baby home. Through methods of trial and error—which, miraculously didn't produce a second explosion—Ike succeeded in getting the 20-ton monster into operation and one of the memorable occasions of his life was hearing the plaudits of the canyon multitude as he brought the tractor triumphantly down the grade into Nelson.

"The old girl was belching smoke, roaring like a catamount, scaring all the Injins for miles around, and traveling like hell . . . Well," Ike qualified that statement, "at least three-and-a-half miles an hour!"

Like the dredging project, the big tractor wasn't an outstanding success, and eventually was abandoned near Emery's Landing, at the mouth of El Dorado canyon. There it stood for nearly 50 years. When the water began impounding behind Davis Dam in 1950, and it was seen that the tractor would soon be submerged, "Pop" Simon moved the rusty old monster to his place of business at Jean, on U.S. Highway 466, in the same county, where it immediately began charming tourists and shutter-bugs, and evoking tall tales from old timers.

Ike Alcock's humor was as roughhewn as the uninhibited days in which he had lived.

One of his favorite stories concerned three "Californy fellers" who came to El Dorado canyon to do assessment work. Water fit for drinking was almost non-existent in the area and after exhausting the meager supply brought with them, the city men began mooching water from Ike. As Ike had to haul his water several miles, this added burden worked quite a hardship on the old man and he soon got enough of the practice. The question was how to terminate it without actually antagonizing the men.

After standing for several days in charred wooden barrels, Ike's water supply invariably took on a dark brown tint which the "Californy fellers" regarded with pronounced disfavor and after numerous subtle hints had failed to discourage the water moochers, Ike seized upon the happy thought that he might get his message across by capitalizing on this discoloration.

Next time one of the men appeared with a bucket and asked to "borrow" some water, Ike cheerfully ladled several gallons of the dark brown fluid into the other's container and the fellow started back toward his own camp.

"Oh, I say!" Ike called after him. "Wait a minute!" Stepping in his cabin he emerged with a piece of dirty flour sack which he handed to the fellow. "Reckon you better strain it," he said, a little sheepishly.

"Why?" asked the city man in alarm. "It doesn't have *bugs* in it, does it?"

"Bugs?" repeated Ike innocently. "Oh, no—no bug could live in *that* water! But several months ago an old stray jackass fell in th' spring an' died, and I noticed this mornin' his hair's startin' to slip."

6

Buxom Belle of the Sixties

LOOPING ACROSS the land—through sage and cedars, and empty space—a long, lonely road spans that portion of the world that lies between Tonopah and Austin, Nevada. Through all its length of 150 miles it serves but a handful of men and the withered husk of a single town—Belmont, the belle of the '60s.

Belmont had flowered and fallen many years before I was born; but even in her ruin she is a pleasant place, and whenever I walk her silent streets it is with the good feeling of having come home. Yet, strangely, my visits to Belmont always are preceded by little gnawings of fear. How much change will I find? How many of the old buildings will have collapsed; how many of the old timers have died?

Not until I enter the foothills at the head of dry Ralston Valley and the first familiar landmarks swim into view, are my forebodings partially lost. There is the tumbled chaos of stone and twisted iron where the big wooden mill once stood. There is the tall, brick chimney, still pointing skyward like a finger of Doom; and the old graveyard, where so many of Belmont's sons lie sleeping.

Another half a mile and I have entered the outlying fringe of the business area—once the sporting district. Then, suddenly, all my forebodings are gone as one quick glance across the ravine assures me that the old Nye County courthouse still stands—still as plain as a three-story bank vault, still as indomitable as the Bank of England. (Plate 1.)

Rounding the Chinese restaurant, with its curling roof and boarded windows, I swing to the left, ease my car through the cottonwood-shaded creek bed and up the short pitch to the front yard of the old county building. For more than 50 years this yard has served as a campsite for prospectors and Indians, and assorted wayfarers, like myself. Once I have gained its familiar shelter, I am at home—and the world is good.

Last time I visited Belmont was in the summer of 1955. My arrival in the courthouse yard found the sun a little too high for starting supper —a welcome circumstance, since it gave me an excuse to prowl once again through the fine old ruin that dominated the town in its ghostliness, even as in its glory.

Examining those splendid walls, still beautifully true and sound after

80 years of buffeting by the weather and the indignities suffered during half a century of abandonment, it seemed almost beyond belief that every brick employed in that construction, every pound of lime used in concrete and mortar and plaster, had been fired in Belmont kilns; that every massive stone in that rugged foundation had been hand-quarried in nearby canyons and hauled to this site by oxen!

It gave me a strange feeling, too, to realize that every man who had labored in that construction is gone—vanished like the winds of yesterday! Judges, juries, attorneys, litigants—all those who thronged the old court-room in search of justice or redress, and even the cases heard there—long are forgotten. But the old courthouse, which listened so briefly to man's tribulations, is still standing foursquare to the world—as rugged as the pioneers who built it, as defiant of Time as the Nevada clay from which it was born.

Picking my way along the ground-floor corridor—through broken lath and plaster and packrat debris, and the desert dust of half a century —I climbed the creaking stairway to the second floor, and yet another flight of shaky stairs to the building's huge, square cupola. There, I looked out on desolation unlimited.

Like a movie set of a bomb-destroyed city rose the jagged fangs of broken rock buildings—foundations without walls, walls without roofs, chimneys without smoke. There was the Cosmopolitan Music Hall, where Fay Templeton had played to applauding throngs. The second floor bal-cony had fallen since I had seen it last, and the roof seemed to sag a little more than I had remembered. Ernst and Esser's big brick-faced mercan-tile was the same roofless ruin it had been for 20 years past. The jewelry store, the saloons, the building where McIntyre and Walker had been hanged—all stood silent and empty, like deserted birds' nests on a dead bough.

Beyond the business section lay the Masonic and Oddfellows hall, the schoolhouse, the big stone office building of the Combination Milling company, the tumbled-down hovels of Chinatown. Prowling through the ruins of those huts, in years past, I had found opium containers and pottery brandy jugs, and Chinese coins turned green with age.

Beyond the last caving cellar and fallen wall, lay abandoned mine dumps, and abandoned shafts and abandoned mills—and it almost seemed as if I could see the abandoned dreams—but in all that chaos there was visible that day not one living, breathing creature; neither man, nor dog, nor horse, nor burro. . .

Belmont was a product of that bright era when the bread of every Western miner was buttered with dreams of a second Comstock. Swarm-ing over the hills in a mad hegira of hopefulness, prospectors had pene-trated, at last, to the Toquima mountains, in Nye County. And there, Destiny had smiled.

The year was 1865. The last volley of the Civil war had been fired but a few weeks before. Lee had surrendered to Grant, Abe Lincoln had been shot—and out in the Far West, a new silver strike had been made, and a new city was due to spring from Nevada's womb!

One day the Toquimas had been speckled by a few men, a few burros, a few ragged tents. Next day, in a manner of speaking, some 6000 boomers had been churning the sagebrush of newly-platted streets! Freight teams and heavy wagons were lurching over the mountains with loads of supplies. Claims were being staked, tunnels driven. Tents were replaced by stout buildings of brick and stone. Business structures rose.

The *Silver Bend Reporter,* a weekly newspaper, was founded by Oscar L. C. Fairchild & Co., and in Vol I, No. 1—issued March 30, 1867 —this fledgling news medium predicted that within a year Belmont would have a population of 10,000 persons.

"Colonel Buel's mill has extracted $100,000 worth of silver bullion from 1000 tons of Highbridge ore, all taken within twenty-five feet of the surface; and there are eighty stamps on the road for the Combination, and Child and Canfield companies, which will make our bullion yield something over $200,000 per month before the summer is over. The hills," exulted *The Reporter,* "are beginning to blacken with prospectors."

Advertisements contained in that first issue offered the professional services of three local attorneys-at-law, a dentist and an assayist, as well as the wares of numerous cafes, mercantiles, livery stables, hotels and lodging houses, sundry palaces of pleasure, and a brewery. Slow freight (oxen) to or from Austin, was quoted at two-and-one-half to three-cents a pound, and fast freight (horses or mules) at four to five cents.

Before the end of April, in that year of 1867, *The Reporter* had advised its readers that a sample of ore from the Combination company's claim, The Highbridge, had assayed $10,247.79 a ton in silver! Colonel Buel had left for Paris with a cabinet of Nevada silver to show at the International Exposition; clay for brick manufacturing had been discovered in abundance four miles west of town, and three large brick kilns were to be built immediately. Crowell and Myers' sawmill was producing 4000 board feet of lumber every ten hours.

H. P. Stimler had opened the Belmont News Depot, and, according to his announcement, would stock *"The Sacramento Union, Territorial Enterprise, Reese River Reveille,* cigars and stationery." Other new arrivals on the business front had included an oyster house, a bakery, two physicians, a drug store, fruit store, and watchmaking shop.

An editorial deplored the fact that there never had been a public school in Nye county, and urged that Belmont be the first county town publicly to recognize the importance of education. Another matter irking the editor at that particular writing had been the high cost of fresh linen.

"The Celestials," it was charged, "have combined against us and demand six dollars a dozen for washing. A few good washerwomen would do well here."

And just as proof that even 85 years ago all editors were not pleased with the administration of government, *The Reporter* had proposed a toast: "Here's to our governor. He came in with very little opposition; he goes out with none at all."

At the time of Nye county's creation, in 1864, the only white settlement within its prescribed boundaries had been the mining camp of Ione, which place, as a matter of course, had been designated as the county seat. And then had come Belmont; and shortly after the tying of her umbilical cord, Belmont had begun coveting the county plum. The hotly contested issue had come to a head in 1867 when Belmont's demands had become louder than the protests of Ione, and the State legislature had awarded to the newer town the Nye seat of government.

As county taxpayers had but barely completed the erection of a courthouse at the earlier capital, they were not in a financial mood to begin immediately the construction of a second building at Belmont. County offices, as a consequence, were housed in various structures leased for that purpose, and not until seven years later was contract awarded for the erection of a new building.

Work of grading got under way in the late summer of 1874, and in September of that year, Belmont *Courier* announced that the joist timbers were on their way from Alpha*, and that a large force of workmen were employed making brick and hauling rock.

"About 60,000 brick are already molded and laid up in the kiln, and a kiln of lime has been burned," reported *The Courier*.

With its completion, the new courthouse had been hailed as one of the finest county buildings in the state.

Belmont's star, by this time, had been gleaming brightly for a full decade. Her rich mines were operating around the clock, and several mills were running at capacity. Largest of these was the Combination Mill, built in the late 1860s at a reported cost of $225,000. (The 250,000 pounds of machinery necessary to the operation of this 40-stamp reduction works had been hauled from Cisco, California, in 14 huge freight wagons, each drawn by 10 heavy mules. Freight costs, alone, had involved more than $17,000!)

But despite her financial prosperity and political prestige, not all was sweetness and light in the City of Belmont. Her history also includes a few dark, grim tales of violence and man's inhumanity.

Of the less laudable episodes, none was so widely publicized as the riot of the Silver Bend miners.

During Belmont's earlier years her mines were worked largely by Cornish and Irish immigrants who had transplanted to the American desert a feud half as old as the British Empire. When suspension of work in the Silver Bend mine was ordered by Eastern directors of the company, Irish

---

*Formerly a station on the now-defunct Eureka & Palisades Railroad.

laborers interpreted the move as a subterfuge to restaff with Cornishmen —then procurable at a lower wage.

The rumor gained momentum. Blood grew hotter, and shortly after dusk on the evening of April 17, 1867, an infuriated mob stormed the office of R. B. Canfield, general agent of the Silver Bend company. When the mine boss refused to sign a check for $3000, drawn in favor of the group, he was overpowered, forced to mount a two-by-four scantling borne on burly shoulders, and a vicious parade through the main streets of Belmont, was begun.

At each saloon en route the inequitous mob gathered to itself additional recruits and downed searing draughts of bottled courage. At each halt, Canfield was held under gunpoint guard until his captors were ready to resume travel—meanwhile being subjected to every vile taunt and indecency the mob could devise.

Upon emerging from the Highbridge saloon, the rioters had ordered the mine boss back on his perch and were making ready to continue with their roistering when a cold, brittle voice cut through the milling crowd.

"I wouldn't do that, if I were you!" came the unexpected words, "It's not right to use a man that way!"

Whirling to determine the identity of the speaker, the rioters closest at hand looked into the steel-hard eyes of Louis Bodrow, a former city marshal at Austin. Quietly contemptuous of the mounting hostility, Bodrow moved in to stand at Canfield's side.

"Pat" Dignon, one of the leading mobsters, spat out a curse and threw a horny fist into the ex-lawman's face. A pistol barked. Another pistol replied; and within seconds the dark mountain street was a roaring hell of flashing knives, flying haymakers and haphazard gunfire.

When sheer exhaustion brought an end to the fight it was found that the mine boss had been rescued by friends. Scores of miners were nursing injuries and in widening pools of crimson lay Bodrow and Dignon.

Both were dead.

To fix direct responsibility for Bodrow's death was impossible, his body and clothing having been riddled by 16 bullets and countless stab wounds. Two shots had been fired from his pistol and it had been one of these, presumably, that had brought death to Dignon.

Returned to Austin, the body of the former law-officer was escorted to its last resting place by the combined membership of Confidence Engine Company, Pioneer Hook and Ladder Company, and the Lander Guard, with the Austin city band leading the cortege. Canfield, the mine boss, addressed the funeral assembly and paid all expenses of burial, and the Rev. J. L. Trefren, Methodist pastor at Austin, lauded Bodrow's courage.

"In his heroic death," said the Rev. Mr. Trefren, "he illustrated the noble qualities which adorned his life, for his brave spirit disdained every thought of peril in defense of the right . . ."

Later that week, in the vital statistics column of the *Silver Bend Reporter,* appeared two succinct notices, in alphabetical order:

DIED—in Belmont, April 18, L. M. Bodrow, aged 36 years.

DIED—in Belmont, April 18, John P. Dignon, aged 40 years.

Another bit of violence to which the better citizens of Belmont never pointed with pride, was the lynching of Charlie McIntyre and Jack Walker, Pennsylvania coal miners, who had come to Belmont to try their hand at silver mining.

Soon after their arrival in town the pair had engaged in an argument with H. H. Sutherland, a local citizen. As frequently happened in such affairs, the discussion had ended in gunplay with Sutherland being shot and wounded by Walker. Another stray bullet had found lodging in the leg of a bystander, Bill Doran. Jailed for his part in the shooting affray, Walker had been bound over to await grand jury action, while his partner, McIntyre, had been sentenced to 80 days in the county jail for drawing a deadly weapon in an angry manner.

The shooting had taken place early in May, 1874. Toward the close of that month the two prisoners had escaped from jail but two days later had been found hiding in an abandoned mine shaft a short distance from town. Recaptured by Sheriff Jim Caldwell, they were returned to the calaboose, then situated in the basement of a brick store building on main street.

About midnight, the sheriff's offices had been filled suddenly with purposeful men. Disarming Caldwell and his deputy, P. E. Turner, and binding them, the delegation had disappeared in the direction of the prisoners' cells.

Subsequently discovered by Night Watchman Gates, the sheriff and his deputy had been released from their bonds and the trio had hurried downstairs to the jail, where the sight that confronted them was not wholly unexpected.

Suspended by their necks from joists in the basement ceiling were McIntyre and Walker, both quite dead. Affixed to the back of each man's shirt was a slip of dirty foolscap bearing the scrawled notation, "301"— the signature of Belmont's vigilantes.

Due to the lurid imagination of a Belmont space-writer for the San Francisco *Chronicle,* one gory phase ascribed to this lynching has been published and republished for 80 years—and all without any foundation in fact.

According to the news report in the *Chronicle,* the men had been brutally beaten and their bodies riddled with bullets, either during or subsequent to the hanging. Both the floor and ceiling of the basement, it was declared, were drenched with their blood.

In a signed statement to the *Chronicle,* on June 17, 1874, Sheriff Caldwell wrote: "There were no marks of violence upon either of them (McIntyre and Walker) with the exception of one bruise on the head of

McIntyre. There were no bullet wounds upon either of the bodies, and I heard no shots fired in the jail at any time during this unfortunate proceeding."

Still another death occurred as result of the episode, but the *Courier* took care to assure its readers that the latter demise was not too regrettable.

"Wm. Doran, who was shot just above the knee . . . during a shooting match between Jack Walker and H. H. Sutherland, died on Saturday last, shortly after the amputation of his leg," reported the frontier news journal, in its issue of May 10, 1874. "He is said to have been a bad man, and although it is perhaps inhuman to rejoice over the death of anyone, it was a fortunate occurrence for him, as his untimely death was a certainty, sooner or later."

While deeds of violence too frequently stained her record, Belmont's daily life was not wholly dedicated to gore and glory. She also had her more genteel moments.

In June, 1874—the same month, ironically, as the lynching of McIntyre and Walker, the *Courier* announced that croquet grounds had been laid out at the lower end of main street. The same issue carried a story concerning the attractive flower garden of one Dr. Moore, and a report dealing with the activities of the glee club.

Cultural center of Belmont was the Cosmopolitan. Here, throughout the late 1860s and the '70s, played such troupes as the Chapman Family, with presentations of *Uncle Tom's Cabin,* and *The Young Widow;* and Stone and Beatty's Combination Star company, starring Amy Stone in *The Female Gambler,* and *Maid with the Milking Pail.* And here, too, came the celebrated child artiste, Fay Templeton, and her theatrical troupe, to play a week-long engagement in July, 1874.

"Their entertainments," asserted the *Courier,* "are chaste, rendering nothing but plays of the first order that can be witnessed by the most fastidious and squeamish."

It was not, presumably, these same "fastidious" and "squeamish" citizens who early in the 1890s elected Old Andy Johnson to the office of Nye County district attorney.

Andy, to put it mildly, was a character. Amusing and likeable, he operated a mule ranch down on Mosquito creek. In addition to the mules, his worldly possessions included a stringy, handlebar moustache, a blissful lack of education, and a penchant for going unbathed, unbrushed, and uncombed.

Due to their dislike for the opposition candidate—School Teacher Charles Deady—a bunch of Belmont politicos had derisively nominated Old Andy for the D.A.'s post. It was only a joke, a piece of satire. Everyone *knew* it was only a joke; but, as jokes sometimes do, it backfired.

Andy was elected.

Fortunately, there was living in the Belmont vicinity at that time, a semi-retired lawyer, William Granger, who agreed to serve as Andy's deputy and handle the legal work for him. Due to Granger's stewardship, the office was managed surprisingly well, and Old Andy gradually developed the idea he had copped a lifetime tenure. As a result, he was quite ruffled when Rancher Jim Butler, of Monitor Valley, yielded to the entreaties of his friends and came out against Andy at the next election in 1896. Jim had but little more education than his opponent and not by any manner of speaking was he a lawyer. However, he was well liked, and he won the election by a neat plurality.

Old Andy was fairly beside himself with wrath! Claiming fraud, he demanded a recount of the ballots; and when the day for inaugurating the new county officials rolled around, he refused to relinquish his office and books to Butler.

For nine days Andy froze to his desk in the old brick courthouse at Belmont. He ate there and slept there, opening the tall, locked doors of the office only to admit proven friends bearing food and liquid fortifications. The county dads were in a divided dither of indecision: Should they force the office doors and remove the ex-district attorney at gunpoint, or should they appeal to the governor for outside assistance?

But Old Andy finally settled the question himself. After holding the office illegally for nine days he at last capitulated, surrendered the keys to his successor, and moved back to his mule ranch on Mosquito creek.

Perhaps Old Andy wasn't so dumb, at that, for the time was nearing when a few good mules would be worth more than half of the town of Belmont. . .

Prior to 1885 the mines of the Belmont (Silver Bend) district, had produced more than $15,000,000 in silver and lead,* but it was becoming increasingly evident that Belmont's days as an active camp were numbered.

Came a morning in May, 1900, and the springtime urge to go prospecting was sinking its spurs in the rump of James L. Butler, aforementioned district attorney. Relegating his ranch duties to his wife and his courtroom duties to a young assistant, Tasker L. Oddie (later to be governor of Nevada) Butler ambled south toward the little camp of Klondyke.

The night of May 18 found him camped at a place known as Tonopah Springs; and on the morning following, Jim made the discovery that launched the stampede to Tonopah—one of the greatest mining strikes in the history of Nevada.

The immediate effect of that boom on aging Belmont was to drain her last remaining strength. The general election of 1903 found her able to muster only 36 qualified voters; and during the year following, Tonopah succeeded in wresting from her the county seat. Shorn of her official prestige, the old camp in the Toquimas gave one last weary sigh and laid down her arms.

---

*Lincoln, Francis Church: Mining Districts and Mineral Resources of Nevada, 1923.

And now, even that "last sigh" was more than half a lifetime in the past. Belmont's last business house, her school, her postoffice, long since had closed; and of her one-time population of 10,000, only two persons then remained in the town. One of these was Mrs. Rose Walter, who had lived in the vicinity of Belmont for all her 60-odd years—her mother having come there from the East, as a young girl. The other occupant of the town was Sarah, a plump and ancient Indian woman who spoke an impossible medley of Mexican, Nevadan and Paiute, and made her home in the big stone building which originally housed the offices of Combination Milling company.

Only two—out of 10,000. . .

Time had been moving forward—not only the years but the time of that afternoon. The sun had slipped down the western sky until it barely was clearing the mountaintop, and long dark shadows were spreading across the land toward my campsite at the front door of the courthouse.

Retracing my way down the stairs, I built a small open fire and cooked my supper of Campbell's soup and boiled eggs and tea—using the concrete threshold of the courthouse as a kitchen cabinet and, later, as a dining table. By the time I had finished eating and had unrolled my sleeping bag on the ground, in the lee of my car, a thin new moon was glinting ghostily from the smooth brick face of the building, and night's chill had crept into the air. A few bats had come to wheel overhead; and down along the creek, a single frog was croaking.

Except for the dying embers of my campfire, the only gleam of light visible in all that deserted city was the faint flicker of a kerosene lamp in the kitchen window at Indian Sarah's.

Belmont, the Buxom Belle of the 'Sixties, is a weary old lady, now. She retires early. . .

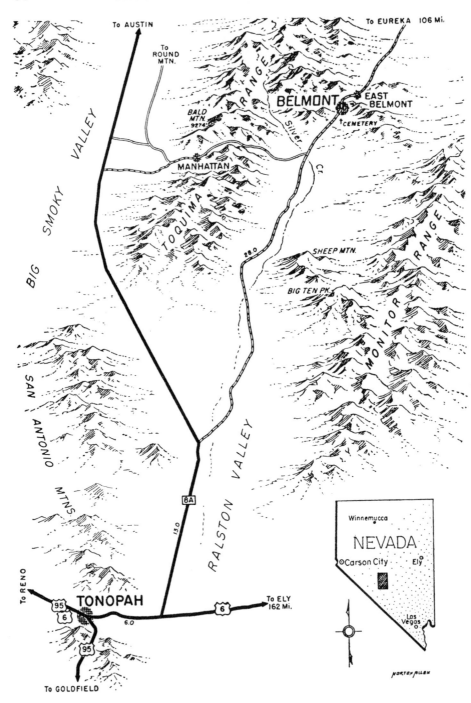

7

Manhattan Is a Spunky Old Gal

A T THE SOUTH END of the Toquima range, nearly a mile and a half above sea level and 14 miles southwest of Belmont, lies the once-important mining camp of Manhattan, Nevada.

Manhattan is a spunky old gal, and to term her a ghosttown—or even potential ghosttown—is to incur the wrath of the Furies; but cold truth sometimes speaks in a cruel tongue. By counting every resident, Indian and white, in all the 36 square miles of Manhattan township, census enumerators, in 1950, tallied only 95 human beings; and no matter how optimistic and charitable one may choose to be, 95 citizens is a far leap from the frontier metropolis that filled this ravine in the days when Teddy Roosevelt was serving his second term as president.

There always is a chance, of course, that the old camp will stage a miraculous rebound from the brink of the grave. Certainly, no one hopes so more than I—but every year finds that hope grown a little dimmer.

Manhattan's career is dated, generally, from 1905; but as early as 1866, the district had attracted a flurry of attention and a small camp had been founded by fortune hunters who poured into the area to scramble for highgrade assaying as much as $2500 to the ton. With that embryo town strangled by the slump of the 1880s and '90s, however, little more was heard of Manhattan Gulch until opening years of the present century.

Following the spectacular strikes at Tonopah and Goldfield, an army of newly-inspired prospectors spread over the surrounding region, hammering and chipping at every likely ledge; and in the midst of this campaign of seeking, a Nye County cowpuncher made the most important discovery of his lifetime.

While returning from Belmont to the Seyler ranch, on Peavine creek, John C. Humphrey and three companions halted beside the road to eat lunch. Finishing his meal ahead of the others, Humphrey wandered off from the group a little way, and within a hundred feet of the road came upon an outcrop containing gold ore of specimen grade. Although the men were carrying no tools, they succeeded in breaking loose a few pieces of the rock, and from samples thus collected reportedly realized some $3200!

But for the phenomenal booms then under way in other parts of

Nevada, the ensuing stampede to the new town of Manhattan would have warranted headlines in every newspaper in the land. Within a few months, three banks were in operation. A newspaper, the Manhattan *Mail,* was being published with regularity, and construction of a large, new hotel was under way. Living accommodations were virtually unobtainable— even tents were renting at fabulous prices—and for seven blocks along the narrow mountain ravine, the plank sidewalks of the burgeoning city were edged with two solid rows of business houses! At Manhattan's elevation—nearly 2000 feet higher than Denver—winter is no humorous matter; yet, not even December's blizzards could stay those in-pouring throngs of 1905.

When the notorious mining promoter, Humboldt Gates, gave the district his implied approval by investing heavily in one of its first major developments, success of the camp was assured. Mining claims in the snow-buried mountains began to enjoy brisk trade—the same properties changing hands, time and again. Such claims, in many instances, were so deeply blanketed by snow that their transitory owners never laid eyes on the ground involved, nor could they have located its site with an Indian guide and compass. Yet, each time a mining claim changed hands it was at a sharp increase in price. Speculation in town property was equally brisk.

"Real estate in the new towns of Manhattan and Central is booming," noted the DeLamar *Lode,* on January 16, 1906. "Lots on Main street, in Manhattan, are now held at figures ranging from $1300 to $1900 each, and frame buildings for saloons, stores and hotels, are being erected as quickly as possible."

Two weeks later *The Lode* still was enamored of the new boomcamp in Nye County.

"There is not a half mile of the 50-mile road between Tonopah and Manhattan over which some team is not passing at all hours of the day," it was stated. "The procession includes autos, stages, private rigs, and countless freight teams."

With such an influx of humanity it is not surprising that Manhattan should have drawn to her bosom a few bad hombres.

Of several gunfights staged in the town, none was more spectacular than the slaying of Sheriff Thomas W. Logan, by Walter C. Barieu, in April, 1906.

One thing that made this case unusual was the fact that no two published versions of it agreed in all particulars. For months after the shooting, discussion of the affray was sufficient to bring men to blows; and, even today, in Nye County, the long-ago murder of Sheriff Logan is a controversial issue.

Tonopah *Daily Bonanza,* in the first published report of the slaying, styled Barieu "a low, Creole gambler . . . an absinthe fiend . . . widely known as a badman." He and another gambler, it was set forth by the

PLATE 1—*Built in the middle 1870s and abandoned in 1903 when the Nye county seat was moved to the rising new boom camp of Tonopah, the old brick courthouse at Belmont, Nev., stands as a rugged memento of that lusty era when battling to acquire or hold the county seat was one of the major activities of every ambitious mining camp.*

PLATE 2—*Last building standing in the former business district of Aurora, Nev., is the Last Chance Saloon—all other structures on Antelope street having been razed by the owners for building material and to effect tax reductions. On the second floor of the Last Chance had flourished a bawdry house made conveniently accessible to patrons by means of an outside stairway.*

PLATE 3—*Chimneys of abandoned smelters stand guard over silent ruins throughout Nevada's mining country. Picturesque stacks may be seen at Tuscarora (above),* Belmont, Newark, Hiko, Palmetto, *and elsewhere.*

PLATE 4—*Antelope street, in Aurora, Nev., was a busy place in the 1860s but is quiet today. Only rubble remains where buildings stood, and town's last resident died in 1955.*

PLATE 5—*With a peak population of 10,000, Bodie, Calif., was one of the wildest and most famous of early Western mining camps, and today finds it one of our best-preserved ghosttowns. Remaining, in 1955, were numerous buildings, two cemeteries, and many ruins, but the town's only inhabitant was a caretaker employed by the Cain family, of Bridgeport, principal property owners at Bodie.*

PLATE 6—*Old freight wagon wheels, such as these in the ruins of the Techatticup mine, near ghosttown of Nelson, Nev., are highly valued by collectors of Western relics who have searched all the more accessible mining towns in quest of them. Five miles down the desert canyon in the rear lies the sparkling water of Lake Mohave, impounded behind Davis Dam, on the Colorado River.*

PLATE 7—*Important early-day adjunct to Western mining was the burning of charcoal, large quantities of which were used in reducing ores into bullion. Made commonly from pinyon pine, juniper, and mountain mahogany (in extreme circumstances from sagebrush) the coal was fired in giant stone ovens, such as these built in 1876 to supply the Martin White smelter at Ward, near Ely, Nev.*

PLATE 8—*Three steam tractors, bought by Pacific Coast Borax Co., proved useless for hauling borax and one of their number (above) was sold to the Techatticup mine, at Nelson, Nev. After unrewarding attempts to use it hauling ore, the machine was abandoned, to be rescued 50 years later by "Pop" Simon, motel owner, of Jean, Nev. As "tourist bait" it is proving completely successful.*

PLATE 9—*Former stage station and postoffice at Schellbourne, Nev., the adobe building below is used as part-time residence by Mr. and Mrs. G. C. Russell, of Tooele, Utah, owners of Schellbourne Ranch. The old town, which functioned successively as a station on the Overland Mail and Pony Express, site of an Army fort, and mining boom camp, embraces several other picturesque ruins.*

PLATE 10—*"Uncle Cell" Bracken, resident of Pine Valley, Utah, for more than 90 years, recalls early days when present ghosttown's economy was based on logging and cattle.*

PLATE 11—*Tom Mulliner, veteran teamster and mail carrier, still likes to be around horses. His summers are spent in a sheep wagon; his winters, usually, at Tooele, Utah.*

PLATE 12—*Still in use at Pine Valley, Utah, is the Church of Jesus Christ of Latter Day Saints (Mormon) built in 1868 by Ebenezer Bryce, Australian shipwright for whom Bryce Canyon was named. It was Bryce's boast that the church was built stoutly as a ship. The pleasantly-situated mountain town is completely deserted in winter, and has but a dozen residents during summer months.*

PLATE 13—*George Tripp, for 86 years a resident of Callao, Utah, married late, fathered 12 children, and has lived to see his descendants populate most of the valley.*

PLATE 14—*"Stoke's Castle," three-story landmark at Austin, Nev., was built in 1897 by Anson Phelps Stokes, Eastern mining tycoon, who occupied it intermittently for several years.*

PLATE 15—*Most of the important banks, hotels, express offices and stores built in Western mining towns in the period 1849-80, were equipped with stout iron shutters which closed over doors and windows and were locked nightly from within, thereby transforming any stone building into a miniature fortress unbreachable by bandits or Indians. Shown is the former Wells Fargo bank building at Silver Reef, Utah.*

PLATE 16—*One of the leading operations in Nevada when this photo was made (c. 1880) the Highland Chief Mill, in Dean Canyon, Lander County, today is represented by only a sprawling waste dump—every building having vanished from its site. Other important producers of gold and silver in the same general area were the Starr Grove, Eagle, Pittsburgh, Morningstar, Dean, and Betty O'Neal.*

PLATE 17—*Columbus salt marsh, 40 miles west of Tonopah, Nev., is known as birthplace of the borax mining industry in the United States —commercial harvesting and refining of the material by Chinese coolie labor having been launched here in the 1870s by F. M. "Borax" Smith. White waste dumps, old metal tanks, and timbers eaten porous by the potent mineral salts, are silent reminders of that now-vanished era.*

PLATE 18—*With neither relatives nor friends remaining in the area to care for graves, ghosttown cemeteries commonly become disheveled places where paling fences lie prone, headboards are splintered and sand-blasted, graves sunken, and all overgrown with thistles and weeds. Shown is a portion of the cemetery at Iosepa, Utah, and the stone of Kapainui Kalauao, Hawaiian colonist, died in 1891.*

PLATE 19—*In towns supported chiefly by a single mine or mill, the leading store was usually owned by the mining company, as was this store at Cortez, Nev. Operators of "company towns" generally banned all gambling, loose women, and sale of intoxicants, whereupon opportunists commonly contrived to cash-in on human nature by establishing nearby a "blow off" town, where the sky was the limit.*

PLATE 20—*For many years after Clifton, Utah, became a ghosttown, this stout log cabin was occupied by Oliver Young, the town's last surviving resident, who claimed the famous Mormon leader, Brigham Young, as his uncle. Since Oliver's death, the old town has been visited only by occasional prospectors, range riders hunting cattle or sheep, and by persons interested in prowling its historic site.*

PLATE 21—*In addition to this "modern" pharmacy, the main street of Gold Hill, Utah, is flanked by an assortment of stores and shops adequate to serve a community of 2000 persons, but none is tenanted. At time of the author's visit, in 1952, the town still harbored five residents, but had lost its postoffice, and not even a telephone afforded connection with the outside world.*

PLATE 22—*In this sandstone building, Wells Fargo & Co. conducted the banking activities of Treasure City, Nev., 80 years ago a place of 7000 inhabitants, perched 9000 feet above sea-level on the bony rump of the White Pine mountains. More metropolitan Hamilton, then seat of White Pine county, lay 3 miles distant and 1500 feet lower, via the now-dim trail at right.*

PLATE 23—*Carson & Colorado R.R., a narrow gauge built by Wm. Sharon and Darius Ogden Mills, ran from Mound House, near Carson City, Nev., to Keeler, Calif., 293 miles. On the day in 1898 when this photo was made at the Candelaria depot, the train crew consisted of Fred Barnes, conductor; Frank Regan, brakeman; Abe Church, engineer (in cab); Johnnie McGillis, fireman, and Chas. Meadows, mail clerk.*

PLATE 24—*In addition to this delapidated building, the former site of Newhouse, Utah, is marked by mill foundations, ruins, and other relics of that period (1905-10) when Samuel Newhouse, Salt Lake City financier, was developing and working the Cactus mine in the San Francisco mountains (rear). Profits from the Cactus financed construction of the Newhouse Hotel and other prominent buildings in Salt Lake City.*

PLATE 25—*Constructed of handsomely-dressed sandstone and lumber ox-freighted from Oregon, the J. B. Withington hotel, at Hamilton, was the most elaborate and costly structure of its kind in Nevada at time of its erection in 1869. Although badly deteriorated, the old hostelry is still the outstanding "show place" of this once-important, but long-abandoned, mining center.*

PLATE 26—*Born at Gold Mountain, Nev., 75 years ago, Douglas Robinson, now of Bishop, Calif., is recognized as an authority on history of Esmeralda county's early mining camps.*

PLATE 27—*At time of his death in 1955, the late Harry Wiley, veteran miner and legislator of Gold Point, Nev., had been a resident of Esmeralda county for 50 years.*

PLATE 28—*Replaced 40-odd years ago by the Ford car, the prospectors' burros which did so much to open the mining country, were turned out on the desert to subsist as they might. Surviving and multiplying slowly, the little jacks are now being slain by so-called "sportsmen," far less deserving of that name than the animals they are killing. (Photo made at Lida, Nev., 1905.)*

PLATE 29—*First stores and shops to appear in every new mining camp were housed in tents. Wagon boxes on their sides became bars and counters; packing cases were remodeled into restaurant tables and barber chairs. Later would come good buildings and furnishings comparable to those seen in Eastern centers. Pictured is a pioneer pie shop at Hornsilver, Nev., early in 1908.*

PLATE 30—*Some mining camps cling to a thread of life long after their contemporaries have died. Such a one is Gold Point, Nev., which began life as Hornsilver (above). For many years the town has had barely a dozen residents, but still supports a small grocery store and postoffice operated by Ora Mae Wiley, widow of the late Senator Harry Wiley, long-time resident of the camp.*

PLATE 31—*All that remains of the jovially-named gold town of Skidoo, Calif., in the Death Valley area, is the former "company" boarding house (left), mill ruins, and a few old cabins—two of them wallpapered with Los Angeles "Examiners," of 1915. During its peak of activity, around 1906, the camp supported a newspaper and stores, and its peace was broken by several murders and one lynching.*

PLATE 32—*Named for the Horn Silver mine, one of Utah's greatest silver producers, this old building originally housed the leading mercantile establishment at Frisco, in Beaver county. More than half the building's front is marked by the ugly but protective iron shutters common to business architecture in Western mining camps of the 1849-80 era. The townsite also embraces other ruins, charcoal ovens, and a cemetery.*

PLATE 33—*Desert-parched throats undoubtedly rejoiced as this 16-mule team delivered its 21,000 pounds of liquid freight to Tex Rickard's Northern Saloon at Rawhide, Nev., in 1908.*

PLATE 34—*Named by its Mexican founders for the day of Candlemass, or Candelaria, when Mary took the Infant Jesus to the Temple, the early camp of Candelaria, Nev., knew little of sanctity. Most of its population was foreign born, water was scarcer than whiskey, and mills, operated with dry battery boxes, blanketed the town in a constant pall of dust. Shown is Main street, about 1896.*

PLATE 35—*Beast of burden commonly employed by desert prospectors of pre-jeep days, was the burro or "jackass." Inured to great extremes of climate, the burro could subsist on dry desert brush, required less water than a horse or mule, and was capable of packing as much as 250 pounds over rough terrain.*

PLATE 36—*Buildings that bloomed in Western mining camps were not always styled along lines familiar to the American Institute of Architects. With its classically-adorned false front and stained glass windows, the former city hall at Midas, Nev., for example, suggests a touch of the Greek—or perhaps Russian, or Latvian. On the other hand, it may be an architectural style found nowhere but at Midas.*

PLATE 37—*Mining camp ruins are rich in poignant effects. Here a lone bird is perched on the skeleton of a dead tree overlooking the crumbling chimney of a two-story home destroyed by fire more than half a century ago. Sagebrush has reclaimed yard and garden, and grows tall within the area formerly occupied by kitchen and parlor. Setting of the scene was at Tuscarora, Nevada.*

PLATE 38—*At time of its construction, in 1906, the depot at Rhyolite served three railroads affording connection with the S.P. and A.T. & S.F., and as the most elaborate depot in Nevada, was styled "The Dearborn Street Station of the West." Abandoned at close of the Rhyolite boom, it now houses a private residence and casino, and is one of the popular show places of this famous ghosttown.*

PLATE 39—*Arriving at Rhyolite at start of the boom, H. D. and L. D. Porter, brothers, opened a general store (below) and by 1907 were doing an average monthly business of $150,000. In addition to groceries, drygoods, men's and women's clothing, and household furnishings, the Porters dealt in lumber, hay, grain, cement, coal, crude oil, gasoline, stoves, Studebaker wagons, T-rails, Hercules powder, and mining and milling machinery.*

PLATE 40—*In 1908, before Rawhide, Nev., was six months old, 50 private autos and auto stages, similar to this rakish model, were shuttling across the desert from Schurz and, together with horsedrawn rigs, were bringing to the new camp as many as 400 pilgrims daily. Auto passenger fare averaged around 25 cents a mile; the makes most favored by boom-camp capitalists, Pope Toledos and Thomas Flyers.*

PLATE 41—*According to the placard displayed in this 1908 picture of Rawhide, a dance was slated for that night by the Eagles' lodge. Every early mining camp of importance was liberally supplied with all the better known fraternal orders; also well represented during their respective eras were the Fenian Brotherhood, Druids, Union League, Knights of the Golden Circle, and Sons of Temperance.*

PLATE 42—*Half a dozen persons still live in the once-rousing camp of Rawhide, Nev., but not for many years has the town embraced an operating business house. Situated on another street, to the north of that shown, are buildings which formerly housed a theatre, postoffice, hotel, store, saloon, and the jail—a stout stone building well-equipped with iron-barred windows and door.*

PLATE 43—*Gaunt hulks of copper mills at Ludwig, Nev., testify to many years spasmodic activity, beginning in 1865 when the main Ludwig mine was opened. In 1911, Ludwig became terminus of Nevada Copper Belt R.R., and for several years preceding and during World War I enjoyed prosperity of an uncertain sort. At Weed Heights, nearby, is the large open-pit copper mine being developed by Anaconda Copper.*

PLATE 44—*Few gladiator jousts were cheered more lustily than the single-jack and double-jack drilling contests that highlighted every mining camp celebration—winner being the man, or team of two men, who could sink the deepest hole into a granite boulder in only 15 minutes. Accompanying photo shows part of an estimated 20,000 spectators witnessing such an exhibition at Goldfield, Nev., about 1906.*

PLATE 45—*Goods destined for the earliest mining camps were hauled chiefly in ox-drawn freight wagons, but this antiquated transportation was not long acceptable to that precocious land. By close of the 19th century, virtually all draft oxen had been replaced with stout, young horses and mules, and covered freight wagons, such as these shown on the main street of Tonopah, Nev., in 1903.*

PLATE 46 — *While prospecting through Northern Nevada in 1912, Charlie Hawkinson wandered into the busy gold camp of Jarbidge, liked the place, and has remained there 44 years.*

PLATE 47 — *Colorful "Diamond-field Jack" Davis, founder of the camp of Diamondfield, shown about 1903 as he arrived at Tono-pah after barely escaping the gallows in Idaho.*

PLATE 48—*Principal buildings remaining in the ghost camp of Berlin, Nev., are (l. to r.) the boarding house, assay office, and mill, all vacant. Not shown are several dwellings, one of which is occupied by Mr. and Mrs. Harold Newman, Berlin's last remaining residents. Just over the far ridge lies Nevada State Ichthyosaur Park, where paleontologists are excavating giant fossil fish-lizards, 160,000,000 years old.*

PLATE 49 — *Arriving at Broken Hills., Nev., at peak of its boom, Maury Stromer mined, operated a store and the postoffice, and after 37 years was the town's last surviving resident.*

PLATE 50—*Ed Green, resident of Lovelock Valley for nearly 65 years, has mined, punched cattle, trapped wild horses, and driven stage to Seven Troughs (below) and other Nevada boom towns.*

PLATE 51—*On the morning this picture was made, in 1908, the stage to Seven Troughs, Nev., had halted at Big Meadows hotel, in Lovelock —possibly to determine if the night train had brought any pilgrims to be transported to the booming new gold camp. Appearance of the Lovelock street has not changed materially since the photo was made— but stages no longer go to Seven Troughs!*

PLATE 52—*Built by Pittsburgh Silver Peak Gold Mining Co., in 1907, this 120-stamp cyanide mill at Blair, Esmeralda county, was the largest stamp mill in Nevada, and Pittsburgh Silver Peak was for years the state's largest producer of low-grade ores. Shutting down in 1915 for lack of ore, the company moved its milling machinery to California, the buildings were razed, and only rubble remains.*

PLATE 53—*Townsite promoters at scene of a new strike frequently realized more net profit than accrued to any individual mine's operator. If a strike proved sufficiently spectacular, price of building sites might skyrocket until raw desert land—available free for the taking, in pre-boom days—would be selling from $2500 to $5000 or more, per lot. Shown is the townsite office at Wahmonie, Nevada.*

PLATE 54—*Built at a cost of $100,000, this marble-tiled 50-rooms-and-30-baths hotel, at Metropolis, Nev., was advertised "Finest Between Ogden and the Coast." After operating only two years it closed permanently in 1913 when local water sources proved inadequate to supply colonists lured hence by Pacific Reclamation Co., sponsors of the project. Only broken foundations and rubble remains.*

PLATE 55—*Even the saloon got "tipsy" at Charleston, Nevada, gold-mining fleshpot of the 1890s. This and a similar log relic, which had housed a general store, are the only original buildings still standing in Charleston's one-time business district. Former site of the town is now headquarters of a large cattle ranch, and the two old log structures are in use for storage purposes.*

Bonanza, had been creating a disturbance in the Jewel Saloon, at Manhattan. The bartender had summoned the sheriff to separate the men. After quieting the pair, according to this account, Sheriff Logan had been in the act of leaving the place when Barieu had whipped out a gun and fired five shots at the lawman's back. Four of those shots had found their mark. . .

The news account carried by the *Weekly Bullfrog Miner,* on the other hand, had attacked the character of the slain sheriff in a manner too potentially libelous to be repeated here, while an altogether different set of details had been offered by the DeLamar *Lode,* with issue of April 17, 1906.

Barieu, it was stated by the Lincoln county publication, had struck an unidentified woman, who had called Logan for help. The Sheriff had thrown Barieu out of the saloon, whereupon the gambler had dashed to a side window and shot at Logan, but missed. As the sheriff ran out the front door to arrest his assailant, Barieu had fired four times—each shot taking effect. Despite his mortal wounds, the sheriff had grappled with Barieu, and disarmed him; and with the pistol taken from him, had beaten him over the head until the other man had fallen insensible. The officer, thereupon, had collapsed, and, moments later, was dead.

Whatever the true circumstances surrounding his demise, Sheriff Logan had been a popular man and his fellow citizens went all-out to lay him away in grand style. The funeral, conducted at Tonopah by the Oddfellows and Eagles lodges, was described as largest in the history of Nevada, to that time, and all Tonopah business houses closed for the rites.

But, Walter Barieu, strangely enough, was not convicted of the Sheriff's murder. Although the state's case was ably prosecuted by Nye County District Attorney Key Pittman—later to be United States Senator from Nevada—the sensational trial at last ended in a verdict of acquittal.

With the Logan-Barieu fracas only about a week in the past, Manhattan's cozy little world was rent asunder by an earthquake centered some 300 miles to the west.

With San Francisco in smoking chaos men came to realize that Manhattan's prosperity had lain not so much in her juniper-clad hills as it had in a building at Montgomery and Sutter streets, in the Bay City. Virtually every speculative mine in the Manhattan district had been backed by San Francisco promoters and San Francisco capital, and with that support suddenly withdrawn to enable reconstruction of San Francisco's own ruins, the Manhattan boom collapsed. Banks closed their doors, merchants took heavy losses, and development ceased.

After several years passed in a comatose state, the town slowly rallied and by 1912 was again going strong. Frank Garside's new weekly, the *Manhattan Post,* was recording the fortunes of the revived camp, and a new 75-ton quartz mill had been erected. When rich ore was found in the lower levels of the White Caps mine, the mill was enlarged and men predicted for Manhattan the greatest era of prosperity in her history. But like its predecessor of ten years before, the anticipated boom of 1915 was short lived.

Meanwhile, another phase of development was being given serious consideration by mining men. Since early in the century there had been sporadic gold placering in Manhattan Gulch—the peak of such activities having been reached in May, 1909, when dust and nuggets to a value of more than $1000 per day had been recovered there by relatively crude methods.* Due to lack of water and other economic factors, all placer mining in the district had been limited to small-scale efforts until 1938, when Manhattan Gold Dredging company—a subsidiary of the far-flung Natomas, of California—placed in operation here what then was the world's second-largest electrically-powered bucketline dredge.

Floating on a pond of water piped from Peavine creek, a dozen miles distant, the 3000-ton desert Leviathan—400 feet in length and 78 feet in breadth—began moving through the alluvial fan filling Manhattan Gulch.

Swallowing around 12,000 yards of cobblestones and gravel daily, the gigantic dredge inched forward, its artificial lake moving with it as tailings were spewed out behind. From each cubic yard of material handled, approximately 21 cents worth of gold was salvaged.

At conclusion of this operation, in 1946, five miles of gulch at the lower end of town was left filled with a mountainous waste of tailings from which had been recovered nearly $4,600,000 in gold, together with a miscellaneous assortment of old coins—mostly dimes—and one gold-nugget stick pin.

With this substantial contribution, Manhattan's known production of precious metals (as of 1949) was boosted to $10,362,289.**

The dredging operation at an end, the big ship was sold to Natomas—already part owner—whereupon was begun the tremendous task of dismantling it and moving it to the next scene of operations at Copper Canyon, 170 miles to the north, in Lander county. Nearly 100 truck loads, scaling as much as 40 tons each, were necessary to complete that gigantic job of removal.

During the period when the dredge was in process of dismantling, reportorial duties had taken me to Manhattan on several occasions; but once the ship was gone there had been no reason for my return to the town—particularly so, since I suspected I wasn't especially popular there since writing a story for the Salt Lake *Tribune* in which I verbally pictured the camp as "knocking at the gates of oblivion."

---

*C. C. Jones, Notes on Manhattan Placers, English Mining Journal, July 17, 1909.

**Kral, Victor E., Mineral Resources of Nye County: State Bureau of Mines Bulletin. Vol. XLV, Jan. 1951.

Thus, six years had slipped by, when like the criminal who feels a compulsion to return to the scene of his crime, I developed an urge to revisit the old town at the head of Manhattan Gulch.

Even to one familiar with the pendulum-like fortunes of mining camps, it was hard to realize that such changes could have been wrought in the relatively short while elapsed.

Departure of the dredge and its payroll had sparked the disintegration of Manhattan's world. All but the barest handful of her citizens had drifted away, and nearly every business house had closed. Some of the better dwellings had followed the dredge to its new scene of activity; other buildings had been moved to the large, new placering operation at nearby Round Mountain.

My return visit fell on a Sunday afternoon. After driving the full length of main street, I was about of the opinion that not one business house remained open, when I noticed a small saloon that exhibited a few feeble signs of life. Not too many years before, this place—and half a dozen others—would have been packed to the sills with roistering miners and dredge men. The walls would have pulsed to a roaring crescendo of juke box music and loud laughing, and boasting and good humor, and the everlasting whirr of slot machines.

But now, as I stepped through the door, it was like entering the cool, dim cloisters of a mausoleum. The only customer in the place was a ragged old veteran who sat at the far end of the bar, nursing a can of beer. He appeared ancient enough to have come in with the first boom in '66. His grizzled thatch of hair swept down to merge with grizzled gray whiskers, and beside him on the bar lay a grizzled felt hat with a hole in the crown.

As soon as my coke had been set before me, the bartender turned back to the old timer, who picked up the continuity of a story evidently interrupted by my arrival.

It was a long, involved tale, having to do with claim jumpers and highgraders, and water rights, and gravel that ran a dollar to the pan.

"What's more," declared the old man, in a thin, shaky falsetto, "It's still a-layin' right there, I tell you—right there in The Gulch! If that sonofabitch hadn't gone and cut off my water, I wouldn't be like this today. I'd be right up there in the blue-chip class with the best of 'em. Yes, siree!"

"Sure, Pop," the bartender nodded mechanically. "Sure, you would."

Going back out to my car I sat for a moment looking up and down that empty, silent street; up past the Toiyabe Club, and the old stone postoffice, both closed; and down past the white Catholic church, and the big gaunt mill, and on toward the sunset, and a landscape torn and tumbled and turned upside down in man's everlasting search for gold.

The screen door of the saloon eased shut with a discouraged thud. The ragged old man, I saw, had emerged from the dim room beyond that door; and now he was speaking to a ragged old dog lying on the porch.

Slowly, painfully, the old dog struggled to his feet and fell into step at the old man's heels, and the two of them pegged off toward a shabby old cabin with a broken gate and broken chimney. From that chimney was rising a thin spiral of smoke, and the flaming glow of the sunset was reflected in the tiny, square panes of the windows.

I hoped that behind those windows some woman was waiting with a good, hot supper; an understanding woman, who was tolerant of an old mining man, and an old dog, and their dreams.

But I doubted if there was any woman in the old cabin at the end of the road. Where there are women, there are curtains—and there were no curtains at those windows.

8

Where Ghosts Swing an Axe and a Lariat

GORDON BECKSTROM was nudging middle age when first I met him. Both he and his father had been born in the little mountain village of Pine Valley, and there Gordon still lived in a sturdy brick house built three generations before by his grandfather. Up the road a piece, stood another house, built even earlier by his great-grandfather. . .

That this little settlement in Southwestern Utah should have exerted such a powerful hold on his family, was not too difficult to understand. Even as a ghosttown, it was a delightful place; and back in the days of its founding it must have seemed the answer to a pioneer's prayer!

Which white man looked first upon the Pine Valley region is a debatable question. Possibly it was Jedediah Smith and his beaver trappers, possibly Fremont. But, in any case, it was Isaac Riddle who brought the valley first to the attention of Southern Utah's Mormon colonists, in 1855.

Riddle and Bill Hamblin, so the story goes, had been given the job of herding the "mission" cattle. One of the cows had strayed; and Riddle, being a conscientious Mormon, started after her. He would have followed her plumb to hell if that had been the only means of returning her to the fold; but the cow was a reasonable beast. Instead of taking him to some less pleasant place, she led him up into the high mountains and down to this valley, which Riddle later characterized, "The most beautiful sight I had ever beheld on God's green earth!"

In a natural amphitheatre formed by high, rolling hills, densely timbered with quaking aspen, oaks and giant pines, lay a small, green meadow. Through its center wound a stream of sparkling water, and the dew-wet grass that blanketed the valley was so tall it drenched the stirrups of Riddle's saddle. . .

Realizing that the region offered an important source of lumber—then sorely needed by the colonists of Southwestern Utah—Riddle, together with Jehu Blackburn and Robert Richey, took steps to procure a small sawmill, which they freighted to the valley by ox teams, and established on Spring Branch creek. The little mill was placed in operation in 1856*,

---

*Deseret News, March 5, 1856.

and that summer saw the arrival of Pine Valley's first permanent residents —all of whom, naturally, were members of the Church of Jesus Christ of Latter Day Saints. Included among these first comers were Jacob Hamblin, later famed as the "Buckskin Apostle," and his wife, Rachel; and on August 3, that year, Mrs. Hamblin gave birth to a daughter, Rachel Tamer, first white child born in the new settlement.

Pine Valley's development as a town was not rapid—not as compared to the mining boom camps—but by 1859 a postoffice had been established there, a church erected, a school was ready to receive pupils, and an open-air dance floor had been built.

"If you want the real, old-time history of Pine Valley, you should talk to my great-uncle, Marcellus Bracken—'Cell', we call him—" said Gordon Beckstrom, in his slow, soft drawl. "Uncle Cell's 95 years old, and he's passed 90 of those years right here in the valley and over the ridge in the next little town of Central. He'd be proud to talk to you . . ."

I found Uncle Cell (Plate 10) spending the afternoon with one of his sundry daughters-in-law. A tall, spare patriarch, neat and clean as a sugar pine, he came equipped with a devilish glint in his eye, and a crooked, infectious grin. When I said I was writing a series of "early settler" interviews for the *Salt Lake Tribune* and would like some information about pioneer times in Pine Valley, the old man jerked his head in assent, and smiled.

"I can give you all of it," he said crisply. "All that's fit to print, and some that's not! What, in particular, did you want to know?"

Marcellus Bracken, I learned, had been born at Payson, Utah, in 1857. With his parents, and five brothers and sisters, he had emigrated to St. George, in 1861—making the 225 mile journey by ox team and wagon.

"If you've never ridden behind oxen, you've no idea how pesky slow those beasts can travel!" said Uncle Cell. "Why," he went on, with a twinkle, "the little girls would hop out of the wagon and build playhouses along the road. They'd play in 'em 'til they got too old for that sort of thing . . . and then, they'd run a short piece and catch up with the wagon again!"

The Brackens located in Pine Valley in 1862, and Cell's father established in Box Canyon the first shingle mill in Washington county. The next year saw three sawmills operating in the valley—these, as well as the fourth mill, being operated by water power and equipped with the cumbersome up-and-down saws, known as "muleys." Fifth mill built introduced the time-saving circular saw; and when the Gardners opened their new mill, residents from miles around gathered to watch its operation with a 40-horsepower steam engine as the driving force.

During his boyhood, said Uncle Cell, as many as seven sawmills had operated in Pine Valley at a single time. Other industries contributing to the town's early prosperity had included a water-powered mill which did a thriving business manufacturing wooden kegs, tubs, buckets, bread bowls, and churns. There had been a tannery, and a cheese factory, and a water-powered flour and grist mill—the first grist through the mill having been supplied by Henry Chadburn who had walked 12 miles to town from his ranch, carrying on his back a 50-pound sack of grain.

While Pine Valley's lumber was used in most of the early buildings in Washington county, it was the mining booms at Silver Reef, Utah, and Pioche, Nevada, that threw the industry into full stride. With lumber in great demand at both camps, Pine Valley millmen found it an easy matter to market their entire output at double the prices formerly received. Among local residents who had turned to lumber freighting as a lucrative source of income, had been young Cell.

"Pioche was a wild town—one of the wildest in the West!" he recalled. "Once, when I was there with a load of lumber, 17 men were killed in a single night, and a murder a day was considered about average! Even Pine Valley was rough—probably the roughest of the Mormon towns. When the logging outfits and the mills were running at capacity, there weren't nearly enough local people to handle the work, so any transient who came along was assured a job.

"Many of these men were fugitives—murderers, horsethieves, and army deserters—who had been attracted to the valley because of its remote location. Since idleness invited suspicion, such men generally worked in the sawmills while in hiding. Among this worldly element, gambling flourished; there was plenty of wine brought in by peddlers from Santa Clara and Toquerville, and"—he grinned—"we even tolerated a pack of saloons!"

For the first 40 years after its founding, the production of lumber constituted Pine Valley's major industry. Toward the end of the century, with the Washington county settlements well established and the mining booms at Silver Reef and Pioche suffering reverses, the demand for building materials fell away, the mills closed, and transient workmen drifted to new fields.

Even before close of the lumbering hegira, a few farsighted men of the valley were beginning to turn to cattle raising. With free range, abundant water, waving acres of wild grass, an assured market, and no restrictions, this was an industry slated to launch a second era as colorful and lucrative as that of the timber harvest.

Due to the deep snows and frigid temperatures common to Pine Valley's high elevation, cattle were wintered in the warm lower country around Dameron Valley and Sand Cove. Ear-marked and branded for identification, the animals were grazed on the open range—the big event of each year being the cattle roundup in which all men and older boys of Pine Valley took part.

Hazed out of the rocks and canyons by hard-riding Saints, the gathered cattle were held at a central bedding ground until completion of the round-up, whereupon they were trail-herded back to Gardner's corral at Pine Valley. In the manner of cattlemen since time of the Pharaohs, local ranchers soon developed a passion for large herds, and the valley and its environs numbered not less than ten men who owned as many as 1000 head of cattle each. During a good season more than two hours' time might be required for the herd to pass the length of main street—the animals bawling and bellering and churning the dust in the best tradition of Dodge City and the Chisholm Trail.

Once the various brands had been segregated and each rancher had claimed his own stock and sold it to waiting cattle buyers, it still remained to trail the beasts down from the mountains and across the desert to the nearest railroad point at Modena, about 45 miles.

In connection with "cow days" in the valley, Uncle Cell recalled the mysterious wild cattle that formerly inhabited the rockiest, most inaccessible canyons, bordering on Dameron Valley and Beaver Dam Wash.

"There were scads of them!" said Cell. "They were a Texas longhorn type—as wild and wicked as any jungle beast—and no one knew where they originated, or how they came to Washington county. Some felt they were offspring of cattle that had belonged to emigrants slain in the infamous Mountain Meadows massacre, which had taken place only a few miles to the north.

"None of the animals was branded, so they were any man's property; but while we occasionally shot one for fresh beef, we never took any of them for marketing. Folks who believed them Mountain Meadows cattle, wouldn't even eat their flesh . . ."

As the 20th century brought mounting herd restrictions, barbed wire, and end of the free range, Pine Valley's cattle kings followed into oblivion her earlier lumber barons. For a time it appeared that agriculture would come to the rescue of the town; but the valley embraced only a few hundred acres of land suited to farming, and markets were a long haul distant. Years went on. Old people died and took their places in the cemetery, young people drifted away to city jobs; and in May, 1952, the once-roaring lumber town of Pine Valley could muster barely a dozen inhabitants.

Even in her decadence, the old town still was pleasant and homey; its setting still was the same beautiful place Isaac Riddle had looked upon nearly a century before. Wild flowers spread over the valley like a yellow carpet, and the dew-wet meadow grass still was cut through by that same sparkling stream. Along the town's single street, smoke curled from the great stone chimneys of a few stout-hearted old homes; 80-year-old apple trees were white with bloom; and tall, gnarled cottonwoods showed the tender green of new leaves.

"The town was completely deserted last winter," said Gordon Beckstrom. "Not a soul here. Too cold . . . too much snow! See that line?" he pointed to a mark on the front of his house. "When I came back to the valley, March 31, the snow was still that deep!"

The line he indicated was nine feet above the ground.

When I had asked if the deer came down pretty close to town, the mountain man grinned.

"They don't have to *come down,"* he said. "They never leave! They do lots of damage to our gardens. You can't fence 'em out. Put another wire on your fence and they only learn to jump that much higher . . ."

In addition to a fourth class postoffice, operated during summer months only, the town still supported a pantry-sized store and a fine old Mormon church that had seen constant use since its erection in 1868.

Designed by Ebenezer Bryce—owner of a Pine Valley sawmill, and the man for whom Bryce Canyon National Park was named—the structure was built of locally-milled pine and hand-hewn timbers fastened with wooden pegs. Bryce, who had been a shipwright in Australia, had boasted that the church was as ruggedly constructed as a ship; that in the advent of flood, it would float; or, if a hurricane struck, it would roll over but would not collapse. (Plate 12.)

In its 85th year of life when I saw it, the old building appeared as sound as the day it was finished, and Pine Valleyans claimed it to be the oldest Mormon church in the United States still being used in its original form.

"You're a Latter Day Saint?" I asked Uncle Cell, knowing it was a needless question.

"Yep!" he nodded. "Been a Mormon for three generations . . ."

"Nice people!" I commented. Again he nodded in agreement.

"You know," he went on, winking at his daughter-in-law, "I figger if I live another ten years or so, I may even get used to Mormon cooking! I've learned to eat everything else fried, and as soon as I learn to drink fried coffee I reckon I'll like it right well!"

I asked if he'd ever seen Brigham Young.

"Oh, my yes!" brightened the old man. "I saw Brother Brigham many, many times! I saw all the early leaders of The Church. They all made it a practice to visit their people—even in little backwoods towns like Pine Valley and Central. But not any more . . ." he shook his head. "It's been ages since I've seen any of the higher officers. I can't go to see *them*—they don't come to see *me* . . ."

"Well, Uncle Cell," I said, rising to leave, "they *should* come to see you. You're the sort of man they'd be honored to know!"

"You think so?" he turned to regard me quizzically. And then, once again, that irrepressible twinkle was flooding the bright eyes of this 95-year oldster. "Tell you what," he said, with a confidential wink, "When you get back to Salt Lake, you might sorta mosey around to headquarters and tell 'em so!"

9

Golden City of the Dawn

BOOSTING THE green shade back from his eyes, the telegraph operator scanned the submitted message. His lips twitched in the hint of a smile. While the message didn't say so in actual words, it made clear the fact that Aurora, Nevada, was in no proper mood for Carson's refining influences.

That was quite understandable. During the three-and-a-half years since her founding, in 1860, the Esmeralda county boomcamp had known nearly two-score deaths by violence. Yet, no sooner had she started cleaning house than Territorial Governor Nye had reared up on his hind legs and sent her a curt warning that order must be preserved.

Chuckling dryly, the operator turned to his key and tapped out Aurora's reply:

"All quiet and orderly. Four men to be hung in half an hour . . ."

Throughout those first years of Aurora's existence the chief thorn in her side had been the Dailey gang—a cutthroat crew whose talents extended into half a dozen fields of outlawry. With her patience already worn thin, the town had needed only the Billy Johnson affair to fire her smoldering fuse.

Billy was a kindly old codger who attended a small stage station on the West Walker river and grew fresh vegetables for sale in the mining camps. Personally, he wouldn't have harmed a fly; but because of his loyalty to another, he was carried afoul of John Dailey's wrath. It all started when Billy's friend, Johnny Rodgers, killed a horsethief named Jim Sears; Sears had been an associate of Dailey, and Dailey had ways of dealing with presumptious citizens who erased his pals.

Soon after Sears' slaying the outlaw and his gang rode up to Billy Johnson's place and began barking questions concerning Rodgers' whereabouts—questions Billy declined to answer. The station being full of idlers it was scarcely an opportune time and place for starting trouble, and the gang leader dismissed the matter with a short, unpleasant laugh. But John Dailey wasn't amused.

From that time forward, Billy Johnson was living on borrowed time —a lethal loan that would be foreclosed on his next trip to Aurora with a wagon-load of spuds.

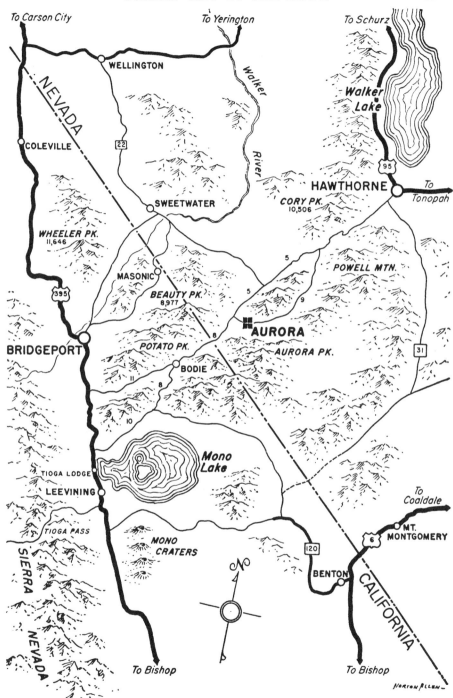

To Carson City
To Yerington
To Schurz
NEVADA
WELLINGTON
Walker
Walker
Lake
COLEVILLE
22
95
SWEETWATER
HAWTHORNE
To
Tonopah
CORY PK.
10,506
WHEELER PK.
11,646
POWELL MTN.
5
395
MASONIC
5
BEAUTY PK.
8,977
9
8
AURORA
BRIDGEPORT
POTATO PK.
AURORA PK.
31
11
BODIE
8
10
MONO
LAKE
Mono
Lake
TIOGA LODGE
LEEVINING
To
Coaldale
TIOGA PASS
MT.
MONTGOMERY
SIERRA
MONO
CRATERS
6
120
BENTON
CALIFORNIA
NEVADA
N
To Bishop
To Bishop
NORTON ALLEN

Winter days are short in the mountains, and by the time Billy had delivered his produce it was too late to start the long drive back to his little farm on the Walker. He accordingly stabled his team, engaged a 50-cent bed, and repaired to one of Aurora's 20-odd bistros.

The old man had barely stepped into the saloon before a sociable-seeming stranger struck up an acquaintance with him and bought him a drink. A little later the pair left the place together.

Neither returned.

In about an hour, John Dailey bellied up to the bar, roared a hearty greeting, called for a round of drinks, and remarked casually that he had stumbled over a dead man in the alley.

Naturally, it was the old spud farmer. Beaten and robbed, his throat had been slashed so deeply his head was nearly severed; coal oil had been poured over his clothes and ignited, and his body had been pumped full of lead.

Dawn found talk of the murder sizzling on every tongue; and every man in Aurora knew, in his own mind, that the slaying of Billy Johnson had been Dailey's pay-off for the Rodgers' episode.

Arresting Dailey and two of his triggermen, Jim Masterson and "Three-Fingered Jack" McDowell, Sheriff B. J. Francis lodged them in jail and charged them with Johnson's death. Thereupon, he and a posse started in pursuit of Bill Buckley, a fourth member of the gang, who had hightailed for the Sierra.

That was fine, said Aurora, so far as it went. But would it go as far as trial and conviction? Punishment? Aurora shook her head and nursed her doubts.

It was not that her citizens lacked respect for law and order, but they had seen too little of either. They had seen too many farcical trials marked by perjured testimony, endless postponements, legal persiflage, under-the-counter transactions, intimidation of witnesses, and eventual acquittal. They had seen too many officials reluctant to prosecute; too many jurymen loath to bring in a verdict of guilty lest they be the next to join those swelling ranks on Boot Hill.

They had seen 27 murders committed in relatively few months—*but they had not seen one conviction!*

Weighing the unsavory situation, Aurora made her decision.

Violence must be cured with violence.

Convening in the Wingate building, 350 male residents were sworn in as members of the Citizens' Safety Committee, and what amounted to martial law was clamped over the settlement. Capt. J. A. Palmer, formerly of Columbus, Ohio, was appointed marshal, and guns possessed by the two local companies of militia—the Esmeralda Rifles—were technically confiscated to arm the new organization. Local peace officers, with exception of those absent on the trail of Buckley, were taken into custody; saloons were ordered closed at nine o'clock in the evening, and members of the Safety Committee began patrolling the streets in well disciplined squads. Never in her short and hectic history had Aurora experienced such utter tranquility.

Having captured Buckley near Mono Lake, the sheriff and his posse returned to the county seat where they were met by a grimly-determined group. After taking charge of the prisoner, the citizens' committee quietly added the sheriff to those in custody, thereby relieving him of responsibility in the events soon to transpire.

Billy Johnson's murder had taken place on the first day of February, 1864. On the ninth morning following, mining tools lay idle and silence hung over shafts and tunnels as Aurora made ready to mete out her new style of frontier justice.

Governor Nye, somehow apprised of developments, likely was dispatching his anti-violence warning at about the same moment Aurora began massing at the doors of the county jail.

Removed from their cells, the four murder suspects were marched to a low knoll on Silver street where a four-man gallows cast its ominous shade on the rocky earth. Guarded by a hollow square of armed citizens, the outlaws were prodded up to the gibbet and invited to "speak their pieces."

Buckley, coolest of the lot, declared he and Dailey, alone, were responsible for Johnson's slaying. This, Dailey confirmed. Masterson denied any complicity in the killing, and Three-Fingered Jack, raving drunkenly, called upon Almighty God to witness his innocence..

All had as well saved their breath. With four of her leading brigands conveniently corraled, Aurora was in no frame of mind to issue pardons. So, Masterson and McDowell had not been involved in the Johnson murder? So, what the hell! There had been others. . .

The four were placed in position. Eight hands were shackled, eight eyes bandaged, and a quartet of nooses expertly adjusted. And at half-past one o'clock, on that gray February afternoon, the armory's pint-sized cannon boomed a signal, four traps were sprung—and despite the governor's warning—John Dailey and his gang plunged into Eternity.

Whenever she wasn't busy disciplining bad boys, Aurora worked hard at her ambition to be known as the mining capital of the West. She even might have realized that ambition if she had not been a contemporary of Virginia City, that scintilating sin center on Sun mountain, 100 miles to the northwest. Virginia's mines were richer than Aurora's; her citizens drank deeper and more frequently; her guns shot straighter; her winds blew harder. In only one respect did the City of the Dawn have her licked four ways from Sunday.

Virginia was the seat of only one county; Aurora was the seat of two!

This circumstance, doubtless unparalleled in American political history, had developed soon after Aurora's founding in 1860. The whole complicated situation stemmed from the town's proximity to the California-

Nevada boundary, then still unsurveyed; plus, of course, her tax potentialities. With riches pouring from her mines and mills, with thousands
of persons thronging her streets and her urban district sprouting substantial
brick stores and fine homes, the new mining camp constituted a juicy
plum which both states were quite willing to pluck.

With the creation of Mono county, in March, 1861, California's
legislature subscribed to the theory that the unsurveyed boundary of their
state lay somewhere to the east of Aurora. In that premise, they designated the flourishing mining camp as seat of the new county, and, three
months later, a full slate of Mono county officials was elected and installed.

Despite this bold step, there were plenty of Aurorans who harbored
doubts concerning the validity of California's jurisdiction. To members
of Esmeralda Union Club—which then regarded most Californians as
potential Secessionists—the state's action in "grabbing" the town appeared
especially significant and alarming.

Stepping into the controversy, Governor Nye set the Aurora region
apart as a "council district," and citizens who questioned the California
mandate, thereupon elected delegates to Nevada's first Territorial legislature, meeting in September, 1861. The pay-off came when those law-
makers apportioned their newly-created Territory into nine counties, and
Aurora—already functioning as seat of California's Mono county—also
was designated the seat of Nevada's Esmeralda!

Difficulties arising from this complex hassle would have guaranteed
a prize crop of ulcers to any ordinary town; but Aurora had coped with
too many unique problems to be thrown by this one. Without too much
difficulty, she geared herself to a political derangement wherein franchises
for toll roads and water lines were granted by California, mining district
affairs were administered by Nevada, and civil litigants were free to carry
their disputes before either Esmeralda's Judge Turner, or Mono county's
Judge Baldwin.

At the next general election, Aurora's voters were offered full tickets
by Republicans and Democrats of both states; and at the same time the
Nevada election was being held at the city armory, the California voting
was in progress at the police station, a couple of blocks down the street.
After balloting at one polling place, voters hilariously moved on to the
other, declaring if they failed to "hit a winner" on their first try, they
might on the second.

This interstate form of government continued to flourish until September 20, 1863, when the California-Nevada boundary survey was completed locally and Aurora was found to lie within the Sagebrush State by
a good three-mile margin. Disgruntled Mono county officials thereupon
packed their records and headed up the canyon for Bridgeport. Along
with their account books they took with them all tax funds collected in
Aurora during their two-and-one-half years of illegal occupancy. As a
matter of fact, about all the abdicating government left for the victors was

a $20,000 indebtedness represented by outstanding warrants; a few copies of the *Esmeralda Star* datelined "Aurora, Mono county, California"; and one sheriff, deceased.

The lawman, who had met an untimely end in the spring of 1862, occupied a grave in the Aurora cemetery where a white marble slab carried the engraved words:

Sacred to the Memory of
N. F. SCOTT
First Sheriff of Mono County,
California
Aged 40 Years

Even though Aurora was not the biggest or brightest of Western mining camps, there must have been occasional times when the Goddess of the Dawn felt stirrings of maternal pride as she contemplated the achievements of her namesake. Despite a rugged climate and remote geographical position, Aurora had not done badly.

Founded in an era when there was not one mile of railroad in the state of Nevada, the town owed her entire existence to freight wagons, oxen, and mule teams. Every round of powder fired in her mines, every stamp in her eighteen great mills, every window and door and joist and brick in her buildings, had been freighted hence over tortuous mountain grades by straining brute muscle and salty-tongued 'skinners. Cost of maintaining a single freight animal in Aurora, in 1863, was calculated at $1.35 a day for hay, alone. Freight rates, needless to say, were correspondingly high.

But even this factor of inaccessibility could not stay the miraculous growth of the town.

By 1863-64, that mile-and-a-half-high mining camp claimed a population of more than 6,000 persons! She further boasted a fine brick courthouse, a brick school, two newspapers—*The Esmeralda Star,* and *Aurora Times*—a brace of brass bands, a dozen hotels, a like number of boarding houses, and two armories with fully-equipped companies of militia.* Her large business section comprising stores and shops of almost every type and description, was constructed mainly of stone and brick— every one of those bricks ox-freighted over the Sierra from Sacramento!

In addition to her material wealth, Aurora possessed most of the hereditaments and attractions of a modern city, including lodges and civic organizations, a cemetery and a racetrack, several literary and "cultural" societies, and a redlight district.

She even had her celebrities, but she didn't know it.

After spending his days pecking grudgingly at an Aurora quartz ledge, a young Missourian found amusement in the evenings writing ludicrous letters to the Virginia City *Territorial Enterprise.* When the city

---

*Thompson and West, History of Nevada, 1881.

editor of the *Enterprise* was called East, suddenly, the desperate publisher remembered this persistent correspondent at Aurora, and wrote offering him a job as cub reporter at $25 a week.

Inasmuch as the proferred position seemed likely to produce fewer callouses and less perspiration than the quartz ledge on which he was working, the young man made haste to accept. Lacking even the price of stage fare to his new assignment, he rolled his few personal belongings into a bed blanket, slung the pack over his shoulder, and hitch-hiked the hundred-odd miles to Virginia City.

From this $25-a-week post on the *Enterprise,* the erstwhile Aurora miner would go on to bigger and better things; and, eventually, under the *nom de plume* of Mark Twain, would win for himself the plaudits of crowned head and commoner.

Of all the organizations that came to flower in the Golden City of the Dawn, few exceeded in popularity her famous Deluge Bucket Company, of volunteer firemen. Following the incorporation of the city, one of the first items of business had been to purchase for this company a brand-new hand pumper resplendent in black and red paint, and gold trimming.

First fire alarm to sound after delivery of the new equipment, found Aurora's volunteers welling with aspirations to equal in fame the celebrated Warren Engine Company No. 1, of Carson City. Leaping to their pre-assigned battle stations, the men rolled the ponderous pumper to the scene of the blaze, which already had gained considerable headway.

The new pump was stiff, the day was hot, the water supply faulty. As strained muscles rebelled, the hose stream fell to a weak trickle, and the flames continued spreading. Men who had entered the fray determined to do or die, gradually developed antipathy to either course.

Seizing upon the opportunity offered by veiling smoke, Aurora's gallant fire laddies—secretly, one by one—climbed down from the pumper and disappeared into the enveloping black folds. Presumably guided by the same beautiful brute instinct that speeds the homing pigeon and guides the migrating lemming, the groping feet of every fireman ultimately deposited him before a swinging, slatted door.

When the distraught fire captain next dashed from the burning building to bark some order, he was dumbfounded to note certain amazing changes that had taken place. Although the pumper still was being operated with vigor the motive power no longer was supplied by his courageous firemen, but by a group of women who had taken charge when their husbands fled the battle! Vocally encouraged by less ambitious spectators on the sidelines, the gals were manning the equipment with grim determination—the angry fire in their eyes far hotter than the fire they fought.

Deluge Bucket Company No. 1 enjoyed a long and effectual life—

but not in the nine lives of a tomcat could the company have lived down the ignominy of that day when the wives took over!

In addition to fighting fires and other sundry chores, Aurora found time to carry on an incessant feud with the tough mining camp of Bodie, California, eight miles distant.

Relations between the two rivals at one time became so strained that two companies of soldiers were assigned to maintain order at the point where the Aurora-Bodie stageroad crossed the state line. But the feud, for the most part, was confined to good-natured mining camp badinage.

On one occasion, an Aurora newspaper published a lachrymose story concerning a local family which had found it expedient to move to the rival camp.

As the family wagon pulled out of Aurora, piled high with household chattels and assorted small fry, one little girl—asserted the Nevada editor —looked tearfully skyward and piped in a sad, childish treble, "Goodbye, God. We're going to Bodie!"

The Bodie news medium, on the week following, carried a scathing rebuke condemning the baseness of any newspaperman who would seek to further his own ends by deliberately misquoting an innocent child.

What the little girl actually said, declared the rival journalist was: "Good! By God, we're going to Bodie!"

Between 1861 and 1869, Aurora's mines produced more than $30,-000,000 in gold and silver bullion. Of that amount, approximately $27,-000,000 was carried down the mountain by Wells, Fargo and company, and another $2,365,969 by uninsured carriers.*

But Aurora's greatness ended with the 1860s. Her mines proved shallow. Veins, that near the surface had appeared as world-beaters, petered out before gaining 100 feet in depth. The 18 quartz mills operating in 1863, by 1865 had dwindled to two. Half the frame buildings in the business section burned the year following. Some were rebuilt, others not. Another disastrous fire swept the town in 1873. By 1880, Aurora's one-time population of 10,000 had shriveled to 500, and three years later, she lost her courthouse to Hawthorne.

Soon after that development, the Golden City of the Dawn was abandoned to chance residents and the weather.

She became a ghosttown—one of the most absolute of Western ghosts. Mine operators in the vicinity removed her ceiling beams for use in timbering their tunnels. Roofs collapsed, walls sagged—and on Antelope street, where shouts of bullwhackers and all-night celebrants once had echoed, desert brush grew tall.

It was this Era that brought to Nevada the Episode of the Mark Twain Cabin.

The Episode stemmed from the fact that Americans have a marked

*Wasson, J., Mining and Scientific Press, San Francisco, 1878.

penchant for bending the knee to lowly beginnings—the log cabins where future presidents were born, the vine-covered cottages that once housed Mr. Great.

In this connection, the people of Reno one day remembered that Nevada's illustrious step-son, Mark Twain, had lived briefly at Aurora.

Ergo! Since Mark had lived at Aurora, Mark must have had a cabin at Aurora! What, then, more fitting than Mark's cabin should be removed from that moribund mining camp to Idlewild Park, in Reno, and there reconstructed—board for board and shingle for shingle—just as the immortal Mark presumably had built it with his own talented digits.

Journeying to Aurora, The Committee discovered a cabin which someone said had been Mark's cabin, and its removal to Reno was duly accomplished in 1927. Relocated in the green stateliness of Idlewild Park, the delapidated shack immediately became a point of homage for thousands of tourists annually who came, saw, and were duly impressed.

But Nevada, herself, was a little dubious. A disconcerting rumor, it seemed, was percolating through the underground. The cabin at Reno, asserted that rumor, was NOT Mark's cabin! The cabin at Reno had stood at the edge of the hills, near the point where the road forked to the Juniata mine and the race track. Mark, however, had lived away down on the lower side of town, not far from the historical jump-off known as Lovers' Leap.

No, Nevada wasn't at all sure that a *faux pas* hadn't been pulled.

One who subscribed to this deleterious school of thought was Arthur C. Davis, a one-time resident of Aurora, who later rose to an executive position with the Automobile Club of Southern California.

Both Art and his father had been personal friends of Calvin H. Higbee, Mark Twain's partner during Mark's brief mining career at Aurora. During that period, Mark and Higbee had shared the same cabin —and the cabin Cal Higbee had indicated as their former residence, said Art, was not the cabin later moved to Idlewild Park.

Possibly the mistake in identity was partly the fault of "Shorty" Jaegers, an old codger who formerly lived at Aurora.

Although not addicted to malicious lying, Shorty was an accommo- dating cuss and was prone to give whatever answer he thought most satisfactory to the inquirer.

"One day some visitors came to Aurora and asked Shorty if such- and-such a cabin—the one later moved to Reno—was Mark's place," said Art. "Shorty, to be agreeable, answered that it was. Mrs. Tourist thereupon removed a shingle from the roof and sent it to Mark with a note saying she thought maybe he would like a souvenir from the cabin he had occupied during his mining days.

"Mark replied, thanking her most courteously for her thoughtfulness. He said he certainly was glad to know that his cabin at Aurora had a shingled roof, because he had been under the impression he and Cal Higbee lived in a dug-out covered with canvas . . ."

But the Reno tourists, of course, didn't know these things; and the forlorn little cabin in Idlewild park most likely was extremely flattered by all the attention and photographic film expended upon it.

After I started writing this chapter it occurred to me that I didn't remember seeing the cabin the last time I was in Reno. The more I thought about the matter, the more it bothered me. Finally I wrote my friend, Clara Beatty, curator of Nevada State Historical Society.

"Is the Twain cabin," I inquired, "still in Idlewild Park?"

Back came Clara's answer.

"Whoever put the cabin in the park," she wrote, "did not put a fence around it. People coming to see it, broke off a souvenir here and one there, and, eventually, they had carried the whole cabin away!

"Just to make sure, I asked the city engineer, this morning, and he said the cabin is entirely gone . . ."

Aurora had been a ghosttown many, many years before that unforgettable day when I saw it for the first time.

My companion on that trip was the late Dora Tucker, of Las Vegas, one of the most wonderful traveling companions I have ever known.

Leaving Hawthorne in a 1935 LaSalle sedan, with a definite propensity for overheating, we headed up the long Lucky Boy grade, then rutted and rocky, shiveringly narrow, and unbelievably steep. Fortunately, it was the spring of the year and melting snow on the higher levels still fed a small trickle of water that coursed down the mountain alongside our road. Wherever it was possible to squeeze to the edge of the grade in a position that seemed even half-way safe, I would halt the car and Dora would leap out and add another gallon or two of snow water to our madly boiling radiator.

Thus we made our way up the hill, traveling more than eight miles in low gear, and using what Dora estimated tentatively as 500 gallons of water.

Whatever the inconvenience of that ascent, it became of no consequence in that delirious moment when we topped the last summit and looked down on the remains of Aurora!

The ghosttown that lay before us was more extensive in scope and better preserved than any we had seen before, or I ever expect to see again! (Plates 2, 4)

More than 100 buildings of dwelling-size and larger—35 of them substantial structures of brick and stone—were ranged along streets in the bottom of a V-shaped canyon, through which threaded a small, bright stream. Sagebrush stood more than man-high in those streets; and in all those 100-odd buildings, there was living that day not one solitary human being!

Dora and I made camp in the lee of the old "Cain Mansion"—a mid-Victorian structure of red brick and "gingerbread lace"—where, in the elegance of French windows and maroon-and-gilt wallpaper, had lived James Cain, Aurora's leading banker, and his family.

During the week that followed, my companion and I moved through a ghosttowner's paradise; a realm of utter delight that I never expect to top.

Here were old homes, long abandoned and open to the weather, but still elaborately fitted with ornate furniture of solid walnut and oak. In one home we found a fine old four-poster bed; in another, a marble-topped ball-and-claw table. There were 50-year-old calendars on the walls, and a leather-covered trunk held some funny old garments with leg o'mutton sleeves, and a pair of high-top button shoes.

In the blacksmith shop were two pairs of leather bellows, each more than eight feet in length, and built throughout with square-cut iron nails. The clinker pile, in the same shop, yielded a double handful of ox shoes. The brick schoolhouse was still furnished with jackknife-whittled desks, and a few old dog-eared textbooks. Blackboards still hung on the walls. In our prowlings over the deserted town we even found cabins lined with yellowed newspapers that chronicled the latest developments in the Civil war—the Battle of Bull Run, the capture of New Orleans, the Union victory at Gettysburg. Papers as fragile as butterfly wings.

Everywhere we turned we were confronted by a wonderful wilderness of relics. In one day's time we could have loaded a railroad box car with material of museum calibre. Yet, the grandest relic of all was this priceless old town, herself!

The big, three-story Exchange hotel was largely in ruins, and the courthouse, armory and postoffice had been partially razed and salvagable material hauled away. Many other business buildings, however, were still standing.

From the fancy brick front of Al Taylor's livery stable and feed store, an oil-painted picture of an Arabian stallion looked out upon the deserted street, his delicate nostrils flaring, head upflung in pride, and every shading of color bright and true. Lettered beneath the portrait was the single word, "Stargo." Possibly the same artist had been responsible for the picture on the front of the Last Chance Saloon—a gigantic stein of beer that still foamed in the imperishability of white lead and pigments. Several of the old brick buildings were fitted with tall, narrow iron shutters and iron doors.

With our allotted week sped and mess boxes grown lean, Dora and I took our departure, both vowing firmly to return the following spring. But that year and more years slipped by and we never got back to the old town.

Then, with the summer of 1948, came a disquieting rumor that the main owners of Aurora townsite—the Cain brothers, of Bodie and Bridge-

port—were going to raze those historic buildings in the City of the Dawn!
Several reasons were cited for that decision.

The buildings were said to offer potential hazard to prowling visitors, and their owners might be held liable for damages; also, the old structures legally constituted "improvements," and taxes on the property would be lessened by their removal. Third, the post-war shortage of construction materials had made the salvaging of used bricks a profitable business.

The last named reason was hardest of all for Dora and me to accept. So far as she and I were concerned, no reason—however justified or logical from a cold-blooded dollars-and-cents standpoint—could possibly have warranted the desecration of this priceless old landmark of Nevada's youth. That we were not alone in that feeling became evident as letters protesting the destruction began pouring in to persons of authority. Letters to the state highway department and state park commission, the state historical society and state museum. Letters to senators and assemblymen, to Governor Vail Pittman, and the D.A.R. But, inasmuch as the old buildings were privately owned, it was the general concensus of officialdom that nothing could be done to halt their threatened despoilage.

Another five years were to elapse before I could bring myself to return to Aurora. I think I was afraid to go back—fearful of what I would find. Yet, all that while, a haunting hope kept nagging at me to go and see for myself whether those rumors had been true or false.

At last, I yielded to that impulse.

It was June, again, as I climbed the Lucky Boy grade out of Hawthorne. This time I was alone, and had a car that didn't boil. All the way up the long hill I tried to reassure myself that the rumored destruction of the town probably had been overrated as rumors generally are. Maybe the Cains had torn down the old Exchange hotel, which had been about to fall. Maybe—Hope whispered—they had found the task of razing so costly they had decided to let the other buildings remain standing.

Maybe—maybe.

Reaching the top of the hill, I again looked down on Aurora, this time with mixed emotions of fear and hope.

And in one black, terrible moment I knew that the rumors were not false.

The Golden City of the Dawn had vanished from the earth. Only her shattered bones, her disintegrating skeleton remained.

There still were a few small frame shacks, half fallen; a few caving dugouts. But, except for these, the grand old frontier landmark had been reduced to a chaos of rubble-filled basements and litter-choked streets, broken rocks and broken brick; broken mortar and plaster, twisted steel and charred timbers. . .

Walking alone through those ghostly streets, I found myself groping back through the years—striving to remember which building had stood on this corner, which over there. Al Taylor's livery stable, with its painted portrait of a gallant stallion; the Sprague-Chappell Tavern Inn, with its stained glass windows; the Mazoa Cafe; A. A. Travis' general mercantile; the saloons, the courthouse, the armory, the police station, the jail, the postoffice, all were gone. All those grand old buildings constructed of bricks ox-freighted over the Sierra from California, 90 years before.

Wandering on up the street, I saw that the sackers of the city had shown no partiality. Even the fine old Cain mansion had been destroyed. Sorting through the jumble of broken bricks and mortar and plaster, I uncovered a splintered piece of the "gingerbread lace" that had graced its gables, and to some of the broken boards still clung brittle scraps of maroon-and-gold wallpaper.

As I pulled back up the short, steep grade leading out of the canyon, I felt a strange sort of hungering to revisit the old graveyard, high on the hill above town.

Here, I could see no evidence of change, of man's despoilage. The family plots still were enclosed by their brown-rusted iron fences and broken palings. Old marble slabs still lifted their serene white faces etched with lambs and lilies and clasped hands, and angels and weeping willows, and lodge emblems, and words. The same words, over and over again. In loving memory . . . here lies our darling . . . suffer the little children . . . safe in the arms of Jesus . . .

Dropping down on the thick carpeting of needles at the base of a huge old nut-pine, I leaned back against its rough bark and let the warm mountain sun beat on my upturned face. It was very quiet. A cottontail rabbit was bobbing around among the rocky graves, pausing now and again to sample some bit of herbage that caught his fancy. Somewhere, nearby, a robin was chirping, and a pair of quail were making plans in the brush along the old stageroad. Except for these, there was no sound but the lonely mountain wind sighing through the pines.

I closed my eyes—and gradually, Time seemed to be turning back; and instead of the robin and the quail and the lonely wind in the trees, I was reliving the days when this old graveyard was being filled. The days when Aurora was in flower; when her streets were surging with good people and bad; when the endless sound of blasting and falling stamps shook the canyon like thunder, and the wheels of ox-drawn freight wagons creaked and groaned through the dust. I was hearing the slap of cards, the clink of glasses; the too-shrill laughter of the night-women, tinny pianos, ribaldry, the deep-throated blare of the mill whistles, the clang of the hoists, the muted roar of massed humanity.

And then word was moving along the street, into the saloons, the gambling halls, up to the third-floor gas-lighted rooms of the Exchange hotel, into the banks, the two newspaper offices:

"Ellen Ferris—Andy Ferris' wife, y'know?—she died, this mornin' . . . . Yeah . . . Too bad . . . nice woman. Only 29 years old, they say. The baby died, too . . ."

It wasn't always childbirth, of course. Other times Death rode in the form of a "widow-maker" in the mines; an accident at the mill, a quarrel over boundary rights, a sheriff pursuing his duty, a child drowned in the stream. It came in the guise of diphtheria, silicosis, scarlet fever, small pox, typhoid, pneumonia. . .

Whatever its cause, the end was the same—a funeral cortege leaving town, crawling up the hill to this quiet God's Acre beneath the nut-pines. The old graveyard had seen funerals when December's snow was whirling angrily from the high ranges to whip and toss the trees, and whiten the coffin, and lash cruelly at eyes already cold and wet. Other graves, here, had been filled as April's rain fell, bleak and dismal, and the mountain sky was sodden and gray, like an empty heart. And there had been funerals, on pleasant June days, like this day, when robins were chirping and quail were making plans, and all the great world around was bursting with new life and hope and promise, and only here in the pines loomed the stark barrenness of Death.

A pine-board coffin lowered into the rocky earth—a coffin built and lined by loving hands. The notes of a beloved hymn drifting through the trees. . .

> Nearer, my God, to Thee
> Nearer to Thee!
> E'en though it be a cross
> That raiseth me,
> Still all my song shall be—
> Nearer, my God, to Thee,
> Nearer to Thee . . .

With the last, lingering note faded from the air, came a moment of hushed stillness; and then, a voice speaking softly, quietly, confidently:
"The Lord is my Shepherd . . ."

Too soon the terrible, grim finality of clods thudding on a coffin lid. Women weeping quietly—widows in black dresses that swept the ground; parents, struck dumb in the loss of their first born; young husbands, staring, dry-eyed and speechless in their bereavement; tiny, motherless children, bewildered by their first frightening experience with Death. Dogs, strangely quiet and subdued; horses fretting a little where they were tied under the pines at the edge of the graveyard.

The last clod, the mound heaped and rounded, the flowers laid— simple wild flowers, gathered along the stream, in summer; tissue paper flowers in winter. Then, a quiet procession winding back down the hill toward town. Miners and gamblers, storekeepers, good women and bad, little children, dogs. Winding back down the hill to their work, their lives, their daily problems, their loved ones, their homes.

But in one of those homes, that night, a chair was newly vacant; a voice, forever stilled.

That was how Aurora's graveyard had been built—how all the

graveyards, in all the frontier mining camps of the West had been built. Mound by mound, prayer by prayer, heartache by heartache. Pine-board coffins lined with tears; grave mounds heaped with regrets, remorse, resignation. . .

But all that had been long ago. So long that the bones of those pioneers—even the coffins and garments in which they were laid away—had returned to dust. The homes where they had lived, were fallen to ruin. The mines they had worked were caved and filled with water; the streets they had traveled were choked with brush and rubble.

And now, even the brave city they had built in the canyon was gone. Gone, vanished, from the face of the earth. . .

The lonely mountain wind was still sighing through the pines and the quail were still making plans as I turned back down the long grade toward Hawthorne.

Like all those sorrowing, heavy-hearted legions who had left the old graveyard in ages past, I felt as if I, too, were leaving behind me something precious; something I had cherished.

I had said goodbye to the Golden City of the Dawn.

I knew I would never go back there again.

CORRECTION:

Sometime after *Ghosts of the Glory Trail* first appeared in print, it was brought to the attention of the author that information supplied by certain Nevada officials relative to responsibility for the razing of Aurora's buildings (Pages 72-73) is not in accordance with the true facts. Mr. Victor Cain, of Bridgeport, California, still one of the major property owners at Aurora, has assured me that neither he nor any member of the Cain family profited by, or condoned, the shameful destruction of that historic town. Almost without exception, he declares, Aurora's buildings were razed by big-scale brick thieves who possessed neither right nor title to a major portion of the material removed and sold.

Naturally, I am happy to make this correction, and, at the same time, tender belated apologies to a fine old pioneer family—the descendants of James Stuart Cain, of Aurora and Bodie.

THE AUTHOR

10

When Brigham Needed Iron

DRAWING TO A HALT at the side of the road, I sat half-chilled by the mighty pageant of industry spread before me. There, in a great open-pit operation—worked by the most modern equipment and methods known to mining science—Columbia Iron Mining company was gobbling away the flesh and bone of a southwestern Utah mountainside—flesh and bone that soon would be re-forged into sinews of twentieth century strength.

In the pattern of Western commerce, Iron mountain's thunderous activity loomed as the be-all and end-all; yet, as I sat contemplating the immense project, I could not but wonder how few of the eyes turned toward that development had ever looked beyond to its nominal "mother" —that sorry old ghosttown on the banks of Little Pinto creek, at the foot of the mountain.

Buried today in her own crumbled ruins, and comforted by her own silence, ill-fated Iron City was the second place west of the Mississippi river where native ore was transformed into the vitally-needed iron of commerce. . .

The "Iron Mission," as it came to be known, had its beginning in December, 1849, when a company of men led by Parley P. Pratt, and commissioned by the General Assembly of the Provisional State of Deseret, had left Salt Lake City to explore the southern section of the state.

While reconnoitering a few miles west of the present site of Cedar City, members of Pratt's party were elated to discover a range of hills apparently rich in highgrade iron ore. Although prospecting for precious metals was discouraged by LDS President Brigham Young, that ban did not extend to iron, lead, or coal, all of which were regarded by Brother Brigham as prime necessities. As a consequence, much interest was exhibited in the report filed by Pratt with the Legislative Council of Deseret, in February, 1850.

As soon as the harvest had been gathered that autumn, a call was issued for colonists to settle in newly-created Iron county; and in December, 1850, there departed from Fort Provo, under leadership of George A. Smith, a train of 129 wagons, bearing a complement of 119 men, 310 women, and 18 children.

Vast coal fields were soon located in Cedar Canyon—only a few miles from the iron deposit—and with this discovery, prospects for developing a domestic iron industry seemed especially encouraging. When apprised of the developments in Iron county, Erastus Snow and Franklin D. Richards, LDS representatives then on a mission in England, took immediate steps to organize the Deseret Iron company for exploitation of the Utah deposits. Among English converts in the ranks of the Saints, were many iron workers and coal miners who were urged to emigrate to Utah to assist in the new field.

By the spring of 1852, two foundries were in operation at Cedar City; and when the French traveler, Jules Remy, visited the district in 1855, he reported both coal and iron mines being worked at capacity and the foundries turning out a ton of pig iron daily from ore yielding 25 to 75 per cent iron.

During the eight years in which the Cedar City foundry was operated, the cost of that operation is said to have exceeded $1,000,000! Not only was the ore exceedingly hard to flux, but it was difficult to obtain a sufficient number of skilled iron workers, and transportation costs were prohibitive. The ultimate result was complete abandonment of the undertaking.

Several years passed before Iron county's colonizers made a second attempt to commercialize their vast iron deposits. The seat of effort this time was on the aforementioned Little Pinto creek, at the foot of Iron mountain, 23 miles west of Cedar City.

The Little Pinto development, according to Wm. R. Palmer, of the Cedar City chapter Sons of Utah Pioneers, was instigated by Ebenezer Hanks, a rugged and resourceful individual who had accumulated considerable collateral while in the course of freighting to and from California.

"Mules were cheap on the Coast and costly in Utah, while cattle were just the opposite—cheap here and high-priced in California," Mr. Palmer explained. "Hanks would load four or five wagons with Utah wool and cotton, and with each wagon drawn by three or four yoke of oxen, would make the long trip overland to the Coast. There he would sell his cargo and trade his oxen for mules—always at a neat profit—and re-loading his wagons with calico, silks, sugar, tea, coffee, boots and shoes, he would make the return trip. Arrived back in Iron county Hanks would dispose of his goods in Cedar City and Parowan, and trading his mules for another bunch of oxen—likewise at a good profit—would again head for California."

This, then, was the man who set about acquiring mining claims on Iron mountain and by 1870 found himself in position to promote the Utah Iron Mining Association, incorporated for "a sum not less than $100,000." The new plant, erected on the banks of Little Pinto creek, was soon operating around the clock and every day saw produced there some 2400 pounds of good quality pig iron.

During the three years immediately following, a major portion of

Hanks' interests were acquired by Thomas Taylor, of Salt Lake City, and in 1873 the business was reincorporated as the Great Western Iron Mining and Manufacturing company with capitalization limit "not to exceed $2,000,000."

Meanwhile, a town of considerable extent had sprung up around the smelter on Little Pinto and had been incorporated as Iron City. In addition to the iron working plant, the settlement included shops and a number of well-built homes—largely of brick-and-stone construction.

A year later saw effected another reorganization in which the name of the enterprise was abbreviated to Great Western Iron company. While capitalization remained at $2,000,000, an appraisal value of $5,000,000 was placed upon the company's holdings, which included 54 iron and coal claims, the plant, real estate at Iron City, and such company property as teams, wagons and tools.

Throughout its fledgling years, southern Utah's iron production industry was, at every turn, confounded by new difficulties. After purchasing a defunct Nevada railroad and moving it intact to Iron City to transport coal from Cedar Canyon to the site on Little Pinto, the coal was found to contain too much sulphur to enable its use for coking. As a consequence, it was necessary to fire the furnace with charcoal, and to supply the prodigious amount needed, three huge beehive-type charcoal ovens were kept in constant operation.

As lateral roads fanned out from the Union Pacific, it became cheaper to import iron from Eastern mills than to mine and mill it under the adverse conditions prevalent on Little Pinto, and eventual abandonment of the Iron mountain project resulted.

Shorn of its livelihood, the town of Iron City disintegrated rapidly. Many of the better brick buildings were dismantled and moved to nearby Newcastle for re-erection there. Other structures were left to crumble and fall.

When large scale development of the Iron mountain hematite deposit was resumed, about 30 years ago, conditions had changed materially and with good roads and motor freight giving rapid access to outside points, there seemed no reason to disturb the slumbering ghost of old Iron City.

Realizing that the ruins of Little Pinto constituted one of southern Utah's most important historic sites, Cedar City chapter Sons of Utah Pioneers in 1948 launched a program aimed at protection and preservation of the remaining buildings. Several of the better intact structures—including one of the original charcoal ovens, the old blast furnace, an open-hearth furnace and Ebenezer Hanks' former residence—together with the land on which they stand, was donated to the chapter by William Lamb, owner. Chapter members subsequently contributed time and material necessary to fence the townsite and to make such repairs as were needed to check further deterioration of the blast furnace and oven.

Preservation of such frontier landmarks, to my way of thinking, is a most commendable undertaking, for posterity has not only a *right* but a *need* to know how laborously ends were accomplished in the days when the West and our pioneering ancestors were young together.

But, so far as the ghosts of Ebenezer Hanks and the other builders of Iron City are concerned, I doubt if they care a rap whether the buildings are repaired or not; as I don't imagine those ghosts spend much time around the old charcoal ovens and furnaces. Progressive, indomitable men that they were, I'm inclined to think that their spirits must be hovering a little higher on the mountain, where vital things are still being done in a vital way, and the mining of iron ore still goes forward.

II

Legal Light of Lida

THE OLD GHOSTTOWN of Lida, in Esmeralda county, Nevada, now numbers barely enough inhabitants to staff a decent game of cribbage, but it was once a place where things happened. Not big, *important* things, such as gang wars and cafe society brawls, but *peculiar* things that didn't happen just any old place.

One of the prime factors in this business of making things happen was Leonard Martin, a disbarred lawyer, who arrived at Lida during the camp's formative years when the county seat was at Aurora—more than 100 miles distant as the crow traveled, and the nearest rail connection was at Wadsworth, 187 miles to the north. Due to exorbitant freight costs, prices of all commodities were terrific; but even after paying mill charges totaling $80 a ton, Lida's ore was rich enough that it still returned a handsome profit to its shippers, and the camp was booming.

Although no longer young at the time of his arrival at Lida, Martin was still a man who delighted in trouble, and local newspaper accounts of the 1870s frequently carried his name in connection with fisticuffs. One of his more spectacular fights occurred one night, in 1874, when he was attacked by three heavily-armed gunmen while traveling the Lido-Palmetto road and, assertedly, minding his own business. Despite the yawning muzzles of three .45s, and the flashing blades of no-one-knows-how-many knives, the unarmed Martin reportedly wrenched a dead branch from a juniper tree, and using it as a club, completely vanquished all three of his assailants.

But men, eventually, grow old; and along with growing old, Martin backslid—mentally, morally, spiritually, physically, and financially. He had been a heavy drinker as long as Lida had known him; now, he degenerated into the "town character," unshaven, unwashed, the butt of everyone's good natured horseplay and rough-hewn humor. Whenever an unpleasant job had to be done, and no one else wanted to do it, somebody always guffawed, "Get Ol' Len Martin!" And Martin could be usually counted upon to do it.

One time, for example, a young prospector died on the desert between Mt. Jackson and the present town of Goldfield. By the time the body was located, little of it was left but a dried-out skeleton and a putrid odor;

but the man's family, in the East, asked that the remains be shipped back there for burial. Fifty dollars was sent for bringing the body to Lida, and Ol' Len Martin inherited the unpleasant chore.

After borrowing a saddle horse from "Blue Dick" Hartman, the ex-barrister succeeded in wangling an advance payment of $10, which he invested in half a gallon of squirrel juice. Thus fortified, he set out into the desert.

Reaching the scene of the tragedy, about dusk, he lashed the skeleton on the saddle behind him and started back to town. Somewhere along the way the head shook loose from the body, but Martin, deep in communion with the desert starlight and the few remaining dregs of his squirrel juice, failed to take note of that loss. As a result, the few spectators who witnessed his arrival at Lida in the chill hour of dawn, rather gained the impression that he had captured Washington Irving's Headless Horseman.

Without a reasonable facsimile of a complete skeleton, the committee in charge of arrangements refused to pay the remaining $40 due; so Martin again rode forth, located the missing top piece where it had fallen beside the trail, popped it in a gunny sack, and galloped triumphantly back to town—thereby providing Lida with conversational material for weeks to come.

Aside from retrieving errant corpses, Martin's chief souce of income was a small mine, which he leased from time to time and thereby retained a precarious credit. One day a mining Big Shot from Carson City came to Lida to inspect Martin's property with a view toward buying. To put his visitor in a happy frame of mind and so help the deal along, Martin set about preparing a sumptious chicken dinner—something of an event in that near-chickenless land.

After the biddy had been boiling for a couple of hours, the Carsonite caught a glimpse of the stew. To his horror he saw that the pot contained almost as many feathers as meat!

"Great day, man!" he exploded. "Didn't you *pick* that chicken?"

"Sure, I picked it!" whined old Len, with a reproachful look. "But, like I allus say, 'Ain't no sense pickin' a chicken too damned close—anybody that don't like feathers can skim 'em off.' "

12

The Little Ghost That Won't
Lie Down

EIGHTY-ODD YEARS ago, the expressive soubriquet "ghosttown" had not entered the Westerner's lexicon of words. Any mining camp not "booming," simply was "dead."

With the year 1867, that term became applicable to Ione, Nevada. In losing the Nye county seat to flourishing Belmont, the older town had slipped into the ranks of the has-beens—the towns with plenty of past but little promise for the future.

Well as Ione recognized the general handwriting on her walls, few of her citizens would have believed that before another two years had passed, less than half a dozen persons would be walking the dusty streets of that erstwhile thriving community which had sprung into life with the first rich discovery of ore in the Shoshone mountains.

The time had been early spring, 1863; the discoverer, P. A. Haven, an out-at-knees prospector who had failed to make his million on the Comstock and had not set the world afire since emigrating to the spectacular new camps on Lander Hill.

As the rumor-gilded facts of Haven's discovery became known, scores of miners from Clifton and Austin had beat a dusty trail up the Reese River to the new strike. The Union mining district had been organized, and before close of that year, the town of Ione had been founded. Situated deep in the heart of Central Nevada's high ranges, the new settlement spread like moss upon the rocky sides and bottom of a narrow canyon just below 7000 feet elevation. Immediately overhead lifted the juniper-grown shoulders of 9000-foot Mt. Berlin, and a dozen miles to the east and southeast towered the bald, white crests of Mahogany Peak and Arc Dome, rising to respective heights of 11,012 and 11,775 feet.

With a continued influx of miners, and with new strikes being made on every side, the isolated camp grew rapidly. Its streets became lined with general stores, a newspaper and hotel, saloons and restaurants and barber shops. Men of the professions found their way thither, and both day and night saw ox-drawn freight wagons rumbling up the Reese River, laden with supplies and mining equipment.

Before her first anniversary, the mountain-smothered town had grown so populous that her citizens demanded the creation of a new county with Ione as its governmental head.

On the premise that here was another rich mining district, slated to rival or even to surpass that at Virginia City, an obliging legislature in February, 1864, performed a major operation on Lander and Esmeralda counties, thereby salvaging a neatly-squared tract of several hundred thousand acres. With this material, the legislators created Nye county, named for Nevada's territorial governor. On April 26, 1864, the new county government was formally organized; Ione, the new county's only white settlement, was named its seat; and $800 was appropriated to build a courthouse.

This desert-mountain kingdom to be governed from Ione exceeded in bulk the combined area of several eastern states. From the California line, near Death Valley, the boundaries of Nye county then extended to Utah Territory on the east, and to Arizona Territory on the south, with only Lander county separating it from Oregon Territory to the north.

Ironically, the same underground wealth that had inspired her prosperity was to write early finish to Ione's political ambitions. Scarcely had the fledgling government begun to function smoothly, before a rich strike was made in the Toquima range, and the new camp of Belmont zoomed into prominence 50 miles to the southeast.

Among early-day miners the lure of "better diggings" elsewhere constituted virtually an occupational disease; and by 1865, so many of Ione's citizens had departed for the later and more sensational strike that Belmont began raising a demand that the Nye county seat be transferred to that place. Two years later, the state legislature acquiesced.

That this action did not carry Ione's approval is evidenced by a quip in the *Belmont Weekly Reporter,* of April 6, 1867. The county officials, it was stated would begin their exodus to Belmont "as soon as the citizens of Ione have reconciled themselves to the fact that they have lost the county seat fight."

Loss of her courthouse marked the beginning of Ione's end. Deterioration of the town was rapid. Several of her mines held on grimly for a few more years, but up until 1880 they had produced only about $1,000,000 worth of gold and silver, and since 1907, around 11,000 flasks of mercury*—not an especially spectacular record among Nevada mining districts.

Possibly the most remarkable thing about Ione is the fact that even as a ghosttown, she has survived while many of her contemporaries have so completely vanished it is almost impossible to locate their one-time sites.

Since her official death, the old Shoshone mountain village has clung stubbornly to a thin wisp of life. Her population at times, has dropped to

*Lincoln, Francis Church, Mining Districts and Mineral Resources of Nevada, 1921.

four or five persons, but in 92 years there has never been a time when pine smoke did not curl from at least one of her rock chimneys. For a number of years the little mountain settlement boasted but a single business house—a kitchen-sized grocery-postoffice-gasoline station. At the same time, a small schoolhouse, staffed by one teacher, continued to serve a handful of pupils—two-thirds of them Indians who moved to "town" at the beginning of each winter, and with the coming of spring moved back to their homes on the upper Reese River.

During the term of 1952-53 the Ione school hit bottom, with a maximum of three pupils in attendance, and much of the time (so I was told) with only two.

"Don't look like we'll have any school here next term," said one of Ione's leading men-about-town. "Well, it's okay by me! By the time we pay the teacher $2400 a year, pay $30 a month for the 'teacherage', and fork out for heat, and lights, and everything else—why, no damned kid's worth it!"

In the immediate vicinity of Ione are situated half-a-dozen other ghosttowns. About five miles to the southeast are the ruins of Berlin— for the past eleven years the home of Harold and Dorothy Newman who, in 1955, were the town's last surviving residents. (Plate 48) Still standing, at that time, were the mill buildings, boarding house, assay office, and several cabins, and an old cemetery contained a few marked graves.

Over the ridge from Berlin is Union Canyon, site of the ghosttown of Union, founded in 1863, and soon thereafter a bustling settlement with a school, stores, ore mills, and a brick kiln. Scattered stone ruins remain, and the canyon also is now the site of Nevada State Ichthyosaur Park.

Three miles southeast of Union lies the weathered skeleton of Grantsville. A contemporary of Union, this place once numbered 42 business establishments, including two newspapers and a brewery, and had a population of around 1000 persons; but all that remains as evidence of that one-time activity are a few old stone buildings and foundations, a huge pile of mill tailings, and a pailing-fenced cemetery so old that not one inscription may be read on its time-scarred boards.

Even less remains at Ellsworth, 12 miles west of Ione, a mining camp formerly connected with that place and with Austin by a "pony express" mail, which continued to function long after abandonment of the original Pony Express between St. Joseph and Sacramento.

"We have in our midst," stated *Reese River Reveille,* of Austin, on April 15, 1869, "an instance of endurance in the saddle, achieved daily without flourish or notice, that we deem worthy of a place in the chronicles. It is that of the mail rider between Austin and Ellsworth . . . by the way of Ione, a distance of seventy miles. The service is tri-weekly.

"This long ride has been made daily, excepting Sundays, for upwards of four months, on three common nags, usually called 'plugs'. The present rider began the service last December, and has kept the saddle six days

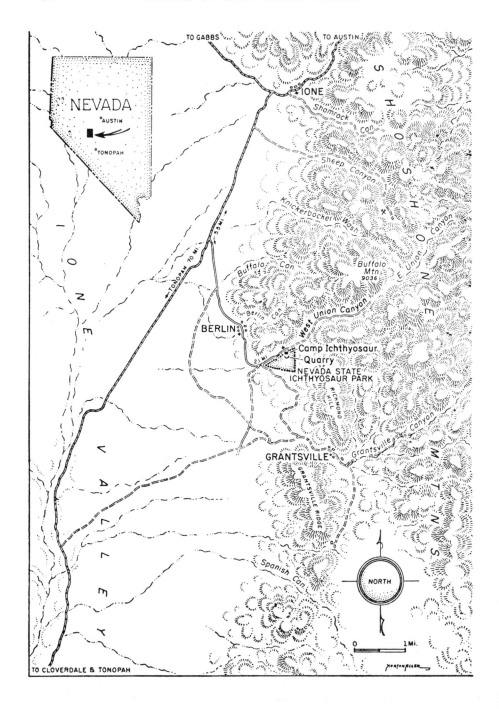

every week since over these seventy miles, frequently in the teeth of the fierce winter blasts that sweep these mountain valleys, and often through snow and rain.

"The rider is named Barnes—a small, sinewy fellow, as tough as a hickory sapling. He is so hardy that he disdains a coat, and rides always in his shirt sleeves, heedless of frost or gales. Besides the mail, he is the 'common carrier' for the people along the route and three times a week he distributes to men and women in the valley from ten to twenty parcels of imperative 'wants'. He receives the orders on his homeward trip, fills them in this city, and distributes them on his outward trip. He carries the mail; buys tobacco for the 'Old Man's' pipe, and medicine for his rheumatiz; picks up all sorts of notions for the 'old woman,' Lubin and hoop skirts for the girls, gimcracks for the boys, and soothing syrup and rubber dolls for the baby; everything indeed, from sole leather to hair pins.

"Do but think of the bottom of this mail rider! He rides seventy miles, six times a week, 1820 miles a month, or at the rate of 21,840 miles a year! He does all this, yet appears to think he has done nothing.

"Pony Express men are proverbially brave and hardy fellows, but we do not know of one whose feats excel those of little Barnes, the modest, model mail rider of Reese River."

More than 80 years later, I found the mail route once carried by Barnes being handled quite as capably by Mrs. Reese Gondolfo, of Austin, who thrice weekly jockeyed an army surplus truck over the long road from Austin to Ione, and thrice weekly—on alternate days—made the return trip to Austin.

Like Barnes, Mrs. Gondolfo carried the United States mail, expressed furs, delivered ore samples to assayers, bought medicine for horse and human, bucked the snows of winter, and the mud of spring. And like Barnes, who 80-odd years before had been pounding over that same arduous route, through the same mountains, and serving the same ghost-towns, Mrs. Gondolfo "thought nothing of it."

13

Time Has Been Cruel to Washoe

SPANNING WESTERN NEVADA from Lake Tahoe to the Oregon border—a distance about the same as that from New York to Virginia —lies Washoe county. Near the southern end of this desert-mountain empire, highway traffic thunders past three old brick-and-stone buildings, leaning drearily, one upon the other. Farther to the rear sulks Washoe Lake, shallow and somnolent; and spread across a grassy slope, lies a lonely graveyard.

A few crumbling headstones and three old buildings. What a sorry end for Washoe City, first seat of Washoe county, and at one time the foremost milling town for ore of the Comstock Lode!

From time of the Lode's discovery, reduction of its rich ore posed a difficult problem. Mexican miners first introduced the use of stone arrastres, long employed for crushing ore in their native land; but in man's impatience to harvest the wealth of a treasure-packed mountain, this ancient method proved altogether too slow. For a time the ore was mule-freighted across the Sierra to San Francisco—another laborous undertaking wholly unsuited to large scale development.

Still groping for a solution, the year 1860 found several of the district's largest operators building quartz mills at Virginia City. But the quartz mill of that day—without fuel—was as impotent as an eight-cylinder motor car *sans* gasoline; and while Mount Davidson was possessed of mineral wealth in untold millions of dollars, she was poor as Job's turkey in anything resembling fuel. Nearest timber worthy of mention stood in the Sierran forests, a long, hard freight-haul distant.

Finding it impossible to bring the timber to the mills in sufficient quantities, and equally impossible to take the mills to the timber—since that would involve dragging the heavy ore wagons up the steep, east wall of the Sierra—millmen settled upon the happy solution of compromising the haul.

It was here Washoe Valley entered the mining picture. Situated at the lowest point between the Sierra crest and Mount Davidson, it constituted close to an ideal milling site, as fuel could be freighted downgrade from the forests, and ore downgrade from the mines—virtually a gravity haul for both commodities.

With construction of mills in the Valley, two towns sprang into life on the shores of Washoe Lake—Ophir on its west shore, and Washoe City, at the lake's north end.

Washoe, by 1861, had become the largest community in the Valley, which then numbered some 5000 settlers, and when legislators met that year to form a Territorial government for Nevada, Washoe City was designated seat of Washoe county, one of the nine political subdivisions into which the new territory was originally divided.

By 1863 the city of Washoe boasted a fine brick courthouse, a jail and hospital, as well as schools, churches, and many types of business enterprises.

That same year saw further distinction accrued to the community when Geo. W. Derickson, esteemed young editor of the three-months-old *Washoe City Times* was involved in a gun duel with H. F. Swayze, one of his subscribers.

In arbitrating the sundry vitriolic attacks that roughened the path of Nevada journalism in the 1860s and '70s, hot lead was a medium far more popular than court action. Relatively few of these disturbances, however, culminated in funerals. One of the notable exceptions was the Derickson-Swayze affair, which had its inception in a humorous skit submitted to the *Times* by Subscriber Swayze.

Although the aforementioned contribution was notably absent from the next issue following, the fact of its submission had not gone unnoted. Having assertedly recognized the proffered gem as a plagiarism from the second issue of his own newspaper, Derickson had seen fit to insert a few lines of sarcastic comment.

"A tall, gawky greenhorn dressed in a buckskin suit," he editorialized, "stepped into the *Times* office yesterday and handed us an article, which he was very anxious to have published. He said he had spent a great deal of time in getting it up, and wanted a dozen or so copies of the paper containing his article, when published, to send to his friends. The article was headed, 'How I Got My Wife,' and was signed 'Ichabod.' The said greenhorn, whose name, he informed us, is H. F. Swayze, is hereby informed that he can have a dozen copies of the *Times,* containing his article, by calling at this office and paying for same. His article, which he says cost him so much trouble and study to get up, was published in the second number of the *Times,* word for word, and we have the same for sale. The same greenhorn, who seems to think printers are as green as himself, brought in a long article several weeks since, ridiculing the town of Ophir and its inhabitants, and was very much surprised because his literary efforts were not appreciated and published. The manuscript copy of the last article of the said H. F. Swayze is at his disposal by calling at the *Times* office; and he can also purchase, for cash, several copies of the *Times,* containing this notice, to send to his friends."*

*Washoe City Times, Jan. 17, 1863.

Since literary artists and would-be artists are inclined to be touchy about their alleged brain children, those words—in the humble opinion of Mr. Swayze—were fighting words. Scarcely had the offending issue of *The Times* hit the street until the maligned subscriber was storming the door of the news office, shaking a fist-crumpled copy of the paper in the editor's face, and demanding full and immediate retraction.

Derickson refused, declaring he had written only the truth.

"You're a goddamn liar!" shouted the challenger.

Over the series of events that followed immediately on that pronouncement, Time has drawn an obscuring and charitable veil. According to testimony subsequently given by Swayze, both men drew their weapons and fired simultaneously, the bullet from Derickson's gun striking Swayze's chin, where it broke the jaw bone and neatly extracted several teeth.

Spitting out the lead bullet and shattered incisors, the wounded man reholstered his own smoking pistol and staggered toward the street, where a crowd of agitated townsmen hovered at respectful distance.

Behind, in a widening pool of blood on the cluttered floor of the dingy newspaper office, lay Editor Derickson.

He was quite dead.

As proof that not all Swayze's fellow citizens credited his version of the shooting (as here taken from the *Virginia City Union* of that period) the dueling victor was convicted on a charge of manslaughter and sentenced to the state penitentiary at Carson, where he served three years.

Ultimate demise of Washoe City came as a by-product of Progress.

When the new Virginia & Truckee railroad began hauling Comstock ore to mills on the Carson River at a rate far cheaper than freight wagons could make the trip down twisting Ophir Grade, the milling town on the lake began to sense her impending end.

Along with loss of her milling business, Washoe was finding it necessary to buck the rising competition of a new place called Reno—a station on the Central Pacific, a few miles to the north. Even Washoe's then-current newspaper, *The Eastern Slope,** had pulled up stakes in 1868 and moved to this upstart community, where, as *The Evening Crescent,* it had become Reno's first periodical.

So rapidly grew the new railroad town that its citizens launched a movement to acquire the county seat, and when the issue was brought to a vote in 1870, Reno swung the election. With the change approved by the state legislature, in 1871, citizens of the dying milltown had no recourse but to watch disconsolately as workmen demolished their fine brick courthouse—for ten years, the pride of the valley. Bricks salvaged from

*Bancroft, Hubert Howe. History of Nevada. Colorado and Wyoming, 1890. At various times in her ten-year career, Washoe City had no less than four newspapers —*The Times,* founded in Oct., 1862, when the town embraced a population of about 2000 persons; *The Old Pah-Utah, The Eastern Slope,* and *The Weekly Star.*

the operation were hauled off to Reno, there to be incorporated in the new city jail building.

Four years later saw the one-time thriving community on the lake dwindled to a village of 70 persons, and passage of the Eighteenth Amendment, in 1919, wrote finis to the town's last remaining business enterprise —a saloon.

Editor Derickson lies buried at his boyhood home of North San Juan, California; his slayer, Horace Swayze, sleeps cold and forgotten, God alone knows where. The Virginia & Truckee railroad, which in its day hastened the death of Washoe City, in time suffered that same fate. Three old brick-and-stone buildings huddle beside a noisy highway, and a few old graves nestle in the tall grass of a hillside cemetery—only but for these, the City of the Washoe has ceased to exist.

14

Canyon of the Tules

AFTER EXCHANGING the usual courtesies concerning the weather, road conditions, and mining affairs, I steered the conversation around to the reason for my visit.

"This place you mentioned in your letter," I broached. "This Tule Canyon—what's the nature of the story?"

"It's a great story!" declared Harry Wiley, Esmeralda county senator, merchant, miner, and general factotum in the little mining camp of Gold Point, Nevada. (Plate 27.)

"Topographically," he hastened to explain, "the canyon's a deep, wide wash, 15 miles long. Most of it lies in Nevada, but its delta stretches across the California state line and into the north end of Death Valley. For your purpose, of course, its chief interest is found in the fact that this ground has been worked for possibly a greater number of years than any other gold placering area in Nevada!

"No man living can remember when Tule wasn't being mined, either by Indians, Chinese, whites or Mexicans," he warmed to his subject. "Official reports have suggested the possibility that mining may have been carried on there even before the California gold rush in 1849; and when Bill Scott and Alexander Palm came to Tule, in 1872, the canyon already was studded with abandoned mines and the ruins of stone walls laid so long before that no one had any idea who their builders may have been!

"Even more amazing, after all these years of being mined, is the fact there's still gold at Tule," the Senator enthused. "Only last spring, Harold Strom was dry-washing on my claim and took out an $80 nugget and a bottleful of coarse gold ranging from the size of turnip seed to nuggets worth $5 and $10 each!

"Well—" he interrupted himself—"How does it sound?"

When I said it sounded like more, he suggested we talk with Fred Green.

"He and the Williams boys hold most of the placer ground in the canyon and Fred's dug up a lot of Tule's early history . . ."

Leaving Goldpoint's last remaining store to its own devices, we ambled down the dusty street to Fred's cabin.

For a man who would make mining and mine engineering his life's career, it was Fred Green's good fortune to have been a son and grandson of miners, and to have been born in Grass Valley, California—possibly the world's greatest cradle of gold mining lore. After passing his boyhood there and in the wild boomcamp of Bodie, he had made the rounds of the mining country until the dream of reviving Tule as a huge dredging project came to possess him.

Greetings barely had been exchanged before we heard the clatter of an approaching automobile, and our impromptu conference was joined by Sheriff Ed Kitchen, of Goldfield—an Esmeralda county old timer, who had known Tule Canyon and vicinity for more than half a lifetime.

As the afternoon slipped away and the sun dropped over the rocky range to the west, Fred and Harry and the sheriff regaled me with tales of Tule and the sundry individuals who had lived and died there— "Honest Tom" Jaggers, "Dutch Chris" Senner, Marijilda, the Mexican; "Happy Days" Alice Diminy, and other characters out of the dim past.

"Look," said Fred, "I've got to take some grub over to the Williams boys. If you want a story about Tule and can spare a few days, why don't you come along? We'll see you get plenty to eat and a shack to sleep in, and you and I can take the jeep and explore the canyon from one end to the other. What do you say?"

Thirty minutes later, Fred and I had taken our leave of Senator Wiley and the sheriff and my car was bumping across the Nevada desert, Tule bound.

Dropping down the mountainside to the wide, brown sweep of Lida Valley, the dusty road bored into the west for ten miles, to the rim of a rocky canyon. Nosing down its side in a sharp, steep pitch, we turned into a sandy wash that floored the cut from wall to wall.

This was Tule Canyon, said Fred; and already I could see old mine workings without end—mountainous piles of tailings and scattered prospect holes, an occasional hillside tunnel. Everywhere were the tumbled ruins of old stone cabins and dugouts. As Senator Wiley had said, it was obvious that a great deal of mining activity had been carried on here over a long period of years—a span which possibly bridged completely the West's great saga of gold.

Five miles down the wash, we came to a halt at Roosevelt Well, an unfailing source of water named half a century before when Rough Rider Teddy was prominent in the nation's news. Turning industriously in the up-canyon draft, a battered windmill sent its spurting stream through a two-inch pipe into a wooden tank, the overflow of which was quickly reclaimed by the thirsty sands of the wash.

On a low bench above the well sat a group of wooden cabins and the ruins of a mill—all that remained of the small mining camp of Roosevelt, established here years before by Harry Stimler who, with Billy Marsh, had made the original strike at Goldfield. Unlike the earlier development, Stimler's efforts at Roosevelt had not been marked by any great success and the camp was short lived. Soon after the close of World War II, its abandoned buildings had become the headquarters of Fred Green and his partners, Oscar and Ray Williams, life-long miners from the vicinity of Florence, Arizona.

Our unexpected arrival found the Williams brothers eating supper; and of all strange sights to encounter in an all-bachelor mining camp, they were eating on a green-and-white checked tablecloth, spotlessly clean and beautifully ironed! Extra places were laid for Fred and me, and Oscar's good cooking found a ready market.

Dusk was creeping down the canyon by the time we had finished supper. Every pocket and ravine in the Slate range, to the east, held its dark pool of shadows; and the 9400-foot crest of Last Chance range, ten miles to the west, was silhouetted blackly against the lingering flame of sunset. Ubehebe Crater loomed as a dark blotch on the mountainside, a little way to the south; and still farther beyond lay the terrifying majesty and immensity of Death Valley—now peaceful and mysterious in the soft glow of the rising moon.

As a net result of several days spent "on the ground" and considerable book-research accomplished since, the most definite thing I have learned about Tule Canyon is the fact that its early history largely is lost. When or by whom its rich gold deposits first were discovered and what its total production has been, are things no man seems to know. The government-sponsored Wheeler Survey of 1871 reported only two men then working "in the once-famous Tule Canyon"—the inference being that this period of "fame" had occurred many years previously.

While examining an old open-cut operation a few days before my visit, the Williams boys had made an interesting discovery with possible bearing on some of the canyon's earlier activities. Near the center of this cut, in an area the size of a dinner plate, lay ten Indian artifacts, eight of which would seem to have no other use than as possible digging or scraping tools. Expertly chipped, they were flatly-oval in shape and roughly three-by-five inches in breadth. Over the entire collection lay a light accumulation of earth possibly blown there by the wind or crumbled down from the bank above.

If these pieces actually were used in mining—as their presence in the cut would seem to indicate—Tule's production would appear to have had its beginning in prehistoric Stone Age times!

Chances are, this is a question no man will answer.

While exploring the canyon in Fred's jeep, we halted at a spring where a stream of clear water poured from a rusty pipe to overflow an old iron barrel and spread across a few square yards of ground. Watercress and other tender plants carpeted the little oasis; and several small willows, grown up around the spring, were swarming with birds. A stone's toss to the east sat a dilapidated wooden barn and a small stone cabin—all that remained of the one-time busy stage station known as Rachfords.

Even after the arrival here of white men, Tule Canyon never had a business district of any great extent, said Fred. For quite a few years, however, it supported a school and postoffice, and at least one store—this commercial center having changed location and name as the store changed ownership. At one period in the canyon's history its "business section" had been at Rachfords. At a time still earlier, when the store had been owned and operated by Christian "Dutch Chris" Senner, both town and postoffice had borne his name.

Leaving Rachfords, we continued on up-canyon, making our way between great heaps of placer tailings and past the ruins of old stone and log cabins and rock foundations. These, for the most part, were virtually obliterated—both time and cloudbursts having claimed heavy toll.

Our way never strayed far from the old Piper Toll road, built in the early 1870s by Sam Piper, of Fish Lake Valley. In the peaceful loneliness of that summer morning it was difficult to visualize this brush-grown trail as a one-time artery of commerce linking the busy mining centers of Palmetto, Tule Canyon and Gold Mountain. Long-line teams and ponderous freight wagons, shouting, swearing 'skinners, and toll gates and activity, all belonged to a period far too dim to be readily recaptured in imagination.

"This was Chinatown," said Fred, waving his arm to include an expanse of stone ruins that differed in no essential detail from other ruins we had been seeing all morning. One ruin, a little larger than the others, he identified as a Chinese hotel.

"At one time—probably during the 1870s—Tule supported a large Chinese population, but all I know about it," he said, "is what I have been told by Douglas Robinson."

I glanced up in surprise, as this was not the first time I had heard of Doug Robinson, (Plate 26) then chief probation officer of Inyo county, California. Mr. Robinson, as a matter of fact, was a valued friend of mine and had given me reams of first hand information concerning the old camps of San Antone, Oriental, Gold Mountain, Candelaria, Silver Peak, Palmetto and Lida. He seemed to have lived in about half the ghosttowns of Esmeralda county, at one time or another; but the fact that his youthful experiences also had included Tule Canyon was something I had not known.

When I mentioned this, Fred grinned.

"Oh, yes!" he said. "The Robinsons really got around!"

Doug's father, H. H. (Bob) Robinson, Fred explained, had operated the Senner store and postoffice from 1891 to 1897—the family having moved to the canyon from Candelaria.

"When the Robinsons came to Tule in 1891, there were about 50 Chinese still living here. According to Doug, they were natural placer miners. They never worked virgin ground—probably were never permitted that privilege. Instead, they bought old claims already 'worked out' and abandoned by the whites; and, even in such unpromising ground, they occasionally hit rich pockets. One claim—mined and re-mined by the whites—was purchased by a Chinaman named Sing Kee, and in only a few weeks time, he had taken out $1400!"

Still drawing on the recollections of Doug Robinson, Fred said the Chinese stayed pretty much to themselves, and had their own stores and observed their own national holidays, and on Chinese New Year, always celebrated with firecrackers and a big feast. Their houses were mainly crude affairs, having mud walls. They cooked on oven-like stoves, made of baked mud; and when they decided to move they traveled light, packing all their belongings in two baskets suspended from a pole carried on their shoulders.

Turning off the road, Fred sent the jeep down a rough side trail leading to a tar-papered cabin on the mining claim of Harry Wiley. Operating a dry washer in the front yard was a husky, middle-aged chap whom my host introduced as Harold Strom—a former engraver and printer who, long before, had exchanged his city job for a gold-pan and pick. According to what Senator Wiley had told me earlier, he had not fared too badly in that pursuit.

After we had visited awhile, and Harold had exhibited the result of his latest clean-up, Fred asked him to show me the place "where the Old Mexican got his big nugget."

Heading out along a foot trail that led to the southwest of his cabin, Harold led us up through the trough of Big Nugget Gulch, a sharply-inclined ravine in the mountain's north slope. Nearly every foot of the way was marked by signs of past mining activity—prospect holes and small tailing piles, broken shovels, square-cut nails and fragments of desert glass. Just before topping the skyline, our guide halted at a spot that seemed to me indistinguishable from a dozen spots passed previously. Here, he said, was where the old Mexican miner, Marijilda, had found his famous $900 gold piece.

Marijilda, according to Fred and Harold, had been quite a miner. While working in Tule Canyon, throughout the 1870s and 1880s, he generally sold his gold at the Harris & Rhine store, in Independence, California, and it was there he had cashed his prize nugget, in 1873.

Strangely enough, said Fred, the old miner was ticketed to a tragic end in the same canyon that so long had provided his sustenance.

Some of the most severe storms ever known in the history of Nevada had occurred during the winter of 1889-90. In the Tule Canyon section, snow eventually lay piled so deeply in the mountain passes that not even a burro train could flounder through to the isolated camps, and with local supplies of food close to exhaustion, Marijilda had battled his way over the range to the mining camp of Lida. There he had reprovisioned and started homeward, carrying on his back assorted groceries, 50 pounds of flour, and a gallon jug of whiskey.

It was a strenuous trip for a man of his years, and the aged Mexican found it necessary to halt for frequent rests. Each time he paused, he presumably took a little swig from the whiskey jug.

Several days later, a passing party of miners found the old man sitting at his last rest stop only a few hundred yards from his cabin. Exhausted by the hard trip, and likely a little befuddled by the whiskey, he had fallen asleep and frozen to death—the partially depleted jug still cradled in his lap.

As the old man had died in a sitting position and his body was still frozen stiff and quite impossible to straighten, there had been nothing the burial party could do but plant him in that rather unusual posture. To have buried even a new-born jackrabbit in that hard-frozen ground would have been a major undertaking; but, by assidious chipping and hacking, the men eventually managed to excavate a hole of sufficient size to accommodate a sitting-up corpse.

Even in view of the terrific thirst this strenuous exercise had inspired, none of the grave diggers appeared to relish the thought of drinking a dead man's whiskey. After due discussion of the situation, the jug and its partially-frozen contents were laid in Marijilda's frozen arms, and the frozen earth was piled over him.

"And I reckon the whiskey's still there," said Fred. ". . . Unless Marijilda's ghost came back to kill it!"

Another of the early characters briefly resident in Tule Canyon had been "Honest Tom" Jaggers. The first I had heard of Honest Tom was during that afternoon jam session in Fred Green's cabin, at Gold Point.

"He always wore a Prince Albert coat and a tall, silk hat," Senator Wiley had recalled. Sheriff Kitchen had nodded and grinned.

"Yeah . . . and a holster with two big guns in it! He claimed to be a right bad hombre, too. Said he had killed more than one man and wouldn't stand for any damned nonsense . . ."

"Tom had a mine he called the 'Dark Secret'," Fred Green had put in. "The shaft's about a mile below our camp. The arrastre where he crushed his ore is still there too, but the rock cabin where he lived is mostly in ruins . . ."

During my second day at Tule, the Williams boys and Fred Green took me down to Jaggers' old cabin and arrastre where we prowled around for an hour or so looking for souvenirs and any possible relics.

Later, I wrote Doug Robinson, at Bishop, and asked what he could tell me of this Tule Canyon character.

"As I first remember him in 1890, 'Honest Tom' Jaggers came to Hawthorne, Nevada, from a small mining camp a few miles distant," wrote Mr. Robinson. "Then past middle age, he was rather small and insignificant, and looked as if a few good meals were what he needed most. He introduced himself as 'Honest Tom Jaggers, from Jaggersville, with a jag on.'

"Jaggersville, according to his accounts, was to become a second Virginia City; the ledges were big and could be traced for miles, while the assays showed better than any other district in the West. Meanwhile, he was short of a little ready cash and would sell to any good friend for $200, a mining claim that would produce good money 'from the grass roots down.' As he built up the jag, the ledges became richer and he let it be known that he was something of a fighting man. Of course, he did not intend to pick on anyone, but, nevertheless, he didn't intend to put up with any damned foolishness!

"Three or four years after I saw him at Hawthorne, he drifted in to Tule Canyon, bringing his few belongings on a very small, and very scrawny burro. Time had not been dealing kindly with Honest Tom— he looked even hungrier and skinnier than the first time I had seen him. This change of location, however, brought a new audience and he expressed confidence that Tule Canyon would soon be the biggest gold camp on the Coast.

" 'All you need here,' he said, 'is a good mining man with a lot of experience . . . like myself!'

"His line paid. He took on all the whiskey he could drink and negotiated for a small grubstake. After that, we always looked for him to come in from his diggings on Sunday. During the forenoon he would talk of his claims; but after 'oiling up' all morning, the afternoon would find him talking both of his claims and his prowess as a fighting man.

"He brought in a little gold—$4 or $5 worth each week—and found time to relocate several dozen abandoned mining claims which he tried to sell to any 'good friends.'

"He was doing fine—at least, he was eating—until he traded a claim 'worth at least $5000' for a Winchester rifle. That rifle put into high gear an imagination already well-primed, and, after acquiring it, there was never any doubt in Tom's mind that he was the original Bad Man of Esmeralda.

"When trouble finally hit him, it hit quick and hard. During an argument over boundary rights, or something, Tom declared war on a man we'll call Smith. Smith, unarmed, started for Tom, and Tom speedily took refuge in his cabin. Since he couldn't break the door down, Smith began tearing boards off the roof. Tom thereupon fired through the roof, wounding Smith in the leg. Smith climbed down and hollered through the door: 'All right, you so-and-so, I'm leaving—but I'll be back in 15 minutes with a couple of sticks of dynamite and blow you plumb to hell!'

"Tom didn't wait for Smith's return. Without even pausing to pack his few belongings, he dashed out of the cabin and started to do a lot of traveling and take but little time about it. Next morning, N. T. Piper— en route between the Oasis and McAfee ranches, in Fish Lake Valley— saw Tom ahead of him on the road. Hearing the rig coming, Tom thought it was Smith on his tail and took a couple of pot shots at Piper, after which he threw together a small stone breastwork and hid behind it until Piper had passed out of sight and hearing.

"Except for this enforced stop, Tom made only one other halt—a brief pause to eat—between Tule and Candelaria, a distance of more than 100 miles!

"Next time I ran across Honest Tom was at Goldfield, in 1905. The big mining boom was on, and Tom was doing well. He had already sold a lot of claims 'worth at least $5000 and good from the grass roots down'. He was rooming at the Esmeralda hotel, eating T-bones and French fries at the Palm Grill, and wearing fancy clothes including yellow, high-top boots, and a wide-brimmed Stetson.

"He was dropping a few dollars in a Twenty-One game when a bystander began to kid him. Tom rared up on his hind legs, looked as mean and ugly as he knew how, put his hand back toward his hip pocket, under his coat tail, and remarked, 'None of that! I'm a man who won't stand for any damned foolishness!'

"When he strode out of the gambling hall there was quite a buzz of comment. 'They say he's mighty mean,' said one fellow. 'Yeah,' answered another. 'He's had trouble all over the country. One day when he was likkered up he told me about killing a man in Tule Canyon . . .'

"I didn't tell them I had ever seen Old Tom before. Here he was, at the pinnacle of his success—money in his pockets, all dolled up, and known as a 'bad man.'

"I didn't figure it was up to me to spoil his playhouse . . ."

15

Miracle on a Mountain Top

IT WAS 1868. Newspapers were filled with the impeachment trial of President Andrew Johnson; the first transcontinental railroad was nearing completion, in Utah; and out in east-central Nevada, men were dipping the knee to a new and shining god—White Pine.

White Pine, the Poor Man's Paradise, was not a single boom town but a mining district embracing a whole gallery of boom towns—Hamilton, Treasure City, Shermantown, Eberhardt, Swansea, Menken, White Pine City, Monte Cristo, California, Mammoth City, Greenville, and Babylon —a wild, rough crop, conceived and born on the bleak hump of a mountain, nearly 9000 feet above sea level!

Any man possessed of half sense should have given wide berth to those winter-wind-swept, elevated eyries; but Silver, in '68, was a shameless siren which caused men to do things no sane man should have done.

So compelling was its Lorelei call that the second year of White Pine's madness had found these dozen new mining camps sprung from the sage, their twisting streets pounded by 50,000 human feet! In that same time, more than 13,000 mining claims had been staked in the district, and San Francisco Stock Exchange had come to deal in nearly 200 White Pine corporations having an aggregate capital of $275,000,000!

As they reveled in the wealth of this new Miracle of Mammon, the Johnny Chloriders of 85 years ago would have deemed it rankest heresy to suggest that their mountaintop money-box ever would be emptied; or that there would come a day when I would walk through the mine-torn streets of Hamilton and Treasure City, Shermantown and Swansea and Eberhardt, and in all that high land would hear not one sound louder than the restless rustle of a lizard's feet, no call more seductive than the thin sighing of a lonely wind.

In all those mountaintop cities, where silver-crazed multitudes had teemed and dreamed, there breathed that day, in 1955, not one living soul but myself!

The stampede to White Pine got off to a slow start. With Austin booming and the Comstock glowing on the Western horizon, little interest attended a newspaper report, in 1865, that two prospectors, Thomas J. Murphy and A. J. Leathers, had discovered silver "in paying quantities" in the White Pine range, 120 miles southeast of Austin, Nevada.

The next two summers following saw a few miners working in the district, and in 1867 the Monte Cristo company erected there a small mill moved from the then moribund camp of La Plata, first seat of Churchill county. But White Pine's ore still was not regarded as exceptional and no one got excited.

Not until the cold winter of 1867-68 did Destiny deliver a surprise package hoarded through all the ages of man!

The agent chosen for that delivery was a hungry Shoshone Indian, Napias Jim.

For Napias to be hungry was not unusual, but this day he was damned big hungry! He had been hungry when he crawled out of his ragged blankets, that morning; and after slogging through the snow all day, in search of wild game, sundown found him still empty-handed— and still hungry.

As he shuffled miserably past Leathers' cabin, Napias' nostrils reached out suddenly to envelope the demoralizing fragrance of hot beans, sowbelly, and coffee!

With hunger shouting, Conscience speaks with fragile voice; and in view of the temporary absence of Leathers, Satan nodded his approval, Leathers' beans vanished quickly into Napias, and Napias vanished into the night.

But because Napias, fundamentally, was a good Indian, it was only a short while until the black vulture of remorse came to roost on his shoulder, and he sought out Leathers and admitted his transient fall from grace. As payment for the stolen beans, he proffered a chunk of silver ore.

After turning the sample over half a dozen times and hefting it glumly, Leathers spat at a crack in the cabin wall and asked casually where had Napias found the piece?

Relieved to have his sins forgiven so readily, Napias guided Leathers and his partners, Thomas Murphy, and Edward Marchand, to the sample's place of origin on the east face of the blizzard-ripped summit of Treasure Hill, nearly 10,000 feet above sea level.

The day was January 4, 1868. The Hidden Treasure mine had been discovered—and Destiny smiled.

Destiny had jolly good reason to smile.

In only 18 months from that January day, the cash sale value of the Hidden Treasure mine, and Hidden Treasure Consolidated, would be more than half a million dollars, and pyramiding rumors would have touched off one of the most fabulous mining stampedes in world history!

Due to the many hillside dugouts occupied by miners, the first town in White Pine district had been named, facetiously, Cave City. On the site of this earlier camp, in May, 1868, was platted the new town of Hamilton, named for W. H. Hamilton, a promoter. Its first frame building —a saloon—was completed the following month. Other buildings shot up, and by that autumn, men were converging upon the new camp from every point of the compass.

In February, 1869, Sacramento (Calif.) *Union* reported: "A private letter from an eminent merchant in Chicago furnishes the information that the Pacific Railroad Company has disposed of 10,000 passenger tickets from Chicago to White Pine for the month of March, alone, and refuses to sell more on account of inability to transport a larger number."

Leaving the train at Elko, nearest point on the railroad, pilgrims made their way to White Pine by any and all means of transportation available. Many traversed the intervening mountains and desert aboard stage coaches loaded to their roofs and drawn by horses and mules at seven miles an hour.

One such stage, which passed through Austin, February 18, 1869, was described by *Reese River Reveille,* of Austin, as "fuller than a stuffed toad. It was chock full inside and nearly out of sight outside. It looked like an irregular pyramid of men, women, cats, dogs, Chinamen, gim-cracks, trunks, bandboxes, parcels, blankets, bottles of whiskey, sacks of flour, fresh beef, a plow, bars of steel and iron—all held together, somehow, and drawn by four horses."

Among the moths lured to White Pine's candle that year was Albert S. Evans, San Francisco feature writer, who found Hamilton a place of seething activity.

"Long lines of mules and oxen, drawing heavy wagons laden with supplies of every kind," wrote Evans in the *Overland Monthly.* "Bull-whackers in soldiers' coats, with whips a dozen feet in length on poles longer still . . . 'honest' miners with salted claims, ready to sell to the newly-arrived greenhorns; footpackers without a cent, who had packed their blankets and luggage all the way from Elko . . . sleeping in snow-drifts, if they slept at all; painted Jezebels from every mining camp from Idaho to Sonora; Shoshone Indians, Chinamen and 'capitalists' . . . crowded the streets of Hamilton. All was bustle and hurry, noise and excitement and confusion. The stores and saloons were crowded with men in huge overcoats, the pockets of which were filled with big specimens, small silver bars, rolls of location notices and assay certificates . . ."

Almost overnight, Hamilton had grown from a few ragged tents and a single business house to a place of violent excitement and extravagant hopes. Nearly every lot fronting on both sides of her mile-long main street was occupied by a building and cross-streets carried the town to a mile-and-a-half in width. New homes and business blocks were being added as rapidly as materials might be acquired. Even lumber of poor quality was selling at $300 and $400 per thousand feet and almost impossible to obtain. Anything which might be converted into roofs, including whiskey barrels and packing crates, was bringing fabulous prices. Store buildings in eligible locations were renting at $500 per month; hay was selling for $250 a ton, ordinary "horse" barley at 33 cents a pound, and common cook stoves were priced at $140.

But transcending all these inflated prices was the price of real estate. Every man from Salt Lake to San Francisco seemed suddenly possessed of a deadly determination to acquire town property at Hamilton, and land, which a year before might have been had for the taking, had skyrocketed until business lots were bringing $5000 and $6000 each!

Even after such property had been acquired, there still loomed the matter of holding possession.

Under the Law of Enclosure the owner of town property could legally protect his title by "fencing"—a term definable in various ways. The act of sticking in the ground, at far intervals, a few crooked branches connected by a single strand of rawhide, rope, or even store twine, usually was interpreted as "constructive possession," and more than one property owner, in the Hamilton of 1868-69, was legally acquitted for killing trespassers on lands so enclosed.

Other quarrels were inspired by less inanimate chattels. A Hamilton correspondent, who signed his communication "H.G.R.," reported to the Reno *Crescent,* in February, 1869:

"A couple of gamblers were shooting at each other all around the streets this afternoon over a woman. I regret to say neither of them were injured, but a faithful horse was shot; the clothes of several people were also shot through, and an acquaintance of mine sitting quietly in his own house received one of the balls through his coat collar over the shoulder. The people are talking of forming a Vigilance Committee."

"Ten thousand men are here now, and 50,000 will be here by the first of July," wrote W. W. Bishop, another Hamilton correspondent to the *Crescent,* that same month. "Real estate is very high, rents enormous . . . It is a faster camp than the Comstock . . . more men are making and losing fortunes . . ."

Into this pot-pourri of humanity had come the *Daily Inland Empire,* a newspaper soon to be recognized as one of the outstanding publications of Nevada. Until more stable quarters might be obtained, the *Empire* was issued from a tent, about 30 by 40 feet in area. The entire editorial force was relegated to one corner of the tent, the remainder of the space being divided between half a dozen compositors, a power press, Washington hand press, two Gordons and a rotary.

Sent to Hamilton, in '69, to obtain an eye-witness account of conditions, a reporter for the New York *Herald* apparently found it expedient to conduct most of his research in the local bistros—the high quality of which was agreeably pleasing to the young man from Manhattan.

"You can see in some of the saloons" (he reported through the news columns of the *Herald*) "as handsome a display of cut glass as in any place of a similar character in San Francisco. And, strange as it may seem, there are some paintings—of nude women, of course—that would not disgrace a well-selected picture gallery. The first class restaurants are good, and serve up a meal in a style similar to Delmonico's, of New York, or Martin's, of San Francisco."

In addition to her *bon vivants,* Hamilton had a commendable number of solid citizens. Before the town was six months old, her people had set up a school district, elected a board of trustees, dedicated a lot for the schoolhouse, and formed a lyceum with debating club and reading room.

With the organization of White Pine county, Hamilton was designated as its seat of government, and a $55,000 courthouse built. Other imposing structures in the town included St. Luke's Episcopal church, erected early in the camp's development, and regarded as one of the handsomest churches in the state; and the J. P. Withington hotel, constructed of Oregon white pine and dressed sandstone, and then recognized as the most elaborate building of its kind in Nevada.

Early in 1869, readers of the *Empire* learned of a new sub-division being opened at Hamilton by W. F. Walton, a real estate developer. The tract, it was said, would embrace some 2000 building lots, with 800 sites zoned for business. Other news included an announcement that the Hamilton Opera House had opened with Miss Olivia Rand in the initial offering. A contract had been awarded for 500,000 shingles to be cut in the Sierra Nevada and brought to Hamilton at a cost of 13 cents a pound for freighting, alone. Other freight outfits and passenger stages, it was said, were pouring in daily from all parts of the state, and each week was seeing the arrival of large herds of cattle, trail-driven overland from Texas.

Hamilton, by this time, had a claimed population of 15,000 inhabitants, and was rated the second largest municipality in Nevada.

And Hamilton, of course, was only one of the jewels in this mountain-top tiara!

Three miles to the south and more than 9000 feet above high-tide lay Treasure City (Plate 22) with a population of around 6000 persons. Shermantown claimed 7000 inhabitants, and Eberhardt but slightly less. Elsewhere in the range were a dozen other mushroom camps which endured for a few months, even for a year or two. Neither the birth nor subsequent demise of these fly-by-nights was accorded much attention by the Queen Bee. With the swansong of one such satellite, Hamilton's *Inland Empire* remarked laconically, "Babylon has fallen!"

But Hamilton's contempt for her satellites was wholly wasted on Treasure City. Treasure was a world unto herself; a cold, rich, draughty, naughty little world.

When a tenderfoot inquired about the climate there, Butcher "Dutch" Schultz snorted in disgust.

"*Glimate?* Ve no got glimate at Dreasure City! Only ve got ten mont's vinter und two mont's damn cold vedder!"

Throughout the winter, embracing more than half of each year, all wheeled traffic was halted at Hamilton by snow-blocked roads, and communication with Treasure City was limited to sleds, sleighs, saddle horses and "shank's mare"—four-horse sleighs making regular trips over the three-mile route at a one-way fare of three dollars per passenger.

During this same snow-bound period, Treasure's chief form of amusement was "betting on the ponies." Arrival of the daily mail stage at Hamilton would find waiting there horseback messengers from Treasure City's rival express companies—Wells, Fargo, and Pacific Union—who would snatch their respective mail pouches and be off up the three-mile grade. Treasure's male population, meanwhile, would be wrapped in the throes of frantic wagering over which rider would first reach the center of town.

As two dark specks rounded the distant shoulder of Treasure Hill, more gold pieces would make their appearance, and shouts of encouragement and derision would shake the mountain, until the snorting, foaming horses skidded to a stop and a great cry of victory resounded. Dragged from his saddle by triumphant hands, the winning rider would be borne aloft to the nearest saloon; and while hostlers threw blankets over the steaming steeds and walked them up and down main street to cool them, victor and vanquished joined in paying and collecting bets, postmorteming the race, and bending the elbow to Bacchus.

Despite the handicaps imposed by her lofty altitude, Treasure City possessed the main business section of the district—the first issue of the *Inland Empire,* in February, 1869, carrying advertisements of 42 business houses at Treasure City, compared with 31 concerns at Hamilton. At Treasure City, too, lived most of the miners, and in her environs were situated a majority of the mines.

And such mines as these were! Although the Hidden Treasure had served as springboard for the mad stampede, its fame and wealth was not to be compared with the fabulous Eberhardt, a later discovery on that same silver-soaked mountain-top.

Worked as an open-cut glory hole, this queen of the bonanzas produced $3,200,000 in silver from an excavation 70 feet long, 40 feet wide, and nowhere more than 28 feet deep—an average of $1000 per ton for 3200 tons of ore! One silver chloride boulder taken from the mine weighed *six tons,* and much of the high grade ore ran eight and ten dollars *to the pound!*

From all over the world came mining engineers to stare incredulously at the Eberhardt's treasure vault, unable to believe what they were seeing with their own eyes!

One who came to see and be convinced was Rossiter W. Raymond, Special Commissioner of Mining Statistics, for the U. S. Treasury department. In a report filed with the Secretary of the Treasury, in 1869, Mr. Raymond wrote of the Eberhardt:

"So rich is this mine that its name has become almost synonymous with that of the cave entered by Aladdin . . . Descending the shaft on a rope, we found ourselves among men engaged in breaking down silver by the ton. The light of our candles disclosed great black sparkling masses of silver ore on every side. The walls were silver, the roof over our heads silver, the very dust which filled our lungs and covered our boots and clothing was a gray coating of fine silver."

In his statistical review of the year following, Mr. Raymond still was slightly overwhelmed by the Eberhardt.

"Large lumps of pure chloride of silver, some of them weighing over a hundred pounds, are found so pure that a nail may easily be driven into any part of them, the same as into a bar of lead," he wrote. "A silver coin laid upon these pieces and struck smartly with a hammer or sledge will leave its impression as distinctly as a seal on soft wax . . ."

Other mines of the district were scarcely less spectacular. The story is told of two late autumn arrivals who gathered rocks on their claim and hastily threw together a single-room stone cabin as protection against the frigid blasts of winter. With the coming of spring and warmer weather, the pair dismantled their cabin and milled its silver-bearing walls for an asserted return of $75,000!

Not even the dead were permitted unbroken rest. In Evans' report to the *Overland Monthly* it was noted that one dead man had been moved twice on account of new discoveries, "and chlorides have been struck again in the vicinity of his last location during the week!"

With 25,000 persons gathered from the ends of the earth, it was inevitable that White Pine should have her gunplay and violence, and columns of the *Inland Empire* and *White Pine News* are sprinkled liberally with reports of citizens hospitalized or buried as result of sudden encounters with hot lead and cold steel. As most of the bullion produced in the district was necessarily freighted to Elko for shipment—a long, lonely haul across 140 miles of uninhabited desert—road agents grew prosperous and impudent. During one two-year period, scarcely a week passed that some bullion-laden stage out of White Pine was not halted and robbed by highwaymen.

But White Pine's downfall came not through highwaymen but as result of those greater evils—Nature's cupidity, international politics, and arson—a trio too frequently met in the Land of Silver and Sagebrush.

Nature struck the first blow when she built the mines "upside down," placing their fabulously rich ore close to the surface, rather than deeper in the earth where mining science expected it to be located. Instead of growing richer as depth was attained, the ore diminished steadily, or petered out altogether.

With "The Crime of '73," the demonetizing of silver, mines and mills began to close, the population to drift away.

One of the first to feel the blight of shriveling trade was Alexander Cohn, proprietor of a cigar store at Hamilton. Operating on the theory that insurance in hand was more desirable than a languishing business,

Cohn one night kindled a blaze in the backroom of his store, and to forestall the efforts of Hamilton's three efficient fire companies, also took precaution to close the city's main water valve—thereby cutting the available supply to a trickle.

Before its discovery the fire had gained a head start and nearly one-third of the city went up in smoke that night.

Convicted of arson, Cohn was sentenced to seven years in state prison . . . but Hamilton's glory was gone forever.

The year following saw Treasure City, likewise, destroyed by fire. Although her mines were still producing in diminished fashion, the town never rebuilt and by 1880 her peak of 6000 persons had dwindled to less than 100. Shermantown, in the same period, dropped from a claimed population of 7000 to a single family.

Even with her satellites crashing all about her, poor Hamilton defended grimly her position as seat of White Pine county; but after her splendid courthouse was destroyed by fire in January, 1885, it was curtains for the old town. White Pine county, by that time, was experiencing a population shift to its eastern portion, and when the new courthouse was erected, its site was at Ely.

Thus was penned the concluding chapter in a 15-year story of greatness. After producing more than $35,000,000 in ore, the miracle cities on the mountaintop tossed in the towel.

Little remains in Hamilton today. A few old dugouts, the buckling walls of the J. P. Withington hotel, (Plate 25) the ruins of a mill or two, a caving cellar where the schoolhouse had stood—only the stale and musty crumbs of a banquet nearly forgotten.

Even as late as 1947, Hamilton was one of the most fascinating ghosttowns in the State of Nevada. Even then, she had not an inhabitant to her name, but a flagless flagpole in the schoolyard still pointed the way to higher things; a few old textbooks of the 1870s reposed in the knife-scarred desks. Some of the old homes held walnut bedsteads and marble-top tables; and in the Wells, Fargo Express office were two massive vaults, long barren of treasure. In front of the old livery stable stood a collection of weather-beaten sleighs and buckboards, and one high-wheeled freight wagon—as solid and stout as the day it had made its final climb up that long, twisting grade! The glass-fronted "call boxes" were still intact in the postoffice, and musty old correspondence and postal records lay a foot deep on the office floor.

As I sorted through that dusty litter—seeking old letters or money order receipts, or anything of historical interest — I was remembering Jim Riley.

Jim was a gambler. Hamilton, during her opulence, had supported many gamblers—some of whom gambled with dice and cards, others with mining stock. It had remained for Jim to gamble with postage stamps—

and because of that unique choice, it was Jim who caught the last, fast ride on Hamilton's Bonanza Train.

Jim and his brother-in-law owned one of the city's main places of business. In addition to operating a general store, they were local agents for Homer King and Company, a stock brokerage concern of San Francisco; they also operated the Western Union office, and Jim was postmaster at Hamilton.

During the dizzy days of 1869-70, when White Pine's star was climbing toward its zenith, the postoffice department had designated Hamilton as an office of the second class, and fixed the salary of its postmaster at $3200 per year.

Time passed. Years of it. White Pine's population gradually trickled away until not more than 50 letters a day were being postmarked at Hamilton; yet, that office still carried its second class rating, and Postmaster Riley still was drawing his $3200 salary!

Inasmuch as the rating of a postoffice was based on volume of stamp sales, this situation at Hamilton seemed rather unusual to some folks.

Even Uncle Sam at last grew suspicious.

Investigation showed that Jim, himself, had been buying the immense volume of stamps necessary to keep the Hamilton office in its preferred rating. In order to finance such heavy purchases, he had persuaded jobbers and wholesalers to accept postage stamps in payment for practically all the merchandise bought for resale in his store! One San Francisco firm, it was disclosed, had for years been supplying him with approximately $2200 worth of goods *each month* and accepting the entire payment in stamps!

Arrested and taken to San Francisco for trial, Jim was subsequently acquitted when the prosecution failed to show he had ever acknowledged the government's notice of a change in the postoffice department's system of computing salaries. It was only a technicality, of course; but to Jim as convenient as a life-raft to a drowning man.

Upon his return to Nevada, Hamilton's ex-postmaster was eager to recount his experiences in the Bay City. The "government boys," he said, had treated him fine all the while he was in custody, even providing him with excellent quarters at the Palace Hotel.

There was only one thing that sort of irked him. As soon as he had been acquitted, he grumbled, the federal officers had refused to be further responsible for his hotel bills and he had found it necessary to pay his own fare back to Hamilton!

And then, Old Jim Riley voiced a classical remark—one that well might serve as an epitaph for all the miracle cities of White Pine.

"Take it all together," Jim had said of his fall from grace, "It was a damned interesting experience!"

16

Seven Somnolent Sisters

BETWEEN NEVADA'S Excelsior range and the cold, bald pates of the Monte Cristos, lies a harsh world of sullen salt flats and grim mountains, warped in the fiery crucible of Earth's creation.

No sparkling streams soften this somnolent waste, no tree-shaded lakes lie cupped in its valleys. It is a hard land that asks no quarter and grants none; yet, even here, are the hallmarks of the prospector—the monuments that mark his mines, the cairns that monument his graves. He came and saw and, briefly, he conquered. He gathered the harvest of the hills and passed on to other hills, other harvests, other worlds.

As proof of that passing he left behind a gallery of seven ghosts. Seven spectral cities in a radius of a dozen miles—Candelaria, Metallic City, Belleville, Marietta, Rhodes, and Sodaville, all in Mineral county; and Columbus, just over the line in Esmeralda.

What changes a few years can effect in the evolution of a mining district! In 1863 there were probably not a dozen white men in all that land between the Monte Cristos and the Excelsiors. Another ten years found seven flourishing centers of sin and silver risen from the sage. Again, time marched on . . . and today, the combined population of all those seven cities—all their nationalities and colors, and creeds and ages —once again does not exceed a dozen persons!

So is the cycle completed: Sage to cities—and back to sage.

Even before Nevada attained statehood, silver values had been discovered in this locality by Mexican prospectors. Many claims had been staked, and a mining district organized. With ore from those first surface workings so rich it could be milled in Mexican *arrastres* which will not ordinarily recover silver values, a boom was not slow in developing. The town of Candelaria was founded in 1865, and through her twisting streets soon surged a cross-section of the United Nations, foreign-born citizens outnumbering American by four to one.

With a potential bonanza under every bush and liquor flowing with the freedom of the surf, the only scarcities in this raw new town were water, stove-wood, law, and churches.

Of churches there was none; of law there was little. Wood—chiefly sagebrush—was cut on the hills by Indians and brought long distances on burro back; and for the first 17 years of its history, all water used in the camp was hauled in wagons from a spring, nine miles distant, at a consumer cost of $1 a gallon.

Over in the rival city of Bodie, California, a newspaper expressed wonder that a lack of water should disturb Candelaria—it being charged that not more than a dozen citizens of the Nevada camp ever used the commodity, either for personal ablution or as a beverage. Bodie further asserted, with an embarrassing degree of truth, that when the telegraph line was extended to Candelaria the operator found it necessary to descend to the 1700-foot-level of the Mount Diablo mine to locate a spot moist enough to attach his ground wire!

Throughout the 1870s and well into the '80s, Candelaria was a tough place where violence rode the night with appalling frequency. Coroner's juries were notoriously lenient, and all but the most flagrant murders won verdicts of "self defense."

One of the camp's more notable blood-lettings was the slaying of Tom Logan, a prominent local saloonkeeper, later eulogized by the editor of Candelaria *True Fissure* as a quiet, peaceful gentleman, "with a disposition gentle as a woman." Logan's death followed a "friendly" card game with Bart Greeley, another prominent citizen "of gentle disposition." Greeley lost, a quarrel ensued, and hot words were supported by hotter lead.

As a mark of respect to two "gentle" citizens, who had behaved in anything but gentle fashion, all flags in the town were flown at half-mast, and all stores and saloons closed for the funeral.

Candelaria, by 1880, was the largest town in what was then Esmeralda county. Flanking her streets were ten saloons, two hotels, half a dozen stores, and offices occupied by three lawyers and a trio of doctors. One of the camp's four shortages was partially alleviated in 1882 by the piping of water from Trail canyon, in the White mountains. As the cost of that necessity plunged from a dollar a gallon to five cents, a Candelaria barber began advertising:

BATHS AT REASONABLE RATES!
Hot water, $1.25; Cold Water 75c

One week after completion of the water line, the Carson and Colorado railroad inaugurated service on its narrow-gauge spur track from Belleville to Candelaria. (Plate 23) Arrival in camp of the first train was cause for great jubilation, since the new transportation facility meant not only a drastic cut in freight rates, but also gave the town a feeling of importance and oneness with the outside world.

Douglas Robinson, a resident of Candelaria in the 1890s, and later chief probation officer of Inyo county, California, often recalls early events in the old Nevada camp—including his boyhood thrill upon seeing great bars of silver bullion loaded into McNaughton's dray to be hauled across town to the railroad station—solid silver, and every pound the rig could haul!

"Candelaria was a great camp!" says Doug. "But it wasn't a good place to live! It wasn't a healthy place. There were no sewers, and few screens on doors or windows. The flies were terrific. The stamp mill was a dry crusher, with no water in the battery box. The result was an endless cloud of dust and bad lungs for the millhands, who put in 12 hours a day. The miners worked a 10-hour day, for which they received $3.50—even in those days far from enough to provide a decent living. Most of them worked seven days a week—few could afford to take Sundays off. Stores were open from seven in the morning until ten at night. There were no churches. The big social event of the year was the Miner's Union dance. Occasionally there were other dances, but not many. About once in three years a traveling show came to town—generally an Indian medicine outfit.

"Nearly every hour of the day and night found heavy freight wagons rumbling through the streets—all fetlock deep in dust. Ore from the Holmes mine was hauled to the mill by 16-animal outfits, while the Mount Diablo freighted to the railroad at Candelaria and shipped to Sodaville for milling. At the same time, marsh borax was being mined at Columbus, and long-line teams brought mountainous loads of the stuff to Candelaria for shipping. Once a 16-animal team ran away when one of the brake rods snapped and turned the two wagons loose. The outfit careened all the way down main street and wrecked itself near our home. The driver and several of the animals were killed.

"Hay, grain and meat were hauled from Fish Lake valley, and poultry and fruit from as far distant as Owens valley, in California. No one could raise a garden—there wasn't enough water. Even after water was brought from Trail canyon, 'the Company' required most of it for their own operations. The big, terraced lawn at Company headquarters caused lots of bitter comment. Mother had a few hollyhocks and a little patch of lawn, about as large as a front porch. This, and the company yard, were the only green spots in town. I doubt if water was piped into a dozen homes. (Plate 34)

"No," said Doug, "Candelaria wasn't a good place to live . . . but she was a great camp!"

Most remarkable mine in the history of the district was the Northern Belle, which brought no shekels to its discoverer. First staked in 1865, the great potential of the property was not fully recognized and the claim was permitted to lapse. Restaked, in 1870, the Belle quickly distinguished itself as one of the great treasure vaults of the state. In 15 years the mine produced close to $15,000,000 in ore, and by close of 1880 had paid 47 dividends without levying one assessment!

After producing close to $30,000,000 — some sources place the figure as high as $55,000,000—Candelaria did a swansong in the closing years of the 19th century. Of the several factors contributing to her end, one of the more important was the matter of wages.

With the price of silver declining steadily, mine operators issued an ultimatum that wages must be reduced to $3.00 daily or the mines would be forced to close. Miners refused to accept the cut. In the resulting deadlock the camp folded; inhabitants moved elsewhere, and the last train pulled out of the station.

Many years have passed since Candelaria has had even one permanent resident. In July, 1955, her twisting main street was edged by a few sturdy stone walls—the leading bank, a restaurant, a hardware store with tall, iron shutters. A litter of broken crucibles and bone-ash cupels marked the site of the assay office; but of the Roaring Gimlet saloon or its nine lusty rivals, nothing remained. Neither was there any way to determine which of those crumbled ruins had housed the town's two newspaper plants—the *Chloride Belt,* and John Dormer's *True Fissure.* On the flat below the terraced "company" garden stood the sagging frame of an old stagecoach; and at several points over the townsite lay great steel vaults that gaped open to the desert wind. But except for packrat litter and layers of powdery red dust, their interiors were empty.

Most important of Candelaria's sister towns was Columbus, five miles over the ridge on the edge of a sombre, white flat.

On that sombre flat, at the foot of the sombre hills, America's borax industry was born.

Development of Columbus was contemporaneous with that of Candelaria. In the old dry lake bed lay an abundant supply of salt, large quantities of which were required in the chlorination milling of silver ore. Salt claims were staked on the marsh and, by 1865, the town of Columbus had been founded. When the slope to the north was found to provide a meager flow of water, a quartz mill was erected by "Colonel" Young, milling equipment was freighted to the site from Aurora, and trains of pack mules began the grueling task of transporting ore from Candelaria's mines across the rugged desert mountains to the mill. With a milling charge of $60 per ton, plus an additional $8.00 for transportation by pack train, only extremely rich ore could be handled in this manner—but Candelaria had it!

As he staked his salt mine, the original claimant of Columbus marsh had noted another substance with silky white fibers and a peculiar taste. Strangely enough, no one bothered to learn the identity of this second mineral until 1871, when there strayed into Columbus a former Comstock miner, William Troup. Taking one look at the silky stuff, Troup borrowed a wash boiler, highgraded a bucket of water, and kindled a sagebrush fire. With this simple equipment he quickly refined enough of the material to prove it was virtually pure borax; technically, ulexite.

Whatever degree of importance Columbus previously had enjoyed as a salt-mining and silver-milling center, was instantly eclipsed by this new discovery. William T. Coleman, for whom the borate, colemanite, later would be named, installed refining equipment and by 1872 the town was deeply entrenched in the borax business.

These operations appear to have marked the first commercial refining of cottonball borax in the United States.

In the years immediately following, Columbus became the headquarters of four men who would subsequently loom large in the borax industry of the world—Coleman, Chris Zabriskie, John Ryan, and Francis Marion "Borax" Smith. Smith, in particular, was slated to fill a large niche in the Western hall of fame. Acquiring the Coleman holdings, he established at Columbus the Pacific Coast Borax company, imported 1000 Chinese coolies to gather and refine the borax, originated the now-famous "Twenty-Mule Team" trademark, and ultimately built and operated the Tonopah and Tidewater Railroad.

Colonel Young's stamps, meanwhile, had continued to pound away at Candelaria's silver ore, which was no longer transported down the mountain by straining pack mules, but was freighted hence in ponderous wagons driven by Chinese teamsters. With their long black queues and "furrin" ways and garb, these Chinese provided the most colorful phase of life in Columbus. They lived, for the most part, in cramped adobe huts and passed their leisure moments in dark opium cellars where they communed with the poppy and wooed the dreams of their ancestors. In addition to those employed in freighting ore, and in mining and refining the borax, many others were engaged in hauling borax—first to the railroad at Wadsworth, some 150 miles to the north, and, later, to Candelaria.

Returning with empty wagons, the weary teams would toil up the long, hard hill between Candelaria and Columbus. Topping the summit of the range, each teamster would loose a banshee scream, lash out with his whip, and literally catapult his outfit down the last steep grade into port.

With every horse and mule snorting and frothing and galloping at full speed to keep ahead of the bouncing wagons, the borax trains careened through Main street—women and children and dogs scattering in every direction, and each black-queued driver screaming and shrieking at the top of his voice, and cursing in all the assorted dialects of the Orient!

It may have been this unique practice—or maybe it was the 1000-man riot in Chinatown over "China Mary"—that prompted the editor of the Columbus *Borax Miner* to observe that the Comstock no longer could claim any form of disorder that Columbus had not experienced!

The town even had its Grade-A lynching, but no Oriental pigtails figured in that affray.

Among those comprising the orchestra at a New Year's Eve dance, in 1873, was a Chilean woman guitarist. Possibly she plunked a sour note, now and then; or, maybe she smiled at the wrong man. Something, at least, proved displeasing to one Victor Monega who eventually reached the limit of his endurance. Snatching her guitar, he threw it on the floor, smashed it to splinters, and strode from the hall. Believing such a display of temper to be somewhat ungentlemanly, one of the town's respected cafemen followed the music critic to remonstrate with him.

For his solicitude, our prominent citizen ended the old year with a thin knife blade parked between his ribs.

Arrested on a murder charge, Monega was lodged in the Columbus jail; but with all the town's manpower assembled at the dance and considerably "likkered up," it is needless to say that he remained behind the bars for only a few minutes.

Due to a complete absence of trees in Columbus' environs, Monega was taken to the slaughter house west of town and there was strung up on a butcher's windlass, ordinarily used for hoisting beeves.

Several days later, when a deputy sheriff arrived from San Bernardino with a warrant for Monega's arrest on a California murder charge, the borax camp music critic already was answering to a Higher Court.

Greatest prosperity in the history of Columbus fell in the years between 1870-75. In addition to the usual accoutrements of a mining camp, the old town on the dry lake was then the site of an iron foundry, a wagon works, and several machine shops. The dining room of Holland's Hotel did double duty as a public hall and theater; and during part of its career, the town boasted two newspapers—the *Borax Miner,* and the Columbus *Times.*

Except for a disagreement between Colonel Young and his partner, A. J. Holmes, Columbus might have flourished for another decade as a silver milling center. From a petty beginning the bad feeling mounted and eventually grew into litigation by which Holmes was forced out of the company. It was a bitter pill; and in taking leave of the town he warned vindictively that another year would see grass growing in the streets of Columbus. Young only laughed at the prediction and put it down as the empty threat of a bad loser.

But the threat was not empty. Gaining control of the Northern Belle, Holmes cut off all shipments of ore to Young's mill; his company immediately erected its own 20-stamp quartz mill at a point seven miles west of Candelaria; and if it had been possible for grass to exist in the mineral-impregnated streets of Columbus, Colonel Young would have seen his ex-partner's threat come true. With the Northern Belle's patronage diverted to the new town, the ore wagons stopped rumbling down the grade from Candelaria, and Columbus' day as a milling center was ended. Borax mining continued to support the camp until discovery of even richer borax deposits in Fish Lake Valley, in 1875. With removal of the Pacific Coast Borax company's operations to the new field, Columbus turned up her toes, until several years later when she climbed back into the news columns with alleged discovery there of a mine yielding pure castile soap! According to the widely publicized report, the "soap vein" was 12 feet in thickness and of unknown length; and it was proposed to build on the edge of the lakebed a huge plant for the manufacturing of soap and cosmetics. Needless to report, no such factory was built.

Sole remaining inhabitants of Columbus are John and Grace Callahan. Arriving in the deserted town 15 years ago, they moved into what is known as "the old Molini place"—an ancient adobe cabin wondrously held together with railroad ties, scrap lumber, cut iron nails, and tin sheathing. Less than a pebble's toss from their front door lies the northern edge of the borax "marsh," which spreads away in 20-square miles of glaring desolation—a sullen waterless world, where scarcely one sprig of green is visible. Spotted over the dry flat are heaps of dead white borax, a few old reduction tanks, and occasional pieces of mining and freighting equipment. All wooden parts have been eaten to a porous sponge by the strong mineral; even iron shows the erosive effect of its gnawing. (Plate 17)

Near the Callahan home stands the caving walls of Colonel Young's big quartz mill, and the ruins of sundry other buildings; and on the barren slope back of town lies the cemetery. General desolation of the old burying ground is emphasized by many open graves from which the bones of Chinese dead were exhumed long ago for removal to their ancestral homes. Of the 300-odd burials the graveyard is believed to contain, only one marker in the cemetery carried a name which still could be deciphered at the time of the Callahan's arrival at Columbus. That last name was Benjamin Rowe, but all pertinent details—who the man may have been, when and where he was born, and how and when he died—had been sandblasted away by decades of the borax-laden wind. Today, even the name has been lost.

Even more anonymous are the sleeping dead of nearby Belleville and Marietta, where not one marker remained standing in either cemetery in 1953; nor was any inscription completely legible. Even the paling fences that had enclosed the plots were lying on the ground.

"Once I figgered to fence the graveyard," said grizzled Matt Obert, one of the last three inhabitants of Marietta. "When I learned what th' job would cost, I said t' myself: 'What th' hell! Them that's in there can't get out . . . and them that's out don't want to get in. So why fence th' place?' "

With construction of the Northern Belle's new mill, in 1873, the town of Belleville came into being and soon enjoyed a reputation as one of the best "sporting camps" in Nevada.

During its career of nine hectic years the town had two newspapers, both owned by Ramon Montenegro, a gambler, who also owned and operated the Club House, Belleville's leading palace of pleasure. One of the celebrated gun battles of the town was a street duel engaged in by this same prominent citizen, and Judge A. G. Turner, the trouble having grown out of pointed remarks made by Montenegro in one of his papers. Meeting on the main street of Belleville, both litigants went for their guns, and Montenegro went down with two slugs in his belly. No charges were filed.

Another local slaying that aroused considerable comment was the murder of Tom McLaughlin, characterized by Candelaria *True Fissure* as "pleasant and genial in disposition and the very embodiment of a gentleman." These genteel attributes had not prevented Tom from making a few footprints in the sands of Marietta when he killed two men and wounded a third—all allegedly members of the Brophy gang. Later, as Tom rode his horse through the streets of Belleville, he was shot from ambush by an unknown assailant. It was presumed that some friend of the Brophys was responsible, but no arrests were made.

With a second 20-stamp mill built at Belleville in 1876, the town continued active throughout that decade, with a brace of hotels, seven saloons, and numerous stores and cafes; but with the arrival of piped water at Candelaria in the early '80s, and transferral of milling activities to points closer to the mines, Belleville cashed in her chips. All that remains to mark her transient presence are the foundation and broken walls of the big mill, the remnants of a few stone cabins, and her nameless graves. Her neighboring hot-spot of Marietta has vanished almost as completely.

And now for a quick leap backward to another of the Somnolent Seven.

Midway between Columbus and Candelaria—in a long, deep canyon between the Mount Diablo and the Metallic and Emperor shafts—is all that remains of the old settlement of Metallic City; or, as she was derisively known to her contemporaries, Pickhandle Gulch.

The Gulch was not famed as an exponent of law and order; even her nickname alluded to the fact that her citizens customarily settled their differences with flailing pickhandles. From visible evidence remaining, her most plentiful building materials would seem to have been native stone and wooden whiskey cases. One of the best preserved cabins still standing in the canyon, in 1950, was constructed of such cases filled with earth, relidded, and laid brick fashion. Stenciled endboards revealed that each of the cases originally had held one dozen quarts, and most of the boxes carried the additional legend:

"Bottled from 1874 Whiskies.
Shipped from Dist. 8, Oct. 17, 1879.
Arrived San Francisco, June 6, 1880.
Ex-Ship Benson."

Despite its isolated position on the shirttail of civilization, Pickhandle Gulch was not wholly ignored by persons of importance, one frequent visitor at The Gulch, being "Lucky" Baldwin, millionaire mine promoter, who was financially interested in several properties in the district. Other big shots who lent their occasional presence included the millionaire Comstocker, Col. James G. Fair.

During his campaign for United States Senator from Nevada, in

1880, Colonel Fair—in red-flannel shirt and wide-brimmed hat—came clattering up the canyon in a dusty buckboard to address Pickhandle's electors. After buying drinks for the town and visiting each of the district's several rich mines, the Colonel trundled back down the mountain, leaving The Gulch unalterably convinced that here was a man's man who talked man's language.

Among the red-letter days of Pickhandle Gulch, this memorable visit was topped only by the day Shagnasty Joe left town.

A frequenter of the Roaring Gimlet saloon in Candelaria, Shagnasty was generally known as a loud-mouthed four-flusher. Pickhandle's Number One bad boy, on the other hand, was Blue Dick Hartman, a drifter from the Comstock, whose face had been permanently discolored by powder burns. The inter-city jealousy between Dick and Shagnasty had created a situation that threatened any moment to break into hot lead.

Word went around one day that Blue Dick had been killed by an unknown assailant and was laid out in McKissick's Saloon, on the south side of the plaza. The news spread rapidly, and soon as the second mine shift came off, Pickhandle convened to pay homage to her departed townsman.

As the delegation filed into McKissick's, every eye was drawn irresistibly to the canvas-covered figure reposing on a billiard table in a darkened rear corner. From the lower end of that impromptu shroud protruded Dick's boots, and beside him lay his familiar slouch hat. Regardless how big a nuisance Blue Dick's presence had been in the past, his absence immediately had the effect of skyrocketing his questionable value to mankind.

"He was a great guy," sighed the shift boss from the Emperor. "A great friend to all of us!"

"That he was!" agreed another from the Mount Diablo. "A gr-r-reat force for law and order!"

Hesitantly drawing aside the canvas covering, one of the miners peered into Dick's mean blue face. As he gazed upon his fellow Gulcher, one of those blued eyelids was stirred by the faintest trace of a wink, and before he replaced the canvas shroud a flicker of understanding had crept into the mourner's brain.

"Yessir!" he remarked dolefully, tossing off another slug. "Dick was a gr-r-reat asset to Nevada, a great name in the West. I figger it's up to us to see he's planted in handsome style. How 'bout it, boys—let's give Ol' Dick a gen-u-ine send-off!"

The idea met with instant approval, and as Dick's hat was circulated, there poured into it a cascade of silver and gold coins. With each subsequent round of drinks, Dick's loss to mankind became the greater, and more coins clanked into the kitty.

The wake was warming up nicely when the swinging doors of

McKissick's were darkened by the hulking figure of Shagnasty Joe. Elbowing his way to the bar, he let out a beller and pounded for service.

"Now, Joe!" reproved the barkeep. "Is that any proper way to act with poor Blue Dick lying dead and cold on th' table, yonder? Ain't you ashamed of yourself?"

"Dead!" exploded Shagnasty Joe, of Candelaria. "That lousy skunk? So somebody beat me to it and plugged him! He may have had you banties buffaloed, but not me! He weren't no gunman! He was nothin' but a lousy coyoty—look at him cross-eyed and he'd run off yelpin' with his tail atween his laigs!"

Shagnasty's incriminations might have become downright insulting if they had not terminated in a hoarse, long-drawn shriek.

The "corpse" of Blue Dick had leaped from the table and both arms were flailing wildly in an effort to throw off the enveloping "shroud" so he might draw his forty-five. Just as Shagnasty cleared the swinging doors, with stark terror lending wings to his boots, Dick got his gun unlimbered and began heating the pants of the departing figure.

Soon outdistanced in his pursuit, Blue Dick returned to McKissick's. There he and his erstwhile mourners dedicated themselves to the business of converting the funeral expense fund into liquid assets.

And that was the last Pickhandle Gulch ever saw of Shagnasty Joe.

17

Where Ghosts Wear Pigtails

GONE ARE THOSE lusty legions who shared in the glory of Tuscarora. The thundering mills, the fan-tan parlors, the great joss house with its silken trappings and fat-bellied gods—all have vanished, like fantasies born out of poppy smoke.

All that remains is an empty husk and great weariness. Weary old buildings on a weary street; weary old benches, bleaching in the sun. Weary old men, warming their bones and puffing their pipes—weary old men, reliving the past when Tuscarora's star shone bright and beautiful.

Those were the days, they'll tell you, when the hills were swarming with prairie chickens and sage-hens, and within walking distance of town were a dozen trout streams packed with speckled beauties. Those were the days when every man's pocket was sagging with gold, and every man was a king.

Those, indeed, were the days. . .

First mining on the slopes of Mt. Blitzen is credited to a pair of brothers, John and Steve Beard. For half-a-dozen years the Beards prospected and placered for gold, hunted and fished in their leisure hours, and reveled in the life of Riley.

And then came 1871, and W. O. Weed's discovery of a mighty silver lode.

Life on Mt. Blitzen was never the same again.

The Elysian fields of the Beards were swallowed by a human avalanche. Claims were staked on every side; shafts were sunk, tunnels driven. The town of Tuscarora was founded. Stores and hotels were erected; a newspaper was born. Despite a severe winter climate and her terrific remoteness from anywhere else, the new town soon had attracted a population of 5000 persons, thereby becoming the metropolis of Elko county and one of the important mining centers of the West. It was a position she would hold through 14 great years.

When old men of the Pine Bench Brigade conduct their daily wake over Tuscarora's wasted cadaver, they speak reverently of her splendid mines—the fabulous Dexter, the Navajo and Nevada Queen, the Grand Prize, the North Belle Isle. They tell proudly of her opulence and mirth and madness; but, most of all, they tell of her Chinatown.

Completion of the Pacific Railroad in 1869 had released upon the Western desert an army of several thousand Chinese previously employed in grading and laying track for this first major western line.

Fearing that the availability of coolie labor would result in widespread wage-cutting in the mines and mills, Nevada's white population adopted a militant stand against hiring these unemployed Celestials. In several communities where they sought to reestablish themselves, their flimsy homes and beggarly belongings were put to the torch and the terrified Chinese sent fleeing before the fury of armed mobs. Because Tuscarora exhibited greater tolerance toward the ex-railroaders, it was but a short while until 2000 of them had congregated in that vicinity. There they devoted their efforts to re-working old tailing dumps and mining low-grade ore in properties already "worked out" and abandoned by the whites.

Tuscarora's Chinatown—despite the fact that it comprised the largest concentration of Orientals in Nevada—was scarcely the answer to a city planner's prayer. Along both sides of a narrow, twisting street rose squalid tenements and flop-houses, many of them extending through several underground stories to open at street level. In these dark, gloomy firetraps, rife with stale air and fetid smells and eerie sounds, the Chinese of Nevada's "Little Shanghai" duplicated as best they might the sensual and spiritual pleasures of the Orient.

Religious center of the colony was an elaborately-appointed joss house, where a smirking idol held court in a setting of gold and silver, carved teakwood and red lacquer. Elsewhere in the colony, opium dens supplied the Nirvana of the Poppy; prayer lights flickered, incense smouldered, and gambling thrived. It has been estimated that every third Chinese in Tuscarora operated a lottery for the others to buck; while games operated by professional Oriental gamblers oftimes saw thousands of dollars wagered on a single play.

White men a-plenty had eyed and coveted those stacks of Chinese gold; but, so far as known, there was only one successful raid on the gambling dens. This, strangely enough, was a one-man job.

Planning his attack with rare cunning, this daring pillager chose a black, cold night when smoke was pouring from the chimney of the colony's largest dive. Climbing to the flat roof he dropped into the stovepipe a long paper cylinder containing five pounds of black pepper and sulphur. Plummeting down the straight pipe, the potent parcel struck the damper and burst open immediately above the roaring fire. Meanwhile, the culprit had dropped a bucket over the top of the stovepipe and leaped from the roof.

With the choking fumes of burned pepper and sulphur spreading through the gambling den, pandemonium broke and every man in the place joined in a wild stampede toward the front entrance. Choosing this strategic moment, the lone raider threw his shoulder against the flimsy back door and lunged forward. As the door went down, he leaped into the room and held his breath as he speedily filled a large ore sack with the stacked coins.

Suddenly suspecting a trick, the gamblers rushed back to their tables —but too late. The thief had vanished into the night, taking with him more than $5000 in Chinese gold!

But stolen gold has a wicked way of slipping through men's fingers. According to the Bench Brigade, it was only a few weeks until Tuscarora's prize brigand had lost every penny of his loot back over the same gambling tables he had robbed!

Most prosperous period in the history of Tuscarora was in the years between 1872 and 1876 when six large silver mills, employing the Reese River process, were in operation in the district. Mining and milling costs were almost prohibitive. As the region was but sparsely timbered, a large part of the fuel used in mill operation was derived from sagebrush and there were times when as many laborers were engaged in cutting and hauling the brush as were employed in all the mines of the district! Pumping constituted another costly operation—a rushing flood of water having been struck almost as soon as the shafts were below ground level. Even despite these heavy costs, the ore of Tuscarora district was sufficiently rich to return a handsome profit until silver's crucifixion by political juggling. Further financial strain was imposed by extended litigation, and the crowning blow came in the form of a devastating fire that halted the pumps and permitted the underground workings to flood with water.

The Dexter gold mine continued to operate until 1898. With its close, the camp on Mt. Blitzen had produced close to $40,000,000 in ore —a large part of it silver.*

It had been a gay, glad song, and the singing had been good. . .

It was snowing as I climbed the long grade into Tuscarora. Earlier-fallen snow laid like a white veil of compassion over mine-torn hills and ravaged ravines; and here and there, that veil was pierced by gaunt skeletons of tall, rock chimneys, by the groping arms of leafless trees, and the broken fangs of stone walls. (Plates 3, 37)

Halting my car in the frozen slush of main street, I ranged my eyes over the business district. Where 2000 Celestials and three times that many Occidentals had formerly walked, there remained that day only 23 inhabitants.

To my left rose the old Masonic Temple—a squat, sullen, stone building, windowless and long vacant. Across the street stood three other buildings—two with wooden awnings and square false fronts and hitch-rails; the third, a brick structure with narrow iron doors. The center unit, I saw, was occupied by a small general store—the last operating business in town.

Pushing open the door of that establishment I entered a cramped

---

*Emmonds, W. H. "A Reconnaissance of Some Mining Camps in Elko, Lander, and Eureka Counties, Nevada." U. S. Geological Survey Bulletin 408, 1910.

room, ringed with ceiling-high shelves. Cluttered and dark, and over-heated by the pot-bellied stove in its center, it smelled of gasoline and apples; of tobacco smoke and wet boots, and new harness leather, and nut-pine wood. The storekeeper and his wife were the only occupants.

After the usual discussion of the weather and current mining conditions, I bought a wedge of cheese and asked if there was an old cabin I might occupy for a couple of nights. The woman thought I might use "Joe's place."

"Joe," she remarked significantly, "won't be needin' it." Her man nodded.

"Sure thing," he agreed. "Ol' Joe won't mind! You'll find the place down on the next street—middle of the block. Frame shack with a 'dobe lean-to . . ."

The cabin looked as if it had not been occupied for a long while. The walls and ceiling were marbled with brown water stains. The floor was littered with rat-chewed newspapers and cast-off garments, and the windows were curtained with cobwebs. In the kitchen stood a pine table, a rusty cook stove with a patched pipe, and several old chairs mended with baling wire. A dynamite box held three lumps of coal. Rummaging through a shed in the back yard I found some wood and kindling dry enough to burn, and it was not long until the old teakettle was remembering how to sing.

After the storm abated in the late afternoon, I walked out through the townsite, making my way over a bewildering chaos of stone and brick, past tumbled walls and caving cellars, and ruin framed by empty windows.

Somewhere in that confusion had stood the first store of the Sewells—later to be the largest grocery chain in Nevada. Somewhere lay the remains of Chinatown, of the theater, the Miner's Union hall, the newspaper office where "Peg-leg Bill" Plunkett had edited the *Times-Review*.

Somewhere—But *where?*

Whether school or church, or gambling den or brothel, all now lay merged in anonymous peace.

Groping through the head-high sage, I came unexpectedly on a small lake as blue as lapis lazuli. Leading through the wet snow to the water's edge were the neat hoofprints of a doe and fawn. Quail were calling from the hillside, and I could imagine that later in the spring the tules alongshore would be a nesting place for killdeers and wild ducks.

As I turned to leave I found watching me a tousel-haired boy and a little brown dog.

"What's the name of this lake?" I asked.

The boy grinned shyly and ground the toe of his boot in the snow.

"Aw, it don't have any name," he said depreciatingly. "It ain't even a real lake—it's just the old Dexter gold mine! After they quit workin' the mine, it caved in and filled with water. Guess you know about the Dexter?" He cocked his head questioningly. "Reckon it was the richest gold mine in the world . . . and now it has the world's biggest rainbow trout in it! Like this—" a pair of sweater-clad arms stretched to their fullest extent and the freckled face again broke into a wide grin.

"Funny, ain't it?" he mused. "Fish in a gold mine . . ."

Thick, gray clouds had settled over the hoary summit of Mt. Blitzen and snow was falling again as I trudged back up the road toward Joe's cabin. At the threshold I paused to range my eyes once more over the town.

In the windows of four homes the yellow glow of lamplight was winking. Four gray columns of smoke were curling from as many chimneys. The wind was beginning to blow; and somewhere down the street, a loose shutter was creaking and banging. Crea-k-k-k, bang! Crea-k-k-k, bang!

Eighty years of history. Eighty years of trials and tribulations and triumphs—all reduced in Time's Crucible to a few tired old buildings, a few tired old men, a few flickering lights—and one creaking shutter.

Closing the door against the gathering fury of the storm, I shook the grate and added a few more sticks of pine wood to the fire.

It would be a good night for sleeping; a good night for ghosts. . .

18

Kingdom of the Elko Prince

W HEN THE PHANTOMS of Tuscarora grow bored with their own spectral company—and, surely, even ghosts must occasionally fall prey to cabin fever!—they have only to wrap their ghostly garments about them and whisk off into the ether. Any way they choose to go whisking, they are certain to encounter another ghosttown long before they have burned up a tankful of whatever ethereal mixture ghosts use for propulsion.

Should they whisk in a northerly direction, for example, they will find a whole Cook's Tour of ghosttowns including, among others, the old camps of Cornucopia, Deep Creek, Aura, Columbia, and Edgemont, while a ghostly swing to the northeast brings Gold Creek, Mountain City, Rio Tinto, Charleston and Jarbidge. To the east lies Metropolis—but Tuscarora's ghosts won't care for Metropolis—and several humps and hollows and 35 miles to the west of Mt. Blitzen, brings Midas. With all these matchless opportunities for whisking, there is no reason why Tuscarora's ghosts should snap and snarl at one another simply because they are tired of the same old haunts.

Take Midas, for example. Any ghost could go a long way without finding a better opening for his talents than in this old mining camp at the edge of Squaw Valley. . .

Forty-two miles of semi-improved road leads northeast to Midas from the little Southern Pacific railroad station of Golconda. Along that road live some of the finest folks in the world; but their numbers are few. Any hostess, even reasonably clever, could seat all of them at one dinner table.

Blacktopped for its first 14 miles to the Getchell Mine junction, and thereafter graveled, the road traverses a wide, sage-covered valley flanked on either side by great ridges of mountains. On the higher peaks of these ranges, and in the shaded ravines of their north slopes, snow lies well into each summer; and over a large portion of each year, nearly every canyon carries its small stream of water, sparkling clear and unbelievably cold.

On an afternoon in July, 1952, that road carried me to the rim of a wide plateau and I looked down, for the first time, on the town of Midas.

Viewed from that distance it appeared to be a rather attractive village. Spread over an alluvial fan at the mouth of a deep canyon, where sheer outcroppings sawed at the skyline, its several streets were bordered by long rows of huge old cottonwoods and poplars. Through the trees were visible a goodly number of buildings.

Not until I rolled on down the hill did it become apparent that these structures, for the main part, were jerry-built wooden affairs, now tattered and shabby. Midas, it was plain to be seen, was not a brick-and-stone mining camp of the 19th century, but a by-product of the leaky-radiator, broken-spring Automobile Era.

Driving to the upper end of Main street, I turned and cruised slowly back. In all that distance, not one living creature made his appearance— not a man, not a dog, not a horse. Of the various business houses along the street, some, evidently, had operated within recent years. But now, all were boarded tightly or were standing open to the wind and empty of anything more tangible than dust. (Plate 36)

In the entire central section of town, there was only one building that gave evidence of being occupied. Even that evidence was sparse. Climbing the rickety steps, I clattered across the loose boards of the rickety porch, and pushed open the door.

The place proved to be a small saloon. Except for the bartender— who appeared to be an Indian—it was quite empty of humanity. As an excuse to hang around awhile, I bought a coke and a sack of salted peanuts and sat down on one of the stools. The bartender was about as garrulous as a pine stump, but I gradually dragged out of him the information that only nine persons still lived in the town, several of these having come there during the original boom of 1907-08.

There was Lou Wilkinson, he said, and Miriam Purdy, and Mrs. Brown. He guessed they were all the original ones still remaining. "Chris" Christenson was another of the original boomers, but he was down at the poor farm in Elko. Chris, he was sure, would be glad to talk to me, if I happened to be down at Elko. No—Midas didn't have a postoffice. It had been discontinued in 1942 when the gold mines closed, and the school had quit in January, 1952, when the town no longer could supply the minimum of three pupils necessary to maintain it.

My friend, the bartender, thought Mrs. Purdy would be the best one to see about the early history of the camp.

Thin and white-haired, and apparently nudging her 70s, Mrs. Purdy lived alone in a little cabin on Main street, a couple of doors from the saloon.

She wasn't especially affable, at first, but after we discovered a couple of mutual acquaintances—Maury Stromer, of Broken Hills, and Josie Pearl, of Leonard Creek—she began warming and invited me into her kitchen where a fire was burning fiercely in a wood range, and a pot was blubbering on the back of the stove.

Yes, it was true she had lived at Midas since the original boom; had been a widow with two little girls and had come there to operate a boarding house for miners. Yes, she admitted further, that had been a good long while ago; close to 45 years. . .

First discovery of gold in the Gold Circle mining district was made in the summer of 1907, said Mrs. Purdy. During that fall and winter the district attracted prospectors in considerable numbers, and a town was started.

"When we applied for our postoffice in the spring of 1908, we asked for the name Gold Circle but the postoffice department refused to approve it. They said there already were too many postoffices in Nevada using the world 'gold'—Goldfield, Gold Hill, Gold Mountain, etc. They said we could call ourselves Midas if we wanted to. So—" she shrugged— "that's what we did!"

By way of proving that the town was started under the other name, Mrs. Purdy produced the original map of the townsite detailing its chief thoroughfares as Main, East, West, and High streets, with intersecting avenues from First to Eighth.

"See—" she pointed. "Right there it says 'The Town of Gold Circle.' "

It was only a short while until business buildings had sprouted along the full length of Main street, and dwellings and assorted shops were lining the other streets. It has been claimed that Midas once had 21 saloons and a population of 20,000 persons, but Mrs. Purdy thought 5000 inhabitants and a dozen saloons nearer right.*

"But I'll have to confess," she said, her old eyes dancing, "I never took time to actually count 'em!"

In addition to her palaces of pleasure, the town also boasted a lively chamber of commerce, city water system, a newspaper, four big general mercantiles, and several hotels and rooming houses—one of the latter accommodating 100 beds. All supplies were freighted to the camp from Golconda and Battle Mountain.

No matter how important a mining camp may be, there always is one mine that stands so far above the others that residents of the district invariably refer to it in capital letters: The Mine. In the case of Midas, "The Mine" was the Elko Prince, located in 1907 by Paul Ehlers, a cook at a nearby ranch. Ehlers, said Mrs. Purdy, later sold to Leslie Savage, of New York, receiving $5000 cash and 100,000 shares of stock in the company.

About 1910, as a result of the so-called "Panic of 1907," money became very tight at Midas and miners at the Prince were notified that the company would be forced to suspend operations unless all employees would agree to take their wages half in cash and half in treasury stock of the company at 10 cents a share. Elko Prince miners, at that time, were

---

*Lincoln, Francis Church, Mining Districts and Mineral Resources of Nevada, 1921 places the peak population of Midas at 2000.

receiving around $4 a day. After accepting the cut to $2 in cash and $2 in stock—which might prove to have no value, whatsoever—the employees of the Prince became the laughing stock of the area and butt of every sucker joke going the rounds.

"But those 'suckers' didn't fare too badly," said Mrs. Purdy, with a sly wink. "None sold his stock for less than 250 per cent profit, and many held on until they realized as much as 500 per cent gain. Which is a lot better," she concluded sagely, "than being hit on the head with a sharp stone!"

First "big" year at Midas was 1916 when gold recovered from 11 mines totaled only a trifle less than $250,000, and with 157,207 ounces of silver, brought the production for that year to $347,107. This yield continued with little change through 1921—the gold and silver output of the Gold Circle mining district in these six years being placed at $1,951,283.*

Diminished mining continued at Midas until 1942 when the props were knocked from under the gold mining industry by the labor priority order from the War Production Board. With that development, the town had no choice but to call it quits.

After we had discovered several more mutual acquaintances and our friendship had been cemented accordingly, Mrs. Purdy brought forth the Midas' register of voters for the year of 1916.

"Many an argument I've settled with this old register!" she declared stoutly. "Indeed, I have! Like folks saying women weren't permitted to vote in Nevada till woman suffrage was approved nationally in 1920. Fiddlesticks! Nevada gave women the vote in 1914! Just look at all the women who were registered to vote in Midas in 1916—scads of 'em!

"Communism's another thing. Could I ever stir up a ruckus! You know Old Man———? Swears up an' down he's never been a Communist? Look here—" riffling rapidly through the yellowed pages she whirled the register around in front of me and pointed to an entry more than a third of a century old. "Right there! That's his jolly old John Henry; and what does it say under 'Party Affiliation'? 'Communist'—that's what!

"Yes, siree!" she said, patting the register affectionately, "I wouldn't take a purty for this old book!"

My departure from Midas the following morning was witnessed by nearly one-quarter of the town's entire population. Two-ninths of that population, to be exact.

One ninth, represented by Miriam Purdy, sped me on my way with a fond farewell and insisted I drop in to see her whenever I happened to be up that way again.

---

*Mineral Resources of the United States, U. S. Geological Survey.

The other ninth—the Indian bartender—stood on the rickety porch of his rickety saloon and impassively regarded my leaving.

If that event brought him twinges of either rejoicing or regret, his poker face didn't betray the fact.

19

Two Hundred Miles from a Dime Store

A T THE WESTERN edge of the Great Salt Desert, I coasted my dusty car into the welcome shade of a Wendover filling station and asked for the best road to Callao.

"BEST road, hell!" snorted the gas man. "There's only ONE road! Follow th' highway south 27 miles to White Horse Pass," he went on, with a southerly wave of his arm. "Leading off from the Pass, you'll see a dirt road that branches to th' left. Follow it another 30 miles to Gold Hill. Nothin' there but some old shacks. Th' road forks at th' north edge of town. Take th' left fork. 'S' rough enough to jar th' hide off an Army mule, but after you've cussed it for 25 miles, you'll be in Callao!

"Hell of it is," he mumbled, as he screwed the cap back on the gas tank, "even when you get there, you'll still be 200 miles from any place a white man oughta live!"

Two hundred miles from a Woolworth store, 85 miles from a high-ball, or a glass of beer—that was Callao, Utah, in the year 1951.

Yet, strangely enough, I have never known another town where it seemed so absolutely evident that God was in His heaven, and all was right with His world!

Nestling in its green, spring-watered, poplar-edged valley, at the extreme western end of the Juab-Tooele county line, Callao was just about the most peaceful place a man could imagine. Each morning the round, red sun burst out of the limitless white flats of the Great Salt Desert sleeping to the east; each night it sat in the high, forested summits of the Deep Creek range, to the West. And during all the hours between, the people of Callao pursued their gentle, age-old ways, cultivating their fields and tending their flocks, rearing their sons, living and letting live. . .

Callao provided her citizens with pure water and peace, and fresh, clean air. She also served them with a church, a school, a postoffice and a cemetery. That was all. Through all the years since her founding, nearly a century before, the old village had never known the luxury of a mayor, a foot of pavement, a sidewalk, or a street light. In all her long years she had never had the services of a resident doctor or dentist, a barber or a druggist.

And, at the same time, she had never felt the need for either a psychiatrist, a mental hospital, or a jail. . .

It was Sunday when I arrived at Callao, and it looked as if some sort of celebration was in progress at the George Tripp place. Parked under the big trees along the lane were a dozen automobiles and trucks. A few saddle horses were tethered to the fence, and children were playing in the shady yard of the old house.

The plumpish, pretty woman who came to the door was enveloped in a big starched apron and her face was flushed and moist with perspiration. Beyond her, in the kitchen, I could see other women in starched aprons, bustling around the big wood-burning range, peeking at pans of biscuits in the oven, and turning the brown pieces of chicken I could smell frying.

"What's going on?" I asked. "A family reunion?" The pretty woman laughed, and passed the tail of her apron across her moist face.

"Oh, nothing special," she said. "Every Sunday's sort of a family reunion at Grandpa's place! He has lots of kids and grand-kids, you know . . ."

I remembered what a mutual friend, at Tooele, had told me about this same George Tripp.

"We were beginning to think George wasn't going to get married," she had said. "He was just an old bachelor. Never seemed to care a rap for the women . . . And then, when he was 50 years old, he up and married a girl of 21! Some folks sorta shook their heads over the match, but George and his wife hit it off fine. She bore him 12 children, and George put 'em all through college with sheep money . . ."

"Won't you come in?" the pretty woman was saying. "We're just ready to sit down to dinner and you can talk with Grandpa while you're eating . . ."

George Tripp, 81-year-old patriarch of Callao, was a light-built man, with a thatch of white hair and grizzled eyebrows, and a desert-browned, smooth-shaven face, where a network of lines fell automatically into use when he laughed. (Plate 13)

"So you write for the Salt Lake *Tribune?*" he said. "Most of us folks out here are *Deseret News* people. Not that it matters," he hastened to add. "Here—have another piece of chicken!"

The story of Callao, I learned, was the story of George's father, Enoch Tripp, and his progeny.

As Willow Springs station on both the Pony Express and Overland Mail line, this future settlement had been staffed only by transient managers during the decade prior to 1869, when Enoch Wallace Tripp had located in the valley. Enoch's father-in-law, George W. Boyd, operator of Boyd's Station, ten miles east of Willow Springs, had held a contract to supply hay and wood to the Overland stations at Dugway, Black Rock, Fish Springs, Boyd's and Willow Springs. Through the summers of 1867 and '68, Enoch had assisted his father-in-law in the haying; and when service was discontinued on the Overland line in the spring of 1869, Boyd had purchased the company's holdings at Willow Springs and his daughter and her husband had become Callao's first permanent settlers.

Prior to her marriage, the young Mrs. Tripp—George's mother—had taken keen interest in dramatic art, and had shown enough talent to win her a place as understudy to Edith Clauson at the old Salt Lake Theatre; and while pioneer life on the western rim of the Great Salt Desert was a far departure from anything she previously had known, the young Salt Lake matron had courageously set herself to the task of making a home and rearing a family.

Like every land-hungry man, Enoch's consuming ambition had been to till his own fields, and hear the rain falling on his own roof, and see the smoke curling from his own chimney. He accordingly had filed on a piece of land immediately west of the station; and, thereafter, every moment he could spare from tending his father-in-law's ranch had been devoted to improvement of his own property—building and fencing, clearing and plowing.

When the new ranch was ready for occupancy, Enoch had moved there with his wife and sons—one of these, a new-born baby, George.

Time marched on. Of the eight children born to Enoch and his bride, seven settled in the valley to rear families of their own. Grandpa and Grandma Tripp passed on; the "new" log house became "the old Tripp place;" and George Tripp, who had come to that place as the "brand new" baby, became Callao's senior resident. Already past 80 years of age, he had lived in the settlement longer than any other man—the closest challenger to that record having been his 83-year-old brother, Enoch, Jr., who had abdicated to Salt Lake City after passing 76 years in the old village at the edge of the desert.

Through all the years since its founding, said George Tripp, Callao had been an isolated place. One of his earliest memories was of making the annual pilgrimage to Salt Lake City for supplies.

"It was a long, hard trip," he recalled. "Four hundred miles, there and back . . . But, golly how we boys looked forward to it! As father always had grain to be taken to the mill for grinding into flour, and other ranch produce to be traded for goods we couldn't produce for ourselves, it was necessary for us to go in a big, covered freight wagon, drawn by four to six horses. In addition to our bedrolls and camping gear, we always carried a couple of 50-gallon barrels of water, as well as hay and grain for our animals. As we moved across the desert toward Salt Lake, we would spot half the horse feed along the way to use on our return trip, a week or so later. It was just as safe as if it had been padlocked. No man, in those days, would have thought of stealing another's horse feed!"

When I asked about early Indian troubles at Callao, he shook his head.

"No," he said. "There was never any Indian trouble, here. The main camp of the Goshutes was right at the edge of town, and the young Indians were the best friends my brothers and I had.

"There was only one time when the town came close to having an Indian uprising," chuckled the old man. "We boys and our Indian pals were playing in the back yard when Mother heard a terrible rumpus and rushed out to see what was the matter. She found that my brothers and I had a little Indian boy in a tub of water. We were scrubbing him for all he was worth and he was screaming bloody murder! When mother asked what on earth we were doing, we said we were trying to wash the brown off of him so he would be white like the rest of us!"

As time went on, other families took up land around the town. The year 1876 brought the Bonnemort brothers, John and Ed, both of whom had been operators for the Overland Telegraph. After Ed's death, his widow, Lizzie Bonnemort, had become known as the Sheep Queen of Utah, and at one time was running more than 12,000 head of sheep.

With discontinuance of the Overland Mail Line in 1869, the little settlement had lost its postoffice, and not until 1892, when a mining boom sprouted in the Deep Creek range to the west, had any particular effort been made to regain it. With the population boosted by an influx of miners, men of the community met at the home of Chris J. Tripp (half-brother to Enoch, Sr.) and appointed him postmaster. As there were several other "Willow Springs" in the state, the name of "Callao" was suggested for the new office. Why a village on the edge of Utah's Salt Desert should have been given the name of Peru's most important seaport, is something no man seems to remember.

After operating the postoffice two years, Chris Tripp surrendered the postmastership to his half-brother, Enoch, who served until 1915 when he relinquished the reins to his daughter-in-law, Mrs. Clara Tripp.

When Clara had arrived at Callao in 1896—a widow, with a small son—she had little supposed she would still be there more than 50 years later, or that she would spend a considerable portion of those years as postmaster of the little settlement! Interested in mining, she had come to western Tooele county as result of the booms at Clifton and Gold Hill. Finding there a great lack of trained assayists, she had returned to her home city of Los Angeles and there had taken a college course in assaying—at that time an occupation little followed by women.

Fortified with her new-won knowledge she had come back to Tooele county and had secured a position as company assayist at the rich Midas mine. Later, she married Roy Tripp, located in Callao, and subsequently inherited the postoffice.

She still had it in 1951. Not officially, of course. Along with other peculiar ideas, the postoffice department in Washington cherishes a notion that folks grow too old for efficient service; so, when Clara reached the age of compulsory retirement, her son was appointed postmaster in her stead. But Clara, at 87, was still doing the work.

"After 36 years of it," she said, "it's got to be sort of a habit!"

In addition to being the only out-of-stater in a community of native-born Utahns, Clara Tripp was the only person in Callao who was not a Mormon.

Due to the town's complete isolation, the Callao postoffice handled a great deal of business—possibly the largest per capita of any postoffice in the state. As in the days of stage coaches and freight wagons, "going to town," in 1951, still involved a 400 mile round trip to Salt Lake, over rough roads. Even in these days of fast travel it was not a journey to be made with frequency, and Callao folks made it a practice to anticipate future needs, and to buy in large quantities.

"There's no store in the community, so everything we don't haul for ourselves must be shipped by parcel post," said the ex-official postmistress. "Sugar, flour, tractor parts, shoes, medicine—everything we use. There's no other way to get it here!"

Possibly the most amazing thing about the town—to an outsider, at least—was the way time seemed to have been frozen in its stride, so that the Past was all mixed up with the Present.

Like the old Pony Express station, for example. Charles Bagley and sons had bought the station property from George Boyd in 1885. And because it had been in use through all its 92 years—and was still being used by third and fourth generation Bagleys—it was one of the best preserved Pony Express stations in Utah. Also seeing daily service on the Bagley premises were a number of log buildings constructed of timbers from the original Pony Express corrals. At one edge of the yard was a pile of planks containing a weathered, roughly-milled pole, tapering from six-by-six inches at its bottom to four-by-four inches at the top.

"See that?" said Dave Bagley, third generation Callaon. "That's one of the original poles used on the first transcontinental telegraph line that put the Pony Express out of business in 1861! Granddad held a contract to supply thousands of those poles. He cut them in the mountains and hauled them by oxen to the point where they were to be used."

Following abandonment of the line, the poles were sold; and to expedite their removal, were chopped off a foot or so above the ground. Stretching away on either side of Callao, those remaining stumps could be traced in a long line across the desert. As for the pole in the Bagley yard, Dave had found it only a few weeks before, while surveying.

"I saw something white shining in the rabbit brush quite a distance away. I thought 'Now, what in the world could that be, away out here?'" he said. "I walked across the flat to investigate, and there lay this old pole—right beside the stump, where it had been cut off!" Evidently the pick-up crew had overlooked it.

As for wire from this original telegraph line—it may be museum stuff elsewhere, but one entire side of the Bagley place was fenced with it, complete with the original splices!

Callao isn't a ghosttown. I doubt, seriously, if it will *ever* be a ghosttown. But even in its prime, it never had been a large settlement. It had reached its all-time peak of population in 1936, with 86 inhabitants. And then had come World War II, and young people leaving for the armed forces, and for high salaried jobs in city defense plants; and by 1951, the old town at the edge of the desert could claim only 40 citizens.

Living on the tag end of civilization, 200 miles from anywhere else, would seem to involve more difficulties than an ordinary Twentieth centurian would care to surmount. But, strangely enough, those 40 citizens of Callao were just about the happiest folks I have ever known! They didn't seem to care a rap that they couldn't get television reception, or couldn't run off to the beauty parlor, once or twice a week, or down to the corner drug store every time they wanted a package of cigarettes or a magazine.

It makes a person wonder. . .

Maybe things of that sort aren't very important, after all!

29

Tybo Was Allergic to Orientals

JUNIPER-GROWN HEIGHTS of the Hot Creek range lift with startling abruptness from the floor of a lonely canyon in central Nevada. Yawning mine tunnels and waste dumps freckle those rocky walls, and along a small cold stream in the canyon's depths grow thickets of wild roses and chokecherries. Here nest chukar partridges, and quail, and mourning doves; deer come down from the hills to drink, and chattering chipmunks collect pine nuts for their winter store.

To Mother Nature, man's struggles and strivings are never of much moment, and here in the canyon her wild creatures pursue their daily ways without regard for the ghost in their midst—the sleeping ghost of Tybo.

Climbing over acres of gleaming slag piles, or browsing among the crumbled foundations of shops and dwellings and the gaunt skeletons of long-silent mills, man instinctively recognizes this as a place where great labor has been expended. Yet, even one of generous imagination scarcely can invest this quiet spot with the roaring life and activity that once was its keynote. Eighty-odd years ago, when furnaces and mills were operating at capacity, and half a dozen mines were threatening to make fortunes for their owners, the Town of Tybo was a lively place!

Attention of white men first was drawn to the district in 1866, by an Indian who had made ore discoveries there the preceding year. Development was fairly rapid, and with discovery of the Two G lode, in 1871, a smelter was erected the next year following. Other mines were brought into production; several of the more important of these being owned by Tybo Consolidated, a London corporation formed by J. B. McGee, previously superintendent of Richmond Consolidated, at Eureka.

Early in 1874, McGee estimated there was on the company dumps at Tybo close to 20,000 tons of ore averaging $60 to the ton.* From 1260 tons of similar ore, smelted during the concluding three months of 1873, the company had realized 153 *tons* of work-lead, running 250 ounces of silver and 1½ ounces of gold to each ton.**

Belmont Courier, Feb. 15, 1874.
**Raymond, Rossiter W., Statistics of Mines and Mining in the States and Territories West of the Rocky Mountains, 1875.

Tybo's ore—while plentiful and profitable to work—was not generally the fantastically rich stuff of fable and fiction. Now and then, however, would appear a rich pocket that would toss the mining world into a tizzy.

One such tizzy was occasioned by the report that a half ounce of pulp from the Slavonian Chief mine, assertedly had assayed at the rate of $20,786.01 per ton.* Another three-alarm tizzy followed a discovery of John Grevich and Tom Meretvich, whose claim on the north side of the canyon had disclosed a ledge varying from 12 to 16 inches in thickness, the "poorest" rock of which was said to carry values of $3000 per ton!**

With her mines and mills staffed largely by Central Europeans and Cornish and Irish emigrants, Tybo—almost from the day of her founding —was beset by racial difficulties. Hot words, too often, were followed by cold steel and whining lead; and far too many of the nameless graves in the cemetery at the mouth of the canyon are filled with the dust of men who believed that the blood of one nation is thicker or redder, or otherwise more desirable, than that of neighboring nations.

High point of the district's racial contention was reached in May, 1876, when charcoal burners with a contract to supply several million tons of fuel to the Two G Mining company, imported into Tybo a large number of Chinese coolies to perform the labor of cutting the wood and firing the charcoal kilns. Angered by this influx of Oriental laborers, white workmen of the district momentarily forgot their own inter-racial disputes and rose in united protest against the Sons of Canton.

Mill owners made haste to clear their own skirts by declaring that the contract price for the charcoal had been based on the premise that only white labor would be used. The charcoal burners countered with the claim that they had been unable to procure white workmen in sufficient numbers, and to escape the penalties set forth for non-fulfillment of contract had been forced to accept any sort of labor available. To forfeit the contract, they declared, would mean their financial ruin. But the whys and wherefores of charcoal economics held no special interest to the Occidental laborers of Tybo, whose chief concern was to emphasize the fact that Coolie wage-cutters were not welcome in the camp.

Assembling in saloons and on street corners, small knots of muttering workmen eventually congealed in a roaring mass meeting with a lust for blood—Chinese blood.

Fortified by raw liquor and mob courage, the howling pack at midnight stormed the sleeping charcoal camp, situated in the canyon a couple of miles above town, and with cracking bullwhips, popping pistols and drunken curses, sent the terrified Orientals fleeing for their lives.

Next morning found the charcoal contractors scouting the nearby hills in pursuit of their scattered woodcutters, reassembling them from

---

Belmont Courier, Aug. 1, 1874.
**Belmont Courier*, May, 1875.

individual points of cover as they might gather a herd of sheep stampeded by wolves. Driven back to the kilns, the still-jittery Chinese were ordered to resume work, and throughout that day discharged their duties under the protection of loaded Winchesters.

Nightfall brought another conclave of 200 miners bristling with guns and indignation. In deference to the armed guards, still vigilantly patrolling the charcoal camp and its environs, the original plan to "clean out the Chinks" lost some of its savor and it was resolved "not to be rash or resort to violence." Instead, the contractors were given 24 hours in which to get rid of the Chinamen.

End of the grace period found the woodcutters still cutting wood and the guards still guarding. Another ultimatum was issued: Either the Chinese leave camp before another nightfall or both they and their employers would be ridden out of town on rails. .

The white laborers, by this time, were so thoroughly aroused that wholesale bloodshed would have been inevitable had the Chinese not grown weary of the whole sordid affair and offered to depart the district in exchange for stage fare to Eureka. With passage money readily supplied by the Anti-Asiatic League, a racial difficulty that had threatened to over-populate Boot Hill was settled to the satisfaction of everyone.

Everyone, that is, except the charcoal contractors, who were left to commune with their forfeited contracts.

Although Tybo had a penchant for taking the law into its own hands, it also had a justice of the peace who ruled the town in a fashion later made famous by the celebrated Judge Roy Bean, of Texas.

Prior to his election as Tybo's chief arbiter of crimes, J. W. Gally had been reasonably busy as the town's leading physician and surgeon. In addition, he owned half interest in the rich Two G mine and operated a prosperous cattle ranch at the edge of the settlement. A soft-spoken, mild-mannered, Milquetoasty, conscientious chap, of painful honesty, no one doubted that Dr. Gally would strive to deal out justice with a fair hand; but neither did anyone doubt that said digit would be an impotent hand.

That it should become an iron-mailed fist, fortified with a double-barreled shotgun, was a development Tybo's electors failed to foresee!

For several months prior to Dr. Gally's election, a loud-mouthed upstart named Newton had been throwing his weight around town and making himself generally obnoxious. If Tybo wondered how her new judge would handle the Newton situation, it wasn't long until she had her answer, for Judge Gally had been scarcely sworn into office until Newton pulled a gun on Rancher Alex McKey, who swore out a warrant for arrest of his assailant.

Time for arraignment was set and Newton and McKey appeared as scheduled. Meeting in the courtroom, the enemies saluted one another with a tirade of invective, and Newton made a grab for his holstered pistol.

A bellowed command froze the draw in mid-air!

Whirling toward the source of that command, amazed spectators saw that its point of issuance had been the erstwhile gentle lips of Judge Gally! And, to the further amazement of the incredulous, a double-barreled shotgun had appeared in the jurist's hands. Both hammers were cocked, and the man behind those hammers looked wholly capable of pulling both triggers.

With the litigants disarmed, the trial was permitted to proceed; Newton, in the end, being held to answer and bail being set at $1000.

"Bail be damned!" snorted the bully contemptuously, slapping his hat on his head. "When you want me, you so-and-so, you can come and get me—in Belmont!"

Again the yawning black muzzle of the shotgun aligned itself with Newton's midsection and once again a neatly-manicured thumb pulled back both hammers.

"Possibly you didn't understand," purred the little justice. "I said '$1000 bail' . . . and you'll stay in this courtroom until you or your friends produce it, or hell freezes over! Is that clear?"

It was clear enough for Newton.

After serving several terms as Tybo's chief justice, Judge Gally—the erstwhile physician—loaded his family into a covered wagon and emigrated to Watsonville, California. There he resumed medical practice, rose to a position of prominence and eventually became director of a California state mental institution—a position for which his years at Tybo had fitted him well.

While the mining town in the canyon eventually would have its own newspaper*, much of the early history of the place was recorded only by the facile pen of one Tristam Feliz, Tybo correspondent for *The Belmont Courier.*

Judged by existing evidence, Tristam must have been quite a lad. Not only did he have a remarkable flair for words, but even when no news existed he could produce reams of readable copy—an unusual faculty that sets journalistic geniuses apart from mere hack writers, such as myself.

Seized by inspiration, for example, Brother Tristam could fill a dozen pages of foolscap with a general discussion of Tybo's then current economic situation.

"Of the subsidiary coin in circulation here," Tybo's correspondent reported to readers of the *Courier,* on June 16, 1877, "half dollars are the most plentiful; quarters are scarce, and the accommodating dime so tenderly cared for at the Bay and elsewhere in the Golden State, is never seen for the reason that it will not purchase anything. It is however, sometime taken by our fruiterers from the noble aborigine and his mahalie as a *quid pro quo* for a Mormon apple; but the man who would be so hardened as to offer it at the bar of one of our high toned saloons for a drink,

---

*The Tybo Sun, founded May 18, 1879, discontinued, six months later.

would be looked upon as a fit subject for some reformatory institution. This unhappy coin is tabooed by even the apparently unappreciative Shoshone, who has a pretty correct idea of its intrinsic significance. Money! money! thou art at once the curse and the joy of the world. The curse is to be without thee, the joy is to possess thee. Thou art called the root of all good; the lightener of our sorrows, the solace of our woes, and the good things of life. Great are the sorrows of the moneyless man. What business has a man without spondulics in this piping world? He should suicide; two bits worth of strychnine will take him to Hades via the route of the grim visaged ferryman. The past week has been an eminently lively one all round. The boys having had plenty of coin, flung care to the winds, and indulged in the insidious potations which generally impart so becoming an incarnadined tinge to the nasal appendages. I heard of several fisticuffs having occurred; but since I saw none of them I am unable to give particulars. The tiger who is nightly bearded in his lair in a couple of places in town is raking into his capacious maws all the vagrant coin in camp. Wherever gambling flourishes is said to be a good place to drive stakes. Tybo then, must be one of these places.

—Tristam Feliz, Tybo Correspondent."

Although a town quite different from that lively camp known to Tristam Feliz in 1877, Tybo, in 1953, still was a good place to live. At that time—and throughout all the preceding years I had known the canyon—it was the stronghold of the Barndt clan, comprised of graying "Dick"— Victor J.—born at nearby Hot Creek; his wife, Martha, and their seven children. Not only did the Barndts constitute the sole inhabitants of Tybo, but they owned the town, lock, stock and barrel, from the old town hall straight through to the big general store that hadn't known a customer in 20 years.

Even though her postoffice had been discontinued and her other channels of commerce had ceased to flow, Tybo still supported a one-room school house. This, in some particulars, was the most remarkable institution of learning in the whole State of Nevada, since its student body was composed solely of Barndt children, and Martha Barndt constituted its entire faculty! She had taught the school even before marrying Dick; and in 1953 she was handling all grades and all subjects from pre-kindergarten pupil, Deborah Ann Barndt, to High School Sophomore, Vicki Jo Barndt.

What made the situation even more remarkable was the fact that Dick comprised half the school board; and there was little chance of his defeat at the polls, since the entire Tybo school district, for many years had embraced only one other person eligible to serve on the board.

I asked how these two managed when a deciding vote was necessary.

"It's never necessary," said Dick. "We never have any disagreements. You see," he went on, "the other board member is sort of a hermit. He lives four miles back in the hills; and because he doesn't have a car, I haul his mail and groceries to him. So—" he shrugged his shoulders—"It's very simple! Either he votes the same as I do . . . or he packs his grub on his back! No," he said, "we never have any arguments . . ."

Both Dick and Martha were possessed of well rounded senses of humor—a prime need of miners and miners' wives who live 60 miles from Tonopah and 118 miles from Ely, the nearest points of supply in any direction.

One day, when Dick and I were going down to look at his lead mine near New Reveille, he was telling me about another mine he owned on the other side of the range.

"I've been trying to sell it," he said. "Several years ago a fellow from Frisco wanted to know what I'd take for it. I told him '$5,000 cash, or $10,000 on a royalty basis.' He just laughed at me. When he said his top offer for the property would be $300, I told him he could go to hell!"

Dick wrapped the old truck around a few more sharp curves and narrowly missed several deep declivities.

"Mebbe I should have taken him up on it," he went on, at last. "God knows, it's the best offer I've ever had for the property!"

21

Forgotten Ghosts of Gold Mountain

IT WAS A MORNING tailored for adventuring. Along the western horizon stretched the 14,000-foot range of the White Mountains, pine-forested and laced by a hundred sparkling streams. Viewed through the clear, thin air of the high elevation, those snowy summits seemed incredibly close; yet for all they had in common with this land I was crossing, they might have been the peaks of another planet.

Here in Lida Valley were neither brooks nor trees, and desert heat lay harshly upon the land. Except for the reassuring throb of the motor in my old desert car, there was no audible sound—not so much as the rustling of a creosote leaf—and all visible movement was embodied in one fluttering sparrow hawk.

Between that silent flat and the shimmering waste of Death Valley, lifted the veiling bulwarks of the Slate ridge and Gold Mountain, and somewhere in those rough ranges lay my destination—two ghosttowns, so long deserted and little known that even history had forgotten them!

First to tell me of those old camps had been Senator Harry Wiley, of Gold Point—a place that comes close to being a ghosttown in its own right.

Mineral discoveries in that vicinity in the forepart of the present century had resulted in the founding of a town first known as Hornsilver.* In 1929, with potential investors more interested in gold than in the sadly-depreciated white metal of Billy Bryan, the camp's original name had been scrapped and the new name of Gold Point adopted.

A contemporary of Rhyolite, Bullfrog, Fairview and Wonder, this stubborn, little twice-named town had continued to muddle through while those more spectacular centers—her one-time rivals and superiors—had reverted to desert. In the course of her struggle for existence she had seen her population shrivel from a lusty 2000 souls to a shaky dozen. She had lost her hotel, her newspaper, her chamber of commerce and water system. She had forfeited her school, her stores, her prestige. Rows of delapidated, empty buildings had come to flank her dusty streets, and a majority of the headframes visible on surrounding hillsides eventually were standing over silent mine shafts and ghostly dumps.

Present at the founding of the town, Harry Wiley had shared in every

---

*Hornsilver: Cerargyrite, a rich chloride ore, containing 75 per cent silver.

phase of the camp's shifting fortune for nearly 50 years and, finally, had become sort of an institution there—an ex-officio mayor and chief of police, and Rotary club, all rolled into one small, soft-spoken package. When past middle age he had married Ora Mae, a comely widow from the Deep South, and the two had remained to operate Gold Point's last business house—a small grocery store, and gasoline station. One corner of this establishment held the Gold Point postoffice—managed by Ora Mae—and through all the years I had known him, Harry had served as state senator from Esmeralda county. He also served nobly, but without pay, as my Number One spotter of Southern Nevada stories.*

Wrapped in the hot blanket of that July mid-day, Gold Point seemed as lacking in life as a painted ghosttown on a desert canvas. Neither dog, nor burro, nor human being—not even a stray breath of air—appeared to be stirring; and but for my own dust-layered car, not a wheel disturbed the silence of Main street.

Parking in the thin shade of a joshua tree in front of the Wiley store, I slapped part of the road dust from my jeans and crossed the splintered porch to the open door. The room beyond seemed even smaller and darker and more crowded than I had remembered from previous visits, but in the greeting of its proprietors lay a welcome as big and honest as all outdoors.

"Last time I was here," I reminded, "you promised to show me a couple of old camps so little known their stories have never been written. Remember?"

"That's right!" Harry Wiley nodded with enthusiasm. "How about this afternoon?"

As soon as we had eaten lunch, had brought each other up to date on current events, and Harry had managed to secretly refill the gasoline tank of my car, he and I headed into the hills, leaving Ora Mae to cope with the assorted commerce of the town.

Following a twisting course, but bearing in a general southwesterly direction, the little-traveled desert trail labored up steep ridges, skirted rocky canyons, clung to one-way curves and wallowed across dry washes. Branch trails led away on either side, and other trails intersected and crossed. Occasionally the main route divided, only to rejoin with itself a few hundred yards beyond.

"Bear to your left," Harry would say. "You'll miss a bad stretch of loose sand." Or, "Take the right fork, it's not so rocky . . ."

Between road instructions, he unfolded the basic story of these places we were about to visit.

Like Gold Point, he explained, each of these towns had been known by two different names. Persons whose knowledge of the area reaches back only 40 or 50 years, are inclined to refer to the earlier settlement as "Old Camp" and the newer as "Stateline," for the Stateline Mine. During

---

*Harry Wiley, 72, died June 15, 1955, a victim of cancer, at the U.S. Veteran's Hospital, in Reno. Burial was in the Masonic plot at Goldfield.

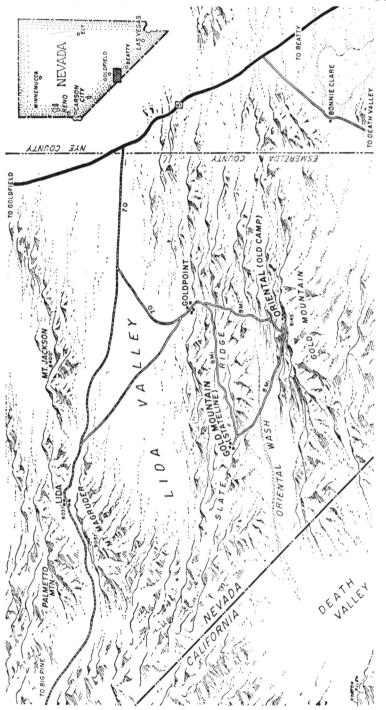

their actual period of activity, however, the camps were known as Oriental and Gold Mountain, and mining reports of the 1870s and 1880s invariably refer to them in that manner.

Original strike in the area had been made about 1866, by one Thomas Shaw. Little outside attention had been centered upon the region, however, until 1871 when Shaw began developing his rich Oriental mine. By that time, several other mines—including the Dusty Bob, Nova Zembla, and Stateline—also were in production, and within a short while, Gold Mountain had become a lively camp with "pony express" service from the nearest railway point—then Battle Mountain, some 250 miles to the north.

In newspaper publicity of the late '70's, the Stateline mine was represented as one of the truly great mines of that day. Ore from the Oriental also showed fabulous assays. In a government report,* it was stated that selected specimens from the Oriental showed a gold and silver content of $1370.79 per ton, while nine "unselected" samples from the same mine averaged $169.19 per ton in silver and $13.47 in gold. The same report credited the Nova Zembla with ore averaging $302.87 to the ton, and the Good Templar, $233.55. Samples from 50 different claims in the Gold Mountain district were said to average $150 to the ton. Sale of stock was being pushed throughout the East, and a long period of prosperity was predicted for the camp.

At this point in Harry's chronicle we topped the summit of a rocky ridge and came in view of the first stone ruins. From crumbled foundations and hillside dugouts— which Harry identified as the former site of Gold Mountain's Chinatown—we progressed into an area where roofless walls stood as high as a man's head; and here and there, a stone chimney stood guard over the site of a vanished house.

"This is it!" said Harry. "This is the business section of Gold Mountain! That chimney and backwall, yonder, is all that remains of Dennis Remeset's bakery; that excavation across the street was the basement of Tallman & Squires' general store, and the postoffice." The store, he said, had closed in 1884, but the post-office had continued to function for another five or six years.

"Here," he remarked, kicking the toe of his boot against a stone foundation, "was the H. H. Robinson home, where our friend, Douglas was born . . ."

The Douglas Robinson he mentioned had been an intimate friend of The Senator since 1905. Prior to becoming chief probation officer of Inyo County, California, Mr. Robinson had lived in half a dozen boom camps in Nevada and, in later years, had supplied me with a wealth of early history concerning those places. The senior Robinsons, according

---

*Raymond, Rossiter W., Seventh Annual Report of Mineral Resources in the States and Territories West of the Rocky Mountains, 1875.

to the Senator, had located at Old Camp in 1880, and about a year later had moved to Gold Mountain.

Contemplating the jumbled confusion that once had been walls, and the fallen foundation that nowhere stood higher than our knees, Harry Wiley shook his head and grinned.

"Seventy years ago, Doug tells me, this was one of the show spots of the town," he went on. "The Robinsons kept a cow for milk, and had a pen of chickens; and after water was brought in, they planted peach trees and grape vines and raised a big vegetable garden . . ."

That fruit and garden produce could have been coaxed to grow on that dry-as-dust mountainside seemed almost past believing! Only stunted joshuas and a few sparse-foliaged desert weeds now graced the slope, and not a single leaf or blade could be termed truly green.

In the earlier years of Gold Mountain, water had constituted the greatest problem—most of it being hauled there from a spring at Old Camp and sold at $3.50 a barrel. That such a tariff can constitute a formidable expense is seen in the fact that a Mrs. Reddy, who ran the company boarding house at Gold Mountain, paid an average of $300 a month for water needed in the maintenance of her establishment!*

In the late 1870s, the Gold Mountain Mining company had erected at Gold Mountain a 40-stamp mill and steam hoist, and for water to operate it had laid 15 miles of pipeline from Mt. Magruder and Tule Canyon. After completion of the line, in 1882, all water for the town had been supplied by the mining company.

Although pioneering conditions at Gold Mountain had not been so rigorous as in some other parts of the West, even here life had been a far leap from Utopia. The nearest doctor had been at Candelaria, 85 miles distant; and not even at Candelaria had there been a dentist! The Robinsons had owned the only pair of dental forceps in town, and when the torture of a throbbing tooth at last exceeded the anticipated pain of its removal, the molar was extracted.

Transportation, too, had posed quite a problem. All material for the big mill, hoist and water system, had been freighted from Wadsworth, near Reno, by long-line 'skinners and 12 to 16-horse teams. Passengers and express had been carried on the Cluggage stage line, operated from Belmont to Gold Mountain by way of San Antone, Columbus, Silver Peak and Lida. After 1882, when the Carson & Colorado railroad was extended to Candelaria, mail and passengers had arrived at Gold Mountain by twice-weekly stage from that point.

Following inauguration of stageline service from Candelaria, Mrs. Robinson had assumed charge of the Gold Mountain stage station and operated it until 1890, providing travelers with sleeping accommodations and meals at 50 cents each.

---

*Robinson, Mrs. Alice, Recollections of pioneer life at Gold Mountain, as described to her son, Douglas, 1943.

"And, believe me," grinned Harry, "those were real hair-on-the-chest, he-man meals! Doug tells about Sam Piper bringing prime dressed beef from his ranch in Fish Lake Valley and selling it for a nickel a pound! Other wagon peddlers, from Owens Valley, in California, brought pork and poultry, eggs, fresh fruit, honey and vegetables."

About the most rugged time at Gold Mountain was during the hard winter of 1889-90 when all roads leading into the district were blocked by snow. With no wagons or pack animals able to make it through to the camp for more than four months, Gold Mountain stores were completely sold out of every type of food. Far greater suffering might have resulted except for the fact that many Indians in the region were virtually starving and would haul flour over the mountains on hand sleds on a 50-50 basis —one sack for the hauler and one for the purchaser.

Relations between Indians and whites of the locality had not always been so amicable. A couple of miners had been killed by Indians in Oriental Wash, a couple of miles from Gold Mountain, in 1868; and periodic Indian scares had been experienced in the area for several years afterward. First time an attack was threatened, every person in camp scurried for cover in one of the mine tunnels. When it was realized that this was not the most advisable safety measure—inasmuch as one or two members of the attacking force could block all escape from the tunnel until its inhabitants had succumbed to thirst or starvation—the camp hastened to build a stone fort around a low knoll, a mile west of town.

As a means of repelling Indian attack, this place must have been ideal. With its summit commanding an unobstructed view over several thousand acres of surrounding territory, it would have been almost impossible for an enemy to have approached the knoll unseen. Further protection had been afforded by a massive breastwork which half encircled the base of the hill. Built as a double rock wall, with center filling of earth, we found its average width to be three to five feet, its greatest inside height about six feet, and over-all length, 225 feet. Between the wall and the knoll behind it had been adequate space for all the frontier inhabitants of Gold Mountain.

Examining the place we noticed the peculiar presence of dead joshua trunks along the top of the wall, and inspection revealed that those trunks had been hewn by axe. The only conclusion we could draw was that the trunk sections had been cut and placed there at the time the fort was built—doubtless as a means of affording additional protection and to provide firing loopholes, which were lacking in the rock portion of the wall. Smaller breastworks, on the shoulder of the knoll and near its summit, likewise were topped with joshua butts—many of them firm and stout despite the 80-odd years elapsed since they had been cut.

With the sun already dropping toward the hills on the west and still another ghosttown to be covered before nightfall, we drew the curtain on Gold Mountain and headed across Oriental Wash toward Old Camp.

"If you were to follow this wash to its mouth, you would come out at Sand Springs, in the northern part of Death Valley," said Harry. "Doug tells some great tales about the old burro prospectors of the Valley who would come up Oriental Wash to Gold Mountain for supplies and a bit of celebrating. For the most part, these fellows were hunting the Lost Breyfogle mine but some were looking for anything they could find.

"Old Jake Staininger, who cultivated a little patch of ground at the mouth of Grapevine Canyon, where Death Valley Scotty's castle now stands, always tried to make it to Gold Mountain for Christmas. One year he arrived five days late because he had forgotten to cut the notches on his 'time stick'. When he learned Christmas was over for another year, the old man was sore as a boiled owl!"

For several miles we had been climbing steadily up a stiff grade. From the joshuas and yuccas of the mile-high desert around Gold Mountain, we had passed through the lower fringe of the juniper belt, and another mile of upgrade brought us to the nut-pines and the outlying ruins of Oriental, just under 8000 feet elevation. Due either to its greater age or briefer period of occupancy, we found here far less evidence of a former town than at Gold Mountain. Except for the roofless walls and fireplace of the Robinson boarding house and postoffice, Harry was unable to identify any of the rock ruins which dotted the hillsides and lined the canyon to the west. Most of them appeared to have been dwellings.

At the junction of our road and the above-mentioned canyon we halted to investigate an old steam boiler—seemingly in sound condition. According to my guide, it had been installed prior to 1871 and had been used to power an arrastre, now vanished. The primitive mill had been operated until 1900, largely on ore brought down the mountainside by pack mules.

As we left Old Camp and headed back across the hills to Gold Point and supper, I asked the inevitable question: What killed the two camps?

Harry shrugged. "The usual thing! The ore didn't hold up to assay figures—partly due to the fact that milling processes were crude in those days and half the values were lost in the tailings. Then, too, there was a strangling amount of litigation. During the eight years from 1882 to 1890, the mill operated a total of only three years, with many starts and stops. Soon after the property was sold, in 1890, the water pipeline was pulled and the camp abandoned. . .

"And I guess that's about all there is to the story!" said Esmeralda's Senator Wiley, as we topped the last ridge and looked out over the darkening expanse of Lida Valley, lying like a placid sea at the foot of the grade. To the west, the high range was silhouetted blackly against the golden splash of sunset, and a few windows in the weathered frame buildings of Gold Point already showed the friendly glow of coal oil lamps.

After we had sluiced the road grit from our faces and hands, and Ora Mae's good supper had been put behind our belts, the three of us continued to sit around the table talking of boom days and borrasca in Esmeralda county. About midnight, Senator Wiley disappeared briefly into an adjoining room and on his return shoved toward me a stack of yellowed newspapers—rare old copies of the *Hornsilver Herald,* and *Goldfield Reviews* and *Tribunes*—all dating from the early 1900s.

"Take 'em along," he said. "Maybe you'll run across something of interest . . ."

Soon as I could make a graceful retreat and Ora Mae had shown me to my quarters back of the store, I wrapped a blanket around me, stretched myself on the bed, and began browsing through that stack of old journals.

Devouring those tattered pages—each as fragile as the spiderwebs of Hope—I found myself reliving the rose-tinted days when this little town was pulsing with vitality and promise; when all her lumber was new, and her hardware, bright; when Big Mines were opening, and Big Deals were in the air. (Plate 29)

The new boomcamp of Hornsilver (later to be Gold Point) had been barely two weeks of age when the first copy of her first newspaper, *The Herald,* had been lifted from the press. Even at that early date, *The Herald's* editor expressed complete confidence that Hornsilver would soon shine as the brightest star in Nevada's crown. By the time *The Herald's* third issue had appeared and the camp had attained the responsible age of five weeks, even the hardshell skeptics were skeptics no longer.

Scanning those brittle, yellowed pages, I read that the Hornsilver Board of Trade had been organized with Harry Wiley as its secretary. The five-weeks-old town then embraced a total of 220 habitations and an estimated population of 700 persons, and M. A. Maher & Company had two four-horse teams and one 16-mule team on the road constantly, hauling lumber hence from the railroad station at Cuprite. A pipeline, to bring water to the new camp from Lida, had been surveyed. Pat Burke, proprietor of the Great Western Saloon, had been elected Hornsilver's delegate to the Democratic convention at Carson City. The town's first "Grand Ball" had been held in the Lime Point Restaurant, with my friend, The Senator, on the dance committee; and Mrs. Sarah Woods, proprietor of the Hornsilver Hotel and Grill, reported a steady increase in business despite the fact that the town then boasted seven other eating houses. On Tuesday of that week, said *The Herald,* Mrs. Woods had served 115 persons at dinner, and on Wednesday, 125.

Hornsilver business concerns that had purchased advertising space in this fifth week of the camp's existence, included an abundance of real estate dealers, stock brokers, mining engineers, assay offices, and most of the town's 13 saloons. The Hornsilver Auto Company was advertising transportation to neighboring camps—"Goldfield, $7.50; Cuprite, $5.00. First Class Machines that go the whole trip and won't leave you stranded on the way . . ."

Also included among those advertisements were half a dozen general stores—The Great Western Meat & Produce Company, West Side Grocery, The Pioneer Store, Barnes Brothers General Merchandise, Exploration Mercantile Company, and the Union Bakery, as well as drug stores, lumber yards, newsstands, etc.

And Crime had reared its ugly head!

M. J. Spaulding, Hornsilver's deputy sheriff, had arrested an unruly citizen who had been mixing with John Barleycorn. "In the absence of a jail," reported *The Herald,* "Mr. Spaulding handcuffed said citizen to the rear wheel of a huge freight wagon, where the party remained until he was able to more fully understand himself . . ."

According to *The Herald* of the following week,* an intensive search of the town had revealed one copy of the Stars and Stripes which had been placed at half-mast in honor of Nevada's governor, John Sparks, who had died the week previous. Justice of the Peace Shannon had received official notice of his appointment as Hornsilver's first postmaster, and new arrivals that week on the gastronomic scene had included the Turf Grill, Keystone Cafe, and Imperial Restaurant. Also, *The Herald* was greatly enthused about a new hotel being built by the Messrs, Scott and Zimmerman. Located at the corner of Orleans Street and Third Avenue, the "superior class" structure was to have double walls throughout, "with building paper between, insuring warmth and being dust proof." Two stories in height, with a ground-floor area of nearly 10,000 square feet, the building, said *The Herald,* would contain 33 sleeping rooms, an office and bar, and a dining room 20-by-30 feet in area.

That Hornsilver's home paper should have thought well of the town was only right and proper; but the fact that this same opinion was held by neighboring journals, spoke volumes for the new camp.

"There is nothing but good news coming from Hornsilver," declared the *Goldfield Tribune,* on May 30, 1908. "New discoveries are reported daily. The town is growing faster than any new camp that has been discovered in this section . . . and additions to the original townsite are being laid off in all directions . . ."

Goldfield Review, appearing that same day, had added its accolade: "Hornsilver is the latest wonder in Nevada mining districts! Hornsilver is a comer! Hornsilver is practically but a month old, and yet it is beginning to astonish the visitors who are flocking to it in an ever-increasing number . . . New mercantile concerns are coming in every week . . . and Main Street is extending in length almost as you watch it . . ."

On and on, I read—through 1908, and 1909, and 1910. And, at last, the oil in my lamp burned dry, and the warm flush of dawn came to glow in the east. For a few fleeting hours I had walked through a gay, glad, impossible world, where the desert sun was a golden aureole spun

---

*Hornsilver Herald, May 30, 1908.

into the sky, where the streets were paved with silver and precious gems, and all the land was pregnant with Hope and Promise.

And now, it was the Morning After; the morning of another day, another era, another world. The fanfare of the trumpets was stilled; the dream, ended; the magic, dead. From a golden aureole the sun had changed to a cruel, red monster, harsh and feverish and devouring. Under the probing of its merciless rays, the old desert mining camp appeared wearier, more drab, more faded, than I ever remembered. (Plate 30)

Of all those brave new dreams that had blossomed in these hills, those bright new buildings that had edged these streets and the buoyant Argonauts who had trodden them, there remained that morning but a few moldy crumbs. A few faded and empty cabins, a dozen men and women, one little store . . . and an old Ford truck.

I had made the acquaintance of the old truck on my first trip to Gold Point, a number of years earlier. After spending the night in one of the deserted cabins, I had been walking across town to the Wiley's when the sound of metal hammering on metal had drawn my attention to a dilapidated vehicle standing in the rear of an empty store building on the first street west of Main. Armed with a monkey wrench, a screw driver, and a pair of pliers, a boy about ten years old was attacking the engine with a zeal I have seen matched only by a hungry squirrel making its way into a nut.

"Are you sure you know what you're doing?" I asked, not to be critical, but simply as a means of opening a conversation.

"Yup!" replied the boy, scarcely glancing in my direction. As he reburied himself beneath the engine hood he muttered something about the bolts being rusted fast. After I had made several suggestions that didn't win me even an E for Effort, the kid again extricated himself from the engine.

"If you're dead-set on being helpful," he remarked, "you can grab that monkey-wrench and hit this cold chisel while I hold it. But be damn' careful you don't hit my hand!"

Overlooking this obvious insult, I grabbed the monkey wrench and hit as directed. Moments later, the kid straightened triumphantly, holding in his grimy fists a piece of rusted iron shaped somewhat like an ocarina, but a trifle larger.

"Jeez!" he murmured in admiration. "I've needed a Ford manifold like this for years!"

"What are you going to do with it?" I ventured.

"Put it on my hot-rod!"

I was developing a queasy feeling that I had been an unwitting accessory to the daylight theft of one Ford part.

"Who owns the old crate?"

Glancing curiously at the truck, as if seeing it for the first time in his life, the boy shrugged.

"Jeez! How should I know? It's been standin' here since before I was born!"

After the young Gold Pointer had disappeared up the dusty street, making like a tommy-gun, and swinging the muzzle of the manifold to liquidate any possible enemies who might by lying in ambush, I turned to examine more closely the source of that versatile weapon.

Judged by appearances, this well might have been the oldest Ford truck in Nevada. Its wheels were chain-powered, its tires, solid rubber; its headlamps dated from that era when the illuminating agent was coal-oil. Battered and rusty and dilapidated, there was nothing picturesque about the old veteran, but I was to learn that in all Gold Point there was no better "conversation piece."

Everyone who glimpsed the truck was fascinated by it. Modern mechanics, probing its four-cylinder innards, were completely captivated by the ingenious manner in which broken parts were repaired—soldered and welded, and wired and friction-taped, and otherwise held together for a few more miles. To every passing oldster, the ancient truck re-awakened memories of 30 and 40 years before, when horseless carriages still were a new-fangled notion; but it was to a few remaining Gold Pointers, the venerable conveyance meant most. To these old-timers it stood as a perpetual reminder that not all desert trails had been blazed by Conestoga wagons and ox teams.

When I mentioned the truck to Senator Wiley, he said it had been purchased during the boom days of the camp by Martin W. Mitchell, then owner of the town's leading mercantile.

Throughout the lush years that followed, Mitchell used the vehicle for hauling merchandise from Goldfield to his place of business—about 30 miles—and for making deliveries of supplies to isolated mines throughout the southern section of the county. During this same period, The Senator recalled, the truck also was used for expressing bullion from Hornsilver to the Wells Fargo office at Goldfield—more than $1,000,000 in gold and silver having been transported by this means.

"No one knows how far 'Mitch' and his employees drove that poor old truck," declared Senator Wiley. "There weren't any speedometers in those days . . . but whether it was 100,000 miles, or 200,000, every one of those miles was a man-killer! We didn't have any roads—only burro trails, over rocks half as big as water buckets, and through bottomless blow sand.

"After she'd been pulling in low gear for miles, with the thermometer away above 100 degrees, I've seen that old bus come roaring into town blowing water and steam like Old Faithful Geyser! But," he added significantly, "she always came in . . ."

Old timers of Southern Esmeralda recall at least two instances in which the truck played an innocent role in desert tragedies.

On one occasion, one of Mitchell's men had been returning from

Goldfield late one night, with a load of supplies. As the truck bounced across the desert, its way only half lighted by the feeble glow of the old-fashioned headlamps, the driver glimpsed in the road ahead what appeared to be a prospector's blanket roll. It was impossible to turn out of the sand ruts, and before the truck could be brought to a stop both wheels, on one side, had passed over the object. Late, and in a hurry to get home, the driver continued on his way without stopping.

Next day it was learned that the supposed bedroll had been a ragged blanket wrapped about the form of "Long-Hair Johnny," a local Indian, who had been returning to the hills after a fling in the hot spots of Goldfield.

As the tragedy was reconstructed by pine-bench sleuths, the old Indian had grown sleepy while riding and, dismounting from his pony, had wrapped his blanket around him and laid down in the soft, warm sand of the wheel ruts. But because of an old truck, groping its way home after dark, the short nap anticipated had become Long-Hair Johnny's last, long sleep. . .

Another tragedy in which the truck figured, involved an old desert rat remembered only as "Scotty, the Pig."

After a week of liquid celebration in Gold Point, Scotty bought his usual supply of groceries and asked Mitchell to take him back to his mine, located about nine miles west, in the hills at the north end of Death Valley. As it was midsummer and hotter than the hinges of Hades, Mitchell refused on the ground that no car could make it through the terrific heat and deep sand to Scotty's mine. Furthermore, he declared, a week of tippling had left the old man in no condition to be turned loose on the desert. But Scotty bided his time and as soon as Mitchell was called away on other business, he succeeded in bribing a green clerk to take him back home.

With the thermometer registering more than 120 degrees in the shade, the truck had battled through six terrific miles of loose sand and rock. By this time, the radiator had boiled nearly dry; and inasmuch as the clerk had failed to bring additional water, it was impossible to continue farther. Telling the old man he would have to wait until nightfall and walk the three remaining miles to the mine, the clerk unloaded Scotty and his groceries in the sparse shade of a joshua tree and returned to the store.

It had been Scotty's habit to come in for supplies about once a month. After one month had passed, and then two months, and still no Scotty, Gold Pointers began to wonder what the trouble might be.

"Some of us fellows finally went out to investigate," said Senator Wiley. "We found the old man's body under the joshua, right where the clerk had unloaded him. After the water in his canteen was gone, he had begun opening cans. He had used all the evaporated milk and other canned goods from his sack of supplies until every can that contained any sort of moisture had been emptied. After that . . ." The Senator paused.

"We buried him there, under the joshua . . ."

Gold Point's senior citizen fell silent as his gaze wandered across the desert hills which had constituted his front yard for nearly 50 years.

"About the old Ford," he went on, at last. "The boom finally collapsed, the mines shut down, and nearly everyone moved away. When 'Mitch' closed the store, about 25 years ago, he drove the old truck behind the building and shut off the engine for the last time . . . and that's where it's stood, ever since!"

22

Frisco, the Devil's Delight

LIKE A ROW of fat Buddhas silently meditating the mistakes of mankind, five old charcoal kilns look down on the shattered husk of the town they once served. A breath of warm air stirs the golden petals of a sunflower, and high in the blue dome overarching the San Franciscos, a lone hawk soars on plush-silent wings. That the ghost of turbulent Frisco, Utah, should rest in a grave so peaceful is the epitome of irony. Certainly there was little enough about her that was peaceful in her day!

By loyal Beaver countians she is characterized "The greatest silver mining camp in the history of Utah"; and even if the superlative is not wholly justified, no one would deny her a place as one of the greatest. . .

Original discovery of ore in the San Francisco mining district came largely as result of blind chance, but in this instance the discoverers at least showed originality. Unlike so many locators of million-dollar ledges, Jim Ryan and Sam Hawkes were not pursuing a band of strayed burros when they came upon the rich outcrop. They simply were seeking an excuse to tarry a bit longer in the vicinity of a good spring of cold water— a wonderful attraction in an arid land where waterholes are few and a long way between.

Packing their burros on a pleasant morning in 1875, Ryan and Hawkes had headed east across the desert from Pioche, Nevada. They were veteran prospectors, and possibly they had their sites set on the mining camp of Alta, then in the throes of its spectacular boom. Whatever their intended destination it has long since ceased to matter for they never arrived there.

After toiling up and across the White mountains, the rugged Needle range, and the dry Wah Wahs, they had at last entered the foothills of the San Franciscos and had gratefully pitched camp at the little desert oasis known to roving prospectors and emigrant trains as Squaw Springs.

With green grass for the jacks and free wood and water in plenty, it was a good camp and Ryan and Hawkes had little enthusiasm for resuming their desert trek. With the idea of postponing their departure as long as possible, one of the pair had suggested it might be well to prospect a bit in the surrounding hills.

According to the story told by old timers, the pair had spent a day or so prowling the slopes in a desultory sort of fashion. As they had trudged back toward camp one evening one of the partners had remarked that a limestone ledge they were passing looked "half way promising."

Idly sinking his prospecting pick into the outcrop he had exposed to view a gray treasure of galena ore so rich in pure silver that it glistened metallically in the evening sun! If man ever looked upon a bonanza this was one, and Bonanza was the name scrawled upon the location notice posted that night by Ryan and Hawkes.

After sinking a 25-foot shaft through nearly solid ore, the discoverers, on February 17, 1876, sold their claim to Matt Cullen, Dennis Ryan and A. G. Campbell for $25,000, and thereupon faded from the picture. Changing the name of the mine to the Horn Silver, the Cullen-Ryan-Campbell triumvirate proceeded to sink the shaft to a depth of 280 feet, in the course of which development work they took out some 25,000 tons of ore averaging $100 to the ton!

As reports of Utah's spectacular new mining development filtered across the miles to Wall Street, that depression-battered camp of the money changers perked its ears.

Particularly did those reports stir the pulses of International Banker Jay Cooke.

Cooke's finances were in a bad way. After underwriting the Civil War bond issues of the United States to the tune of $2,000,000,000 Cooke had committed himself to build a railroad from Duluth to Seattle. Midway of that undertaking had burst the Panic of '73, and the simile "Strong as Cooke's Bank" had changed from a proud boast to an epithet of scorn. The great financial institution had fallen like an overripe plum; work on Cooke's Northern Pacific railroad had been necessarily suspended, and even the Cooke mansion in Philadelphia had been seized by creditors to satisfy claims.

Into this unenviable situation had stepped Lycurgus Edgerton with a glowing account of the Horn Silver property and its potentials. Cooke had seized upon that report like a doomed man scenting a pardon, and he and Edgerton had entrained immediately for Utah. En route there, Edgerton had suffered a heart attack and died. Cooke had continued the journey alone, and in 1879—by pulling a few financial strings—had purchased the Horn Silver for a neat $5,000,000.

Upon acquiring the mine, the New York financier threw himself into the problem of improving transportation facilities to enable shipping lower grade ore than had been financially feasible with mule-drawn wagons. At Salt Lake City his forceful argument at last convinced The Powers that the Utah Southern railroad—built from Salt Lake to Provo in 1873 by the Church of Jesus Christ of Latter Day Saints—should be extended to serve the new mining district far to the southwest. More persuasive powers, abetted by Sidney Dillon, president of the Union Pacific, convinced Jay

Gould he should take a half interest in that railroad and supply the money for its construction.

Thus financed, the line was extended 176 miles, and in the summer of 1880 reached the Horn Silver mine.

Several years before Cooke's entry upon the scene, a shirttail settlement had begun accumulating on a barren flat a mile east of the mine. Although situated in the San Francisco mountains and the San Francisco mining district, this spawn of the Horn Silver had few of the characteristics attributed to Good St. Francis of Assisi; and even if the gentle saint's name had been conferred upon her, men would have dubbed her "Frisco" before the ink had dried on her charter. Thus, both time and confusion were saved when that abbreviated title was officially adopted from the beginning.

Fledgling Frisco, from the very outset, had been inclined toward looseness and unruliness; and when rails of the Utah Southern Extension pushed into camp in 1880, the immediate result was to change an outpost of civilization into a satan's paradise.

Gamblers, gunslingers and goodtime women poured in from every decadent boomcamp between Colorado and the Coast. Street brawls and bashed noggins, knifings and gunplay, became matters of small moment to any but the participants. Liquor-fortified tempers flared on slight provocation, and holstered guns were altogether too accessible for the promotion of longevity. Each of the town's 20-odd saloons and gambling dives boasted of killings—generally over matters too trifling to warrant even a rebuff. One Frisco saloon actually boasted that two of its patrons had shot and killed one another over a 50-cent bet in a faro game! Every morning saw the "dead wagon" cruising the streets in search of human "meat" slain during the night—and seldom was the search in vain.

After enduring this unsavory state of affairs for nearly a year, law-abiding citizens of Frisco rebelled and demanded the introduction of law and order. For the important and highly lethal task of restoring some semblance of peace to their fair city, they imported a gunslinger named Pearson, from Pioche, Nevada.

Not only was Pearson quick on the draw and a crack shot, but he was cold-blooded as a rattlesnake. Also he was too smart to turn his back on the door—a trifling matter of frontier etiquette that only five years before, in Deadwood, S.D., had cost the life of Wild Bill Hickok.

To the Bad Boys of Frisco, Pearson's ultimatum was simple and to the point: Get out or shoot it out! Something about the manner in which he said it caused most of the trouble-makers to choose the first alternative. Those who failed to heed the warning became the new marshal's personal clay pigeons to be picked off, one by one—as many as six in a single night! Most victims of his gunfire were buried without either inquest or funeral announcement.

It was drastic medicine, but it cured the patient. Before too many weeks Frisco's deportment was showing a definite improvement and her mortality rate was verging on normal.

Even with the establishing of law and order, this Beaver county town was never an ideal place in which to reside. Laborers in the mines oftimes dropped from heat exhaustion as underground temperatures rose as high as 110 degrees, and rock dust in the ore sent as many as 40 men a month to the hospital with "miner's con."

All water used for domestic purposes was necessarily hauled seven miles, and, in the camp's early period of development, sold at four cents a gallon. After coming of the railroad, water was hauled in by train and toted from door to door in a large barrel mounted on two wheels. Bumping over the rocky streets the waterboy shouted his ware and housewives hurried from their homes to flag him down. There were a few hard-water wells; but although animals could drink their product, it was not considered fit for human consumption.

Throughout her brief and hectic career, the town of Frisco bent her knee to only one idol—the Horn Silver mine, the district's one big producer.

According to local legend, more than $54,000,000 worth of ore was removed in ten years (1875-85) from a hole 900 feet long, 900 feet deep and only 400 feet wide! Records of the U. S. Bureau of Mines, at Salt Lake City, place the total yield at a figure considerably lower; bureau statistics showing that the Horn Silver's production of silver, lead, and other metals, from 1875 to 1913, had a total value of $20,768,471. During this same period, dividends paid stockholders amounted to $6,-892,000.

To Jay Cooke, the Horn Silver's first big time promoter, the mine repaid many fold. Over a long period of years Cooke enjoyed from it an annual income of $80,000, and finally sold his interest for close to $1,000,000.

Frisco's finish was written by a cave-in that only for blind luck might have ended in one of the worst mine disasters in the history of Utah.

Work had been going forward at a killing pace, and, some said, with too little regard for proper timbering and the tenets of mining safety. On the morning of February 12, 1885, the night shift had just emerged from the mine and day men were waiting at the hoist house to descend, when mine bosses noticed a trembling in the main shaft. While the men were being held back momentarily, to see what might develop, the entire mine caved to the seventh level with a reverberating crash that broke windows at Milford, 15 miles away!

Following the cave-in, a new shaft was sunk through 910 feet of solid rhyolite at a cost of $26 a foot. During the course of this protracted work, a majority of the miners were necessarily laid off. Without ore to process, the two big smelters were forced to call it quits; and without the hungry maws of the smelters to consume their product, the charcoal camps followed suit.

Miners, millers, charcoal cutters and burners, moved to other jobs; the camp followers followed them, and business houses closed for lack of patronage. Even after the Horn Silver resumed production, the town of Frisco was never rebuilt.

Speeding along State Highway 21, between Beaver and Ely, motorists today bisect her remains.

Five old charcoal kilns, the iron-shuttered company store, (Plate 32) a few board shacks, a dozen or so stone foundations, and remnants of walls —only these mark the grave of a mining camp men once hailed as Utah's greatest.

23

Placer Gold and Man's Perfidy

I N THE MIDDLE 1870s—more than a dozen years after the founding of Schellbourne and Egan Station—a transitory mining slump at Hamilton was responsible for a number of new ore discoveries in the far Eastern portion of White Pine county, in Nevada. Pre-eminent among the boom camps that blossomed as result of these strikes, were Osceola, Ward, Taylor, and Cherry Creek—all of which are now ghosttowns.

As a Ghost of the Glory Trail, Osceola casts a thin and spectral shadow, and only for her production of both lode and placer gold, as well as silver, lead, tungsten and phosphate, is she unique among mining centers of the state.

Situated about 15 miles west of the Utah line, in White Pine county, the deserted townsite is so thoroughly inundated by mountains it seems incredible that desert-roaming prospectors of 80-odd years ago even should have found the place!

Overshadowing the townsite, the rugged Snake Range rises to heights of 9000 and 10,000 feet; and seven miles south of Osceola, culminates in 13,058-foot Mount Wheeler, highest peak lying completely within the boundaries of Nevada. For nearly two decades prospectors had been nibbling at the fringes of this mountain stronghold, but not until 1872 were their efforts rewarded by the discovery of lode gold.

By the spring of 1875 there were operating in the district several important mines, including the Western Slope, Osceola, Exchange and Pilot, but until 1878, when the district's first stamp mill was installed, all ores mined locally were pulverized laborously in Mexican-type arrastres. Even with this primitive type of recovery, quartz mining at Osceola was fairly profitable, but it was not a poor man's game. As a consequence, the first major rush to the district did not occur until 1877 when flakes of placer gold were discovered by John Versan in gravel deposits of the area. Before close of that summer, gold washers and dip-boxes of every description were scattered through the ravines, and with stores, a boarding house, Chinese restaurant, and two stages running regularly to Ward, the canyon settlement was assuming the appearance of a lively mining camp.*

---

*Ward Semi-Weekly Reflex, June 21, 1877.

By virtue of an abundant supply of water, it was possible to introduce here the hydraulic system of placer mining—the Osceola district being one of the few regions in Nevada where this method of gold recovery has been practiced. Extensive hydraulic operations were conducted here for 20 years, beginning in 1880, during which time a considerable amount of gold was recovered.

Estimates of Osceola's mineral production are strangely at variance. Weeks places the camp's yield, prior to 1907, at $2,000,000;* Stuart estimates it between $3,000,000 and $5,000,000,** and Francis Church Lincoln neatly sidesteps the issue by quoting both of the earlier figures.

While a little mining was in progress in the district in 1950, Osceola had ceased to exist as a town. Following a disastrous fire of two years before, the only business building still reasonably intact was the old Marriott general store—an abandoned stone structure with tall, narrow, iron shutters and doors. Of the town's other business establishments, only cracked foundations and blackened rubble remained. Not far from the store, the old Marriott home was still standing in a jungle of fruit trees and roses, and from a rusty iron pipe across the empty street, gushed an unfailing flow of cold spring water.

In this peaceful scene there is nothing to show that only for the perfidy of man, Osceola might have won for herself considerable fame as home of the largest gold nugget ever found in Nevada. But due to the aforementioned perfidy, even that honor was denied her.

The nugget in question was found in the placer mine owned by three partners, John Versan, J. C. Poujade and W. B. Garaghan. The discoverer was one Charles Keisel, an employee in the mine.

Chances are, Mr. Keisel was an average sort of man who was kind to his wife and kids, and stray dogs, and practiced an average sort of honesty; but Mr. Keisel, like many other average men, was blinded temporarily by the glitter of gold. When he looked upon the mighty nugget he had found in his employers' mine, he grew understandably covetous; and when it occurred to him that no one knew he had found the treasure, he just naturally decided to keep it for himself!

With the aid of an assayist unencumbered by scruples, the purloined gold piece was melted and run into bars having a value of $200 each.

If Mr. Keisel had not been fundamentally honest, the story of his fall from grace might have remained forever unknown; but due to this latent quirk, he had developed a bad case of conscience trouble. Result was that early one morning he had appeared at Poujade and Garaghan's store, in the nearby town of Ward, whence he had been convoyed by the dark angel of remorse.

Rousing Mr. Garaghan from sleep, Mr. Keisel had begun raining on

*Weeks, F. B., Geology and Mineral Resources of the Osceola Mining District, White Pine County, Nevada, USGS, B-340, 1908.
**Stuart, E. E., Nevada's Mineral Resources, Carson City, 1909.

his bed a shower of small gold bars, at the same time sobbing out the whole bleak story of his transgression. Before he had finished, Mr. Keisel had surrendered to Mr. Garaghan some $4000 worth of treasure; yet, even this sizable amount, he declared, did not represent the full worth of the single nugget—his confederate having retained an undisclosed portion of the whole as his payment for melting and casting it.

The windfall having come at a most fortuitous time when the partners were desperately in need of funds, they did not find it in their hearts to be too severe with Mr. Keisel. Not only did they refuse to prosecute, but they even rewarded his belated honesty by restoring to him one of the $200 bars, and John Versan later gave him $1000, thereby cutting him in as an equal partner in the great gold piece.

And thus was lost to posterity what is believed to have been the largest nugget ever found in Nevada, and poor Osceola's greatest potential claim to fame.

The aforementioned Mr. Garaghan long was regarded as one of the leading citizens of Nevada. In addition to his mercantile business at Ward he owned far-flung mining interests, and was a prominent political figure in White Pine county, which he represented in the lower house of the Nevada legislature.

Once in the 1880s, while attending a funeral at Taylor, the legislator was introduced to the officiating sky pilot, a man only newly arrived in Nevada. In the discussion that followed, the preacher mentioned, rather undiplomatically, that Nevada had more saloons than churches and declared, if there were more houses of worship, there would be less crime.

Rallying to the defense of his state, Mr. Garaghan declared there were not one-half as many known criminals in Nevada as in the state of New York where churches were plentiful.

"When a man commits a crime in New York he is generally sent to prison, Mr. Garaghan," retorted the minister frigidly. "In Nevada, I understand, he is sent to the legislature!"

Another story told on the popular politician had its setting in Hamilton in 1888 during Mr. Garaghan's campaign for the office of county treasurer on the Democratic ticket. Among those who made the rounds of the town with the campaign party and bellied up to every bar, in turn, was one of the most worthless old soaks in eastern Nevada.

As evening approached and the tippler had not missed a single round of drinks, Garaghan dropped his hand on the man's shoulder and made some jocular remark concerning "my good Democratic friend, here."

Opening his rheumy eyes in amazement, the old barfly shook his head. "Oh, no, Mr. Garaghan," he said, "you got me all wrong! I'm a *Republican.* I'll admit I'm dirty and ragged, and worthless, and that I *look* like a Democrat . . . but I'm not! No," he added, hastily gulping down the last remaining snort, "I've fallen pretty low; but, thank God, not *that* low!"

24

Treasure in a Sandstone Reef

I T WAS A BIG morning. The winding road I had followed through the Utah foothills was smooth and white and spattered with sunshine. Cottonwoods and locusts bordering on Quail creek were rouged in October's gold, and the lonely wind that rustled their leaves carried with it a hint of frost.

But the beauty of the morning was largely wasted on the old mining camp of Silver Reef.

Even at first glance it was painfully evident that far more than frost had laid a blight on that once-famous place, for of all the buildings that once flanked her mile-long main street, only two structures were standing intact on that pleasant morning in 1947.

Before the larger of these survivors, the little mountain road drew up and stopped.

It was the former home of Wells, Fargo bank—a bleak sort of building, faced with mustard-colored sandstone and fitted with tall, narrow doors, and iron shutters. (Plate 15) There was something almost hostile about its appearance; yet, muffled voices that issued from within, suggested tenancy.

My sharp rap on one of the iron shutters brought no reply. Again I pounded on the shutter and called, "Anybody home?"

The indistinct talking broke off as though sheared through by a knife. After a moment of dead silence, a man's voice thundered, "Well, damn it! Come on in—the door ain't locked!"

Crossing the worn threshold, I groped through a dim hall to a second door, which opened on a warm, old-fashioned kitchen. There were braided rugs on the floor; the windows were framed in checked gingham, and a rousing pine fire was burning in a fat stove. At an oilcloth-covered table in the center of the room, an elderly man and woman sat eating their breakfast.

Alex and Mayme Colbath were the owners of Silver Reef—every stick and stone and stope of it. And very early in our conversation, I learned it was not advisable to refer to The Reef as a "ghosttown."

"Silver Reef's no ghost!" the white-haired Alex bristled. "It's *never* been a ghosttown. Somebody's always lived here!"

And it was true. But for more than 20 years the permanent population of the town had been limited to Alex and Mayme; and long before their marriage, Alex had lived at the Reef, alone. Passionately dedicated to the mission of restoring these mines to their one-time greatness, this man had cleaved to the camp for more than a third of a century, seeking and striving and waiting, and forever feeding on the unbuttered crust of Hope.

Old Alex was not much on talking; not like the warm-hearted Mayme who was literally saturated in stories of the early days. From Mayme and other old-timers of Washington county—particularly Mrs. Marietta Mariger, of Leeds, who had passed nearly 70 years in the shadow of The Reef —I gradually fitted together the story of this famous old mining camp.

In the course of that effort I learned only one thing, for certain: No matter how many historical oracles I might consult, I seemed fated to end with an equal number of versions concerning "true facts" of the Reef's discovery. After nine years of research, I am still unable to authenticate a single one of the anecdotes told in that connection; and so I am taking the coward's way out. I am going to scrap the whole kit of them and start fresh with John Kemple, miner-assayist from Montana, and the first Anglo-American definitely known to have prospected this area in search of precious metals.

Appearing in Washington county some time between 1866 and 1869, Kemple passed considerable time in the vicinity of the white sandstone reef above Leeds. In the course of these prowlings, he reportedly found a piece of float carrying hornsilver values that several published accounts have placed as high as $17,000 per ton! After long and fruitless search for the sample's point of origin, Kemple shook the red sand of Utah from his shoes and wandered on to Nevada and Arizona. While working in those states, he presumably picked up more know-how, and the early 1870s found him back in Washington county, where he took the lead in organizing the Harrisburg mining district.

Southwestern Utah then, as now, was a Mormon stronghold; and although members of that faith were not encouraged by their leaders to join in the scramble for precious metals, a few of the area succumbed to the seductive call of Mammon. Among these straying Saints were Elijah Thomas and John S. Ferris, both of Leeds, who soon afterward located a rich deposit of silver on the white reef. Staking a claim, the partners gave several samples of the ore to J. B. Francis of Kanarra; and Francis, in turn, sent the specimens to Walker Brothers, Salt Lake bankers.

When Walkers opened that bag of samples from the white reef, they looked in amazement upon the first ore of its kind ever known in the United States.

The silver values it carried were fantastically high—and those values were locked in sandstone!

Now, the mining experts of 1875 were deeply learned and extremely positive chaps; and they "knew," inasmuch as sandstone is a sedimentary formation, that silver *did not* and *could not*, occur in it.

Possibly Walkers placed more faith in seeing than in science. In any case, they believed what they saw, and the sandstone samples looked good enough that they ordered an investigation of the Harrisburg district by three of their ablest mining men. When one of that trio—William T. Barbee—found horn-silver even in petrified wood, he staked 22 claims, sped back to Salt Lake for additional supplies, and returned to Washington county where he founded the new camp of Bonanza City on the flat east of Tecumseh Hill.

By the time Barbee's new town was three weeks old it embraced an assay office, boarding house, blacksmith shop, and various other appurtenances, and its founder was realizing a comfortable income from the sale of town lots. And then, up the road from Pioche, Nev., came a team of horses and a buckboard driven by Hyrum Jacobs, Pioche merchant. Hyrum expressed his wish to establish a general store in the new camp. Bill Barbee extended the warm hand of welcome, and quoted his price on choice business lots. Hyrum listened, and Hyrum declined—with emphasis.

Climbing back in the buckboard he clucked to his horses, drove up the ridge a few hundred yards, selected a site for a new town, named it Silver Reef, and established his store as its first business house.*

Another year found Bonanza City a fading memory, and Silver Reef roaring with life. Bisecting the town was a mile-long board walk, flanked by stores of nearly every type and a marvelous collection of saloons, gambling dives and dance halls. A weekly newspaper—the Silver Reef *Echo* —was being issued with regularity. A brewery, volunteer fire department, and brass band, were functioning—each in its own fashion. A school had been built by public subscription; there were three cemeteries, a race track, a miners' union with 300 members, and branches of the Oddfellows and Masonic orders.

For a man with no previous experience in the founding of cities, little Hyrum Jacobs had not done badly at all!

Among those who rode into Silver Reef by muleback in 1877 was Father Lawrence Scanlan, later to be bishop of the Salt Lake diocese of the Catholic church. Looking about him, Father Scanlan saw a place having need for both church and hospital. Determined that this lack should be remedied as rapidly as possible, the earnest young priest had circulated through the saloons, the lowest gambling dives and brothels; and from this level of society came the funds for his projected undertaking. Actual work of construction found Father Scanlan toiling alongside the day laborers, laying stones, and sawing and nailing boards.

Favorably impressed by the young padre's sincerity and industry, Washington county Mormon leaders offered him the use of their fine new tabernacle at St. George as a place to hold divine services until his own

---

*Mariger, Marietta: Saga of Three Towns, 1952.

church building might be complete. And because the new priest had been too busy to organize a choir, "Brother" John McFarlane's Mormon choristers graciously supplied his music, even learning to sing difficult Catholic Masses in Latin! Similar evidence of good-feeling and social tolerance is found throughout the early history of Silver Reef; and only the friendliest of relations seem to have prevailed between Gentiles of the rough mining camp, and Mormons who had settled in the adjacent valleys some 25 years before.

"Naturally," said Marietta Mariger, a life-long Mormon, "the economics of the situation had something to do with it. Silver Reef sought laborers, the Mormons sought labor; Silver Reef needed what the farms produced, and the Mormons needed a market for their goods."

At a meeting of Saints in the tabernacle at St. George, Apostle Erastus Snow, leader of the Virgen Valley settlements, publicly thanked God for sending "Brother" Barbee and his mining camp to provide outlet for Mormon farm produce, thereby ameliorating the struggle these colonists had long endured due to poor transportation facilities and limited markets.

"The Mormons have had a hard time serving the Lord in this God-forsaken country," responded Barbee, the Gentile. "It was about time something turned up to take the place of sorghum and wine as a circulating medium!"

With many operating mines and mills, a heavy payroll, and a population of several thousand persons, Silver Reef's star reached its ascendancy in the period between 1877 and 1880.

Working ore from the Buckeye mine, the Pioneer mill was producing 1000 ounces of silver bullion daily, for a monthly gross of $34,500. More than 10,000 tons of ore valued at nearly one-third of a million dollars were run through the Christy mill in 1878; and during the year following, the camp reached its all-time peak of production with the milling and shipping of 995,315 ounces of bullion.

With such stakes in the game, it is only natural that the Reef should have been the scene of considerable claim jumping and litigation. Even the original mine of Thomas and Ferris, the first on the Reef, was jumped by Piochers wiser in mining ways. In their haste to sell the stolen claim for $30,000, the jumpers lost almost as much as they "jumped," for not long afterward the mine produced more than its sale price in a single month!

From a devil-take-the-hindmost city, the decadence of Silver Reef followed a familiar pattern. The ore became leaner with depth. The mines began filling with water, and production costs skyrocketed. When wages were cut 12½ per cent to partially offset the increased costs of pumping, some 300 miners walked out on strike. With the manhandling of Colonel W. I. Allen, head of the Stormont company, United States marshals were called into the case and 36 strike leaders were jailed.

Experienced miners and mill hands began leaving for other camps.

Merchants who had extended heavy credit on the assumption of continued paychecks, found themselves holding the bag. Business failures multiplied, and one store after another closed its doors. Disheartened by the outlook, original developers crawled out from under, saving such skin as they were able; and under new owners, working with inexperienced help, production went into a nosedive.

Virtually every mine and mill on the reef had ceased operation by 1891; and during the entire subsequent decade, the district's total recorded production of silver was only 206,069 ounces.

With mining at a standstill and revenue no longer forthcoming, abandoned buildings of the town were sold at public auction for taxes. Little interest was shown in the sale until the purchaser of one old saloon assertedly came upon an overlooked cache of $10,000 in gold coin. Bidding thereupon became brisk, and even stone buildings were bought and torn down with fervor. But no other treasure caches were reported found.

Early in the present century, Alex Colbath became interested in the sorry old camp. In 1916, with World War I bolstering silver prices, he managed to raise $160,000 and with that for a nest-egg organized the Silver Reef Consolidated Mining company. At conclusion of the war, the property was leased by a New York concern and elaborate plans were made for building a mill and reactivating the mines. Another slump in silver prices effectually squelched those hopes.

Came 1928 and controlling interest in the company was purchased by American Smelting and Refining. After sinking a single test hole to a depth of 541 feet, American Smelting charged its loss to experience and retired from the field. Despite this and other costly fiascoes, Alex Colbath's faith in the mines remained unshaken. He mapped underground workings, he studied formation; he ate and talked and dreamed only Silver Reef. And, eventually, he acquired full ownership of the property.

From that day forward, his life was dedicated to a single end: To find someone, somewhere, who would work the old mines as Alex felt they should be worked.

"One time we were closing a deal to sell the property when Alex learned that the prospective purchasers were going to turn the mine over to leasers, strip the highgrade ore and abandon the rest. That settled it," said Mayme. "There wasn't any sale . . ."

On another occasion, a motion picture company wanted to lease the townsite, restore it to its original form, and use it as a setting for Western movies. The company had offered nearly as much for use of the site as Alex was asking for the whole place, but when they stipulated that the mines were not to be worked as that might interfere with their plans, the deal was off.

We had left the kitchen; were wandering over the old town, around and between the fallen walls and crumbled ruins—the Harrison hotel, the Empire saloon, Lauder's store, the Rice bank.

"On that flat was Chinatown," said Mayme, indicating a section of hillside barren alike of buildings and Orientals. "More than 250 Chinese lived there. They wore their hair in long black queues, and had their own Chinese mayor, and their own societies and holidays. Mother often said how exciting it had been to come up to the Reef and visit the little Chinese shops with all their strange-smelling foods, and glass chimes, and incense . . ."

The woman fell silent. Brushing a strayed wisp of gray hair from her eyes, she looked off across the desert toward the purple peaks of Zion; and, suddenly, a strange radiance came over her face. In the quiet loneliness and everlasting faithfulness of those hills, she seemed to see a parallel to the dream so long cherished by her man.

"Some of our friends have said we should farm the place," she went on, softly. "We could irrigate the whole flat from Quail creek. Others think we should start a dude ranch . . ."

"Farm—dude ranch—hell!" exploded Old Alex. "I'm a mining man —been a miner all my life!—and when Silver Reef comes back, it'll be as a mining camp—not as a damned hawg ranch!"

Years went by. Fair years and lean years; and Alex Colbath eventually passed over the Great Divide to richer prospecting, still holding tight to his dream.

With her loyal champion gone, the old town gathered her ghostly shrouds a little closer to her bony frame—and Zion's purple peaks still look down in compassion.

25

Big Store in the Wilderness

EIGHTY YEARS AGO one of the most extraordinary settlements in the state of Utah, the former town of Ajax is today so completely vanished that only by luck and careful searching may its one-time site be located.

William Ajax, founder of the town, had emigrated to Salt Lake City from Wales, in 1862, and soon after his arrival had established a general store. Although he stocked merchandise of good quality and priced it more reasonably than the then existing stores, Ajax soon incurred the disfavor of church leaders and a general withdrawal of patronage resulted.

Closing his Salt Lake establishment the Welsh merchant moved west to Rush Valley where he began making hay for freight teams then engaged in hauling supplies to the booming gold camp of Ophir. Observing a need for additional trade facilities in that isolated section, Ajax, in about 1872, took it upon himself to found a new settlement, 24 miles southwest of Tooele, and nine miles south of the present station of St. John. There he re-established himself in business.

Never in the history of Utah has there been another store like that built by William Ajax in this new community that bore his name. Located entirely *under ground,* the mercantile portion of the establishment consisted of one huge room with a 15-foot ceiling and mezzanine floor, plus sundry alcoves, side-rooms, and "L's," the whole embracing a floor area of roughly 11,000 square feet! Second floor of the building—actually the ground floor—consisted of living and sleeping rooms where Ajax and his wife reared their family of nine children and supplied lodging and meals to travelers.

Dealing in practically everything under the sun, from baby rattles to blasting powder, the Ajax emporium carried a stock that inventoried constantly between $125,000 and $150,000; and for a number of years the store is said to have enjoyed a larger daily sales volume than any mercantile establishment then located in Salt Lake City! Not only residents of Ophir and Mercur, but sheepmen, ranchers and miners from as far distant as the Nevada line, made it their point of supply. As the store flourished, a railroad station and postoffice—both bearing the name of Ajax—came into being.

With the death of its founder, about 1899, management of the business passed to his son, Ivor. But the glory of "The Big Store in the Wilderness" was nearly ended. One large segment of trade was lost when several nearby mining camps became depopulated by the closing of their mines and mills; another large trade potential was lost to Progress. As better roads and, eventually, automobiles, brought to isolated settlers a more rapid form of transportation, there was a growing tendency to drive to Salt Lake City where, along with buying his supplies, a man could see a few sights and enjoy a little fling.

With its former patronage dwindled to a trickle, The Big Store gradually failed, and early in the present century, closed its doors forever. Tramps, bumming on the railroad, began camping in the old building, and one night it burned to the ground—presumably ignited by some itinerant's campfire.

By diligent searching, in the summer of 1954, I located the former site of the town—the sole reminder of the one-time settlement being a ragged, rounded depression marking the excavation that had housed the big store. The south wall of this depression still retained a few partially-burned planks fastened together with cut iron nails; and scattered over the surface of the ground were fragments of hand-painted china dishes, and iridescent slivers of choice crystal and cut glass.

"Yes . . ." said Mrs. Blanche Ajax, the aging widow of Ivor, and now a resident of 2732 Imperial Street, Salt Lake City, "That would be the Big Store. Father Ajax always carried a large stock of fancy dishes . . ."

26

Cattle Rustlers and Rolling Rocks

WITH CREATION OF Lincoln county, in 1865, Governor H. G. Blasdel and a party of state officials left Carson City bound for Crystal Springs — an important stage station pre-selected as county seat. Roads through Southern Nevada being then few and far between the official party was forced to follow a round-about route through Death Valley, and their food supply had grown dangerously scant even prior to their arrival at Ash Meadows—more than 100 miles from their point of destination.

Leaving most of the party at The Meadows, Governor Blasdel and one companion made their way across the desert to Logan City—a mining camp ten miles west of Crystal Springs—and there procured supplies. Their return to Ash Meadows found one member of the official party already dead from starvation, and the others reduced to eating lizards and any small desert creatures that came to hand.

Recuperated in strength, the party resumed its interrupted trek, but upon arriving at Crystal Springs, the governor found their arduous trip had been largely for nothing, as the population of the area still lacked the number of voters required to establish a county government. Further steps to organize the county were postponed for one year—Crystal Springs being permitted to fulfill its prescribed function during that probationary period and until March, 1867, when the Lincoln seat of government was moved to Hiko. Hiko, in turn, retained the courthouse until 1871, when the political plum was carried away by booming Pioche, some 70 miles to the east.

Crystal Springs, today, is only a cattle ranch, and virtually nothing remains as evidence of its one-time official status. Hiko has fared a trifle better. The last time I was there (in 1948) its fourth class postoffice was serving around a dozen patrons, but no other business house was in operation. The interior of the long-vacant Murphy store building was papered with *Ladies Home Journals* of a generation past; and up on a knoll overlooking the town stood a tall, brick chimney, and the ruins of a mill formerly used in reducing ore from the Magnolia mine, at DeLamar.

But nowhere in that town was there any tangible reminder of the lusty days when these same cottonwood-shaded streets resounded to the tread of 3000 persons, and the night hours were broken by the snort of hard-ridden mounts and punctuating stabs of gunfire.

Conceived in violence and suckled on sin, Hiko was a frontier fleshpot of the first skimming. Although founded in 1866 as a result of mineral discoveries in that region, the town never gained any special prominence as a mining and milling center. Rather, her strong forte was cattle. Stolen cattle.

Attracted by the plentiful grass and abundant water of the Pahranagat Valley—and especially by the region's paucity of law enforcement officers —cattle rustlers of three states seemed drawn irresistibly toward this 30,-000-acre bedding ground cradled between the rugged Hiko range and the Silver Canyon mountains. Here, in these pleasant surroundings, stock brands might be altered at leisure, jaded horses rested, and stolen beeves safely fattened prior to sale. As result of this splendid adaptability, thousands of animals stolen from ranges in Nevada, Utah and Arizona, ultimately found their way hence. During the decade immediately following the Civil War, rustling operations became so flagrant, it has been said that a single day's ride through the valley generally would reveal as many as 350 different cattle brands!

The fact that legitimate ranchers also were endeavoring to graze their herds in the same region, brought about constant clashes and bloodshed; and every ranch in the valley has been the scene of killings.

The story is told of a horsethief once trailed to the Pahranagat by a group of irate Utah ranchers. Encouraged by these unexpected reinforcements, harassed local settlers formed a posse, caught the thief, and gave him a perfunctory midnight trial. With the hemp fitted snugly about the robber's neck and the free end of the rope passed over a barn rafter, the self-appointed executioners were awaiting the word to hoist-away when a voice from out of the darkness commanded the thief's release. Inasmuch as the order was backed by the unwavering muzzle of a double-barreled shotgun, there was little choice but to comply.

With great shouting and pistol-popping the renegades and their rescued comrade headed at full gallop for the bistros of Hiko, there to dedicate the night to lively and liquid celebration.

Enraged by this piece of defiance, the long-suffering ranchers of the Pahranagat hastened to organize a local chapter of the notorious "Committee of 601," a vigilante group then wreaking vengeance upon evil-doers in Nevada mining camps. Although "justice," as meted by the Committee, was scarcely consistent with the finest traditions of Sir William Blackstone, it should be remembered that Sir William's experience had never included such a place as Hiko.

One of the first to feel the whiplash of the new Committee was L. B. Vail, professed horse trader and suspected cow-thief and gunslinger.

That Vail had slain several men, including a brace of his confederates and, further, was addicted to the cozy caper of sleeping on their graves, had been a matter of common rumor in Eastern Nevada. Private feuds between bandits scarcely constituted a matter for concern by the "601," but the disappearance of Robert Knox—a cattle buyer last seen with Vail —had inspired the Committee to swing into action.

With motive and opportunity established, any evidence needed to clinch the case was supplied when Knox's saddle was dug up by coyotes at a site where Vail had recently camped. Further probing nearby disclosed a shallow grave containing the body and personal effects of the missing man.

Arrested, Vail was hauled into Hiko and lodged in its crackerbox jail. If events were to follow their normal course, there were good odds that the accused murderer would be freed by his pals—or would effect his escape in some other manner—long before time of trial. This had been the custom in the Pahranagat, and there was little reason to believe that history was through repeating herself.

To forestall any such development, the newly-formed "601" took charge.

On a sizzling day in July, 1867, the vigilante trial of L. B. Vail was conducted at Hiko with legal flourishes and punctilio that would have done credit to the Messrs. Gilbert and Sullivan.

With court assembled in a saloon convenient to the courthouse, a judge and jury were appointed by the Committee, and the protesting prisoner was removed from custody of the sheriff.

Using his pistol butt as a gavel, and an upended whisky barrel as a "bench," the jurist *pro tempore* banged loudly for order and declared court in session. Bending upon the gathering a fierce look, the judge warned all present that this august tribunal was not, in any manner of speaking, to be confused with a necktie party. That point of law having been established, the hearing proceeded.

Witnesses were called, sworn and questioned; and even the doubts of a skeptical man might have been allayed, in part, if more of the testimony had been audible. A great deal of it, unfortunately, was lost in the noise of certain construction then in progress immediately outside the door. To-wit: one gallows.

Adding to this noise was more hammering and sawing in the rear of the saloon where fabrication of a pine-board coffin was under way.

Upon conclusion of the trial, the veniremen filed solemnly into a rear room. There, with the aid of 52 rectangles of cardboard, they managed to occupy their time until a halt in the hammering indicated that the gallows had been brought to completion. The panel, thereupon, filed solemnly back to the jury box and a verdict for conviction was rendered.

The defendant did not appeal the case. Even if he had been *naive* enough to believe such a course worthwhile, he was a little too pressed for time.

Less than 60 minutes after returning its verdict, the jury was irrigating its tonsils in a toast to civic duty fearlessly met, and L. B. Vail, late nag-swapper, was pushing up rocks in Hiko's boothill.

The Pahranagat was not easily won. Even as long as ten years later, many of her citizens still regarded lynchings as the only form of justice that could not be bribed, bought, or otherwise corrupted.

One of the later coups of Hiko's Committee of 601, involved "Tempiute" Bill and a sullen-faced bruiser remembered only as Moquitch. This pair had been suspected of several robberies and even a killing or two, but no action had been taken against them until the robbery and murder of a harmless old duffer at Crescent Wash. As all evidence pointed toward the unsavory two, the Committee had tagged them with the Indian sign.

With "grapevine" notification that the heat had been turned on, Tempiute and Moquitch fled into the desert ranges of Nye county, where they managed to elude capture for five months.

Soon after their apprehension by Nye county officers, the fugitives learned that Hiko's "601" had neither forgotten their sins nor forgiven them.

As the prisoners were being returned to Lincoln county, Deputy Sheriff J. A. Bidwell was waylaid by a grim delegation and forced to surrender his captives.

Convoyed into Hiko by the committee, Tempiute and Moquitch subsequently admitted several other murders, in addition to that of the Crescent Wash miner, whom, Tempiute said, they had beaten to death with a stone because he had refused to divulge the whereabouts of a rumored gold cache. As their accomplice on that particular job, the culprits named a man known to them only as "Johnny."

Trial of the two defendants was recessed momentarily while a well-heeled delegation of members from the "601" descended upon Johnny's camp and called upon him to surrender. Inasmuch as Johnny elected to shoot it out, the Committee obliged; and by the time the smoke of battle cleared, not only Johnny but half a dozen of his followers were permanently *hors de combat*.

With that errand neatly dispatched, the "601" trundled back to the improvised courtroom and the trial was resumed.

Reporting the incident in its issue of Jan. 15, 1875, the Pioche *Record* said:

"Moquitch and Tempiute Bill were placed in a wagon, with ropes around their necks, and taken to a two-story building, and from an upper window a plank was run out and the ropes attached. The horses, it is supposed, took fright at something and dragged off the wagon, leaving the two hanging by the neck.

"As no one relieved them, they soon died."

After a dozen years of such demonstrations, Hiko's lawless element gradually dispersed—its members presumably heading for places where ropes were fewer and peace-pursuing citizens did not shoot so straight or so frequently.

Through all the years since only redmen roamed the Pahranagat, the valley's greatest asset has been its phenomenal springs.

Hiko Spring, most northerly of the valley's three major flows, pours forth at a rate of approximately 2700 gallons a minute; Crystal Springs has a volume nearly double that figure, and Ash Springs, still farther down the valley, has a flow of 22.89 cubic feet per second—nearly 10,000 gallons per minute.

Adding to these major sources the flow of numerous smaller springs, the Pahranagat's annual water production has been estimated at 30,000 acre feet—a lot of water in a land fundamentally desert!

Strangely enough, however, it was neither her phenomenal springs, her cattle, nor even her rough-shod justice, that brought to the Pahranagat her greatest tidal wave of publicity. For this bit of world-wide notice, the valley must thank The Rolling Stones—those perambulating pebbles that never existed save in the fertile brain of Dan DeQuille, then a reporter on the *Territorial Enterprise,* at Virginia City.

In the course of Comstock journalism there occasionally fell days when no new bonanzas were discovered nor any new millionaires made. As these distressing periods brought to editors the same appalling number of columns to be filled with news matter, both DeQuille and his contemporary, Mark Twain, were given to fabricating "whoppers" to bridge the gaps. On one such occasion, DeQuille came up with his later-to-be-famous report on the aforementioned pebbles.

Couched in highly erudite terms, the article described a phenomenon allegedly restricted to the isolated Pahranagat.

Certain stones there, declared the writer, were periodically drawn together by some mysterious power, later scattering wide apart, only to regroup in quivering masses at what appeared to be the magnetic center of the valley.

"These curious pebbles," wrote DeQuille, "appear to be formed of lodestone or magnetic iron ore. A single stone, removed to a distance of a yard, upon being released, at once started off with wonderful and somewhat comical celerity to rejoin its fellows."

On the basis of these alleged observations, their author predicted a completely new doctrine of electrical propulsion and repulsion.

National wire services seized upon the story. Sweeping across the land in a blaze of headlines, it ultimately found its way to Europe where it created a furor among the world's leading physicists, then deep in the study of electro-magnetics. With the master minds of two hemispheres belaboring him for additional details, the Virginia City newsman at last sought to end the controversy by admitting that the Pahranagat story was a complete hoax. By this time, however, no one would believe that the story was not true! Least of all, the great scientists of Europe. Refusing to accept the author's renunciation, they went so far as to brand it a bald-faced attempt by the United States government to withhold from the world invaluable scientific knowledge. For a time the matter even threatened to become an international issue.

The final *coup de grace* was the hooking of Phineas T. Barnum, world's greatest baiter of suckers, who offered to DeQuille a contract calling for a salary of $10,000 per year.

All DeQuille had to do to earn the neat little stipend was to collect a few of his famous Rolling Stones of the Pahranagat and cause them to do their stuff under Barnum's Big Top!

27

Six-Toed Chinaman of Charleston

IN THAT WILD, perpendicular land where Nevada rubs shoulders with Idaho and snowdrifts lie in the canyons for eleven months out of each year, the ghosttown of Charleston sleeps in the dust of oblivion.

With only two of her original buildings still standing—a log saloon (plate 55) and a log grocery store—the Charleston of today bears little resemblance to the trigger-happy camp which flourished here in the 1880s, when the town's natural bent for outlawry was aided and abetted by nearness of the state line. Any miscreant who found conditions momentarily too hot for him in Nevada, had only to trickle down the Bruneau river and over the border into Idaho, where he could lose himself like an ink blot on a dark night. Once in the wilds of Owyhee county, the fugitive evildoer might marry and sire six bantlings before the red tape of extradition could be untangled and reknotted in the form of a hangman's noose. Now and then, of course, one of Charleston's delinquents tarried long enough to tie his bootlaces, and thereby won for himself stellar billing in a subsequent necktie party.

One of the lads who failed to leave camp in time, was the Six Toed Chinaman, liquidator of "Allegheny" Mardis.

Allegheny—no one ever bothered to call him George Washington Mardis, as a hopeful Pennsylvania mother had named him—was a character. Bewhiskered and one-eyed, with a face resembling a relief map of the Badlands, it was he who had made the original gold strike on 76 Creek, thereby launching the district; and, despite certain idiosyncrasies, he was regarded as the "father" of the town and its leading citizen.

The aforementioned aberrations stemmed largely from the fact that the old man considered himself somewhat of a preacher and philosopher. A back-door, left-handed preacher, if you insist; but, nonetheless, a preacher.

In a time and place where nine men out of every ten thought only of gold and silver and the sensual sinnings those commodities might finance, Allegheny Mardis found his chief delight in the beauty of hills and streams, the pleasurable perfume of mountain posies, and the tremolo of birds. All this he confided to his burro, Sampson. He also preached long and eloquent sermons to Sampson, and read him fiery denunciations from the Old Testament; and Sampson, being a good burro, cocked an appreciative ear and listened patiently and uncritically. If his master wished to preach for the sweet sake of preaching, it was perfectly okay with Sampson.

One day in the 1880s, as Allegheny was preparing his wagon to make the long drive to Elko, he was asked by a Charleston Chinaman to deliver to the county seat some $250 in gold in payment of a debt. It was the last favor Allegheny Mardis would ever undertake for any man.

Miners, next day, found his team and wagon abandoned along the road below town, and a search in the nearby brush revealed the old man's body, riddled with bullets. The $250 in gold, entrusted to him for delivery, was gone.

When amateur sleuthing in the vicinity of the crime revealed the tracks of a barefooted male, the search narrowed automatically to China-town—it being the contention of the sleuthers that only a Chinaman would be fool enough to go without shoes in that rigorous climate. When those tracks were further noted to exhibit six toes on the left foot, a volunteer posse of witch hunters swarmed over Charleston's Chinese quarter in a bloodthirsty pursuit that saw slippers yanked roughly from scores of Oriental feet.

Their search, at last, was rewarded by finding a Chinaman who possessed the damning malformity of a surplus toe on the near foot!

Despite eagerness to get on with the case so they might return to their tunnels and faro layouts, members of the vigilante posse allotted two full days for the extra-toed Oriental to devise any possible alibi. With that time elapsed and no alibi offered, the suspect was duly convicted on circumstantial evidence.

Next day, with most of the population of Charleston either looking on or taking part, the murder and robbery of George Washington Mardis was avenged in one of the last lynchings to take place in Elko county.

Among Elko county pioneers, a favorite story concerns an early-day sheriff whose tour of duty frequently called him to the north part of the county. Returning to Elko after one such trip he remarked that he had enjoyed a most gratifying experience.

"Got your man, eh?" inquired a bystander.

"Hell, no!" blustered the sheriff. "I didn't GET anybody . . . But I rode plumb through Charleston without getting shot!"

28

Place of the Star Hill Pony

ALTHOUGH THE BOOM camps of Ward and Taylor contributed substantially to the mineral and anecdotal wealth of Nevada, chief mining camp of eastern White Pine county was Cherry Creek, situated in the foothills of the Egan range, across Steptoe Valley from Schellbourne.

Over an eleven-year period, between 1872 and 1883, Cherry Creekers ate high on the hog. The town enjoyed a wide reputation as a place where a man could have himself some fun. Entertainment—anything from cockfights to fast women—was always available, and it was not unusual for fun seekers to drive or ride horseback as much as 100 miles to attend dances at The Creek. Such visitors, in many instances, stayed over a day and danced both nights until dawn.

Throughout the prosperous years of the camp, when her mines were rich and productive and three mills were operating at capacity, every Saturday night saw the streets thronged by miners, their pockets sagging with money and souls bleeding for action. While poker and faro provided partial outlet for this welling vitality, Cherry Creek was a rugged town that regarded such indoor sports as fit only for after-darkness hours when it was no longer feasible to indulge in the Sport of Kings—for the Cherry Creeker, above all else, was a turf fan!

Several groups, as well as numerous individuals, owned fast-stepping nags and competitive spirit ran high. The only upsetting detail lay in the fact that all horses in the vicinity had been matched and rematched until every local sportster knew their relative potentialities as he knew the face cards of a poker deck.

Unbested champion of the area was a shapely bay owned by a group of Star Hill miners who were so confident of their pony's ability they invariably backed him to the bottom of the poke. Pat Keough, a rancher in Butte Valley, a dozen miles west of Cherry Creek, saw in this loyalty a chance to garner a nice crop of shekels, provided he could ring in a strange horse whose speed was not known to local track fans.

At Hamilton, 60 miles across the range, lived Dan Morrison, owner of a horse named Muggins, which Keough had seen in action and knew to be faster than the Star Hill bay. A little connivance between Keough and Morrison, and Muggins appeared at Cherry Creek — making his arrival in the guise of an unkempt pack animal loaded to the crupper with camp gear.

As Cherry Creek was always willing to accommodate any man bent on losing his shirt, it required no particular finesse for Morrison to strike up a match between his trailworn "packhorse" and the unwhipped pride of Star Hill. A few drinks and a little bar-side braggadocio was sufficient to bring forth the awaited challenge.

Now, the Creek's turf fans were not complete simpletons. The more they thought about the matter, on the night before the race, the more they realized that the newly-arrived horse scarcely had the appearance of a pack animal; and before tossing in their respective pokes, they decided it might be advisable to stage a little preliminary heat between the newcomer and the local favorite.

Slipping into the livery stable in the chill midnight hours, the Star Hill delegation stealthily removed Muggins from his stall and taking him to a lonely flat below town, gave him a clandestine workout. To their relief, the stranger's performance was clumsy and slow, and the Star Hill pony romped away from him like Citation leaving a dray horse. Word was eased around to back the bay to the limit. Morning of the race found every pocket bulging with track money, and before the two contenders went to the post, nearly $10,000 had been wagered by local miners.

The smug confidence felt as the animals got under way in a burst of dust, soon was usurped by stark dismay.

Muggins, at the half-way mark, was loping down the track as strongly as the north wind sweeping through Steptoe Valley—and several lengths to his rear, pounded the losing hooves of the Star Hill bay!

At the finish line, the only change in position was an increased lead for Muggins.

The joke, naturally, was too good to keep. The stakeholders barely had paid off before Pat Keough confessed that he had relied on the Star Hill gang to pull some sort of shenanigan to learn the speed of the alleged packhorse. As a prelude to any such coup he had removed one of Muggins' front shoes, leaving him one-fourth barefooted, and had replaced one of his rear shoes with a cumbersome four-pounder—thereby throwing the animal off stride and slowing his pace. As soon as the trial heat had been run, the regular light shoes had been restored so that the Star Hill tricksters had succeeded only in tricking themselves.

Between 1872 and 1883, Cherry Creek was at its zenith with an estimated top population of 6000 persons. In addition to numerous saloons and gambling houses, the place boasted a hotel, a newspaper—the Cherry Creek *Independent*—a Wells Fargo office, G.A.R. post, and all the other appurtenances of a frontier metropolis, including the only two dentists in White Pine county. One of these was Pete Cannon, the druggist, who pulled refractory molars with a pair of fence pliers. The other was Old Man Leonard.

An outspoken athiest and loyal consort of the Demon Rum, Old Man Leonard rambled over the countryside in a delapidated sheep wagon drawn by a pair of lean donkeys. In addition to his camp gear, personal belongings and dental equipment, he transported in the wagon a choice collection of lizards, snakes, tarantulas and scorpions, all of which he alluded to as his "pets." Needless to say, Old Man Leonard was not popular with the frailer sex.

But to return to the subject of Cherry Creek. After a decade of greatness, the town, in 1882, made an ambitious play to cop the county seat from Hamilton—a proposal that lost by only a few votes. Could the town have continued prosperous for another few years, there is good possibility that she might have grabbed the courthouse honors. But it was not so written in the tea leaves.

With the crash of 1883, Cherry Creek was finished forever.

Today, the town is scarcely an echo of its former self. When I saw the place, last, in 1949, a few old wooden buildings still huddled along the main street. One of these housed a fourth class postoffice opened briefly each day at 2:30 o'clock in the afternoon. A vacant building nearby carried on its false front a faded sign, "Cherry Creek Barrel House Saloon," and across the street stood the only operative business in town —a small dimly-lighted building that functioned as a combination general store, soft drink parlor, service station and bar.

A few old buildings, most of them empty; a few old timers, living in the past; a small schoolhouse, a cemetery, and tangled thickets of choke-cherries in the ravine west of town . . . Only these remain of Cherry Creek, the town that took its whiskey straight, and lost its shirt on the Star Hill pony.

29

Man With the King-Size Dream

NEWEST MEMBER OF Nevada's ghosttown circuit is Mountain City, a town that has flared and faded for 85 years. Before this appears in print, Mountain City may again be a mad metropolis—her returned prosperity founded on titanium or some other mineral—but at the present writing, she's a very quiet old lady.

After Jesse Cope's original discovery here of ore values, in 1869, the town developed rapidly—fortune hunters from all over the West being lured into the district by the Terrific Trinity of placer gold, lode gold, and silver. Included among these boomers were large numbers of Chinese, previously employed on the new Pacific Railroad, brought to completion earlier that year. Bucking the gold placers by day and the fan-tan parlors by night, the pig-tailed Orientals added color and atmosphere to the narrow streets of this remote mountain settlement, only a dozen miles south of the Idaho line.

One of the first official reports of the place was written by Rossiter W. Raymond, United States Commissioner of Mining Statistics, in August, 1870.

"This city is located on the Owyhee river, 85 miles north of Elko," observed Mr. Raymond. "It is now a trifle over one year old, has about 200 buildings, among which are to be found specimens of cloth, adobe, log, frame and cut stone, and the hammer and saw are to be heard on every side. The population, including Chinese and a few Indians, is not far from 1000 . . ."*

Inasmuch as the Raymond analysis made no mention of any palaces of pleasure, it must be assumed that the government mining engineer was interested only in life's higher planes. Certainly, Mountain City never was lacking in spirits to cool the fevered tonsil, and even that embryonic period covered by the report found the town supporting comfortably 20 saloons and two breweries!**

That her population pyramided in spectacular fashion is evidenced by the fact that only three years after founding of the town, her electors

---

*Statistics of Mines and Mining in the States and Territories West of the Rocky Mountains for the Year 1870. Washington, D.C., 1871.
**Owyhee Avalanche, Aug. 26, 1870.

cast more than 1800 votes in the Grant presidential election—and this before woman suffrage!

Costs of mining, milling and ore transportation were terrific; but due to the happy circumstance that the ore was rich and lay close to the surface, more than $1,000,000 in silver is said to have been recovered from shallow workings prior to 1881.* With political downfall of silver, however, the once-busy camp went into a decline, and by the early 1890s, only one lone Chinaman remained.**

In 1900 (after most of the town's buildings had been torn down or moved away) new ore discoveries and better prices for metal brought about a revival of the district, and for a little while the hills again echoed to hammering, sawing and blasting, but in only half a dozen years, the ore that could be mined profitably was exhausted, and once again the dust of oblivion settled in the streets and Mountain City became a place where but three families lived.

It still was a three-family town in 1920 when a wandering prospector, S. Frank Hunt, became interested in certain iron gossan showings in the hills, three miles south of town.

Beneath that gossan, contended Hunt, lay one of the greatest copper deposits in the world!

For 50 years the Mountain City district had been prospected and mined for gold and silver without any significant indications of copper. And now, here was a man who had the unmitigated gall to claim that copper, eventually, would transcend in value all the other metals Mountain City had produced!

As copper, then, was only five or six cents a pound, it was little wonder that Hunt became a laughing stock, an object of ridicule—not only to promoters and capitalists, but to fellow prospectors, as well—and for another dozen years, Mountain City remained a three-family town.

All that while, Hunt never ceased to hammer away at his dream. Nothing could dissuade him. Lacking funds of his own to prove the field, he was grubstaked for a considerable time by Vivian P. Strenge, Salt Lake City mining man. But even Strenge eventually lost faith in the proposition and withdrew his financial support.

After several other promoters had investigated the property and turned it down, Hunt succeeded in gaining the interest of another Salt Laker, Ogden G. Chase, and in the early-Depression year of 1931, the Rio Tinto Mining company was formed. Name of the new concern had been chosen in honor of the world-famous 3000-year-old copper mines on the border between Spain and Portugal.

Chase's resources were so limited that little promotional advertising could be given the proposition, and the unique method adopted by the

*Lincoln, Francis Church, Mining Districts and Mineral Resources of Nevada, 1921.
**Miller, B. F., Nevada in the Making, Nevada State Historical Society Papers, 1924.

company to raise funds for development forms one of the fascinating chapters in the history of Nevada mining.

Two million shares of stock were issued, half that number assessable, half non-assessable. Thereupon, adopting a plan that has since been employed successfully by numerous Christmas-seal charities, Chase mailed unsolicited blocks of assessable stock to hundreds of persons who might conceivably be interested. The stock was offered completely without cost —persons accepting it being obligated only to meet periodic assessments until the full five-cent limit had been paid.

Many of the letters, together with the stock they contained, were thrown in the fire; other certificates were returned with polite—or not so polite—refusals. Occasionally, however, some reckless soul with a penchant for gambling would signify his willingness to take a chance on the strange proposal.

Other shares were peddled over the bars in the beer parlors, the hotels, and redlight houses, of Elko. Not because they entertained any faith in a rich copper deposit beneath the Mountain City gossan, but because they liked the lame prospector, Hunt, merchants accepted the stock with a shrug and a grin. In some business houses the certificates piled up in stacks.

Eventually, a major portion of the stock had been placed; and out of proceeds from the initial assessment of two cents a share, work was begun on a road from Mountain City to the claims, equipment and supplies were purchased, and operations started at the mine head.

With little assurance of ever being paid, every man on the crew— as well as the company's office force in Salt Lake City—worked that entire first winter without wages. Frank Hunt, president of the company, cooked for the men while the general manager, in addition to his supervisorial duties, worked a full shift daily alongside his crew, mucking, drilling, and timbering in the shaft. The new "town" of Rio Tinto, established near the mine head, then consisted of two log cabins and a tenthouse.

At a depth of 227 feet—23 feet short of the level predicted by Hunt —ore was reached on February 26, 1932.

And just as Frank Hunt had predicted, a dozen years before, that ore was a sulphide running 40 per cent in copper!

Only a few months after the recipients of those Rio Tinto shares had chucked most of them in their respective wastebaskets, the stock was rocketing madly, and shares that hadn't cost anyone more than a nickel apiece, eventually were quoted at $17!

With the field proven, International Smelting bought controlling interest, and less than five years after Hunt's discovery of ore beneath the concealing gossan, the mine was producing 450 tons of ore daily with earnings at the rate of $4,000,000 annually.

Reporting on the Rio Tinto operation in 1938, C. W. McCullough, mine executive of Park City, Utah, wrote:

"The population of the district is not centralized in one town but in three thriving communities a few miles apart—Mountain City, Rio Tinto and Patsville, the latter two lusty infants kicking away the sagebrush from around their cradles, at the workings of the Rio Tinto and Copper King properties, respectively . . . Each of these towns boasts the usual mining camp business houses: drug stores, garages, shoe shops, cafes, boarding houses, and, of course, the ever-present saloon, there being eleven of these in the three towns at this writing.

"One of the few buildings that survived the two ghosttown periods is one originally built for a bank but never used. Another monument of the old and new is the hotel at Mountain City, a two-story structure moved from Gold Creek after discovery of the Rio Tinto mine. The building has been repaired and modernized to some degree but makes few pretensions toward being a first class hotel. (The plumbing is still outside!) Nearest rail point is Elko, some ninety miles to the south . . . But, today, the travel is northward across the Bruneau Desert in Idaho to the town of Mountain Home, 117 miles . . . this because of the better highway.* About 600,000 pounds of ore and concentrates are being hauled over this route daily . . .

"Rio Tinto . . . has been assuming proportions of a model town through the housing and building program fostered by Mountain City Copper Co. In the wake of Frank Hunt's dream-come-true has sprung up a hospital, an accredited high school, a fine grade school building, a movie house, social center, athletic field, a newspaper plant, and other modern facilities. Seeking to eliminate the floating class of miners, the company has erected ten modernistic apartments to attract men of families to Rio Tinto. These apartments, consisting of eight suites of three rooms and bath each, bring metropolitan comforts and conveniences to this isolated Western frontier. Numerous cottages and duplexes cater to those requiring larger dwelling places. The town has electricity, running water, and a sewage system. The company buildings and the apartment houses enjoy the advantages of a central heating plant. On every side is a note of permanence that reflects the confidence of the operators in the enormous ore reserves waiting to be mined . . ."**

But, despite these optimistic predictions, Mountain City was not destined to endure for long.

Nine years later, readers of Intermountain newspapers one morning learned to their shock and surprise that the workings of Mountain City

---

*Under pressure from the company, the road from Dinner Station to Mountain City was hard-surfaced, about 1938, at a cost to Nevada of approximately $2,000,000. Following this development, Elko became trucking terminal for the operation. (N.M.)

**McCullough, C. W., and June Metcalf, Story of the Mountain City Copper Co., The Mining Journal, Feb. 28, 1938.

Copper Company, at Rio Tinto, were to be closed immediately. According to Frank A. Wardlaw, Jr., president of the company, the closing order had been issued by the board of directors "because efforts to find new ore bodies have been unsuccessful and further operations cannot be carried on at a profit."

Once again, Mountain City's cycle had been run.

On this occasion, the running of that cycle had resulted in the production of more than 1,000,000 tons of ore—some of it running as high as 60 per cent in copper—for a total gross return of more than $23,-000,000.** In addition to laying the groundwork for several new fortunes, one lasting result of those millions was creation of the S. Frank Hunt Foundation at the Mackay School of Mines, in Reno. Endowed to the extent of nearly $200,000, the express purpose of the fund was to finance field trips, and to further the study of geology, mineralogy and mining—thereby fulfilling the late Mr. Hunt's dream of making more "good prospectors."

But all these high ideals and fine results were largely wasted on the poor old town that had seen them made possible.

When I passed through this district in 1954, only one man remained in residence at the once-thriving camp of Rio Tinto. One family remained at Patsville; and proud Mountain City had shriveled to a sleepy village.

**Production figures from Nevada's Metal and Mineral Production, (1859-1940) University of Nevada Bulletin, 1943 and from Jay A. Carpenter, Director, Nevada State Bureau of Mines.

30

Three-Time Loser in the Utah Hills

LOOSE GRAY CLOUDS had been hovering over the Toanas since early morning; and now, as I neared White Horse pass, a mixture of snow and sleet came whirling from a leaden sky to whiten the junipers. The month was June, but calendars mean little in that high, wide land, where Nevada and Utah join.

Watching closely, I spotted an old road leading east from the vicinity of the pass, and, easing into it, settled back for the last 30 miles of this pilgrimage to the mining camp of Gold Hill, on the Utah side of the border.

The road dropped rapidly in elevation. The chill of the high country yielded to rain; the rain, in turn, to bright sunshine and the glaring immensity of Great Salt Desert. Here, on these barren flats was a different world—a somnolent, white, empty world—where the air hung heavy and lifeless, and heat lay in rippled waves on the skyline.

Skirting the salt flats for 20-odd miles and winding through a spur of the Deep Creek mountains, the old road climbed to a low summit and headed downward through a long, dry ravine. Midway of that descent, the scattered outline of a town began taking form on a distant slope to the south. Viewed from afar, the old buildings appeared small and dark, like specks of black pepper in the great brown bowl of the desert hills. Some of those specks, as the road drew nearer, became identifiable as business buildings and dwellings. Three dark specks at the north edge of town resolved themselves into a depot and two box cars on a siding; and other specks, on surrounding slopes, took form as shaft houses and the headframes of mines.

But when the old road merged with main street, one glimpse was enough to show that Gold Hill was not prospering.

The windows of the depot were boarded tightly; the rails leading to it were brown with rust. The two old freight cars had been converted into living quarters, and even these were abandoned. Midway of the deserted street stood a large brick building that still bore the identifying signs of a mercantile company; but its windows were draped in cobwebs and barren of goods, its doors were padlocked. Only the scattered clutter of disuse filled other structures that had functioned as poolhalls, and cafes and

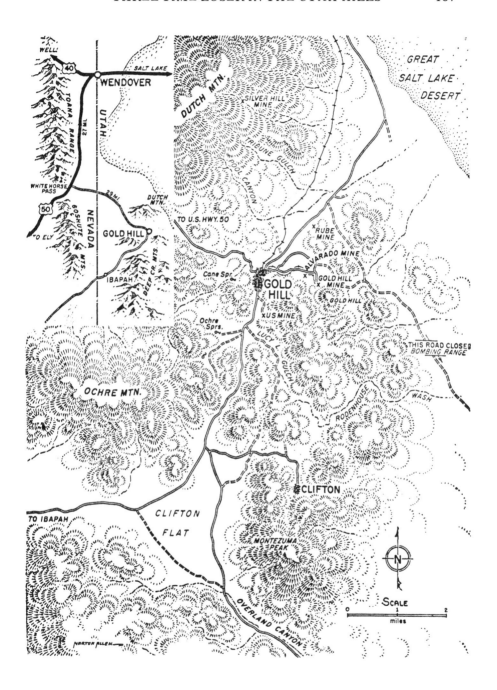

drugstores. (Plate 21) I had been prowling over the town for possibly half an hour when my ears caught the first faint sound of life—a dull thump-thump-thumping from the backyard of a frame cabin.

Investigation revealed a small, determined blonde, of uncertain age. She was seated a-straddle a pine bench, her attention centered on an old iron mortar and pestle with which she was pulverizing a sample of greenish ore. On the ground at her feet lay a prospector's pick and a battered gold pan.

Two minutes after our exchange of introductions, Leatha Millard's home was my home, and Leatha had become my chief source of information concerning the past, present and potential of Gold Hill.

Since her arrival there as a young woman, in 1907, Leatha had seen many changes. From a city that had boasted its own newspaper and hotels, and representatives of all the trades and professions, she had watched it shrivel to a ghosttown, where, in that year of 1952, not one business house remained in operation, no telephone afforded contact with the outside world, and she and four other persons comprised the entire population . . .

Presence of mineral in the Deep Creek mountains had been learned nearly a century before when travelers on the Overland Trail were approached by Indians who proffered ore samples in exchange for food and tobacco, said Leatha. Among the many California-bound goldseekers were a few who had halted their journey to investigate the source of those samples.

They had found the ore—plenty of it—but mainly lead and silver, which offered small chance for profit in a land then so far removed from mills and smelters. Some mining had been done, but nothing of importance until 1864, when Col. Patrick Connor erected Utah's first large smelter at Stockton. Although sale at this plant meant a haul of 125 miles by mule teams across the Great Salt Desert, the immediate result had been a mining boom in the Deep Creek mountains and founding of a town called Clifton, about five miles southeast of the present site of Gold Hill. Many mines had been opened and, in 1872, a mill and small smelter had been constructed locally.

But Clifton was too far ahead of her time. Her ore was composed too largely of the base metals, while the precious metals for which men sought were limited to rich pockets, too far between. Unable to operate profitably under conditions then existing, Clifton's major mines had ceased production; the smelter had closed after reducing some 1500 tons of highgrade lead-silver ore; business houses had locked their doors, and the camp had died.

The years that followed had been marked by sporadic revivals. Old mines would reopen, mining journals would carry optimistic reports, and Clifton again would bloom with the ephemeral vigor of a resurrection plant.

But none of these revivals was of long duration and, in time, they ceased altogether.

Feeling that the story of Gold Hill should begin with Clifton, Leatha and I headed for the older town. At the summit of the divide, south of Gold Hill, we turned into a nearly-forgotten side trail—rocky and rutted, and generously supplied with high centers—and in another mile we were entering the ruins of a settlement which had flourished before either of us was born.

Here were all the familiar accoutrements of an 1870 ghosttown—the hollow rock squares of old foundations, the tumbled heaps of stone where shops and dwellings had stood, the lonely desolation of ancient fireplaces long before robbed of the homes they had served. In the weedy yard of an old log cabin, the rutted trail gave a last gasp and died. (Plate 20.)

"This was Ollie Young's place," said Leatha. "He was the last living resident of Clifton . . ."

Oliver Young and his brother, Brigham, who claimed the original Brigham Young as their uncle, had located in Clifton during one of its periodic revivals, explained my hostess-guide. After the boom collapsed and everyone else left, the Youngs remained.

"They were fine, clean old men," said Leatha. "But although completely devoted to one another, they lived in separate cabins—Ollie, here, and Brig about 30 yards up the canyon. Brig died first; and that left Ollie the last inhabitant of this lonely old town. He had to walk to Gold Hill for all his supplies. I was running one of the stores there, at that time, and if I could get away, I always brought him home.

"For years after Brig's death, Ollie kept both cabins immaculate—even kept the cupboards stocked with food—just as if his brother were away on a prospecting trip and due to return at any moment. But, one day, some hunters set fire to the place and it burned to the ground. After that, Ollie seemed to lose interest in living, and it wasn't long until he died, too . . ."

The open door of the old cabin revealed an interior dirty and cluttered and almost barren of furnishings. An old cook stove was balanced precariously on one leg and two bricks; its pipe had fallen to rust. In one corner stood an iron bedstead with part of a corn-shuck mattress still on its springs. There was a rickety pine table, with a half-empty can of condensed milk, and a half-burned candle stuck in a medicine bottle. Over the stove hung an orange-crate cupboard, its interior lined with yellowed sheets of the *Intermountain Republican* and *Salt Lake Herald,* of 1908. The entire place was befouled with packrat litter and multiple layers of white dust blown from the Salt Desert.

"I wish you could have seen it when Ollie lived here," said Leatha. "It was like a doll's house . . ."

After prowling around the site of the vanished smelter, where we found some crucibles and a couple of old "spice pots" used for molding

the skimmings, we floundered on up the brush-choked canyon in search of
the old well which had formerly supplied water to the town. The canyon
eventually became so rough we abandoned the search and were heading
back toward the car when a break in the heavy undergrowth revealed an old
iron pump, heavy with accumulated rust.

Simply because it seemed the natural thing to do, I gave the old
handle a few vigorous strokes. It sounded like all the ungreased pump
handles in Creation, rolled into one; but from the rusty spout leaped a
bright stream of cold clear water! Even though its town had gone where
the woodbine twineth, the old well was still putting forth.

I remained with Leatha Millard for nearly a week. During that time
we visited all the historical mines of the district, interviewed old timers
for twenty-five miles around, browsed through brittle newspaper clippings,
and scanned musty mining reports without end. From it all, I gradually
absorbed the story of Gold Hill.

Although mining claims on nearby Dutch mountain had been recorded as early as 1882, Gold Hill's first development of importance had
not occurred until ten years after that date when an amalgamation mill
had been constructed for treating ores of the Cane Springs, Alvarado and
Gold Hill mines. One of the guiding lights in this development was Col.
James F. Woodman, owner of valuable mining properties in the Tintic
district, and discoverer of the notorious Emma mine, at Alta.

Due to the many successful mining ventures he had fathered, Colonel
Woodman's nod of approval was sufficient to light the fires under any
new district. Therefore, when he turned his attention toward Western
Tooele county, attention of the mining world turned with him; and the town
of Gold Hill was born in 1892. A lusty and precocious offspring, it soon
was to take its place among the famous mining towns of the West.

Gold Hill's mines adhered to no cut-and-dried pattern. In addition
to occasional showings of fabulous richness, a dozen different minerals
and metals were yielded in commercial quantities. One rich shoot in the
Alvarado carried $1100 in gold to the ton of ore. The Copper Queen
carried 1800 ounces of silver to the ton. Copperopolis ore ran $400 per
ton in copper; and the Lucy L produced thousands of dollars to the ton
in bismuth.

During 19 months of operation, Colonel Woodman's Alvarado and
Cane Springs mines produced for their owners some $200,000, in addition
to large amounts lost to highgraders. Even at that, the operation had been
seriously handicapped by transportation difficulties.

Arrival of Leatha and her parents at Gold Hill, in 1907, had found
everyone in camp completely confident that the projected Western Pacific
railroad would be routed via Gold Hill, thereby ending the extreme isolation under which the town had operated for the first 15 years of its life.

But the Western Pacific, as it built across the Great Salt Desert,
elected to by-pass Gold Hill some 50 miles to the north; and the town's

remoteness continued unabated. Access roads were impassible to autos; and even with most of the West largely motorized, Gold Hill still was dependent on freight wagons and horse-drawn stagecoaches.

Not until 1917 did the town get the railroad service she had sought for so many years. Built south from Wendover, the Deep Creek Extension was planned as the beginning of a line which would, ultimately, continue through Nevada to Southern California. For the moment, it was enough that it had reached Gold Hill.

Construction of the branch line was barely started when a dozen new mines had opened, closed mines had been reactivated, and frantic stockpiling of ore was under way throughout the district. With opening of the line for operation, ore shipments had been made in such terrific volume that sampling and smelter plants of Salt Lake valley were swamped and it was found necessary to declare an embargo on shipments from the district. Despite this curtailment, the Deep Creek railroad, in its first year of operation, carried out of Gold Hill some $1,000,000 worth of ore. Without the embargo, it was estimated that the year's shipping would have doubled that figure.*

Coincident with advent of the railroad came Uncle Sam's entry into World War I. With that development, Gold Hill's previously idle deposits of tungsten and arsenic came to transcend even her gold in value.

Of several tungsten properties in the district, the most spectacular was Reaper No. 3, owned by the Seminole Copper company. The Reaper was fabulously rich, some of its scheelite carrying as much as 78 per cent tungsten. From a glory-hole 45 feet long, 50 feet deep, and nowhere more than 15 feet wide, more than $80,000 worth of scheelite was reportedly mined during 1917.

With railroad rates based on "per ton" value, it proved virtually prohibitive to move this highgrade tungsten by freight, a circumstance that led to the Reaper's unique practice of shipping its ore to Salt Lake City by *parcel post!* Packaged in small quantities to comply with postal weight limits, tons of the concentrates began pouring through the Gold Hill postoffice. Mail stages were swamped, financial ruin faced the contract carrier, and postal facilities at both ends of the line were strained to the breaking point. But the mail—and the Reaper's scheelite—still went through.

Strangely enough, it was arsenic that fathered the two greatest booms in the history of the district.

Throughout World War I, and for half a dozen years following its close, the great arsenic mines of Gold Hill poured forth their lethal treasure—much of which was channeled to the Southern states for combatting the cotton boll weevil. In 1923, one mine in the district was

---

*Salt Lake Tribune, December 30, 1917.

estimated to hold a reserve of 250,000 tons of ore averaging 20 per cent arsenic, and years of Grade A prosperity loomed ahead.

Less than 12 months later the arsenic market collapsed, and with it collapsed Gold Hill.

Plans for extending the Deep Creek railroad to Nevada and California had been abandoned, long before; and in 1938, the last train clattered over the line. In 1940, all miners remaining in the district recovered but a single ounce of gold, and there seemed no doubt but that Gold Hill was gasping her last.

And then came World War II—and, once again, a beleaguered nation was crying for the old town's tungsten and arsenic!

Uncle Sam stepped in. Things began to hum. Mines closed for 20 years were returned to production. Electric lights appeared on the streets of Gold Hill. Old buildings were reconditioned and equipped as barracks for workers. Four new apartment houses were built and soon were filled to overflowing with miners and their families. Long-closed business houses reopened. The poolhall and bowling alley were thronged with men; shouting youngsters packed the schoolyard, and music and hilarity again sounded in the streets on Saturday nights.

But suddenly as it had begun, it was all over.

In January, 1945, the Gold Hill mine—the district's chief producer of arsenic—was ordered to halt production. In the 16 months it had operated during World War II, it had yielded 98,784 tons of ore running from 18 to 30 per cent arsenic.*

And that was all the arsenic Uncle Sam needed . . .

The flames of a prairie fire could not have emptied the town more rapidly. Released miners sped to new jobs. Business houses closed their briefly-opened doors. The four new government apartment houses were yanked from their foundations and moved to other sites where men still had need for places to live. With close of the 1946 term, the district lost its school; in 1949, its postoffice.

With sacrifice of these last remaining symbols of urbanity, the old mining camp in the Deep Creek range gave up its long struggle to repel the hovering ghosts.

To the west of Leatha's cabin stood the ruins of Colonel Woodman's old mill. The machinery—originally imported from France at great cost—had been long before removed to another site; but the rock foundation and backwall, and two adobe-and-stone charcoal kilns, still remained as evidence of past activity.

In the desert hills, half a mile from town, gaped the open stopes of the original Cane Springs and Alvarado mines; and down the wash to the north stood the silent headframe of The Rube.

Even those who labeled him a "queer duck" and made cracks about

---

*Matthews, Allan F., and Bryson, R. Louise: Minerals Yearbook, 1945.

"missing marbles" were obliged to admit that Loeffler Palmer's mine was a very satisfactory substitute for the United States mint.

In 1920, after half a lifetime of fruitless prospecting, Palmer had staked this claim a couple of miles below Gold Hill. He had named it The Rube, and had worked it as a one-man operation, each year taking out a single carload of ore, for which he received around $6000 or $7000.

And then, instead of mining another carload, or, better still, forming a $10,000,000 stock corporation and mining thousands of carloads, Palmer would take his paltry six or seven grand and retire until the next summer; and not until then would he do another lick of work!

All of which was why folks made the comments about "missing marbles."

Palmer's one-man mine was too good a story to escape notice. From Gold Hill the tale spread to Salt Lake newspapers, and eventually to mining journals; and, by and by, the world was making a beaten path to his door.

Despite floods of attractive offers, Palmer consistently refused to sell The Rube. Gold stored in Mother Nature's bosom, he averred, was safer than in a national bank; and by removing only as much as he needed, each year, he always would be assured a living.

But a group of California capitalists began eyeing the property and making fantastic offers. As each offer was refused, they would go a little higher; and Palmer eventually weakened and sold. His ownership of The Rube had extended over a long period of years, during which time he had taken out around $112,000.* With proceeds from sale of the mine, he retired to the Coast, bought a fine country estate, and presumably dedicated the remainder of his life to clipping coupons and growing daffodils.

And now, for a quick backward glance at The Rube.

Upon acquiring title to the mine, the new owners did exactly what everyone always had said Loeffler Palmer should do.

They took steps to develop it. By installing great quantities of costly mining equipment, they paved the way to operate on a colossal scale and thereby reap millions where the mine's former owner had been satisfied with peanuts.

It was then folks began wondering if they could have been wrong about the "missing marbles."

Almost before the colossal new wheels started turning, Palmer's vein pinched out.

And that was the end of The Rube.

Salt Lake Tribune, December 20, 1936.

31

De Lamar Was a Widow Maker

THE DAY WAS A SCORCHER.

Since early morning July's brassy sun had beaten a fierce tattoo on that world of grim playas and burned mountains, and sinuous dust augers that slithered across the land like Balinese dancers. But for those writhing columns no movement was visible—not one fluttering leaf, or one soaring hawk. Even the hoary Joshua trees seemed gripped in a strange, hypnotic spell.

My road, drawing nearer the foothills, shriveled to a single track, sandy and rocky by turns and crowded upon by desert brush. An old cemetery moved into view. Granite slabs and wooden headboards and half a century of neglect—all enclosed within three looping strands of barbed wire.

Passing between the graveyard and "Old Man" Nelson's toll station —now, nearly 50 years abandoned—the rutted turnpike continued on up the mountain.

Coasting my car to a stop at the summit of the grade, I ranged my eyes over the desert empire stretching away on every side. It was a harsh, hard land. Beyond the wide flatness of DeLamar Valley and the Pahranagat lifted tier upon tier of parched mountains—the Pahrocks, the Pintwaters, the Hikos—treeless, waterless, hopeless realms, as gaunt and forbidding as the gates of hell.

How early desert prospectors could have known the courage to probe these satanic strongholds—gambling their lives on the meager store of water they might pack on the backs of their burros—was impossible to comprehend. Yet, every wild canyon in those wild ranges had known the footsteps of bearded Argonauts. They had laced the earth with their tunnels and pierced it with their shafts. They had come and gone; and, behind them, they had left one enduring memento of their passage—the skeleton of a city that had ceased to be!

Looking down on that city from the top of the grade, I saw a sepulchre of deserted streets bordered by hollow shells of brick and stone. It was a place of broken roofs, of vacant foundations and cold chimneys; and in all those silent halls there was not one curtain to add grace to a window. Not one laughing child or barking puppy played in those yards, not one green tree spread its shade upon the ground.

This was DeLamar, 50 years before the greatest gold producer in Nevada.

This was DeLamar—City of the Dead.

Close under the road, at the head of the grade loomed the dark frame of the old mill; and down in the ravine below, lay a mountainous heap of white tailings. Something about those tailings had seemed unusual from the first I had glimpsed them. Now, it came to me—it was the dust. No breeze was stirring on that hot afternoon. The sullen air lay upon the land like a smothering blanket, and even the creosote boughs hung strangely limp and lifeless; yet, from that tailing dump was rising a fantastic spiral, as white as sea-fog!

Strangely fascinated, I watched as that dust column mounted into the sky—mounted, and mushroomed, and disappeared. Again, it would hover low along the face of the dump; or, like an ominous smoke pall, would drift restlessly over the valley below.

This was no ordinary dust—not the clean, earthy dust the winter wind whips across the desert.

This was "Devil Dust"—the man-killer, the maker of widows—the Death Dust of DeLamar!

Old timers, such as Frank and Vilate Pace, of Caliente, had told me of the camp's early years, when its ore had been worked in a barrel chlorination plant, and had passed dry through a coarse crusher to Griffin mills. As DeLamar's pay-streak had lain in Cambrian quartzite, more than 80 per cent silica, the volume of dust produced by this method of handling had been terrific; the mortality rate, tragic.

Bulk of the work in DeLamar's mines and mills had been performed by raw farm boys lured from the Mormon settlements of Southwestern Utah by the prospect of "high wages"—$3 a day. They had never heard of silicosis, those strapping lads; but "miner's con" doesn't wait for a formal introduction.

Three or four months in the DeLamar mill and the boys would be coughing. Only a little hacking cough, at first—"nothing serious." Another month and the attacks would be occurring more frequently, and lasting longer; and, finally, the days and nights and noons would be merged in a single, red hell of wracking pain.

The fortunate died quickly. The others clung to life with grim persistence—empty husks, too far gone to work, too stubborn to die.

Frank Pace had been luckier than most. He had emigrated to DeLamar from St. George, Utah, in 1900; had obtained work at the Whitehead & Miles general store. Frank remembered the "Death Dust"; the sound of coughing in the night, the funerals, the widows.

"Unless a man saw it himself, it's impossible to imagine what it was like when the mines and mills were operating!" Frank had said. The air, he declared, was so impregnated with powdered silica that even women and children who never went near the mines succumbed to the dread silicosis; even horses eventually died from effects of the dust.

Little wonder men called that camp, "The Maker of Widows."

The original strike at DeLamar was made in 1892. Shortly afterward, several of the leading claims were purchased for $150,000 by Capt. John De La Mar—a prominent mining promoter of that day—and when a new town was laid out, it was given an Americanized version of the captain's French name.

DeLamar grew rapidly. Most of her original settlers and merchants moved there from Pioche—which was then experiencing a slump—and many of her first buildings were brought there intact from the older town. Threat of disaster is little deterrent where gold is the goad, and even the "Death Dust" did not keep DeLamar from being a lively place where liquor and money flowed freely and men lived fast.

What is probably the most authentic picture of contemporary life in this Lincoln county boomcamp is that presented in the pages of the DeLamar *Weekly Lode,* a nearly-complete file of which is preserved in the archives of the county recorder's office, at Pioche.

The Lode's purpose, as set forth at the head of its editorial column, involved devotion to "Free Coinage, Progress, Politics, Society, Mining and News." It might be worthy of mention that the publication also was devoted to Capt. John De La Mar.

In the issue of March 7, 1899, we find that the Palmer House— "DeLamar's Finest"—was offering First Class Meals, three for one dollar, or board at $25 per month. Other advertisements offered the wares of various general mercantiles, drug and hardware stores, jewelry and millinery shops, and sundry saloons and cafes, as well as the professional services of a dentist, a lawyer, several midwives, and a stock brokerage office operated by Senator J. A. Clark.

The Oddfellows and Masons already had active lodges, and a Knights of Pythias chapter would be organized later. The Hebhurn Opera Company was playing an engagement at the $10,000 Max Schaefer Grand Opera House, then the most elegant theatre in Southern Nevada; the gun club was having regular shoots every Sunday afternoon, an orchestra was available for dances or other festive occasions, and the DeLamar Brass Band was presenting weekly concerts.

Also serving the temporal and spiritual needs of the community, were a hospital, a school, and two churches—Protestant and Catholic.

("If we do our duty during the week, at home, and go to church on Sunday," read one church notice in *The Lode,* "we shall all be happy— even in DeLamar.")

The town's greatest deficiency was water. After it was piped over the range from Meadow Valley, it was still necessary that it be hauled from the end of the pipeline to each home at a consumer cost of 50 cents a barrel. As a result of this lack, the threat of fire forever hung over the town like the sword of Damocles. Small blazes were of frequent occurrence, and the camp lived in terror of the day when such a blaze should coincide with a hard wind.

The axe fell on the afternoon of May 29, 1900. The air had been hot and dry for weeks, the town was like tinder. Moments after the fire was discovered in a lean-to on Edwards saloon, the flames had spread to buildings on either side, and everyone knew that the camp was doomed.

One of the first major structures to go down was the splendid Schaefer Grand. Sweeping on through main street, the fire devoured every building in its path, and by supper time the entire flat was a rolling sea of flame and smoke.

John Roeder's big mercantile at the upper end of main street, was well-built, with thick rock walls. It had been considered "fireproof," and the more hopeful were counting upon it to check the progress of the fire; but with the terrific heat surrounding it on every side, the interior of the store suddenly was rocked as if by an explosion, and the entire structure burst into flames.

By blasting buildings in the path of the blaze, the roaring inferno eventually was brought under control, but not before most of the business section lay in ruin and many persons had been left homeless. Armed guards patrolled the streets throughout the night, and the De La Mar company, according to *The Lode,* "added five extra incandescent lamps on each pole for the more complete lighting of main street as a precaution against lawless citizenry and marauders."

Like an evil genii released from its imprisoning bottle, there arose from the ruins an ugly and persistent rumor.

The De La Mar company, it was whispered, had diverted the town's supply of water in order to assure better pressure for protecting the company's woodyard. It further was claimed that when the fire department tried to telephone for more water, the call could not be put through because the telephone wire had been cut.

Rising to the defense of Capt. De La Mar, the editor of *The Lode* angrily refuted these rumors and rebuked his fellow citizens for harboring such wicked suspicions.

"It was reported that the company turned the water off the town and this prevented the stopping of the fire where it started," stated *The Lode,* on June 12, 1900. "The fact is that every pound of water the company had was turned on the town pumps all the time . . . As for keeping their men at work protecting the wood yard . . . only six men were kept there who were absolutely indispensible."

The newspaper further pointed out that as soon as Capt. De La Mar learned of the fire he had cabled his local agents, Mr. Cohen and Mr. Swindler, to see that everyone who had lost by the fire was taken care of, and that, above all, "there must be no suffering allowed."

DeLamar was "down," but it did not necessarily follow that she was "out," since frontier mining camps were possessed of amazing resilience. Work of rebuilding the town was under way before the embers had cooled, and by 1901 the camp was largely restored to its former glory. During this same period of reconstruction, it had gained recognition as the leading gold producer in Nevada. Handling around 400 tons of ore daily, the De La Mar mill each month was turning out from $100,000 to $200,000 in bullion. The April Fool mill also was operating, and around 400 men were employed in the mines.

But the feast was too good to last; the famine was nearing. Before the new century was two years old, the DeLamar mines were beginning to curtail operations. Many of the released miners joined the stampede to Tonopah. Another year, and the exodus would be channeled toward Goldfield.

As the mines failed, DeLamar's business district shriveled; but even with its advertising lineage dropping steadily, *The Lode* remained faithful to its trust. On January 23, 1906, it still found the courage to declare stoutly: "The day is not far distant when DeLamar will be the greatest gold producing camp in the world!"

It was the cry of Job's comforter. It was the small boy whistling in the graveyard.

Less than five months later, *The Lode* suspended publication. The editor announced he was moving to Caliente and would establish a newspaper there. The future of Caliente, he believed, "held more promise" than that of DeLamar. By this time there were many who believed that the future of almost anywhere held more "promise" than did that of De-Lamar; and when the machinery in the great mill ground to a stop on September 1, 1909, only a handful of residents remained in the town.

In her 16 years of life, DeLamar had added to the wealth of the nation some $25,000,000* in gold and silver. And now, as the final shift streamed off duty, the mill whistle was tied down and permitted to scream 'til the last spark of power was exhausted.

DeLamar was through. The chips were down.

During the four decades following, several of the old mines were reopened briefly, and the old mill tailings were re-worked with fair success. But the camp never returned to life.

Last surviving resident of the town was Mrs. Agnes Horn, an elderly widow, who styled herself. "Mayor of DeLamar." Living alone in the little board cabin she had occupied with her husband back in the boom days, Mrs. Horn dedicated her declining years to the task of maintaining life in half-a-dozen fruit trees, a handful of currant bushes, and a tiny

---

*G. W. Miller, "The DeLamar Mines of Lincoln County, Nevada." Mining Science 58 (1908) 347-8.

vegetable garden. In all the ghostly ruin that once had been a prosperous city, her yard was the only spot of green remaining.

With Mrs. Horn's death, about the time of World War II, she was laid beside her family in the lonely old cemetery west of town. Soon afterward, her little cabin was moved to the kaolin plant, near Las Vegas; and now, even the trees and garden she cherished have died for lack of care and water.

"What about the treasure that's supposed to be buried at DeLamar?" I once asked Frank Pace, as we stood on the summit of the grade looking down on the old town and the restless tailings.

"Treasure?" inquired Frank innocently. "What treasure?"

"Why, old 'Squinty' Thomas, up at the Jackrabbit mine, mentioned something about it," I went on. "He said one of the mine officials, back in the early days, had connived with an assayer and they had highgraded a lot of company bullion—$70,000 worth, I think he said. This official had buried the loot; and then, presumably, had died before he could repossess it and make his getaway. Something of that sort . . ."

"Yeah . . ." Frank nodded, slowly. "Something like that.

"Folks have been telling various versions of that tale for almost 50 years," he continued. "Hundreds of men have hunted for the bullion. They've combed this whole area with doodlebugs and metal detectors, and every fool gadget under the sun. They've dug up horseshoes and old buckets and railroad spikes . . . but, so far as I know, the gold is still lost.

"One old man swore he helped bury the loot and could go back to the exact spot. Several times I almost had him 'mellowed up' to the point of showing me the place . . . but he never quite did it. And now," said Frank, "he's dead, too . . ."

Pausing, the old desert miner let his gaze travel over the bleak ruins of the mill, and on toward the Southwest, where mountain-hemmed flats were welling with the purple haze of evening.

"Y'know," he continued, almost as if thinking aloud, "that ol' codger dropped some powerful strong hints. I've always had a sneakin' idea I know just about where that bullion's cached! Some day, when it's a little cooler—" a slow smile crept over the man's weathered face and puckered the skin at the corner of his eyes—"Some day, I figure I'll mosey back up here and do a little prospectin' on my own!"

32

Iosepa, The Forlorn Hope

A S THE NUCLEUS of an agricultural colony the town of Iosepa was not destined for fame.

As an example of man's courage, it must stand forever unchallenged.

That native Hawaiian Islanders should forsake the green glory of their homeland for the barrenness of Utah's Skull Valley seems beyond all reason, and only by probing far back into the past does that circumstance become partially understandable.

Since early in the 19th century, the South Sea Islands had been a fertile field for religious workers of several denominations. Even as early as 1844 the Church of Jesus Christ of Latter Day Saints had sent missionaries to carry the gospel and suitable garments to Hawaii, and several thousand Islanders were converted to the Mormon faith.

Much as the devout Mohammedan feels drawn toward Mecca, so 50 of these converts eventually expressed a yearning to visit Salt Lake City, world center of their newly adopted creed.

Arrived in the new land, they were received royally by Church leaders. They were accorded the rites of the temple and entertained lavishly, and every day their eyes beheld sights more wondrous than ever were looked upon before by any of their people. But like riding on a perpetual merry-go-round, the excitement of this urban whirl soon palled on the simple Islanders. If they were to remain in this strange country, they declared, they must have a colony site of their own—preferably a tract of farming land, such as the fertile, productive valleys, they had been shown in the vicinity of Salt Lake City.

To Church authorities, the Islanders' ultimatum came at a most inopportune time. Utah's arable acres had been none too plentiful, even in the beginning; and now, after 40 years of colonization, nearly every foot of ground capable of producing crops was being farmed to the limit.

In this circumstance, alone, lies the only possible extenuation for the site ultimately selected.

In Skull Valley—a long, dry, semi-barren expanse near the eastern fringe of Salt Desert—the Church purchased 960 acres of land. At a point 50 miles west of Salt Lake City and 20 miles south of Great Salt Lake, a townsite was platted and named for the Saints' major prophet,

Joseph Smith. Here were built a few houses, a store, a combination school-house and church. And because the Hawaiian tongue has no sound of "J," the town's name was necessarily compromised as "Iosepa." Compared to all the compromises stretching ahead, this was a minor concession.

What qualms must have assailed those gentle Islanders as they gazed upon the land allotted them for a home! For countless generations their race had known only the luxuriant beauty of a carefree South Sea paradise; a place where surf sparkled on white coral strands, where wild fruits could be had for the gathering and fish for the catching, where midnight was as warm as noon and winter never came at all.

And now—Skull Valley.

But for a few stunted junipers on the desert hill to the east, there was not a tree or shrub as far as the eye might range. In summer the heat of the Salt Desert would beat mercilessly upon them, and the icy grip of snow-laden winds would assail them in winter. Here were no fish, no fruit, no gleaming surf; here were no gay tropic blossoms an island maid might tuck in her hair.

Only men of magnificent heart and deep religious faith could have had the courage to take up the cross of Iosepa. . .

A city water system was installed. A small stream in the Stansbury mountains was channeled to the site for purpose of irrigation; a few natural springs were developed for the use of cattle. Streets were graded and flanking rows of poplars and cottonwoods set to shade them. And in lieu of hyacinths to feed the soul, every sidewalk was edged with the old-fashioned yellow roses originally brought West in the covered wagons of pioneer homemakers.

Time passed. Babies were born. Old men died. Crops were good and bad, by turns, as the Lord willed. During the colony's best year its farmers sold more than $20,000 worth of hay, grain and cattle. Other years found scarcely enough food in the fields to keep starvation from Colony doors.

As soon as Iosepa was fairly well established, additional Kanakas were brought from the Islands. Only in this way could the colony show a growth, for those who peopled it were not adapted constitutionally to the unremitting labor demanded of men who would conquer the desert; neither were their systems capable of adjusting to the violent climatic changes of Skull Valley.

Sickness and death was the payoff. The cemetery at the foot of the brown hills, a mile east of town, soon held lengthening rows of neat bare mounds, guarded by paling fences and wooden markers.

Darkest of Iosepa's dark days came in the middle 1890s when it was discovered that the dreaded scourge of leprosy had followed its people, even to this far new land. Seeking relief and cure, the first Kanakas to become afflicted had covered their bodies with black mud from a warm mineralized seep below town. But warm mud is no combatant for a malady that has haunted mankind for more than 1000 known generations of time.

Iosepa, eventually, took the old way out. The afflicted were removed to a building well separated from the main colony and there were confined in isolation until merciful Death released their tortured souls.

With the cemetery growing faster than the town, and the flat dry bosom of Skull Valley remaining as inhospitable as in the beginning, it is little wonder that the Islanders at last lost heart. A few of the younger ones strayed away to Salt Lake City and the mining camps in search of employment; and in 1916, with completion of the LDS temple in Hawaii, a majority of those remaining returned to their native land.

Iosepa, the Forlorn Hope, was deeded back to the desert winds and desolation.

Fifty miles west of Salt Lake City, a road turns south from Timpie Junction. Although improved and partially religned, this is the Route of the Pioneers. Through this same high, wide valley cradled between the Cedar and Stansbury ranges, passed Jedediah Smith, in 1827—first white man to cross Great Salt Desert. Eighteen years later, across the north end of that valley, strode John Charles Fremont, "The Pathfinder;" next year following brought the Bryant-Russell party, and the overloaded wagons of the doomed Donners; and another three years found Skull Valley echoing to the shouts of California-bound gold seekers. Still later, across the south tip of the valley had pounded the wheels of Overland stages, and hooves of the Pony Express; and eventually, through here would creep the Lincoln Highway, and cars with boiling radiators and thin tires.

But all this belongs to the distant past. The road of the pioneers— the road that leads south from Timpie—is traveled today by only a few ranchers, and now and then by some history-probing pilgrim with an affinity for ghosttowns and gone days.

The arid brown slope where Iosepa once stood is now included in the vast holdings of Deseret Livestock company. Many of Iosepa's original buildings were moved away; others were razed and their materials used in construction work at the ranch headquarters, nearby. Only one building, square and starkly plain, was still standing when I last saw the town, in 1952. From a high standard at its front hung an old bronze bell.

Elsewhere over the townsite were caving cellars and crumbling foundations almost without end. With abandonment of the colony the cottonwood and poplar trees planted along its streets had gradually succumbed for lack of water. In time they had been felled for wood and fenceposts; but still their ghostly stumps remained, like accusing fingers upthrust from the dry earth. Lost in the smothering sage and cheat grass were neatly-laid flagstone walks that led to non-existent houses; and the entire length of main street could be traced by a line of heavy fire hydrants, shorn of both the water that fed them and the town they served.

Like leaves scattered by November's wind lay mute reminders of those who once had called this place home. Desert brush had grown through the frame of a little writing desk with delicately-milled legs. Fragments of glass, turned purple by the desert sun, lay strewn upon stone-encircled mounds that once were flower beds. Elsewhere lay twisted horseshoes, old wagon wheels, a hand-forged shovel, a walking plow, the broken head of a tiny, China doll. . .

Most poignant of all were the old roses. Displaying the dogged tenacity of their kind, they had continued to thrive through drought and cold and heat. With neither pruning knife to shape their destinies, or human hand to guide them, they had spread to form impenetrable thickets, their thorny hands stoutly interlocked as though to repel the ghosts. Untended and unloved for nearly 40 years, they still greeted the desert summer with a courageous smile and a shower of golden bloom.

Not for many, many years had a man been buried in Iosepa's cemetery. The paling fences that once enclosed the grave plots were largely fallen; and from every wooden headboard the inscriptions had been scored clean by abrasive action of wind and sand and storm. Of all those buried here, I found only six markers that might still be identified with their proper owners. On these the chiseled names and words were in the strange tongue of Polynesia—soft, vowel-lightened words, that read like summer surf breaking on the strand at Waikiki. (Plate 18)

Enclosing one grave was an iron grill fence. This, together with the white marble tombstone, seemed to stamp its owner a person of greater than average importance and affluence. Under a bas-relief of clasped hands, I made out the wording:

J. W. KAULEINAMOKU

Hanau ma ka la

27 Oct. 1837, ma Hilo, Hawaii.

Make ma Iosepa,

Skull Valley, Utah

Julai 21, 1899.

Who he was, what his young dreams may have been, and why, among all those legions buried here, he should have been honored with the most impressive tombstone and the only iron fence, is only another lost fragment in the story of Iosepa, the forlorn hope of Skull Valley.

33

Queen City of Bonanza Road

WAILING ACROSS THE desert of the Amargosa, the night wind draws mournful music from a thousand greasewood lyres . . . and thin gray ghosts keep rendezvous on Golden Street.

Up from the nameless graves at the foot of Ladd mountain, down from the dim vagueness of the canyons, the shadows come dancing. Frolicking, rollicking, roistering, they whirl over the empty streets and silent ruins, on to a spectral world of gayety and glitter.

Ah, but where is that gayety? Where that glitter? The jeweled gowns, the sparkling cafes, the Nirvana of golden dreams . . . Where is it all?

As well you might seek the smoke of Yesterday's campfire!

The gray lizard lies cold and unblinking in the crumbled halls where Bacchus reigned. The packrat prowls where silver slippers tripped; and champagne bottles—like man's starry hope—lie shattered in the dust.

A silent street, a lonely wind; a song without music, a drama without players . . . This, sir, is the Queen City of Bonanza Road!

This is Rhyolite . . .

Rhyolite had her birth in that era when "the late war" was the Spanish American, and the Big Names in the mining world were Tonopah and Goldfield. Search for Jake Breyfogle's missing gold and the Lost Gunsight silver lode had been drawing men into the wild ranges at the head of Death Valley for nearly 50 years, but few of those treasure-seeking pilgrims had given more than cursory glance toward a group of nameless knobs on the north rim of the Amargosa desert. Yet, there had been lying in those hills since Time's beginning a piece of gold float that was slated to make history.

Destiny was saving that piece of float for a kid from Iowa—a kid named Eddie Cross.

Eddie, still in his 20s, had wandered west to Utah and there had teamed up with that inveterate desert roamer, "Shorty" Harris. Time, the wanderlust, and five burros ultimately brought the pair to Southern Nevada; and a sizzling day in the summer of 1904 sent them trailing through the rough hills fringing the Amargosa.

And there, Eddie found his float—just as Destiny intended he should!

Eddie didn't know beans about ore, but the sample had a strange appearance. He decided to show it to his partner, who had slumped down on a rock and was fanning himself with his battered hat.

One glimpse, and the old desert rat let out a whoop and sprang to his feet, his eyes bulging, his horny hands a-tremble.

"Hell-fire, Eddie!" he shouted. "We've struck the richest jackpot this side of the Klondyke!"*

The old man's estimate was not far wrong. If it wasn't the richest jackpot south of the Klondyke, at least it was a jackpot men would parlay into one of the greatest promotional extravaganzas in the history of mining!

Because the ore sample found by Eddie was roughly frog-shaped and greenish in color, the partners dubbed their potential mine The Bullfrog, and headed for Goldfield, 75 miles away, to record their claims.

Shorty—like many old-time prospectors—seldom was reticent about his strikes. Before the partners had been in town half a day, even the swampers on the freight wagons knew about "Shorty's discovery" down on the Amargosa. Everyone wanted to hear about it. Shorty wanted to tell about it. The tarantula p'isen flowed, elbows were bent—and the sharpsters gathered 'round.

Before removing his aching head from the bright lights of Esmeralda's metropolis, Shorty had sold and gambled away his half interest in the mine.

All he had to show for the transaction were $500 and a mean-faced mule. But, what the hell! The old desert rat shrugged. Never could tell about a mule. Might be a purty fair jackass, at that! The Short Man always could use another jack.

Unfortunately, no mule was worth what that mule cost Shorty.

Only a few months later, the Bullfrog Mine would be listed on the San Francisco Exchange at $200,000. . .

The new Bullfrog bonanza was situated 75 miles south of Goldfield and 120 miles north of McWilliamstown—which place soon would be much better known as Las Vegas. In the 200 mile splash of desert separating those points lived virtually no man, Indian or white. It was a land grown to spindly joshua trees and creosote brush, and broken by rough volcanic ranges and sterile flats; a land where the best trails were dim and uncertain, where July temperatures soared to 130 degrees in the shade, and water was non-existent save in a few widely-separated springs. And now, this wilderness was about to be shaken by a major gold rush!

Eddie's and Shorty's discovery had been made on the torrid afternoon of August 9, 1904. Before close of that year, boomers were converging upon the new strike from every side—south from Tonopah and Goldfield, east out of Death Valley, north from the settlements along the Colorado River. They were coming by nearly every mode of land transportation known to the West; by horseback and burro-back and afoot, by surreys

---

*Lewis, Lucien M., personal interview with Eddie Cross; *Desert Magazine,* Dec. 1946.

and democrat wagons and mule teams, by stagecoach and freight wagons. Yes, even by automobiles . . . rugged old Pope-Toledos and Desert Flyers, and Fords with carbide lamps and brass trimmings.

Passage to the new bonanza from Goldfield was priced at $18 by horse-drawn Concord, $25 by auto, while freight from McWilliamstown (Las Vegas) cost six to ten cents a pound, and a full week was required for the jolting journey. Despite this factor of isolation, a rash of towns soon appeared in the shadow of the discovery—Bonanza, at the south end of Ladd mountain; Orion, to the east; and spang in the middle of the excitement, rose The City of the Bullfrog.

Bullfrog—where the winter of 1904 found 1000 boomers shivering in drafty tent houses and earthen-floored stone cabins and dugouts; 1000 men and women stripping the surrounding hills of their thorny desert brush to be burned in cookstoves or open campfires; 1000 men and women paying from $2 to $5 a barrel for water hauled from the brackish Amargosa river, three miles distant.*

But all this was slated to change—and soon.

On the cold, gusty day of January 18, 1905, with Bullfrog and her sister boomcamps still less than six months old, an Opportunist pitched his tent at the edge of the hills a mile up the wash from Bonanza. Looking over the desert emptiness about him, Pete Busch sensed that here on this slope—and not in the valley below—was the place where a city should rise; and he knew, further, that he was the lad who could start that city to building.

Next morning found Pete and his burro plodding up the rocky trail toward Tonopah, 100 miles to the north. Pete was headed for Tonopah because he had "connections" there where he might borrow the $300 needed for platting his new city of Rhyolite, named for the granite-hard igneous rock of which these desert mountains were composed.

As he scuffed along the trail on that midwinter day in 1905, Pete made plans for his new city.

It would be a city of dignity and decorum, a credit to the state. Unlike Bullfrog and Bonanza, it would not be fabricated of adobe and canvas, but of cement and stone, and brick. It would have fine schools and churches, an elegant opera house and sumptious hotels and cafes— places where gentlemen and their ladies might assemble without rubbing shoulders with the unwashed masses.

Rhyolite, in short, would be everything Bullfrog and Bonanza were not.

Operating under the firm name, Busch Brothers, Pete and his brother, Ed, were about to father a city whose name would echo around the world!

Never did a miracle spring into life with more enthusiasm and zeal!

In February, 1905, Rhyolite's main thoroughfare—Golden Street— was only a bold mark on an engineer's map and a series of stakes set in parallel lines across a desert slope. Less than one year later, those stakes

---

Rhyolite Herald, Special Pictorial Supplement, March, 1909.

had been replaced by a wide, smooth street pulsing with traffic, and flanked on either side by substantial buildings two and three stories in height!

Neither were residents of the district any longer domiciled in drafty tents or forced to depend on the bitter water of the Amargosa river. On June 26, 1905, the first piped water had been brought to Rhyolite through lines of the Indian Springs Water Company. Arising in natural rock springs, five miles north of town, the water traveled to its destination by gravity, in a flow assertedly adequate to supply "a town of 10,000 persons, and a 20-stamp mill."*

Six weeks after service had been instituted by the Indian Springs company, residents of Rhyolite and Bullfrog had waited with candles, lanterns and bated breath for the after midnight arrival in town of the first water to flow through the extensive system of still another company —the Bullfrog Water Company. Piped from Goss Springs, a dozen miles up the Oasis Valley from Rhyolite, this system had instituted service with a daily capacity of 200,000 gallons, and claimed its springs could be developed to produce double that amount. Third company to enter the business of supplying water to the embryo metropolis was Bullfrog Water, Light and Power, whose source of supply consisted of 13 springs flowing an aggregate of 1,000,000 gallons daily.

From a place so devoid of water that a man might have sold his soul for a glass of it, Rhyolite, in less than one year's time was being served by three separate systems having a capacity so completely adequate that water stood in the city's fire hydrants at 70 pounds pressure!*

In addition to development of water and power, this same first year saw progress sweeping triumphantly through every street, every place of business. Enveloping the town was a tingling of surcharged energy so potent it prickled the skin. Wherever man turned he witnessed the birth pangs of a new world, wherein all facets of community life were developing independently, but simultaneously, and all were driving headlong toward a perfect culmination of the City Ideal.

Rhyolite's civic progress, in many cases, did not emerge full-winged, like a moth from its chrysalis, but was attained through a series of steps, each representing some slight improvement over the one before.

First mail addressed to camps in the Bullfrog district was carried by rail to Goldfield, thence by Kitchen's Stage to Amargosa, four miles from Rhyolite, where Len McGarry's store did double duty as postoffice. Whenever the "boys from Bullfrog" had a bit of leisure time, they would amble across the hills to McGarry's, sort through the packing box in which

---

*Bullfrog Miner, Dec. 21, 1907.

the Bullfrog-Rhyolite mail was kept, remove any letters addressed to themselves, and leave the remainder for the next comer.

This system of mail delivery was followed until the middle of February, 1905, when Bill Parker opened a grocery store at Rhyolite and the ex-officio "postoffice" was moved nearer home. With arrival of the stage, Bill would mount a box and call the names on incoming letters until he grew tired or dry, whereupon some volunteer would take over and finish the job. Due to the fact that this extra-curricular mail service was not authorized by Uncle Sam, it was necessary that the town make up freewill offerings to pay the stage company for carrying the Rhyolite mail to and from Goldfield. Such collections never amount to less than $50 a week. Patrons wishing to post or receive registered mail were obliged to go to Beatty, the nearest official postoffice.

In March, 1905, petition for a postoffice at Rhyolite was forwarded to the Postmaster General by J. C. Lynch, manager of Amargosa Trading Co. The application was approved, Mrs. Anna B. Moore was appointed postmaster; and on June 10, that year, Rhyolite's postoffice opened officially in a 10-by-12-foot tent. No boxes or sorting cases were available; nor could any be procured immediately, due to the fact that incoming stages and freight wagons were loaded to capacity with higher-priority goods such as lumber, hardware, food, and drinkables. Mail distribution in the new office, as a consequence, offered but little improvement over the system previously followed at Parker's store. Upon arrival of the stage—often as late as 10 o'clock at night—the postmaster would open the mail bags and begin calling the names on the letters, a ceremony which frequently dragged on until after midnight.

In view of these primitive beginnings, it was considered a great step forward when Postmistress Moore received a shipment of 200 lock boxes ordered two months earlier from San Francisco. Freight charges on the shipment (from Las Vegas to Rhyolite, only) were 11 cents a pound, and 18 days were required for transporting the boxes over this last 120-mile leg of the journey.

And when the boxes at last made their appearance, it was found that the existing postoffice was entirely too small to accommodate them— the boxes taking up virtually the entire floor space and leaving no room for the postal crew! Rallying to the emergency, enterprising citizens hastily moved the postoffice to a larger tent, whereupon the 200 boxes were set in place and made available for rental. Long before nightfall every box had been engaged, and patrons who had failed to obtain one were offering fancy inducements and bonuses for "transfers."

Within a few weeks time the postoffice had outgrown its second tent, whereupon citizens again came to the rescue and subscribed sufficient funds to erect a frame building which was presented to the postmistress, rent free. Summer of 1906 found even this building outgrown. Due also to the phenomenal growth of the camp—something the officials in Washington couldn't seem to understand—the postmistress was out of stamps and supplies a good share of the time and was forced to supplement her stock by requisitioning extras from the postoffice at Goldfield.

From an office of the fourth class, Rhyolite climbed to third, and to second class; and by March, 1907, this office that had not even existed two years before, was rated officially the seventh-largest postoffice in the State of Nevada!

Schools were another matter smitten by growing pains. With Rhyolite only three weeks old and its population still limited to 45 adults and five children, a mass meeting had been called to consider the general welfare. Among problems discussed was the need for school facilities and a committee of three, with Walter Smith as its secretary, was appointed to "investigate." Soon afterward, when in San Francisco on other business, Mr. Smith took it upon himself to purchase $400 worth of school supplies, including desks, blackboards, a flag, bell, et cetera. The material—shipped C.O.D.—arrived at Rhyolite before a school district had been organized there, and before any funds were available to pay for either the supplies or their freight charges. Rather than permit the goods to escape to some other camp, Judge L. O. Ray, Ed Busch, and several other public-spirited citizens, signed personal notes to cover their cost. One of three members comprising the first board of trustees of the Rhyolite school district was "The Grand Old Man of Nevada," ex-Senator William Stewart, an 80-year-old pillar of Comstock days, who had come to this raw, new camp to open a law office.

A school house was erected at a cost of $1000, and, again, personal notes were given to cover the expenditure. By the time this house of learning was ready for occupancy, the town's original five children had increased to 20 and end of the first month found that number zoomed to 40! Long before close of the term, the school enrollment had climbed to 100 pupils and the county school tax allotment (based on the opening enrollment of 20 pupils) had disappeared like a snowflake in the hot place.

With funds to keep the school in operation during that first term acquired largely through public subscription, arrival of vacation time found the new district with a deficit of considerable proportions. As a means of remedying the situation, women of the town decided to sponsor a basket social and dance.

Auctioning of the filled lunch baskets began at midnight; and as the purchaser of each basket automatically acquired a supper companion in the person of the female who had packed the lunch, each man present felt domestically-bound to purchase the offering prepared and contributed by his own wife or sweetheart. No bid for less than $5 was accepted by the auctioneer; and as good-natured rivalry generally developed, most of the lunches brought not less than $10 or $15.

Top bid of the evening resulted when the editor of one local newspaper attempted to buy the supper basket prepared by the other editor's wife. Increasing $5 at a clip, the auctioneer was calling for $40 when the contributor of the basket began tugging at her husband's sleeve.

"Let him have it," she whispered, hoarsely. "There's nothing in it but a couple of sandwiches!"

But the husband had his own ideas on the subject. No rival pencil-pusher was going to eat midnight supper with *his* pretty, young wife! As a result, the bidding continued to mount until the prized basket eventually was knocked down to the husband for $70—possibly establishing a record price for sandwiches!*

With $640 cleared by the social, Rhyolite's school budget again was balanced.

Opening of the 1907 school term found enrollment at 258 pupils, and that same year saw a $20,000 bond issue voted for construction of a new school.

Even the strangling bogie of transportation had been licked by 1907.

From that cold, January day in 1905 when Pete Busch pitched his tent on the barren site where Rhyolite would rise, scarcely a year had gone by until three rival railroads were under construction—each leveling grades and stringing ties in a frantic endeavor to be the first to bring rail service to the new town.

Winner in this devil-take-the-hindmost bout was the so-called "Clark Road," the Las Vegas & Tonopah. Affording connection with the Union Pacific, the L.V.&T. ran its first regular train out of Rhyolite, December 16, 1906.

Midsummer 1907 found the district also being served by the Bullfrog & Goldfield Railroad, and close of that year brought initial service of F. M. "Borax" Smith's Tonopah & Tidewater. Although this last mentioned road fell several hundred miles short of serving either Tonopah or "tidewater," it gave the new district direct rail connection with the Atcheson, Topeka & Santa Fe, which it intersected at Ludlow, California.

At their Rhyolite terminus, the three rival lines shared what was then the most elaborate depot in the state—an edifice referred to in the press of that day as "The Dearborn Street Station of the West." As the only town in Nevada with railroad competition, Rhyolite was considered the most important railroad center in the state. (Plate 38)

With the advent of rail service, there had begun to pour into Rhyolite a flood of potential investors, speculators, and self-asserted capitalists. Arrived in that miracle-sired city at the head of the Amargosa, such investors looked upon a place that was rapidly fulfilling the most grandiose dreams of her founders. With more than 10,000 persons surging through her streets, she was already the largest city in Southern Nevada, and a definite power in state politics.

Stepping from the luxurious palace car which had whisked him across the desert with a minimum of annoyance and discomfort, the 1907 visitor

---

*Death Valley Magazine, Aug. 1908.

found his way beset by ten hotels and innumerable cafes which bid for his favor with such lures as "Free Sample Rooms for Traveling Salesmen," and menus that opened with oyster cocktails and ox-tail *Madeira,* and ran through eight courses to close with imported champagne and Havana Perfectos.

Strolling up Golden Street, Mr. Nineteen-Seven was properly impressed by the Southern Nevada Banking Company block, three stories in height and built entirely of flawless white granite! Not far from this noble structure he craned his neck at the four-story height of the John S. Cook and Company bank building, erected at a cost of $90,000. The Rhyolite Mining Stock Exchange, our visitor was told, had been organized with 75 charter members, and in less than 30 days boasted a paid roster of 300 active members in half the major cities from San Francisco to New York!

Already beginning to feel a bit light-headed, Mr. Nineteen-Seven continued along the street, passing 45 saloons whose doors were never closed. He noted a great number of elaborate gambling palaces and dance halls, even an opera house! Local residents called his attention to a fine, modern electric light plant, an ice plant, four bustling newspaper offices, a soft-drink bottling works, and a Miner's Union Hall, the last named building two stories in height and fronting for 60 feet on the street. Common mine laborers, he was told, were receiving $4.50 a day and up; skilled artisans, $7 to $10. In evidence along the street were stock brokerage and real estate offices almost beyond counting. Second-floor windows presented the names of scores of professional men—most of them mining engineers and attorneys-at-law.

Inquiring judiciously into the matter of "business opportunities," Mr. Nineteen-Seven was told that Jack Conley and Charles Crismor, proprietors of the Southern Hotel Grill, had walked into Rhyolite with only $13.35 between them. Eleven months later they were the owners of a business tentatively valued at $35,000! He was told, also about H. D. and L. D. Porter, brothers, who had come to Rhyolite when it was still a "rag village" of tents. Establishing a general store, (Plate 39) they had begun dealing in everything mortal man might need—lumber, hay, cement, coal, T-rails, candles, Hercules powder, stoves, furniture, fresh and dried foods, clothing, millinery, boots and shoes. By that summer of 1907, they owned real and personal property in the town to a value of $150,000 and were doing a gross business of that amount every month!

"Why, they pay their errand boy a greater sum than the floor walker in a city department store receives," Mr. Nineteen-Seven was told. "As for their head clerk—his monthly salary check would make a flash roll for Death Valley Scotty!"*

As he gazed in rapt admiration at the magnificent homes lining Magnolia avenue, our visitor was reminded that all this elegance and

---

*Death Valley Magazine, Aug. 1908.

ostentation was a far cry from the primitive conditions of only two-and-one-half years earlier, when half the population of the camp was domiciled in tents, many persons were sleeping on the bare, rocky ground, brackish water was being sold by the gallon, and ice—shipped by stage all the way from Goldfield—was so costly its addition to a bar drink doubled the price of that concoction!

Picking up a copy of the *Bullfrog Miner,* our perambulating pilgrim read of $1,000,000 mining strikes, and $1,000,000 stock promotion deals; of new buildings being erected on every hand, and that four carloads of Utah livestock and poultry had been received that week by one Rhyolite slaughterhouse. Reading further, he learned that *The Miner* was available on the newsstands of 24 cities, from Los Angeles to Houston, Texas; north to New York, Boston and Pittsburg, west to Vancouver, British Columbia, and back down through Seattle and Tacoma.

Engaging a $5 room at the Southern Hotel, Mr. Nineteen-Seven settled himself in an easy chair upholstered in leather a quarter-of-an-inch thick, and picked up a copy of a handsomely-bound brochure published earlier that year.*

Any remaining skepticism our visitor may have harbored was put to rout by the incontestable sincerity of the publisher, who had prefaced his volume with an eloquent discourse on the beauty and sublimity of Truth.

"The publication of this booklet must fail in the accomplishment of its purpose if the truth be not rigidly adhered to and the story told without any of the ornate embellishment, which is so often the habit of municipal enthusiasm . . ."

Well, now! Here was something a man could sink his teeth in! Settling back in the luxurious leather folds of his chair, Mr. Nineteen-Seven read further:

"Untold centuries ago there was locked away in these mighty mountain vaults, the meed of precious metals that belonged to this day and age . . . The massive doors of these mountain vaults were fitted with Time Locks, and the hour has struck when their bolts may be shot back. Some half hundred of these vault doors have been thrown wide open, and the gleaming heaps of precious stuff revealed have quickened the whole world's pulse. Some half thousand other doors are enough ajar to show the glint of hidden treasure. From one vault alone, during the year 1906, $1,350,000 in the coin of the realm was taken by stockholders in the form of dividends. The total investment in this case was $300,000, and the return thereon for the year, 450 per cent. And this was only one of many . . ."

With his breath coming shorter and faster, his pulse quickening, Mr. Nineteen-Seven read on:

---

*Rhyolite, Metropolis of Southern Nevada, Pub. Feb. 1907, by Richard R. Sinclair.

"The monstrous mineral ledges of the Bullfrog District are quite without parallel in this country. The discovery of veins measuring from 20 to 30 feet in width are much too common to excite any unusual interest or attention, while 60 and 80-foot ledges, although not frequent, are by no means rare . . . Never before, and nowhere else on earth, has there ever been such a showing made in the way of real demonstrative development work within the two years next succeeding original locations, as in the Bullfrog District . . ."

The visitor's breath had accelerated to short, hard pants, and prickles were clattering up and down his spine like shod horses on a cobbled street. Feverishly moistening his dry lips, his eyes raced on to the next paragraph:

"A wonderful country, this Bullfrog District, this erstwhile unknown desert land, now famous the world over for its fabulous wealth. Broad and free and rich, a-quiver with bursting potentialities, astir with movement, pulsing with power, aglow with the radiant dawn of a glorious future. The natural habitat and field of action of men who are altogether alive. Men of red blood, quick wit and coiled energy. Men who love to see action for action's sake, and who delight to see things come to pass beneath their vigorous hands! The land of a legion of imprisoned opportunities that await only an unbarred door to spring forth to meet you! Who would not breathe its vital air, and have a hand in its stirring affairs and a share in its splendid destiny!"

That did it! Never should it be said that he was not a red-blooded man of action who wanted to see things come to pass beneath his vigorous hands!

Catapulting from the deep enfoldment of his leather chair, Mr. Nineteen-Seven thundered down the stairs, out through the chandelier-lighted hotel lobby, into the brilliant incandescent glow of Golden Street.

His mortal wants, of a sudden, had become very few: A telegraph office, a stock broker, a dotted line. . .

In these basic desires, our feverish visitor was not without company. Many visitors to Rhyolite in 1906 and 1907 became investors in dotted lines and faultlessly-engraved stock certifiicates printed on the best quality water-marked rag bond and beautifully edged in gilt.

That these certificates should be masterpieces of the printer's and engraver's art was only right and proper, since, in many cases, they represented all an investor received for his money. If mines of the Bullfrog-Rhyolite district were not phenomenal for any other yield, they, at least, produced plenty of that costly intangible known as Experience.

Soon after the original discovery of gold by Eddie Cross and Shorty Harris, every canyon in the Bullfrog Hills—as well as all the area between those hills and the Amargosa Desert—had been plastered with mining claims, only a few of which ever developed into mines. Of these few, it was the Montgomery-Shoshone which yielded the most shekels—as well as the most sleepless nights.

Due to mining involvements elsewhere, Bob Montgomery was unable to join the first wave of prospectors to the new strike area, so hired a Shoshone Indian to go to Bullfrog and locate some ground for him—a common practice among prominent mining men of that day. In exchange for the service, Bob is said to have offered the redman $5 and a new pair of jeans—an arrangement completely satisfactory to the Indian.

When he arrived on the scene a little later, Bob didn't have an especially high opinion of the ground staked for him by his red brother, but he paid off, as agreed, and started to do the location work.

Almost immediately he ran into a deposit of talc—sticky, stubborn stuff that gold miners considered about the heaviest cross one of their profession could be asked to bear. With this development, Bob thought still less of his potential mine. He said, later, he might have quit the claim altogether but Rhyolite was booming and he figured his ground was near enough town that he might, in time, realize a tidy sum from the land. Meanwhile, he kept pegging away.

One rainy day, as he was drilling a round of holes in the talc, a stranger ambled into the tunnel.

"Pretty tough, eh?" remarked the newcomer, after a bit. "What's it worth to you if I show you some good stuff in this ground of yours?"

Bob struck a deal with the stranger, who took him outside and pointed to the face of the dump where the talc was being dissolved by a trickle of rainwater.

At the bottom of the tiny rivulet lay a thin streak of flour gold!

After one incredulous look, Bob started to curse and then broke out laughing.

"Stranger," he said, "you sure pulled a fast trick on me . . . but it was a damned good one!"*

During the two years next following that momentous disclosure, the chronology of the Montgomery-Shoshone, as recorded in contemporary news mediums, forms a blow-by-blow history of a mine of great potentials, of Wall Street manipulation, and a few—but very few—great profits.

"The biggest strike in the history of the Bullfrog Mining district has been made during the present week in the tunnel on the Montgomery-Shoshone," stated *Rhyolite Herald* in its issue of May 5, 1905. "After cutting through more than 50 feet of ledge matter, all good ore, the tunnel encountered a very rich streak of white talc—now exposed for about six feet—that assays from $3000 to $6000!

"The Denver Post recently published a story from Goldfield to the effect that Robert Montgomery and Malcolm Macdonald had refused an

---

*Bob Montgomery died at Clovis, N.M., in Aug. 1955, at the age of 92 years. At time of his death he was operating a mine in the Mogollon Mountains, of New Mexico.

offer of $10,000 a day and 25 per cent royalty on the net production, for a lease on the Montgomery Shoshone mine."

"The Montgomery-Shoshone proposition is so new, yet so startling, that even the best mining men who are privileged to visit the property, can scarce believe what they see with their own eyes," said the *Rhyolite Herald* on May 12, 1905.

In its issue of Feb. 16, 1906, the *Herald* announced that Charles M. Schwab, of Pittsburg steel fame, had purchased the Montgomery-Shoshone, Polaris and Crystal, at a reported price of $5,000,000. Shoshone stock then was selling at $4.

In connection with that transaction, the financial magazine, New York *Commercial,* reported: "Mr. Bonbright (of Wm. Bonbright & Company), said yesterday that as yet no estimate had been made of the earning powers of the mine, though the ore in sight was easily thought to amount to $10,000,000, without counting the potential possibilities of the property."

One week after Schwab's purchase of the mine, Montgomery-Shoshone stock sold on the New York curb as high as $23 a share and was withdrawn by the company. Rather than finance the mine from sale of treasury stock, it was announced, Mr. Schwab had decided to "lend" the company close to $500,000. With this money was erected a mill, completed in September, 1906, at a cost of $225,000; water rights, and other assets were acquired from time to time; and in November, 1907, when the first official report was issued, the books showed receipts of $734,225.52 and disbursements of $747,592.59. And the mine still owed Mr. Schwab $428,093.02.

In addition to the Montgomery-Shoshone, the Bullfrog-Rhyolite district embraced a few other fairly good mines, but far too much of their ore failed to pay the costs of mining and milling—and too much of Rhyolite's wealth was centered on the Atlantic seaboard in that man-made canyon known as Wall Street.

Thus was Rhyolite a fertile field for the Panic of 1907, the full brunt of which was not felt in Nevada until a couple of years later.

Through all the days of her pampered life, Rhyolite had never known a morning when she lacked cash in plenty and credit without limit. Now, suddenly, she found herself bereft of both—her paper wealth dissolved, her credit vanished.

Rhyolite didn't have what it took to weather that blow.

The mines and the mills closed, the banks, the hotels. Business houses were abandoned with stock still lying on their shelves and unpaid accounts lying heavily on their ledgers. The exodus began. Twelve thousand persons streaming out by train, by automobile and stagecoach, by horseback and mule-back and afoot. Twelve thousand persons streaming out as rapidly as they once had streamed in!

It was the old, familiar story—except that Rhyolite told it in a setting of grand opera.

The town, of course, wasn't entirely deserted. About 700 were living there in the fall of 1910—some prospecting, some working for the Montgomery-Shoshone, some operating the few remaining shops and saloons.

Then came a morning in March, 1911, when subscribers to the Rhyolite *Herald* found the entire front page of that news medium devoted to the obituary of a mine.

"To all appearances," read the account, "Montgomery-Shoshone is dead.

"The big hoisting engines are lifeless and the rumbling of the mill has ceased.

"Presumably it is all over . . .

"Its career has been short but checkered; full of sensations and disappointments.

"It has startled the world with its richness, commanded the respect and homage of the greatest financiers, and dumfounded its admirers by its erratic behavior.

"It has proven a successful failure; a mine of great resources; promoted on the get-rich-quick fashion; touted as 'the one best buy'; heralded as 'Nevada's infant wonder'; and nursed ultimately from month to month until it has expired from sheer exhaustion.

"Credited with almost $1,500,000 in net bullion return, Shoshone today faces an indebtedness of more than $200,000 . . .

"With a gross production of more than $2,000,000*, . . . Shoshone doubtless would have been a dividend payer had not the frenzied finance methods been employed in its construction.

"Burdened by a debt of almost a half million dollars advanced by the steel king for the building of the mill and for other improvements, Shoshone's profits have gone a-glimmering in liquidation and interest . . .

"There seems to be no doubting the statement that Shoshone would have made good in every sense of the word, had a small mill been built with funds from the sale of treasury stock. There would have been no indebtedness, no interest, no immense investment for improvements . . .

"The history of Shoshone has been a case of trying to make a world beater out of what would be considered ordinarily a 'mighty good little mine.' "**

One year after the appearance of that death notice, a shotgun might have been fired down the center of Golden Street without claiming one casualty, Indian or white.

---

*$1,388,398 is the gross production credited to Montgomery-Shoshone by B. F. Couch, Nevada's Metal and Mineral Production: Nevada State Bureau of Mines, Vol. XXXVII, No. 4, 1943.

**Rhyolite Herald, March 25, 1911.

Almost before the main outpouring had ended, the three railroads had discontinued service to Rhyolite and Bullfrog. Their rails eventually were pulled, the cross-ties sold as salvage to the highest bidder. ("Death Valley" Scotty eventually paid $1500 for all the ties from 70 miles of Tonopah & Tidewater line. After coughing up another $2500 to have the ties hauled to his $3,000,000 castle at the north end of Death Valley, Scotty corded them in a ravine for use as fence posts and for burning in the castle's multiple fireplaces.)

With Rhyolite offering no further market for electricity, the power company scrapped its line in 1916. Rabbit brush and creosote crept back into the streets. Dust settled over the gambling tables, the ornate chandeliers, the roulette wheels, the bars. Birds came to nest in mahogany-fitted offices, and a jealous desert wind began gnawing at those elegant buildings so briefly thrust upon its domain.

Today finds poor Rhyolite and Bullfrog entombed in their own devastation. Far better the quick, clean fate of Bonanza and Orion, whose superficial scars have vanished completely from the face of the earth!

Shimmering Golden Street is a sorry wraith, her once-proud structures reduced to hollow shells of twisted steel and shattered concrete. Robbed of their supporting timbers, roofs and floors have tumbled into their basements. Outer walls and partitions lean dizzily, and under the buffeting of winter gales, sometimes may be seen to sway.

Beaten upon by the Amargosa wind, weakened by rain and frost and human vandalism, the city will continue to crumble and fall until the last weary arch and heading is lost in the anonymity of rubble.

As late as 1925-30, the visitor to Rhyolite and Bullfrog might gather in one afternoon as many souvenirs and relics as he cared to carry away. The floor of the First National Bank was layered knee-deep with canceled checks, old correspondence and business forms; textbooks lay in the ruins of the $50,000 school building, and furnishings were in place in many of the abandoned dwellings.

But not today. By close of World War II, relic hunters and scrap dealers had ransacked the area so thoroughly that almost nothing of value remained in the ruins of either town. At the sites of former assay offices, it still is possible to find fragments of broken crucibles and cupels. There are scraps of china and crockery where cafes once stood, and broken glass bottles where were once saloons. But that is all.

Of the hundreds of fine buildings spread so briefly upon these slopes, the year 1955 found only two structures tenantable.

One of these was the old union station. Formerly known as The Dearborn Street Station of the West, it is now termed "the largest railroad depot in the world without either trains or tracks." Nearest rail connection, at the present time, is at Las Vegas, more than 100 miles to the south.

About 1924 the old depot was purchased by N. C. "Wes" Westmoreland, a colorful character who had operated the Old Arizona Bar, at

Vegas. Upon taking possession of the depot, Wes found in the ladies' waiting room the mummified carcass of a cow. The story was a great favorite around Beatty, where wags claimed the cow had missed the last train out of Rhyolite and had starved to death while waiting for the next one.

After transforming the old station into a roadhouse—The Rhyolite Ghost Casino—Wes lived there alone with his dogs for 23 years. Throughout that time he offered to visitors a diversified program of intoxicants, gambling, and Western hospitality, and his unique establishment became famous all over the world. In addition to tending bar, Wes served the place as doorman, cook, chambermaid, porter and janitor.

"When there ain't any wind," he boomed, "I even blow to keep the flag flying!"

In April, 1947, Wes leased the casino and said he was going to spend the remainder of his life in a kindlier climate, closer to civilization. Six weeks after leaving the desert, he was dead.

During the probating of Westmoreland's estate, the casino was placed on the market. While only the old depot was involved in the sale, newspapers mistakenly reported that the entire ghosttown of Rhyolite was to go under the hammer. Soon after the circulating of this misinformation, Las Vegas Chamber of Commerce received a communication from a group of ex-Nazi soldiers, in Hamburg, Germany. They wished to buy the town—lock, stock and barrel—and offered as payment $10,000 in United States money. Whether the men were seeking to gratify a lifelong desire to own a ghosttown, or whether they believed the place could be rehabilitated and restored to activity, was not disclosed.

Rhyolite's other main tourist attraction is the Bottle House.

Back in 1905, when Saloonkeeper Tom Kelly built his now-famous dwelling, it is unlikely that he had any knowledge of the health-giving rays admitted by glass. Doubtless his choice of bottles, as a component of masonry, was inspired solely by the fact that in Western mining camps no other commodity was so readily obtainable as a bottle; most particularly, an empty bottle.

Architecturally, the idea proved sound.

Embedded in the outer walls of the dwelling are 51,000 quart liquor containers laid in adobe-mud mortar, their bottom ends to the outside. Main body of the walls is comprised of Anheiser-Busch and Reno & Company beer bottles, with a small representation of Hostetter's Stomach Bitters. Gordon's Gin bottles form the corners. Containers originally of clear glass have been roasted to a deep purple shade by the elapsed decades of desert sun; but those of greenish or amber cast, have remained unchanged.

For more than 50 years the old bottle house has stood on the parched hill slope between Rhyolite and Bullfrog. Its 51,000 glass eyes, unblinking and emotionless, saw ground broken and footings laid for Rhyolite's four bank buildings. They saw those handsome walls pushed upward, two and three stories above the desert plain; and they watched those walls weaken and collapse, and saw packrats and desert birds come back to live in the great steel vaults. . .

In whatever realm of the Hereafter he may have found eternal lodging, Saloonkeeper Tom Kelly might be interested to know that the house he put together in jest is one of the last survivors in the Queen City of Bonanza Road.

34

Fortune in a Low-Cut Gown

L IKE THE GODS of mythology, whose feats grow grander with each retelling, so not all glories attributed to the National mine are fully supported by government statistics.

One notable variance between the inflexibility of the printed page and the greensward of man's memory, concerns the richness of the National's ore.

According to report of Francis Church Lincoln*, large quantities of the mine's highgrade assayed between $10 and $75 to each *pound* of ore. But to loyal champions of the National, such a niggardly estimate verges on libel.

"Seventy-five dollars!" exploded one old-timer, when I asked him to confirm that estimate. "Why, jumpin' Judas! I've seen highgrade from the National that assayed $200 *to the pound* in gold! Even the rock we used for surfacing roads carried $4000 to the ton!"**

So it goes . . . But whether her ore ran $200 a pound, or $2; whether her total production was $8,000,000 (as credited by conservative sources) or $12,000,000, as claimed by others, there is no doubting that the National was a treasure vault whose like has been known to few men.

With mining activities being pushed throughout Nevada since the middle 19th century, it is a mystery why this incredible deposit should have been overlooked until 1907, when values were first located in the district by J. L. Workman, an automobile-borne prospector. Encouraged by Workman's report, other miners strayed into the region, and less than two years later—at an underground depth of only 40 feet—the two Stall brothers discovered the fabulous National vein!

By telephone and telegraph and train, by newspaper headlines and word-of-mouth, spread the wild tidings:

Gold! Gold in Humboldt County!

---

*Mining Districts and Mineral Resources of Nevada, 1923.

**Waldemar Lingren, U. S. Government geologist, reported that the National's best ore averaged $30,000 per ton; and a single shipment of only 4500 pounds, made in 1911, netted $365,000 or a total of $81.20 a pound—this at the "old" price of gold and silver. Metallurgically, the ore was almost pure electrum, an alloy composed of about half-and-half gold and silver.

To every down-at-the-heels prospector, every Hard Luck Harry, the new strike loomed as Opportunity in a low-cut gown. To every gambler, every tin-horn promoter, the fragrance of easy money came drifting across the sage—and the mad scramble was born.

With the fantastically rich ore of the National as a corrupting influence, highgrading came to flourish. Armed guards were engaged to patrol the mine; and nighttime found blinding searchlights playing over its entrance, their hot fingers probing restlessly through the dark in search of skulking figures with few scruples and heavy pockets.

Months passed; and out of that dark hole in the mountainside, down a narrow, twisting trail to the valley, and on to Winnemucca and the railroad, poured the National's gold. One million, two millions—yes, possibly even twelve millions of dollars.

And then came a morning when the shift whistle failed to blow.

That the mighty National had been milked of its treasure was almost more than Nevada could believe; but the street corners of Winnemucca and National and McDermitt became meeting places for miners who gathered in dismal groups—groups that nodded grimly and laughed little.

There was still gold in the mine—everyone said so! But it was like the meal that clings in the seams of its container and lies powdered over the ground where men have spilled it. There is meal—but so far as the hard-headed cook is concerned, the barrel is empty.

Since that day when the engines were silenced and the last shift streamed off duty, many changes have come to the National mine and the lusty camp that adopted its name.

Last time I walked through those ghostly precincts, a foul-smelling stream of greenish water was trickling from the mouth of the caving tunnel and losing itself in the weed-choked canyon below. Two old ore cars were standing on their rust-corroded tracks. Alongside the forge, in the blacksmith shop, lay six dull picks that would never be sharpened; and in the littered yard of the machine shop, a killdeer had made her nest and laid her speckled eggs. . .

At the rear door of the company boarding house and hotel, an iron dinner gong swung idly in the wind. Two desks were standing in the schoolhouse. Cluttering the assay office were broken crucibles, and bottles of acid, and other trivia pertinent to the metallurgist's trade; and spread upon the floor of the paymaster's office lay a wilderness of 40-year-old correspondence and sheets of production figures.

But in all that accumulation of chaos, I found not a single page of National's former newspaper, *The Miner;* and in all the canyon, there was no sound louder than the creak of a loose door, swinging in the wind.

Sitting alone on the front porch of the old hotel, I looked across the deserted townsite, past tar-paper shacks and caving cellars, and great heaps of rusted tin cans and broken bottles. And as I contemplated these day-by-day cast-offs that testify so eloquently to man's one-time occupation,

I was remembering Joe Davis, of Winnemucca, and a story he once told me.

"My introduction to National was in 1913 or '14," Joe had said. "I didn't know exactly where the town was located, but I followed the wagon road up the canyon till I came to a place where music was blaring from five saloons. Gambling tables were running night and day, with the sky the limit. Everybody was flush with money, and the place was swarming with good-time women and dancehall girls.

"I was getting nicely organized for the evening, when a friend of mine from Winnemucca happened along. He sat down and we fell to gassing, and I said I hadn't expected to find National such a lively camp.

" 'National?' the feller repeated, in surprise. 'You're not in National —this ain't nothin' but a soo-burb! The main camp's a mile-and-a-half farther up the road!'

"Well, y'know," Joe said, a little smile twitching at the corners of his eyes, "I looked around at all the women, and the bright lights, and all the miners whoopin' it up, and I said to him, 'What th' hell, bub! Call it a suburb if you want to . . . but *it's deep enough for pappy!* ' "

35

Rawhide, The Ringtailed Roarer

FOR MORE THAN 40 years Nevada had watched new mining camps rocket out of the sage to shine and sin for a day and revert to sage; and as each ephemeral camp had died on the vine, she had seen two newer and brighter constellations risen to take its place. If this program of hail and farewell was not one that offered the most stable political economy and long-range security, it was, at least, a stimulating life that kept the state awake and on its toes. It was a he-man's life—and Nevada liked it!

Even the economic facet of the program operated well enough so long as there had been Virginia Cities and Auroras, and Austins, and Belmonts, and Eurekas, and Tonopahs waiting to be discovered. But after nearly half a century dedicated to burying the old king in sackcloth and toasting his successor in champagne, Nevada, in 1907, found herself assailed by vague little pricklings of doubt.

The picture was changing—and in that change Nevada could foresee a threat to her whole mad pattern of existence!

It was the same old story of too many men, too many mines, too many bars of bullion, too many years—and it all added up to the fact that established camps were being "worked out" after briefer lives, no new El Dorados were being discovered, no lusty new towns were being born to replace the ones that had sung their song.

Maybe the ore's all gone, ran Nevada's troubled whisper. Maybe there won't be any more big strikes, any more great camps! What then, pardner, what then?

It was a horrible thought to contemplate—and Nevada was worried.

Thus had the stage been set for the Act III denouement that broke in the form of Rawhide—Rawhide the doomed man's reprieve, the shipwrecked mariner's sail; Rawhide, the ringtailed roarer that burst over the sagelands in the closing weeks of 1907!

Within a matter of hours after news of the strike had been made public, half the citizens of Nevada were talking of little but those rich stringers of gold Someone had found at the foot of the Sand Springs range, 100 miles northwest of Tonopah. And despite the fact that winter in that high country, is a time of icy winds and deep snow and sub-zero temperatures, every trail leading toward that isolated Golconda was soon blackening with traffic!

First comers found the site of discovery marked by a post to which had been wired a tin box and a cow's tail; and to the box had been affixed a crude sign:

DEPOSIT MAIL HERE FOR RAWHIDE

It was a simple, honest beginning—but Rawhide's tolerance of the rude and rural was to be short-lived.

Three months after her birth, the new camp's population had leaped to 5000 milling boomers. Another three months and that number had increased to 10,000, and all roads to the desert rendezvous were jammed with crawling vehicles and men and animals—foot travelers and mule trains, freight wagons and horsebackers. Fifty private autos (Plate 40) and half a dozen horse-drawn stages were shuttling passengers over the rough, dusty roads from outside points; and in a single day, four hundred men and women sought to book passage to the new camp from Schurz, twenty-five miles to the west. Nevada was having her last big fling before settling down to the cold boiled potatoes of grim reality. . .

Arriving at Rawhide in his chauffeur-driven Thomas Flyer, Sports Promoter "Tex" Rickard paid $8000 for a corner "business lot," grubbed away the sagebrush, and launched construction of a fabulous fleshpot modeled along lines of his ultra-successful Northern Saloon, at Goldfield. Rushed to completion in ten days, the Rawhide Northern rang up bar receipts of $2000 on its opening night, and its gambling tables were soon yielding to the house an average of $25,000 per day!

By February, 1908, newspapers of Tonopah and Goldfield were giving the new camp more space than they were their own communities. The Rawhide Coalition Company had been purchased by E. W. King for a cool half a million, and shares in Rawhide Consolidated were bringing ten times their par value. A half-inch seam of gold in the Grutt Hill mine was running $300,000 to the ton—$150 a pound—and a single waterbucket full of ore from another Grutt mine had yielded $2800 in gold.*

Midsummer, 1908, (Plate 41) found Rawhide boasting 1500 wooden and stone buildings, 1000 tent houses, and a greater number of hotels and rooming houses than any other city in Nevada. And still accommodations fell short of the demand, and every night saw men sleeping in the streets and on the sawdust-covered floors of saloons.

Citizens of Rawhide had a choice of three local daily newspapers— *The Rustler, The News,* and *The Times.* The last mentioned, a 20-pager, was composed on a Merganthaler typesetting machine and printed on the largest Miehle press in the state; but it was W. W. Booth's little *Rustler* that claimed honors as the pioneer news medium of the camp. At the top of his editorial column, Editor Booth observed: "This paper is different

---

*Weight, Harold O., (quoting Leo Grutt) When Rawhide Roared, *Desert Magazine.* June, 1947.

from other newspapers; and I thank the Gods of Verse and Prose that it IS different."

During the same summer of 1908, there were operating in Rawhide three banks, open daily until midnight. There were half a dozen theaters and variety houses, telephone and telegraph service, an electric light plant, and a mammoth refrigeration plant to cool champagne and beer—but there was no water save that freighted across the desert from Dead Horse Well and sold by the gallon. Standard price of a hot bath was $5.

In Stingaree Gulch flourished a sporting district rivalling in magnitude the notorious Barbary Coast, of San Francisco. Cheap orchestras played all night in flimsy dancehalls that reeked of smoke and sweat and Florida Water and whiskey, and too much human brawn in too little space; and flanking both sides of a twisting street for half a mile were bagnios and bawdry houses, with 500 chippies of all races and colors working the line.

There were 90 saloons that never closed their doors—and there was a church.

"Ninety sch'loons — one schursh," hiccupped an old lushington. "Where'n hell you find a better percentage?"

Few Western mining camps have been favored with a more accomplished set of promoters than was Rawhide—particularly after she won to her support that Terrific Trio, George Graham Rice, Tex Rickard, and Nathaniel C. Goodwin.

Nat Goodwin, famous Broadway comedian, had received his first taste of mining camp life when he was brought West to appear on the opening night program at Goldfield Theatre. It had proven a life to his liking, and after close of the engagement he had elected to remain in Nevada.

Later, when the popular showman followed the boom to Rawhide, *The Weekly Miner,* of Bullfrog, took occasion to remark editorially: "We trust that Nat's exalted opinion of Nevadans will not be too abruptly shattered by running afoul of countless wildcat promoters who sell worthless mining stocks . . ."

Chances are, that was the last time anyone ever doubted Nat's ability to hold his own in the wicked world of commerce. Joining the Rice combine, the Broadway thespian not only bought worthless stocks, but proved himself uncommonly adept at unloading them—and always at a handsome profit!

Elinor Glyn—whose sensation novel, *Three Weeks,* had been but recently suppressed as indecent, thereby assuring its success—telegraphed to Nat that she was entraining for Rawhide to procure additional first-hand knowledge of life in the Rugged Raw.

Determined that there should be no muffing of this priceless opportunity to gain international renown, the Rice-Rickard-Goodwin triumvirate swung into action. In one of the speediest organizational jobs on record, arrangements were perfected for a dozen saloon brawls and street fights, complete with flying steel, popping pistols, and clobbered corpses. Super-maudlin touches were added to Stingaree Gulch, and every beef-eater in town was enlisted in the task of making Miss Glyn's sojourn one to be remembered.

Elinor came and saw, and was properly palpitated—and galloped home rejoicing to write another best seller.

Though her life on this mad sphere was brief, Rawhide was to crowd into her few months a larger measure of excitement and color than most mining camps experience in an equal number of years. Considering how thoroughly she was geared to sensual pleasures, there seems to be more than a touch of irony in the fact that the most imperishable of Raw-hide legends should concern the death of a gambler, and a funeral sermon preached by an unfrocked minister.

When Riley Grannan clattered into Rawhide in a horse-drawn stage, in 1907, he was known as one of the greatest plungers the world had produced. Among his more notable accomplishments was that of having laid what was then famed as the largest wager in track history—$275,000 on the outcome of a single horse race; but whether Riley was betting on a war in Europe, or the number of beans in a 100 pound bag, the sky was the limit. Verily, Riley Grannan was a man after Rawhide's own heart!

Upon his arrival at Rawhide, Riley had begun making plans to erect there the queen of all pleasure palaces; but, pending consummation of those plans, he was temporarily operating the gambling concession in a local saloon, when stricken by pneumonia in April, 1908. A prominent Reno physician was rushed to the isolated camp at a cost of $500; but the Grim Reaper beat him to the punch.

As befitted a man of his stature, the internationally-known gambler was laid out in a satin-lined casket; and as befitted the frontier camp of Rawhide, that fancy casket with the silver handles was mounted on a pair of rough pine saw-horses set in the back room of the Variety Show House —a gambling hall and saloon on Nevada street, near the entrance to Stingaree Gulch.

It was only natural that Riley's Nevada friends should wish to give him a handsome send-off, with a 24-carat sermon and all the assorted props—floral, vocal, and instrumental—but in the accomplishing of that ambition lay a measure of difficulty.

Any minister capable of preaching a sermon thought worthy of the occasion might very logically take a dim view of this wayward son who had looked too seldom on the altar cloth and too often on the black-and-red pasteboards, the toteboards, and the galloping dominoes.

In her determination to do the right thing by Good Ol' Riley, Raw-hide enlisted the aid of Herman W. Knickerbocker.

Knickerbocker was something of an enigma. According to barroom gossip, he had been pastor of a large Methodist congregation in Los Angeles, but upon his subscribing to certain views contrary to the Methodist credo, his church had unfrocked him in disgrace. Emigrating to Nevada, he had built a small theater at Tonopah and there had endeavored to organize a Shakespearian group. With failure of that altruistic effort, he had turned to wandering the desert as a prospector, and Time had brought him to Rawhide. All this, of course, was only Brass Rail Biography. "Knick" was never one to talk about himself, or his past.

And now, this clergyman of the Sullied Cloth was to deliver an eulogy over the chill clay of a plunger known around the world. . . .

Possibly there lies buried in the soul of every man some latent spark of genius. If that be so, then Herman W. Knickerbocker's hidden flame must have burst into its full glory on that raw, gusty day, in April, 1908, as he stood with bowed head beneath the garish lights of the Variety House, and with words drawn from his heart sent Riley Grannan down the dark, uncharted road toward Eternity.

Speaking extemporaneously to that motley throng of boomers and gamblers who had gathered to pay final respects to the greatest of their kind, the vibrant voice of this admitted agnostic—this Bob Ingersoll of the Sagelands—rose to impassioned heights as he probed the everlasting enigma of life and death, and God and man. It was an eloquence that caused hardened men to weep unabashed, and sent scalding tears to furrow the painted cheeks of the Jezebels of the Night.

Recorded in shorthand by a down-and-out court reporter known as "Rattlesnake Shorty"—a booster in Tex Rickard's saloon—that 2000-word tribute to Riley Grannan has come down through the years as a Western classic, and today is regarded as one of the most famous funeral eulogies ever delivered in the United States! Published and republished in book form and pamphlet, and sold by tens of thousands of copies, those words of Herman W. Knickerbocker have been read and quoted wherever the English language is spoken. . .

Another colorful character to grace the local scene was "Rawhide Jack" Davis, who dealt himself in early in the game, and after dabbling in several properties, disposed of his interests in Rawhide Consolidated Mining company in May, 1908.

In part payment thereof, he received $250,000 in what bankers of those days termed "hard coin."

Upon receipt of the money, paid to him in Reno, Davis announced his intention of dedicating the whole wad to the business of having a good time and seeing the country. To that end he contracted for the most powerful and costly automobile the day provided, and engaged the services of two liveried chauffeurs. Delivery of the vehicle had been promised for an early date, stated Goldfield *Review*.

"Then will begin what promises to be one of the most exciting races across the continent ever undertaken by an automobile. Davis wants the world's record. The best time made thus far was 14 days. Smith (one of the brace of chauffeurs) is one of the best known and most experienced automobile men in Nevada, has made seven transcontinental trips, knows the roads like a book and believes the time can be cut to 12 days. This will be the aim of the party. No expense is to be spared in the effort.

" 'Rawhide Jack' Davis is not related to 'Diamondfield Jack' Davis. (Plate 47) He is another type of man, a gentleman, every inch. He was born in Eastern Oregon and came to Nevada a little more than a year ago. He was prospecting and struck the Rawhide country before the excitement started. One day, while walking over Hooligan Hill, he picked up a piece of rock. It contained free gold, the first to be found in the camp; so—Davis enjoys the distinction of being the discoverer of the first gold in Rawhide.

"He is 30 years old, has been married seven times, and takes his good fortune as a matter of course."*

With his triumphal departure from Nevada, Rawhide Jack Davis appears to have dropped through a hole in the earth. If there is any further record of him or his exploits, I have been unable to locate it.

In less than 12 months, the meteoric career of Rawhide had transformed desert wasteland into a frontier metropolis.

In less than two hours that same metropolis was leveled back to desert waste.

The Big Fire—grimmest event in Rawhide's history—had its inception on the morning of September 4, 1908, when a wind-blown window curtain was ignited by a gasoline stove in the backroom of the Rawhide Drug store, on Nevada street. From this point of beginning the flames spread rapidly to the adjacent roof of the Ross hotel, and to buildings beyond.

Four companies of the Rawhide Volunteer Fire department rushed chemical engines to the scene, but all efforts were in vain. By the time the fire had reached the new quarters of Freiman clothing store, the heat had become so intense that the building occupied by Nevada meat market, on the opposite side of the street, burst into flames. With this development, there vanished all hope of saving the business portion of the town.

Under the direction of J. G. Flynn, superintendent of Rawhide Coalition Mines, more than 3000 pounds of dynamite was used for razing buildings in an effort to bring the blaze under control. In order to save the elaborate plant of the Rawhide *Press-Times,* all other structures around it were blasted; and with wet blankets, and what little water was available, it proved possible to turn the trick.

"As the last big building to be devoured by the flames—the Gill Terrace—was razed to the ground, the force in the *Press-Times* office heaved a sigh of relief," reported that news medium. "Our magnificent $25,000 plant and building were saved, and thus it was made possible to run off a special edition of the paper, which was being set on the

---

Goldfield Review, May 10, 1908.

Merganthaler while everything around the building was at white heat . . ."*

By the time the fire had burned itself out, not one building remained standing within a radius of nine square blocks (about 15 acres) in the heart of Rawhide's business section.

Among the more important losses were 27 assorted stores, including general mercantile, clothing, hardware, furniture, jewelry stores, bakeries, and meat markets; 26 bars, cafes and restaurants, three hotels, three banks, the stock-exchange building, office and plant of the Rawhide *News,* the postoffice, two telegraph offices, express office, stage depot, Hazen lumber yard, two photo galleries, two barber shops, and the water company office. Also destroyed were several large buildings that had been occupied by lawyers, mining engineers, and other men of the professions; as well as a number of warehouses, private dwellings, and smaller shops.

As the demolition crew had moved through town, only a few yards in advance of the spreading fire, Tom McCauley, superintendent of Rawhide Consolidated Telegraph, had stuck by his chattering instrument, sending and receiving messages and occasionally darting a quick glance out the window toward that nearing sea of red flame and rolling black smoke. Only when a building three doors distant had been dynamited and his own office was smoking with heat, did McCauley wrench his instrument and necessary connections loose from his desk and flee for the comparative safety of the street. Outside the building, he bumped into W. P. De-Wolf, staff correspondent of *Nevada Mining News,* at Reno. Together, the two men dashed to the south end of town, McCauley climbed a telegraph pole, and made an emergency wire connection; and with batteries borrowed from Rawhide Morning Star company, telegraphic communications were soon reopened with the outside world—DeWolf writing the messages and McCauley transmitting them to the *Mining News.*

(DeWolf, incidentally, had written the first telegraphic news concerning the disastrous fire at Cripple Creek, Colorado, in 1896. His operator, on that occasion, had been Frank M. Conehay. Like DeWolf, Conehay had followed the boom camps, and the big fire at Rawhide had found him operating a key in the Rawhide Telegraph office, a business rival of McCauley's outfit.)

With the information sent out by McCauley and DeWolf, the destruction of Rawhide by fire became the No. 1 news story in the West on that black Friday in September, 1908.

Tonopah *Daily Sun,* on the afternoon of the fire, carried a six-column banner line:

RAWHIDE IN ASHES

Reno *Evening Gazette* proclaimed the dread news in a seven-column banner:

RAWHIDE IN RUINS

*Rawhide Press-Times, Sept. 4, 1908.

while *Nevada Mining News* issued a special "Rawhide Fire Extra," with an eight-column, three-line streamer filling the upper third of the front page:

RAWHIDE, THE CAMP, BURNS: MINES UNHURT;
LOSS, $1,000,000; REBUILDING IN HOT EMBERS;
NEVADA MINING NEWS RUSHED FIRST AID

Upon learning that 3000 persons had been left homeless in the camp, *The News* had immediately opened a subscription campaign for Rawhide Relief. All Nevada responded nobly, residents of Reno, alone, in less than one hour, contributing nearly $5000. Tonopah's citizens were called together by tolling of her fire bell, and under the eloquence of Key Pittman, later to be governor of Nevada, more than $1900 was raised on a single street corner in only a few minutes time. Even California towns and cities rallied to the cause; and San Francisco Stock & Exchange Board sent a contribution of $4500.

All the provisions in Rawhide's stores having been destroyed, with exception of the stock of one small grocery, *The Mining News* appealed to the wholesale and commission houses of Reno for prompt action, and from the Southern Pacific company secured the donation of a relief train which was given right-of-way to Schurz. On its departure from Reno, the "Rawhide Relief" carried 20 barrels of flour, two tons of ham and bacon, two tons of potatoes, a ton of beans, four tons of evaporated fruit, one ton each of butter and lard, a ton of coffee, and 100 cases each of canned tomatoes, corn, table fruits and evaporated milk; as well as 500 loaves of bread and a large contribution of fresh fruit.

Governor D. S. Dickerson rushed to the stricken city a shipment of government tents and blankets for use by the homeless, and offered to dispatch state police to maintain law and order.

Rawhide's telegraphed reply was typical of that rugged time and the fighting spirit of the frontier:

RAWHIDE SEPT 4 1908
D F. DICKERSON
CARSON CITY
TOWN ORDERLY. WILL BEGIN REBUILDING
TOMORROW. CITIZENS NOT DISCOURAGED.
H F BREDE and H B FULLER

That Rawhide's citizens were not discouraged was a masterpiece of understatement.

With smoke still rising from the hot ruins on the day of the fire, a mass meeting of townsmen was called, and E. W. King, president of Coalition Mines, was elected to head the relief committee. Reporting that meeting, Rawhide *Press-Times* stated:

"Jack Hines made a motion that no telegrams going to the outside through the committee should be worded so that the impression should get abroad that Rawhide was seeking relief or aid on account of being destituted; that all necessaries sent into the camp would be thankfully received, but should be paid for. This motion received numerous seconds . . . and was unanimously carried."

The Coalition company, it was announced, further, would begin erection immediately of a substantial brick building to replace their offices destroyed by the fire, and Grutt brothers reported their intention to rebuild with stone.

But Tex Rickard scooped the town in the matter of rebuilding.

"Before the fire had reached his premises," (stated *The Mining News*) "he had placed an order with one of the lumber companies for the material with which to erect a larger and better building than the one which was about to be destroyed. Within an hour after the fire had cleared his building site, he had closed his contracts with the carpenters, painters and paper-hangers . . . and had wired to San Francisco for a new stock and fixtures."

In admiration of Rawhide's courage, telegrams expressing good wishes began flooding the town from persons in every corner of the nation. Typical of these was the message from Charles A. Stoneham, then president of O. F. Jonasson & Co., New York Mining Stock brokerage concern.

"From the ashes of the lumber piles of Yesterday will be reared the granite walls of the permanent and enduring Rawhide," wired Stoneham. "Investors should not be alarmed, as actual ore, Rawhide's greatest asset, cannot be eliminated by fire . . ."

As the New York financier had predicted, Rawhide rose from her ruins to glow again on the Western horizon . . . But not for long.

The mad saturnalia, the sky's-the-limit stakes, the reckless extravagance, the runaway ride on the merry-go-round, was nearing its end. A nation-wide panic was sweeping West from the Eastern seaboard—and Rawhide was in no position to weather a panic. Too little of her wealth reposed in her mines; too much of it in the golden tongues of her promoters. While her surface ore had been, perhaps, the richest ever discovered in the West, it had not held up with depth; and with only about $1,500,000 of actual gold production to her credit, Rawhide folded her tent.

But for stories contained in old newspaper files, and harbored in the memories of a few men still living, Rawhide, today, has practically ceased to exist.

Last time I returned to the town was in 1949 when I went there to interview S. W. Conwell, veteran Rawhider and perennial political candidate, who was then campaigning for the governorship of Nevada, on the Independent ticket. At that time there were only nine or ten persons living in the old camp, and of all the hundreds of buildings that had lined these streets, not more than a dozen remained and not one business house was in operation. Structures still standing included a two-unit building formerly occupied by the postoffice and a theater; adjoining it was a two-story structure that had been a hotel. Elsewhere over the townsite stood the old stone jail, the Barrel House saloon, Grutt Brothers office, the office of Wonder Lumber company, and several other small structures and cabins. (Plate 42) Seventy-three-year-old Frank Hopkins was using for storage what he claimed had been the wine cellar of Tex Rickard's Northern—but of the old Northern, nothing remained but a bare space on the ground.

Frank said prospecting around Rawhide was terrible; that he and his dog, Cap, hadn't made a dollar—"honest or otherwise"—in a long while.

Before leaving town, I drove out to the old cemetery. I hadn't expected to find Riley Grannan's grave, of course, as Riley had been shipped back to Paris, Kentucky, for burial—but I had hoped to find a little more than the old graveyard proved to offer.

It had been a large cemetery; but in all its dry, thorny, desert-reclaimed space, diligent search revealed only four grave markers on which inscriptions were legible. Two of these dated from 1908, the others from 1914 and 1922.

As I made my way back toward town, I paused for a bit to prowl over an immense area literally buried in rubble. Bank vaults, bedsteads, broken thundermugs, grocery scales, oil drums, bottles, silverware, fragments of glassware and dishes, chains, cables, broken concrete—everything a man might need in this world or the next—but all of it melted and welded and heat twisted in the Big Fire in 1908.

Wandering idly over the sites of what had been hotels and banks and saloons and shops, my eyes fastened on a metallic crescent barely protruding from the ashes and charcoal. Even before I stooped to retrieve it, I knew it was a 50-cent piece.

As I stood there in the ruins of Rawhide, turning in my fingers that old, fire-blackened half dollar, I was deeply grateful for having found it. Thereafter, when my miner friends started fanning the breeze over the Wonderful Had-Been Days, I would be able to hold my own with the best of them.

Speaking loftily, but none-the-less truthfully, I could murmur, "Ah, yes—Great old camp, Rawhide! I picked up a nice piece of money from the Rawhide boom . . ."

36

Bad Boys of Bovard

SITUATED IN THE vicinity of Rawhide were several contemporary boom camps, none of which distinguished itself by achievement or longevity. One of these flashes-in-the-pan was Bovard, on the northeast flank of the Gabbs Valley range, 24 miles northeast of Hawthorne, and about a mile from Bovard, lay Lorena. Vivid recollections of both places were retained by my good friend, the late F. A. "Gus" Goodale, of Los Angeles.

A civil engineer and surveyor, Gus was one of the first to pitch his tent in the embryo boomtown of Rawhide—arriving there Oct. 27, 1907. During that winter, he and his partner, A. J. Koerner, were employed in platting and surveying a number of additions to the original Rawhide townsite; and the next summer following, they took part in the rush to Bovard.

"In 1907, several months before the Bovard boom got underway, a group of prospectors had been grubstaked by 'Tex' Rickard and a man by the name of Smith—one of the officers of the Coalition company," recalled the former engineer. "These fellows had located some claims in the Rand district, and Mr. Smith asked my partner and me to go there and survey the properties. 'Tex' had his chauffeur drive us to the new camp in his Thomas Flyer automobile.

"It was about eight o'clock in the morning when we arrived at Bovard, which then consisted of only a few tents. We went on back into the hills to do our surveying; and to illustrate how fast these boomcamps grew, when we drove back through town that same afternoon, we found a street nearly a mile long, with plenty of tent saloons!

"It didn't take long for trouble to get started, either! As we were preparing to leave town, someone came out of one of the saloons leading a man whose head was wrapped in a bloody towel. He had been in a fight and his opponent had broken a whiskey bottle over his head and then jabbed him in the face with the jagged shank. We got him into Rickard's machine and rushed him to a doctor in Rawhide for treatment. I'll never forget that trip—the injured man moaning and groaning, and dripping blood over everything, and the chauffeur sending the Thomas Flyer over that rough, sandy road at 50 and 60 miles an hour!" Gus

Goodale shook his head and grinned weakly. "I was never so scared in my life . . .!"

During the first three days of the Bovard boom, some 800 persons flocked to the new camp, and city lots enjoyed brisk sale.*

But Bovard, as a town, was not long for this world, and Lorena, her stepdaughter, was even shorter lived.

During that summer of 1908, when Bovard was booming, several men from Mina and Luning became piqued with the town—for some reason now forgotten—and vowed they would shake its dust from their heels forever. Moving out into the desert about a mile, they founded a new camp which they christened Lorena. Streets were platted, building sites surveyed, and a tent saloon opened for business.

While neither Bovard nor Lorena had any water supply save that hauled into town by teamsters, this was not an unusual situation in Nevada mining camps, and the new place began to enjoy a sleazy sort of boom.

And then, one morning the water wagons failed to make their usual appearance. The desert camp grew steadily dryer, as the day progressed and by the second morning the water supply of every man in town was down to the settlings. There being neither team nor wagon in camp with which water might be hauled, the situation—to put it mildly—was grim.

One by one, the settlers of Lorena subscribed to the theory that metropolitan Bovard might be, after all, a more desirable place in which to live; and, one by one, they pulled stakes. The camp eventually shriveled until the only residents remaining were its founders—still determined to hold out to the last ditch.

For their final meal in Lorena, these stalwarts emptied the tent saloon of its last remaining stock; and by using beer and ginger ale as substitutes for water, they managed to mix their flapjacks and brew their coffee. Thereupon, they swallowed their pride, struck camp, loaded their packs, and headed back across the desert to the despised rival town.

Not until some while later was it learned that Bovard's fun-loving boys had bribed the water haulers to remove Lorena from their daily schedule!

Ely (Nev.) *Mining Expositor*, April 23, 1908.

37

City of the Broken Hills

MAURY STROMER was a boomer—a breed of men whose day is done, whose like will never come again. All but a few of his 70-odd years had been spent in successive Nevada camps where hope roosted high on every ridgepole and no man was more than half a pick's length from fame and fortune.

Maury had been justice of the peace at Aurora. He had followed the treasure trail to Candelaria and Tonopah and Goldfield, and on to Rhyolite and Rawhide—and, finally, he followed it to Broken Hills, in northeastern Mineral county. There he had remained, operating a general store and the postoffice as long as there had been any need for either. He had watched the camp progress and retrogress from sagebrush back to sage. He had buried his wife, and buried or said goodbye to his fellow townsmen; and after 37 years' residence, had come a day when he found himself the last surviving resident of the town. (Plate 49)

It was Maury who gave me the history of Broken Hills.

Possibly the camp would have proven more permanent if the original strike had been made on some date other than April 13, 1913. At the time, of course, no one gave any heed to the double jinx. It was enough that Joseph Arthur and James M. Stratford had struck paydirt in the rough hill country north of Mina. Fingering samples from the new prospect, men transcribed that ore into a second Tonopah, another Tuscarora. The belated discovery came to glow like a shimmering rainbow of promise, and a town soon had sprung into life.

"It was a nice little town," recalled Maury. "Good, decent folks, peaceful and law-abiding. We had saloons, sure—a few gambling houses and bawdy houses, too—but they didn't dominate the place. There were stores and homes, a nice school, even a hotel. Our greatest lack was water. Except for that hauled in and sold at $2.50 a barrel, there was none to be had. Later, I acquired a small truck and hauled water for $1 a barrel."

Due to this scarcity of water, Broken Hills—like Rawhide—lay under constant threat of fire. On several occasions the camp was swept by blazes of major calibre—one of these resulting in destruction of the hotel and a tragedy not soon forgotten. With exception of a 16-year-old girl, all residents of the building had managed to escape the roaring inferno but in his frantic efforts to save his entrapped daughter, the father, too, suffered burns which later proved fatal.

"Another sort of tragedy," recalled Maury, "was the death of Old Matt Costello. Fine old man, Matt—a prospector. After working like a dog for most of his life he finally struck something pretty promising and sold the claim for $1500. He was tickled as a kid with a new red wagon! Had a thousand-and-one ideas about how he was going to spend his money.

"One day it occurred to us that we hadn't seen Matt for quite a while. We went out to his cabin to investigate. We found him sitting at his table, his head resting on his arms, as though he might have fallen asleep while eating his breakfast. He had been dead several days.

"We figured he'd be happier here in the hills, so we buried him up near his cabin. All the good he ever got out of his money was what we spent for him. We bought him a neat little headstone, all engraved nice and proper, and an iron fence to keep cattle and varmints away from his grave. . .

"Another funeral I'll never forget was that of Alfred Jacques, our leading saloon-keeper.

"Jacques—or 'Jake', as we called him—had said he wanted to be buried at Eagle Rock, in the hills north of camp. Naturally, he had to go and die in the middle of January when the ground was frozen hard as billy-be-damned. I didn't think we'd be able to sink a hole deep enough to plant him; but we fixed him up the best we could, loaded him in a truck, and started up the hill—everybody in camp traipsing along behind.

"The trail was rocky and steep; there was no endgate in the old truck, and Jake's coffin kept bouncing and jouncing and threatening to slide out the open rear end. Every now and then we'd have to stop the truck and push him back where he belonged.

"We finally got him up the hill to Eagle Rock and got him planted," continued Maury, a cryptic sort of smile playing over his lined features. "When we got back to town we all lined up at the bar—Jake's bar—and h'isted a few, on the house. God knows, we needed 'em!"

Broken Hills was no bonanza. Only the original discovery claim of Arthur and Stratford ever produced wealth in such quantity as men had anticipated. Before its sale to the Broken Hills Silver corporation (backed by George Graham Rice's Fidelity Finance and Funding company) the Broken Hills mine had produced around $65,000 for its discoverer.

"Rice paid $20,000 for the mine," recalled Maury. "He made only one shipment from it—35 tons of ore assaying $225 to the ton. Soon afterward he pulled out for Butte, Montana, got involved in some fraudulent stock promotion deal, and was sent to the penitentiary."

Several other outfits operated the mine, later, but none with phenomenal success.

It was the early years of the depression that killed the camp. With the mines closed, the town's population drained away until only a few old timers remained. The others, eventually, passed on to Better Prospecting, and, in 1950, Maury was the last one left.

Formerly operator of the camp's leading mercantile establishment, and postmaster at Broken Hills until the office was discontinued about 1930, Maury still retained much of his original faith in the district, and still managed to wrest a living from his silver-lead mine, "The Badger." At that time he was stopeing on a four-foot vein that carried $2 worth of gold and 40 ounces of silver to the ton. He aimed to take out a couple of tons daily.

Working alone, the old man would descend his 140-foot shaft by vertical ladder, shovel 350 pounds of ore into a bucket, reclimb the ladder to the surface—a distance roughly equal to that of a 12-story building—start his engine, hoist the ore and dump it. Thereupon, he would relower the bucket and climb back down the ladder for another load.

"Judas Priest, Maury," I said, when he had explained the procedure. "Doesn't that program get terribly tiresome?"

"Oh, I don't know," replied the old ghosttowner. "I reckon it would —if a man carried it to extremes. But, you see, I only make about a dozen trips a day!"*

From Maury's cabin I wandered across the empty street to the weather-beaten store building where he had held forth so long as general factotum.

The winter afternoon was dismal and dark. The sun, barely visible through gathering storm clouds, seemed weak and cold and terribly far away. The desert wind that wailed down from the high ranges shook the old building, and pummeled it and rattled it. It whistled around the eaves and banged the door, and ran impatient fingers through the long, loose strips of tattered muslin that hung from the ceiling in ghostly shrouds.

Suddenly there was snow in the air—small angry flakes that swirled through the glassless windows at the front of the store and sifted through every crack in the broken walls and roof. Drifting to rest inside the cold building, the icy flakes mingled soundlessly with the undisturbed dust of two decades.

Strewn over the floor of an annex which had housed the postoffice, lay a bewildering assortment of rubble. Old letters, canceled checks, 20-year-old circulars and newspapers, still in their wrappers. On the shelves were out-moded postal forms, and one of the postoffice boxes held an unopened letter. Running my finger under the flap, I withdrew a yellowed sheet of foolscap. Some chap in Kansas City, 20 years before, had been inquiring about the mining boom at Broken Hills. . .

Standing in the rear of the building was a decrepit poker table, and lying in the dust beneath it, a torn ace of diamonds and an eight of spades.

---

*Maury Stromer died in March, 1956, at Paso Robles, Calif., where he had spent the winter with his daughter. Burial was at Mountain View cemetery, in Reno. He was 75 years of age.

An orange-crate cupboard on the wall held a few dog-eared novels of the Mary J. Holmes era; another packing box supported an ancient phonograph with a broken spring.

Still in place on the turntable was an old wax record, as warped and brittle as a potato chip. Taking it to the front of the store where the weak, thin light was a little stronger, I brushed the layered dust and cobwebs from its faded label and made out the title of the song: *There's Nobody Home But Me.*

Glancing toward the cabin across the street, I could see Maury Stromer hustling about the yard, his grizzled head bent to the whipping gale as he made things secure against the lowering night and the storm.

Placing the warped record back on the phonograph, I made a firm resolution never to be the last survivor of a ghosttown.

It's a lonely business. . .

38

Death Rode the Jarbidge Stage

FROM THE OLD stage station of North Fork, on the headwaters of the Humboldt river, a graded road leads northeasterly to Jarbidge, Nevada, and on to Idaho. It is a lonely road that serves few towns. Sage chickens patter along its dusty ruts, or whirr away heavily on stiff wings, and jackrabbits and half-wild range cattle turn to stare curiously at the human intruder. Crossing the West Fork of the Bruneau the road leads on through the little ghosttown of Charleston and up into Humboldt National Forest where the scraggly brush of the desert gives way to tangled thickets of small quaking aspen and mountain mahogany. These, in turn, give way to dark aisles of alpine fir and limber pine and high, wide, barren expanses where it seems possible to look past the edge of the world half-way into Eternity.

After looping over the tumbled ranges for 50 miles, the road noses sharply down the south wall of Jarbidge Canyon—dropping more than 2000 feet in five miles of hairpin turns—and deep in the basement of that shadowy gorge it deposits itself in the old mining camp of Jarbidge, population 23.

Should the spirit of adventure ever lead you to Jarbidge I hope you find it much as I did in the summers of 1950 and 1954—a pleasant little ghosttown, its single street flanked by two rows of faded log cabins built during the gold mining boom days of 40-odd years ago. I hope your visit falls in June or July when every old porch is latticed with morning-glory and hop vines, and the old picket-fenced yards are buried in hollyhocks, and the canyon air is sweet with wild roses, and chokecherry blossoms and creek dogwood, and the brush is filled with quail talk.

I hope, especially, you'll find Charlie Hawkinson (Plate 46) or George Urdahl at home, for both Charlie and George have lived at Jarbidge since 1912, and both know this region like the insides of their own pockets. They'll show you the ruins of the great Pavlak mill and tunnel, the Bluster and Success mines, the Flaxie and Starlight. They'll tell you about the Lost Sheepherder gold mine, and the night Death rode the Jarbidge Stage; and they'll tell you about the boom. . .

Although placer gold had been emanating from the district over a considerable number of years, it was discovery of that gold's source which launched a stampede to the Jarbidge river country and gave birth to the boomtown in the canyon. Even newspapers of that day were in disagreement concerning the author of the discovery, but the honor was generally conceded to D. A. Bourne, of Boise, Idaho (formerly of Steptoe, Nevada); and the time of Bourne's discovery, was November, 1908.

The Jarbidge country, however, is a long way from anywhere else, and it took quite a while for the boom to get started. As late as September, 1909, only six or seven men were prospecting in the area; but by January, 1910, Jarbidge was a name with which to reckon! The Escallon group of claims had been bought by Twin Falls-Jarbidge Mining and Development Company for $250,000, and Bourne said some of his assays had run as high as $73,000 per ton!

"Before I had dug a hole 10 feet deep in the property . . . I had been offered $2,000,000!" said Bourne in an "exclusive" interview given to a Los Angeles newspaper. "Then I was given a chance to sell 100,000 shares for $1,000,000. But as there is ore valued at $27,000,000 in sight, I am not selling!"*

February found 500 persons in camp, and the first wheelbarrow made its arrival by muleback. Due to general remoteness and mountainous snowdrifts, all supplies were scarce and costly. Most of the buildings in camp, as a result, were constructed of hewn pine logs—but seven business structures were built of dressed lumber brought in on burro back over virtually perpendicular miles. The Commercial Club was housed in a log building 24 by 60 feet in area—a structure that did double duty as a public hall. It was claimed there was no finer dance floor in the state.

Time marched on. New mines were discovered, and existing mines developed. New businesses came into existence, and population of the town multiplied—but still its inaccessibility remained. In 1917, with nearly every hamlet in the United States linked by fast rail transportation or all-weather highways, Jarbidge still clung to its precarious perch in the northeast corner of nowhere. Nearest rail connection was Rogerson, Idaho, 65 miles to the north, and throughout the winter months, any resident of Jarbidge who had business at Elko, his county seat, necessarily made the journey hence by train, via Pocatello, Idaho, and Ogden, Utah!

"On grades leading into Jarbidge Canyon the road averages not more that a foot wider than a wagon, and the slightest accident means a fall of thousands of feet," declared *The Elko Independent,* on Jan. 31, 1917. "When this grade is filled with snow . . . the danger of passing over it can be better imagined than described."

Only the week previous, it was stated, the stage team had gone off the grade, the driver saving his life by jumping. The four horses, the sled, and its cargo, had rolled down the mountain 150 feet and lodged against a tree, killing the two leaders and injuring the wheelers, which landed on top.

---

*Quoted in *Elko Free Press,* Jan. 21, 1910.

"Had it not been for the tree, the whole concern would have gone to the bottom of the canyon, a distance of at least 2000 feet."

In view of these circumstances, it isn't especially surprising that the 800 residents of Jarbidge were then paying $100 a ton for hay, and 75 cents a gallon for gasoline!

"Fresh eggs," remarked the *Independent,* "would undoubtedly be worn as watch charms by the wealthy people of the camp, if they could be secured."

Before close of that rugged winter, the people of Jarbidge must have truly believed that the Wrath of God had descended upon them.

After long weeks of isolation and food famine, March was ushered in by devastating avalanches—more than 100 slides occurring in the immediate area of the camp, within only 24 hours! In the course of their thunderous descent, these slides piled themselves across the streets of the town, or dammed the Jarbidge river and thereby threatened to flood both canyon and camp. Born on the precipitous canyonside, 1500 feet above the town, one such avalanche rushed downward with the speed of a runaway express train, sweeping from its path huge boulders and great trees. Reaching the main street home of William Perkins, "one of the finest residences in camp," the slide hurled that building a distance of 200 feet, and smashed it into the side of the Hudson home.*

While Time didn't improve the climate or topography of the area, it changed other factors. The Guggenheim interests became heavy owners of mining property in the district; electric power was brought to the camp from a distance of 80 miles, and summer of 1917 saw a wagon road opened to Deeth on the Southern Pacific—the people of Jarbidge subscribing $10,-000 in cash toward that $68,000 project, with remainder of the cost being shared by Elko county and the U. S. Forestry service.

With the stumbling blocks of transportation, communication, and accessibility conquered, at least partially, Jarbidge spiraled into fame as the greatest gold producing camp in the State of Nevada. . .

But, after producing no-one-knows-how-many zillion dollars worth of ore, the great mines shut down, most of the camp's population trickled away, the stores and business houses closed, and Jarbidge became a ghost-town.

All these things are remembered by Charlie Hawkinson and George Urdahl; and Charlie, especially, remembers the night Death rode the Jarbidge stage, for Charlie was one who took part in that midnight manhunt. . .

It was in the closing days of 1916, when all the big mines in Jarbidge canyon were pouring forth gold, and the town was booming. Every saloon, on that night of December fifth was packed to its thresholds. The cracking and popping of pine-gorged heating stoves mingled with the slap-slap of cards, the whirr of spinning roulette wheels, the clink of shot

---

*Elko Independent, March 5, 1917.

glasses and silver dollars on polished bars, the scuffing of heavy boots, and the constant roaring overtone that comes from big voices and big laughter, and too many men in too little space.

There was only one disturbing detail.

The incoming stage was hours overdue—and Jarbidge knew it was no night for a stagecoach to be traveling the hazardous road that led south from Rogerson, Idaho. Driving four skittish horses over that road offered danger enough, even in fair weather—and the weather this night was anything but fair. Thin, dry snow had been spitting through the pines since mid-afternoon, and as winter's early dark settled over the canyon, an icy wind began whistling around windows and doors and rattling stove-pipes, and banging loose sheets of corrugated iron roofing. Even before this present storm there had been three feet of snow on the narrow, twist-ing Crippen Grade, over which the stage must travel; and only two days earlier, several large freight teams out of Jarbidge had met a bunch of incoming teams from Rogerson and it had been necessary for the outfits to work all one night and half the next day before they could pass on the grade.

Fearful that the stage driver had experienced similar trouble, Post-master Scott Fleming, about sundown, asked Frank Leonard to take a saddle horse, ride up the grade till he met the stage, learn what the difficulty might be, and bring in the first class mail.

But when Leonard returned, several hours later, he was empty-handed. He said he had ridden all the way to the top of the grade but had not sighted the stage.

This development threw the town into a tizzy of conjecture, the con-census being now that the stage had run off the grade and plunged into the Jarbidge river—a theory that was held until about nine o'clock that night, when word of the missing stage reached a Mrs. Dexter, who lived at the north edge of town.

"Why, no," said Mrs. Dexter. "The stage didn't run off the grade—it passed my place about suppertime! The driver had his coat collar turned up around his face, and was huddled on the seat as if he was terribly cold. I called to ask if he wasn't about frozen, but he didn't make any reply . . ."

The driver hadn't made any reply—and three hours later, he still hadn't arrived at the postoffice, only half a mile up the road from Mrs. Dexter's house.

Only now did Jarbidge begin to realize that the stage had not been delayed by the forces of nature, but by human forces of evil.

Defying the storm that was now wailing through the dark streets of the mountain mining camp, a volunteer searching party, lighted by kerosene lanterns, began combing the canyon between the postoffice and Mrs. Dexter's place. Minutes later, the missing stagecoach was found in a dense clump of willows, 200 yards off the main road, and only a quarter of a mile from the business section of town.

Slumped on the seat of the coach sat the driver, F. M. Searcy. In the back of his head was a round black hole made by a bullet fired at close range. Three inches of snow lay piled on the body, and both the seat and the floor of the stagecoach were caked with frozen blood. The horses, still in their traces, and tied to a clump of willow brush, were shivering from cold. Near the stage lay the second class mail sack, which had been slashed open and its contents scattered; but the sack containing the first class mail—including $3200 in cash consigned to Crumley & Walker's Success Bar and Cafe, and other smaller amounts to a total of nearly $4000—was nowhere to be seen.

Darkness and the mounting fury of the blizzard prevented any further investigation that night, but armed guards were posted on every trail and no one was permitted to leave camp. It wasn't a good feeling to know that the man responsible for this foul deed was probably one of those aiding most actively in the search.

When the vicinity of the crime was examined the morning following, it was discovered that the murderer had lain in wait along the road, only a short distance below Mrs. Dexter's house. He had, evidently, swung aboard the coach as it passed; and, according to blood stains in the snow, had shot the driver almost immediately. Startled by the shot, the nervous horses had started to run away, causing the stagecoach to careen wildly along the edge of the road for a hairlifting 100 yards, whereupon, the murderer evidently had been able to seize the lines and bring the animals under control. Continuing bloodstains in the snow indicated it had been he who was driving when the vehicle passed Mrs. Dexter's house, which accounted for the fact that he had not shown his face or responded to her greeting. Shortly beyond her place, he had turned the horses and coach off the road into the secluded thicket of willows, and there had tethered the animals and gone calmly about his business of robbing the mail.

From the point where the stagecoach had been found, the footprints of a man and dog were found to lead to the river where the murderer had washed the blood from his hands and discarded a blood-stained shirt. The tracks then led through the willows to a path that crossed a footbridge over the river into town.

Like most mining camps, Jarbidge had an old tramp dog who was owned by no one but was everyone's friend. As the volunteer posse conducted its grim investigation, the old tramp was frolicking alongside, and when the group reached a point about 100 yards from the bridge, the animal bounded off into the brush, and began pawing at a small mound in the snow.

It was the first class mail sack. The bag had been slashed open, blood-smeared letters were scattered through the snow, and the registered parcel containing the $4000 in cash, was gone.

The dog's apparent knowledge of the mail sack's location inspired someone to match his paws against the crusted prints of the animal which had accompanied the murderer on his grisly trail of the previous night. When the paws and prints were found to be the same general size and shape, it remained only to figure whom the dog might have been following.

Thus did the finger of suspicion first point to Ben Kuhl, an employee at one of the mines.

The old dog was especially fond of Kuhl. As a matter fact, he was about the only friend Kuhl had in camp, for Kuhl just wasn't popular. He had been in trouble a few weeks previously—something about "jumping" a piece of real estate—and was then free on bond while appealing a $400 fine assessed in that connection. This understandable need of money, coupled with the dog's friendship for him, and the fact that he wore shirts "similar" to the blood-stained shirt found under the bridge, was judged sufficiently incriminating that Kuhl was arrested on the day following the crime and was charged with robbery of the United States mails and murder.

Searchers, later, found a coat buried under the bridge—a coat which Kuhl's partner, a Mr. Kirby, said had hung in their cabin and would have been available to Kuhl, had he wished to use it. In the same cabin was found a gun with one chamber fired. It wasn't Kuhl's gun. It had belonged to a gambler, who had loaned it to a friend to shoot rats, and the friend had loaned it to another friend . . . And even though it had turned up in the cabin shared by Kuhl and his partner, there was no proof it was the gun which had killed the stage driver. Kuhl swore he had spent the entire evening in one of the saloons, and several men substantiated his story. Later, however, they said maybe it had been some other evening they had seen him in the saloon. . .

The whole case was very confusing.

About all anyone could say for certain was that young Searcy, the stage driver, had been very popular in camp, and now he was dead—shot in the back of the head by someone who had not given him even a fighting chance for his life.

Kuhl *could* have done it—and Kuhl had not been popular.

So Kuhl was it.

If there was any talk of lynching, no one remembers it, now. Everything was strictly legal. Taken to the county seat at Elko, Kuhl was tried, convicted on circumstantial evidence, supported by bloody handprints on the mail, and was sentenced to life imprisonment in the state penitentiary at Carson City.

Throughout his trial and subsequent imprisonment, Kuhl never failed to plead his complete innocence of the crime, and after serving 27 years he was released, in 1944.

Given even half a chance, Charlie Hawkinson, or any other of the old timers of Jarbidge, retell the story of the holdup. They point out the spot on the road where the murderer swung aboard the stage, the clump of willows where the driver's body and the horses were concealed, and the bridge where the assassin washed his murder-stained hands and removed and discarded his bloodied shirt and coat. They also tell that the $4000 in stolen money was never found, and that it still must lie buried somewhere in the canyon near the lower end of town.

But even this angle of buried loot is not exceptional in the annals of Western stage coaching and, in the final analysis, the Kuhl case stands unique for only one reason.

It marked the closing of an era.

For more than 100 years, highwaymen had preyed upon carriers of the United States mails, striking from ambush, robbing and killing, and living to kill again.

But that night of December 5, 1916, when Death rode with the Jarbidge mail, is said to have been the last time in the history of the West that a horsedrawn stagecoach was held up and robbed and the driver slain.

30

"... and the Desert Shall Rejoice..."

HOWEVER FORLORN AND forgotten other ghosttowns may be, the loneliest skeleton in Nevada's closet is that of Metropolis.

Metropolis is lonely and forlorn because she is a pariah—an agricultural ghost in a mining world.

Even her brief hour of glory was little touched by mirth or madness; and now, as the wild wind whistles down Emigration canyon and sends its probing fingers through the gray sage of her sepulchre, it finds there only gaunt ruins and cold chimneys, and desolation and dead hope.

From the first day they learned of that alluvial slope in northeastern Nevada, the alert boys of the Pacific Reclamation company could hear in fancy the symphonic rustle of sales contracts, the crackle of mortgages. If ever was a perfect pitch for the land shark it was here on the headwaters of the Humboldt, where sagebrush grew higher than a horse's back! Best of all, that land might be had for a song—a short song, quickly sung.

Securing title to some 40,000 arid acres, the promoters drafted plans for a concrete diversion dam across Bishops creek, and a fanning network of canals. Except for a little stage scenery, the curtain was ready to rise on Act I.

Most important of those missing props was a town. True, the settlement of Wells lay only a dozen miles to the southeast; but the plank-sidewalked Wells, of 1910, was scarcely a place to favorably impress potential capital, and the next nearest trading point was Elko, 50 miles to the west. Prospective settlers—Easterners, especially—were inclined to regard 50 miles as a right-smart distance from doctors, ribbon counters, and the assorted niceties of civilization.

The only answer was to create a shining new city in the heart of the development.

The thought was parent to the deed.

In a matter of weeks, the Pacific Reclamation company had platted a townsite. Streets were graded and paved, building lots surveyed. Cement sidewalks and electric lights blossomed throughout seven blocks of the intended business district, water was brought under pressure from mountain springs, and like a moth emerging from its chrysalis, the city of Metropolis was born.

As the aforementioned investors could scarcely be expected to pitch their tents on the windy plain, the PRC then built a three-story stone-and-brick hotel of 50 rooms— 30 with private bath—the whole erected and furnished at a cost of more than $100,000! Decorative tile formed elaborate mural designs along corridors and balconies; and from broad picture windows fronting on the elegant lobby, it was possible to witness man's triumphal conquering of the desert wastes. (Plate 54)

Sale of land was begun in 1911.

In the Salt Lake City office of Pacific Reclamation Company, the high ceiling was swept by the feathery top of an 11-foot sagebrush with a trunk like a young redwood—a Metropolis sagebrush, naturally, and one invariably cited to potential purchasers as irrefutable evidence of that land's fertility. Were any further proof of that fact required by Doubting Thomases, same was amply supplied by the company's magnificent brochures replete with photographs of brimming irrigation canals, attractive farm homes, tight fences, prize-winning poultry, trim orchards, and undulating fields of grain that topped a man's head.

That such miracles had been accomplished on raw desert, loomed as an inspiration and personal challenge to every man who had ever yearned for a piece of God's good earth. Office workers, factory hands, farmers, dreamers, men in every level of society, every· corner of the land —even to Canada and the Old World—seized upon those brochures as they might have embraced a new faith. They turned the pages with hands shaken by emotion; their eyes devoured the story and the pictures—and heavy-laden hearts swelled with new hope!

As soon as the development promised to become an important source of revenue, Southern Pacific built a spur track from its main line, eight miles to the south, and at the Metropolis terminus erected a $10,000 depot with handsomely-landscaped grounds and ever-flowing fountain.

The town, in time, began to grow of its own volition. The Metropolis *Chronicle,* a weekly newspaper, brought out its first issue September 15, 1911. A city hall was built, and Consolidated Wagon Works erected a huge structure for the furtherance of its activities. On a slope overlooking the business district rose Lincoln school—an architectural gem of brick and stone and concrete; and between the hotel and the school burgeoned Madison city park, with winding pathways and flower beds, and emerald lawns and spreading shade trees. Washington city park—with more winding ways and flower beds, and a cannon, besides—spanned that portion of the world between the hotel and the depot; and just over the hill rose a new cemetery. Stores of every type came to flourish. Men of the professions hung their shingles in upper-floor windows. Five saloons irrigated the dusty palates of the populace, and ambitious citizens began casting covetous eyes at the Elko county courthouse.

Irrigable lands of the reclamation company were available at $75 per acre, and up, according to location. But not all pilgrims who came to

Metropolis were equipped with money of that shade. Many were the sort of small fry a good sportsman would have thrown back—but not the silver-tongued salesmen of the PRC! Before a potential investor was permitted to escape the net, he was offered a glowing picture of the pleasure and profits to be realized from dry farming "above the ditch." Such tracts, it was pointed out, could be had for $10 per acre, payable in easy installments, with interest at 10 per cent.

It was a great piece of music as arranged and played in the plush office with the fancy frills and the giant sagebrush.

A great piece of music—a great opportunity.

But most of the settlers were licked before they even set foot on their land. Too many costs piled up too quickly. Before any crop might be planted, the heavy growth of sage must be cleared. Neighbors would pool their draft animals and hitch several teams to a length of railroad rail. As this heavy drag was pulled broadside over the land, the brush in its path would be uprooted, later to be raked into piles and burned. For months at a time the air was never free of the acrid bite of sagebrush smoke.

With the ground cleared and ploughed it was possible to begin planting; but before there could be any hope of harvest, all fields must be fenced. Fenced not only with good posts and barbed wire to turn the ravenous hoards of range cattle and sheep that swept down from the hills to live at the colonists' expense, but fenced tightly enough to turn back the jackrabbits that swarmed over the land in gray battalions.

Any settler who got squared away so he could harvest a crop by the second year was more fortunate than most. Yet, all this non-productive while, money drained away like water through a sluice. The "easy" payments on the land, the 10 per cent interest—which once had appeared so inconsequential—houses and barns that must be constructed against the biting blasts of winter; taxes, grocery bills, doctor bills, feed bills, seed bills . . . Every outlay of money, however small, came to tower like a spectre of doom.

And then, Dame Nature took a hand in the game.

The "average annual rainfall of 13.8 inches" as assured in brochures of the reclamation company, became only an interesting piece of mythology.

Year after hopeless year, dry farmers "above the ditch" saw the fragile blades in their fields turn yellow and wither beneath the blast of midsummer's sun and wind. Other years failed to bring even enough moisture to sprout the seed in the ground. Three years, virtually without rain and with the mountain snow-pack diminishing steadily, left the Bishops creek reservoir so far depleted it was no longer possible to supply the water needs of the colony. Irrigable land, bought at premium prices, became no better than waste acres on the open desert.

The fountain at the depot ceased to flow. The palatial hotel closed its doors. Washington and Madison city parks were reclaimed by the sage. The Cooperative Marketing System was disbanded; merchants packed their stocks and withdrew. The railroad abandoned service and pulled its tracks.

As taxes became delinquent and land payments lapsed, one farm after another reverted to the promoters—and disillusioned settlers piled their possessions into lumber wagons and battered Model-T's and headed back down the dusty road toward Wells. Behind them they left their cabins, their fences, their drought-blighted crops, their parched orchards, their hope.

Of the hundreds who had streamed to Metropolis with high aspirations, the colony soon dwindled to a few hardy souls too stubborn to toss in the towel of defeat.

One of these few had been Mrs. William Glassman—and in 1950, Mrs. Glassman was still holding the fort.

She was a tiny wisp of a woman who wore faded blue jeans and a wide-brimmed hat, and referred to herself derisively as "a jack-Mormon." Her voice was soft, but as she spoke, she seemed to grow in stature until she became the reincarnation of all the visionaries and pioneers, all the Empire Builders, who have forever dedicated their lives to pushing back the wilderness.

It was May as I walked through the ruins of Metropolis with this aging woman who had clung there through thick and thin for 37 years. Patches of snow were still lying on the surrounding ranges, but here on the south slope of the hill it was soft and warm.

We wandered past the ruins of elaborate Lincoln school where the last pupil had walked down the steps several years before and the building had been closed. After most of the timbers and bricks had been salvaged for use elsewhere, the gutted structure had been left as a plaything for the desert wind. The standards for swings and high bars were still standing in the school yard, and a scattered heap of weather-warped textbooks lay at the foot of the front steps. Site of the Consolidated Wagon factory was marked by a caving basement and stone foundation. The roof and outer walls were gone from the big hotel, but a few ragged partitions still rose above the rubble. In the crumbled plaster at the top of one partition, a family of owls had its nest.

At one corner of the hotel stood a lone fire hydrant; and leading through the head-high sage to the former site of the depot, stretched 300 yards of cement sidewalk. But of the depot or its ever-flowing fountain, not a trace remained. Neither was it possible for a stranger to know where the newspaper office had stood; where the saloons and barber shops and millinery stores and cafes had welcomed their respective customers, or where the boundaries of either city park may have lain. Gardens and orchards, streets and homes and hopes, all had been swallowed by the repossessive blanket of the sage.

"It wasn't much like this when I first came here," said Mrs. Glassman, ranging her eyes over the crumbled ruins, the dry slope, the few small shade trees she had nurtured and kept alive with water hauled from the hills.

"I left the Southern Pacific at Deeth and came to Metropolis on the branch line. There was a homesteader on every quarter-section of land throughout that distance, and I was told that the country was settled equally well for many miles to the north. Everything was green. When the wind rippled through the grain fields it looked like waves running over a green ocean!

"The depot set yonder about a 100 yards—" her pointing finger indicated a section of the hill where a solid stand of gray sage was broken only by the blackened corpse of one dead tree. "There was a fountain in the depot yard. For several minutes after I got off the train I stood and watched the silvery spray of the water—something about it fascinated me! And then, I walked through Washington park and up to the big hotel . . .

"I was 22 years old, and I had never seen a more beautiful town! Everything was green and golden, and every man thought Prosperity had come for all time.

"And then the drought . . . and hardship and heartbreak. Most of the settlers left. For the few of us who stayed on our land, life became a nightmare of jackrabbits and range cattle, and litigation over water rights. For six years the Mormon crickets took everything we tried to raise. They even chewed the fence posts and ate our shoes and curtains!

"Why did we stay?" she shook her head in answer to my question. "I've asked myself that same thing a thousand times . . . and I still don't know the answer!"

In the broken partition of the hotel, the owl family was raising a noisy fuss over some morsel of food. A meadowlark had lit in one of the dead cottonwood trees and was singing, just as meadowlarks have sung through every May that has come to Nevada. A gray lizard pattered across the warm sidewalk and ran a little way up the side of the rusted fire hydrant.

"No . . . I can't tell you why we stayed," the woman continued, looking across to the foothills where her cattle were grazing and a small field was greening with the spring. "Maybe we had to prove to ourselves that we were tougher than the ones who had left. Maybe we considered it sort of a challenge and wanted to show we could meet the desert on its own terms, and win!

"Maybe that was why we stayed," she said. "I don't know . . ."

But, even as she spoke, this tiny woman's head lifted in an attitude of defiance, and her thin shoulders straightened with the determination and courage of a crusader. Into those desert-faded eyes surged a new bounty of strength and faith and hope, and the shadow she cast across the land grew broad and tall. . .

40

Guide for Ghosttowners

BELIEVING THAT MANY readers of this book may be interested in exploring a few Ghosts of the Glory Trail, I am including a directory listing 277 of the more important ghosttowns of the Great Basin. In addition to giving a thumbnail history of each camp, I have spot-located each in relation to some existing town or landmark found on any road map of the area.

In this "Who's Who" directory, it should be noted, I have not included any of the famous and highly-publicized "tourist ghosttowns" such as Virginia City, Austin, and Goldfield, Nevada. No member of this trio, so far as I am concerned, merits the title of "ghosttown," since each still functions as the seat of its respective county, each has churches, a school, active business concerns, homes, and each a local newspaper—Jock Taylor's *Reese River Reveille,* at Austin, founded May 16, 1863, being the oldest newspaper in Nevada of continuous publication; and the *Territorial Enterprise,* of Virginia City, claiming the largest circulation of any weekly paper in the entire West.

Go and see these three old towns. You'll find them interesting, extremely historical, highly photogenic, and well worth your time. But after you have seen them, I hope you'll go off on some dim little road to a remote region, far from bars and juke boxes, and slot machines and picture postcards and people, and there visit a real, honest-to-goodness *ghosttown,* where no commerce has functioned for possibly 70 or 80 years. When you have walked the silent streets and prowled through the deserted buildings in such a place, you'll understand why I can't find it in my heart to apply the term "ghosttown" to any of the tourist-conscious centers on the paved highways.

Prospective ghosttown visitors should observe a few rules of caution. As many of the older towns are situated on back roads little frequented by travelers, motorists using such byways must be capable of changing a tire, and have with them the equipment necessary to that job —a bumper or scissors jack, good lug wrench, and a spare tire full of air. A shovel also is a necessity, and an armful of burlap sacks can be very helpful in extricating a car bogged in soft sand. Before leaving the last point of supply, check your car—or have a service station attendant check it—to make certain it is in good mechanical condition, particularly as to fan belt, generator belt, battery, water pumps, fuel pump, wiring system and tires, and have your gasoline tank filled to the brim. (In the back country of Nevada and Utah, even on designated county and state roads, are many sections where gasoline stations are 100 miles apart.)

Most important "must" for ghosttown explorers is a 5- or 10-gallon can filled with water. The water cans made for use on Army jeeps are very satisfactory. Glass carboys are too subject to breakage, and use of canvas waterbags is not advisable in rough country since they must be hung on the outside of the car frame and a jutting rock or sharp branch may rip the bag and result in loss of the water. Even though you plan to return nightly to a point of supply, it is well to carry at least a small box of food. Choose imperishables and leave them in the car from one trip to another, replacing as used. Canned meat, cheese in vacuum-sealed jars, hardtack, raisins or other dried fruits—anything of this sort helps "take up the slack" in case a breakdown makes it necessary to lay over for a day or so in some isolated area. Candy bars are not satisfactory in hot, desert climates.

As many ghosttowns are situated in country ranged by sheep or cattle, it is a good rule to leave each gate as you find it. If closed, reclose it behind you; but if a gate is open, do not jump to the conclusion that it *should* be closed. To do so may result in trapping cattle in a portion of range devoid of water supply.

Unless there is in your party a cautious, experienced miner who knows and respects the risks involved, *do not venture into abandoned mines.* Timbering in many such mines is badly deteriorated, and hammering or picking at the side walls or roof of an old tunnel may precipitate a cave-in. Neither is it safe to venture too near the mouths of open mine shafts. The rim may be far undercut by caving, and the additional strain imposed by even one person's weight may prove sufficient to send another section of the surface crashing downward for hundreds of feet.

Never reach into or under any place not fully visible to the eye—rattlesnakes like to lie in the shade afforded by rocks and old buildings.

Don't destroy the old towns, or desecrate their graveyards. Always remember that if the folks who have visited those towns in the past had destroyed their buildings, they wouldn't be there for you to explore today. Don't break into buildings that are locked. They may appear abandoned, to *you;* but in the eyes of the sheriff, the lock on a ghosttown door is just as inviolate as your own locked door in the city. And be careful of buildings posted prominently with "Keep Out" signs. There may be a coyote gun or other booby trap set to fire when the door is opened.

If you find an unlocked, unposted building, containing furniture, foodstuffs, and other evidences of occasional occupancy, don't disturb it. Chances are it is being used as some stockman's "line camp," or by some old prospector who may be working a mine in the next county, or is otherwise absent on business, or even confined to a hospital. When he returns to his home he deserves to find things as he left them. In case of inclement weather, of course, you are welcome to the use of such cabins; but before leaving, be sure to replace the fuel you have used, so that the next man who stays there will have wood and kindling, even though he arrives in the dead of night, or the midst of a blizzard.

Folks who write me concerning ghosttown etiquette ask frequently if it is permissible to take relics and souvenirs found in these towns. That's a hard question to answer, since circumstances vary. As a general rule, no one will object if you limit your "larceny" to actual relics having no other use than as museum specimens or "collector's items." If any article looks as if it might be *owned,* and still useful for its intended purpose— leave it alone! Abide by the Golden Rule, and let your conscience be your guide.

Excellent maps of the mining country, showing the locations of many former boom camps since become ghosttowns, may be purchased from the U. S. Geological Survey, Federal Building, Denver, Colo., at 20 cents each; or at slightly higher prices from assigned dealers in leading cities throughout the country. Drawn to scales ranging from 1:24,000 (1 inch=2000 feet) to 1:125,000 (1 inch=approximately 2 miles) these maps indicate mines, mills, cemeteries, streams, and other natural and man-made features, and are accurate. An index showing sections mapped may be had on request to the Denver office.

With this preliminary briefing, a standard passenger car, pick-up, or jeep, some shoe leather, and determination, any able-bodied person should be able to visit a major portion of the 277 ghosttowns embraced in the accompanying directory.

Good luck, and good hunting; or, perhaps I should say, good *haunting!*

Ghosttown Directory

(Unless specifically noted "by road," all mileages quoted are based on approximate airline distance between geographical points mentioned. In many cases, no direct road exists between town described and point of location cited in the text. Persons planning to visit any off-the-beaten-track ghosttown should first make local inquiry concerning best routes, road conditions, and other factors.)

NEVADA

ALPHA, Eureka Co., 35 m. N.W. Eureka. During construction of Eureka & Palisade R.R., in late 1870s, Alpha embraced stores, saloons, freight barns, depot, and hotel for 75 guests. Almost nothing remains.

AMADOR, Lander Co., 7 m. N. Austin. With 1500 inhabitants, and 700 qualified voters, Amador, in 1863, was a candidate for location of Lander county seat. Losing the decision to Austin, Amador languished, and by 1869 was completely deserted.

AMERICAN CANYON, Pershing Co., 12 m. S. Unionville. For 15 years, beginning 1881, Chinese placer miners worked gold deposits in this area for a total production of $10,000,000. During this period, the canyon was site of a large camp, embracing shops, lodging houses, and a joss temple. Rock ruins.

ARABIA, Pershing Co., 7 m. N. Oreana. A small mining camp supported by the rich Montezuma mine which, prior to 1875, had yielded 3150 tons of lead, and $455,000 in silver, from only 7000 tons of ore. Rock ruins and extensive mine workings remain.

ARROWHEAD, Nye Co., 12 m. S.E. Warm Springs, on U.S. 6. A small camp (store, boarding house, P.O., blacksmith shop, etc.) abandoned in 1930s. All that had survived in 1954 were cement foundations, rubble, and the wooden building that had housed the smithy.

ATWOOD, Nye Co., 25 m. N.E. Luning. Discovery of gold-silver ore, about 1901, led to the birth of a small town and P.O., and sale of town lots was boomed by a Tonopah realty firm. Little remains.

AURORA, Mineral Co., 28 m. S.W. Hawthorne. (Plates 2, 4; Map p. 63)

AURUM, White Pine Co., 30 m. N.E. Ely. Discovery of silver ore in 1871, caused the founding of a small camp with stores, P.O., hotels, saloons, ore crushing mill, etc.

BANNOCK, Lander Co., 14 m. S.W. Battle Mountain. After Alex Walker, in 1909, discovered surface ore assaying $180,000 in gold to the ton, the town of Bannock was founded and within a few months embraced hotels, dance halls, saloons, P.O., and stores. Later discoveries of placer gold yielded nuggets weighing up to 20 ounces each, but the excitement was short lived. Ruins.

BARCELONA, Nye Co., 50 m. N. of Tonopah, 8 m. W. Belmont. In 1876 this town embraced 3 boarding houses, store, blacksmith shop, and assay office. Deserted by 1877.

BAXTER SPRINGS, Nye Co., 18 m. S. Manhattan. Founded in 1906, Baxter soon numbered 400 inhabitants, with restaurants, grocery, hardware and general stores, lodging houses, and saloons.

BELLEHELEN, Nye Co., 5 m. S. of U.S. 6 at point 50 m. E. of Tonopah. A camp of the early 1900s, with a peak population of 500.

BELLEVILLE, Mineral Co., on Rte. 10, 12 m. S. Mina. (Page 115)

BELMONT, Nye Co., 48 m. N. Tonopah. (Plate 1; Map, p. 50)

BERLIN, Nye Co., 5 m. S. Ione; 55 m. S.W. Austin. (Plate 48; Map, p. 86)

BERNICE, Churchill Co., W. slope Clan Alpine Mtns., about 90 m. (by road) E.N.E. Fallon. Considerable antimony and silver were mined here during last third of 19th century, but few evidences of that activity remains.

BETTY O'NEAL, Lander Co., 14 m. (by road) S.E. Battle Mountain. A small camp established 1880, with peak reached in 1920s when Noble

Getchell reopened the old Betty O'Neal mine. After producing several million dollars in bullion, operations ceased in middle 1930s. Equipped mill, vacant boarding house, sundry ruins, and no inhabitants, remained in 1955.

BIG CREEK, Lander Co., W. slope Toiyabe Mtns., 12 m. S. Austin. Established 1863, with mills, stores, school, justice court, P.O., express and telegraph offices, and stages connecting with Austin. The famed humorist, Artemus Ward, once lectured here in the Young America saloon, where 150 miners paid $2 each to hear him. Boom was short lived, and Big Creek has been a ghosttown since 1867. Stone ruins.

BLAINE, Elko Co., 20 m. S.E. Elko. A town that flourished briefly in early 1900s.

BLAIR, Esmeralda Co., 2 m. (by road) N. Silver Peak. Formerly location of Nevada's largest ore mill— 120 stamps, operated by Pittsburg-Silver Peak Mining Co. (Plate 52) Blair, in 1907, was a clean, well regulated camp, with numerous stores, a bank, two-story hotel, water and sewer systems, a weekly newspaper, *The Press,* and was served by the Silver Peak R.R., connecting with Tonopah & Goldfield R.R. at Blair Junction. Foundation of the big mill, cellars, rubble, and 2 cement buildings, remained in 1954.

BONNIE CLARE, Nye Co., on State Rte. 72, 5 m. (by road) W. of U.S. 95. A small mining and milling town of early 20th century. Cabins and mill ruins remain. (Map p. 143)

BOVARD, Mineral Co., 15 m. S.W. Rawhide, 23 m. N.E. Hawthorne. (Page 232)

BRISTOL CITY, Lincoln Co., N. end Cedar Range, 25 m. N.E. Pioche. Known originally as National City, this was a lively place in the 1870s when it boasted a smelter, P.O., stores, 3 boarding houses, livery stable, and other business houses patronized by 700 miners and millhands.

BRISTOL WELLS, Lincoln Co., 20 m. N.W. Pioche. By 1953, this smelter town of the 1870s had vanished except for 3 beehive-type charcoal kilns, a pile of slag from the smelter, and two stone cabins.

BROKEN HILLS, in a narrow sliver of Mineral county, closely bounded by Churchill and Nye; 2½ m. E. Rte. 23, at a point 50 m. S.E. Fallon. (Page 234; Plate 49) Old cabins and foundations.

BUCKHORN, Eureka Co., S.E. side Cortez range, 30 m. S. Beowawe. Following discovery of gold-silver ore by Joe Lynn in 1908, principal claims here were acquired by Geo. Wingfield, who erected an 800-hp electric power plant at Beowawe, and a 300-ton cyanide mill at Buckhorn. Mill operated through 1914-15, shut down in 1916, and was dismantled for lack of ore.

BUCKSKIN, on Lyon-Douglas Co. line, E. slope Pine Nut range, 12 m. S.W. Wabuska. Grown up around the Buckskin mine, located 1906, this town supported briefly a P.O., chamber of commerce, telephone and telegraph offices, 2 lumber yards, numerous stores, and paid $1.50 a barrel for its drinking water. A victim of the Panic of 1907.

BULLFROG, Nye Co., 5 m. (by road) W. Beatty. (Page 204) Extensive rock ruins.

BULLION CITY, Elko Co., on Bunker Hill, Pinyon Range, 28 m. S.W. Elko. Following ore discoveries in 1869, Bullion City became an important camp which remained active until the 1880s (as long as smelters owned by the Empire City Co., of NYC, and A. J. Ralston & Co., of San Francisco, were in operation.) Prior to 1884 the district had produced $3,000,000 in gold, silver, copper and lead.

BULLION, Lander Co., 25 m. S. Beowawe. Bullion, in 1906, was one of the bright stars in Nevada's mining firmament. A townsite was platted, lots sold, and business houses erected. It must have been a very good town, as "the good die young."

BULLIONVILLE, Lincoln Co., 1 m. (by road) W. Panaca, 12 m. S.E. Pioche. In 1869, by virtue of an abundant water supply, this place became milling center for the rich Pioche mines. Growth was stimulated by completion of Pioche & Bullionville R.R., in 1873, and by 1874, the town had a population of 500, and a lively business district. When water was struck in the Pioche mines, two years later, it became unnecessary to ship the ore to Bullionville for milling, and the town died. Scarcely an "X" marks the spot.

CANDELARIA, Mineral Co., 15 m. S. Mina; 7 m. (by road) W. of U.S. 95. (Page 109, Plates 23, 34) Extensive rock ruins and cemetery.

CANYON CITY, Lander Co., W. slope

Toiyabe Mtns., 7 m. S. Austin. As early as 1863 this town had a hotel, store, 2 restaurants, 3 saloons, meat market, notary public, recorder's office, and according to the *Reese River Reveille,* of Austin, "a marvelous future." Ledges proved to be small and less valuable than expected, and the town died young.

CARRARA, Nye Co., E. side U.S. 95, 10 m. (by road) S. Beatty. Quarrying of marble was begun here in 1904 by American Carrara Marble Co. Later, gang saws were installed and the townsite dedicated May 8, 1913. When the marble proved too fractured for satisfactory use, the plant was dismantled in 1936, and Carrara died of malnutrition. Stone foundations and partly-sawn slabs of marble remain.

CAVE CITY, White Pine Co. (See HAMILTON)

CHAFEY, Pershing Co., 10 m. N.E. Mill City. Established 1908 on the site of the earlier mining camp of Dun Glen, Chafey was briefly an important center with assorted business houses and a newspaper, *The News.* Rock and adobe ruins, and a small cemetery.

CHARLESTON (nee MARDIS) Elko Co., 45 m. N.W. Wells. (Page 176, Plate 55)

CHERRY CREEK, White Pine Co., 45 m. N.W. Ely. (Page 178; Map, p. 29)

CLAN ALPINE, Churchill Co., 20 m. (by road) N. Eastgate. A stamp mill built here in 1866 operated but a short time, and town was deserted by '67. Rock ruins of the mill, company offices, dwellings, and a few old fruit trees, remained in 1955.

CLIFFORD, Nye Co., S. of U.S. 6, at a point about 50 m. E. Tonopah. After discovery of ore by James and Ed Clifford in 1905, and sale of discovery claim for $250,000, the camp boomed and soon had population of 500 with P.O., hotel, stores, saloons, and boarding houses.

CLIFTON, Lander Co., at mouth of Pony Canyon, below present town of Austin. Town developed with the discovery of rich silver ore in 1862, and soon had 500 inhabitants, P.O., Wells Fargo office, and several places of business. With founding of Austin, in '63, Clifton was absorbed.

COLUMBIA, Elko Co., 10 m. S.W. Mountain City. Prior to mill's closing in 1870, a busy mining camp with stores and offices. Now headquarters of a large cattle ranch. Rock ruins.

COLUMBIA, Esmeralda Co., 1 m. N. Goldfield. Only a fading memory today, the Columbia of 1905 boasted numerous two-story brick business buildings, and a Chamber of Commerce incorporated at $10,000. Ruins.

COLUMBUS, Esmeralda Co., 5 m. W. of U.S. 95, at a point 20 m. (by road) S. Mina. (Page 112, Plate 17)

COMO, Lyon Co., 15 m. (by road) S.E. Dayton. After discovery of gold-silver ore and erection of a mill, in 1863, Como boomed, became first seat of Lyon county, had a lively business district, a newspaper—*The Sentinel*— and enjoyed a peak population of about 700. By 1874 the town was completely deserted except for one man, Judge G. W. Walton, who burned to death in his cabin, on Nov. 22. that year. Extensive mine dumps, mill tailings, and ruins of stone buildings remain.

COPPER BASIN, Lander Co., 10 m. S.W. Battle Mountain. Since early 1860s, the surrounding region has been mined for gold, silver, lead, copper and turquoise. Wooden buildings (several still occupied in 1955) mark former site of the town.

CORNUCOPIA, Elko Co., 15 m. N.W. Tuscarora. In the 1870s a town that embraced numerous stores and shops, a two-story hotel, and a population of 1000, including 400 voters, Cornucopia died when most of its citizens joined the stampede to Tuscarora.

CORTEZ, on Lander-Eureka county line, 40 m. S.E. Battle Mountain. First ore out of this district was mule-freighted to Austin where it helped found the Geo. Hearst fortune. With erection of a mill, in 1865, Cortez began to boom and soon numbered 1000 inhabitants of mixed racial groups, chiefly Mexicans and Chinese. Production continued until close of the century and several unsuccessful efforts have been made to revive the camp. Vacant cabins, boarding house, cemetery, extensive and picturesque mill ruins, and 6 residents, remained in 1952. (Plate 19)

CRESCENT, Clark Co., 15 m. W. Searchlight. After turquoise mining operations were begun here by Toltec Gem Co., of NYC, in 1897, the leading mine was found to have been worked in prehistoric times by miners who had used stone hammers and other primitive tools. The town of Crescent, which grew up around the operation, consisted of one vacant building and mill ruins, in 1951.

CRYSTAL SPRINGS, Lincoln Co., 40 m. W. Caliente. (Page 170)

CUPRITE, Esmeralda Co., E. side U.S. 95, near jct. Rte. 3. In 1908-9 the nearest railroad town to the booming gold camps of Lida, Hornsilver, Bonnie Clare, and Tule Canyon, once-busy Cuprite, in 1955, had been reduced to one old fireplace chimney, partially fallen.

DANVILLE, Nye Co., E. flank Monitor range, 95 m. N.E. Tonopah. A small town that developed in 1866 and was active for a number of years. By 1880 the place was virtually deserted, and only a few old cabins and graves marked its site in 1948.

DEAN, Lander Co., near the head of Dean Canyon (a tributary of Lewis Canyon) 15 m. S.E. Battle Mountain. Marking the site of this small mining camp, which flourished in the 1880s and '90s, are a few old cabins, ruins of the Highland Chief Mill (Plate 16) and the tunnel of the Dean mine.

DELAMAR, Lincoln Co., 14 m. (by road) S. of U.S. 93, at a point 17½ m. (by road) W. Caliente. (Page 194)

DEVIL'S GATE, Lyon Co., near the present site of Dayton. Developed soon after 1859 this town soon embraced a P.O., two hotels, brewery, stores, saloons, two shoe shops, barber shops, and livery stables. Stone ruins.

DIAMONDFIELD, Esmeralda Co., 3½ m. N.E. Goldfield. A small town, promoted by "Diamondfield" Jack Davis, spectacular character of the early 1900s, who arrived in Tonopah, about 1903, from Idaho, where he had been convicted of murder and was standing on the scaffold, noose adjusted and black hood in place, when a last-minute pardon from the governor cancelled the execution. Throughout the remainder of Davis' life, the episode formed one of his favorite anecdotes. (Plate 47)

DOUGLASS, Mineral Co., 5 m. S.W. Mina. A small camp active around 1900-5.

DOWNEYVILLE, Nye Co., E. slope Paradise range, 4 m. N.E. Gabbs. Site of one of the state's first lead smelters, Downeyville retained its P.O. and some show of life until after turn of the century. Partially-fallen stone cabins, caved cellars, old foundations, rubbish dumps, and mill ruins remain.

DUN GLEN, Pershing Co., 10 m. N.E.

Mill City. Settled in 1862, Dun Glen experienced several raids by Indians, and in '63 became site of a small fort staffed by U.S. cavalry. Most colorful era in the town's history was in the 1870s and '80s when Chinese placer miners, engaged in recovering an estimated $4,000,000 in gold from nearby canyons, supported here opium dens, fantan parlors, and a joss temple. Rock ruins and old graves.

DUTCH CREEK, Mineral Co., S. end Walker Lake. Founded 1906, when Walker Indian Reservation was opened to mining, Dutch Creek boomed and by 1907 had a population of 500 and a lusty business district, including a newspaper, saloons, stores, eating houses, etc. Daily mail service was supplied through Hawthorne, and steam launches provided passenger and freight connection with other points on Walker Lake. (Former site of town is included within the U.S. Naval Ammunition Depot and is not accessible to civilians.)

EAGLEVILLE, Churchill Co., 52 m. S.E. Fallon; 10 m. S. Frenchman's Station, on U.S. 50. A small village of early 1900s.

EBERHARDT, White Pine Co., 30 m. W. Ely; 5 m. S.E. present ghosttown of Hamilton. A small town that grew up in 1870s around the Stanford mill, engaged in handling ore of the rich Eberhardt mine. At its peak the camp still had about 200 citizens, with P.O., store, blacksmith, wagon and carpenter's shops, "and an active temperance organization." By 1954, the big mill and other buildings lay in ruin, and the temperance society had triumphed — the town was completely "dry." (Page 104)

EDGEMONT, Elko Co., W. slope Bull Run Mtns., 92 m. N.N.W. Elko; 5 m. S. White Rock, on Rte. 11. Developed following discovery of gold in 1890s, Edgemont was scourged by yearly snowslides, one avalanche, which thundered down the mountainside in 1917, demolishing a 20-stamp mill, assay office, and boarding house. Despite this drawback, the district produced more than $1,000,000 in gold. Ruins.

EGAN, White Pine Co., 40 m. N.E. Ely; 12 m. W. of U.S. 93. A famous relay station on both the Pony Express route and Overland Mail lines, Egan became an active mining camp with nearby discoveries of silver, in 1863. Stone ruins.

EL DORADO, Clark Co., 29 m. (by paved road) S.E. Boulder City. (Page 36, Plates 6, 8) Most of the original townsite today is covered by waters of Lake Mohave.

ELLENDALE, Nye Co., 2 m. S. U.S. 6, at a point 30 m. E. Tonopah. High grade gold float discovered in 1909 by Ellen Clifford Nay inspired a "rush," a townsite was laid out, and homes and shops built. After producing around $1,000,000 in bullion, the camp died, and in 1951, only a single house marked its former site.

ELLSWORTH, Nye Co., on Burnt Cabin Summit road, 12 m. W. Ione. Founded in 1864 as result of silver-gold discoveries the previous year, Ellsworth enjoyed its peak of population around 1870. Stone walls of a former store building, and ruins of several stone cabins, remained in 1955. (Page 85)

EMPIRE CITY, Ormsby Co., on Carson river, 3½ m. N. Carson City. Town was platted in 1860 and three years later became site of a large sawmill, for which timber was cut in the Sierra and rafted down the Carson River, until 1865, when V-flume transportation was introduced. Mill ruins.

ETNA, Pershing Co., formerly a small milling town on left bank of Humboldt river, 3 m. N. of present S.P.R.R. station of Oreana. Active in the middle 1860s.

FAIRVIEW, Churchill Co., 42 m. (by road) E.S.E. Fallon. Following discovery of rich silver ore in 1905, a stampede developed and surrounding hills were soon blackened by 2000 prospectors. Spring of 1906 found business lots in the new town selling for $100 a front foot, and for ten years Fairview was a lively place with numerous stores, a weekly newspaper —*The News*—hotel, bank, dancehall, and 27 grog shops. After the Nevada Hills mine closed, in 1917, the town declined rapidly. Remaining in 1954 were the Dromedary Hump mill, many stone foundations, and two inhabitants —Ed and Sylvia Stratton.

FARRELL, Pershing Co., 5½ m. N.E. Seven Troughs; 25 m. N.W. Lovelock. A small, rowdy camp of early 20th century.

FLETCHER, Mineral Co., on Rte. 3-C, 18 mi. S.W. Hawthorne. Former stage stop, way station, and P.O., on Carson City-Aurora road.

FRANKTOWN, Washoe Co., on U.S. 395, 10 m. N.W. Carson City. Second town settled in Nevada, and formerly an important milling town for Comstock ores, Franktown also was the site of Sandy and Eilley Bowers' fabulous mansion, now embraced in a county park, and open to the public on payment of a small admission fee.

GALENA, Lander Co., 14 m. (by road) S.W. Battle Mountain. As platted in 1869, Galena's townsite embraced wide streets, public squares and parks. The camp grew rapidly, and by 1871 was served by a city water system, substantial business district, a good hotel, public hall, etc. A smelter was built to treat the rich silver-lead ores of the Duck Creek mines, and the camp knew several years of opulence. Eight persons still resided there in 1953.

GALENA, Washoe Co., E. slope Mt. Rose, 14 m. S. Reno. Three years after Galena's founding, in 1860, 11 sawmills and a sash factory were operating in her environs, and with loggers, millmen, bull-whackers, woodcutters, charcoal burners, and teamsters thronging her streets, the town lived lavishly. Her timber barons swung a heavy axe, however, and within a few years all nearby acreage had been stripped of its timber. After major fires in 1865 and '67, Galena threw in the towel, and scarcely a scar marks its former site.

GENEVA, Lander Co., E. slope Toiyabe Mtns., 10 m. S. Austin. Founded in the early 1860s as result of gold and silver discoveries, Geneva flowered briefly and by 1864 numbered 500 citizens, numerous cabins of stone and log construction, and many tents. Ruins.

GILBERT, Esmeralda Co., Monte Cristo Mtns., 25 m. N.W. Tonopah. News of the Gilbert strike reached Tonopah late in 1924 and by close of that year nearly 100 outfits were prospecting in the area. Before its first birthday, the town boasted 500 residents, a good business district, electric-lighted streets, and a newspaper, the *Record,* which reported that 12 sacks of picked sample ore, taken to Tonopah by the Gilbert brothers, assayed $96,000 to the ton! When the vein of the Gilbert's Black Mammoth mine was lost by faulting, the boom collapsed. Wooden ruins.

GLOBE, Lander Co., E. slope Toiyabe Mtns., 17 m. S. Austin. A small, very old ghost, once supported by a sawmill.

GOLDBANKS, Pershing Co., E. base East Range, N. end Pleasant Valley, 35 m. S. Winnemucca. Gold discoveries in 1907 made this a place of great promise and many leasers worked feverishly for about a year, after which the boom subsided.

GOLD CENTER, Nye Co., 5 m. S. Beatty. With its townsite officially platted in 1905, Gold Center became briefly a prosperous place. Served by the L.V. & T.R.R., its commercial district included an ice plant and brewery, hotel, bank, brokerage offices, saloons, and mercantile establishments. Ruins and debris.

GOLD CIRCLE, Elko Co. (See MIDAS)

GOLD CREEK, Elko Co., at confluence Penrod and Gold Creeks, 70 m. N. Elko. Attention was drawn to this district in 1873 when several $50 nuggets were yielded by Gold Creek, but the main boom did not develop until 1896. Within a year the town embraced a P.O., 3-story hotel with 40 rooms and a liveried bellboy; a weekly newspaper, The *Gold Creek News*, numerous stores, electric-lighted streets, and a city water system. Ruins.

GOLD HILL, Storey Co., 1 m. E. Virginia City. Founded 1859 as result of placer gold discoveries, Gold Hill ballooned in stature with the rush to the Comstock diggings in 1860, and her streets were soon flanked by a town hall, stores, lodge buildings, firehouse, churches, a school, and substantial dwellings. After waning of the Comstock excitement, the town still clung grimly to life. Time took away her railroad (Virginia & Truckee); she lost her P.O. in 1943; her firehall was demolished by snow in 1951; and in 1955, the old town could muster but six residents. Extensive and picturesque ruins.

GOLD HITT, Esmeralda Co., Oneota mining district, 6 m. from Basalt. *Tonopah Bonanza*, in 1906, characterized this "a town with a future." The camp, at that time, embraced a general store, meat market, restaurant, lodging house, feed corral, and 3 saloons; a daily stage line to Basalt was in operation, a telephone line was being built from Summit, and Ogden

capital was installing a mill. It's all gone, now.

GOLD MOUNTAIN, Esmeralda Co., on Slate Ridge, 30 m. S.W. Goldfield. (Page 141; Plate 26; Map, p. 143)

GOLD MOUNTAIN, Esmeralda Co., 6 m. S. Tonopah. After the original town of this name (see above) was dead and forgotten, the same name was given a second camp which burgeoned in 1901, and soon included a boarding house, general store, and three saloons. Some mining is still in progress, but the town has vanished.

GOLD POINT (nee HORNSILVER) Esmeralda Co., 30 m. (by road) S.W. of Goldfield. (Page 148; Plates 27, 29, 30; Map p. 143) In 1955 Gold Point still embraced a combined store and P.O., 13 residents, and many old wooden buildings.

GOLDEN ARROW, Nye Co., 40 m. S.E. Tonopah. The Golden Arrow company was capitalized at $1,000,000 in 1906, and the townsite incorporated. A few stores and a hotel were built but the excitement was short-lived.

GOLDYKE, Nye Co., 25 m. N.E. Luning. Values were first discovered in this district in 1901—gold, silver and mercury being the principal metals, with some lead and copper. Of the small camp developed in 1906, only one vacant dwelling, and a 5-stamp mill, remained in 1954.

GRANITE, Mineral Co., 6 m. N.W. Schurz. A promising camp in 1908, when many leasers were working actively in the vicinity, Granite supported several business houses and a small newspaper, *The Times*.

GRANITE, Nye Co., S. tip Lodi hills, in N.W. part of county. First gold discoveries were made here in 1875, the camp had two smelters, at different times, and some production continued until 1916.

GRANTSVILLE, Nye Co., 55 m. S.W. Austin. (Page 85; Map, p. 86)

GREENVILLE, Lyon Co., A prosperous farmer-supported town in Mason Valley, Greenville, in 1880, embraced a P.O. (known as Mason Valley); a Methodist church seating 200 persons, school, Wells Fargo office, 5 stores, 3 hotels, 2 saloons, 2 restaurants, 3 livery stables, and 3 blacksmith shops. Only the memory lingers on.

GUADALAJARA (or SANTA FE) Lander Co., E. slope Toiyabe Mtns., 18 m. S. Austin. First gold and silver discoveries in this district were made by Mexicans in late 1850s or early '60s, and a small sawmill was established. Walls and foundations of 8 stone cabins mark the spot.

HAMILTON, White Pine Co., 30 m. W. Ely. (Page 100, Plate 25)

HANNAPAH, Nye Co., 15 m. N.E. Tonopah. Sale of business and residential lots was thrown open here, Feb. 6, 1906, but the town failed to distinguish itself, and only diligent search reveals its former site.

HARDIN CITY, Humboldt Co., 45 m. (by road and trail) N.E. Gerlach. Founded 1866, as result of a masterly hoax inspired by reported discovery of rich silver float by covered-wagon emigrants, in 1849. Three mills were built and thousands of dollars expended in development, but by the summer of 1868, the district was deserted. Ruins of 3 rock-and-adobe mills, traces of other buildings, and several graves, remained in 1954.

HIGHLAND, Elko Co., 2 m. S.W. Bullion City; 30 m. S.W. Elko. A small camp of the 1870s and '80s.

HIGHLAND, Lincoln Co., on summit Bennett Spring Mtn., 12 m. S.W. Pioche. Founded 1869, this town soon embraced a boarding house, brewery, saloon, store, and dwellings.

HIKO, Lincoln Co., 4 m. (by paved road) N. U.S. 93 at a point 43 m. W. Caliente. (Page 170)

HOBSON, White Pine Co., 45 m. N.E. Eureka; 55 m. S.E. Elko. Situated on site of earlier Fort Ruby, its P.O. (since discontinued) was established during the Spanish-American War, when Admiral Hobson was cutting capers in Santiago Harbor. Former townsite, now headquarters of Harris cattle ranch, still marked by several interesting old buildings. (Ask owner's permission to visit.)

HORNSILVER, Esmeralda Co. (See GOLDPOINT)

HOTCREEK, Nye Co., 70 m. N.E. Tonopah. After rich ore discoveries in 1865, a town developed, was granted a P.O. in '67, and by '68 had 300 residents, 2 stamp mills, and assorted business houses. Several of the original stone-and-adobe buildings are still in use on the Hot Creek ranch.

HUMBOLDT CITY, Pershing Co., 2 m. (by road) S. of U.S. 40, at a point 33 m. N.E. Lovelock. (Page 10)

IONE, Nye Co., 50 m. S.W. Austin. (Page 83; Map, p. 86)

JACOBSVILLE, Lander Co., 8 m. (by road) W. Austin. Established in the late 1850s as a station on the Overland Mail line, Jacobsville served later as a Pony Express station, and in 1861 became first seat of Lander Co. The town, at its peak, had a population of 400, with P.O., 2 hotels, 3 stores, telegraph office, courthouse, and 50 residences. With transfer of the courthouse to Austin, in 1863, Jacobsville died of a broken heart. A few stone foundations are still faintly visible.

JARBIDGE, Elko Co., 70 m. N.W. Wells. (Page 238, Plate 46)

JEFFERSON, Nye Co., 60 m. N.E. Tonopah; 6 m. (by road) N.E. Round Mountain. Silver-gold values were first discovered here in 1866 but district did not become active until '74. By close of that year the town boasted two operating ore mills, P.O., hotel, large general store, 3 restaurants, 7 saloons, a brewery, 2 bakeries, butcher shop, barber shop, lumber yard, 2 livery stables, blacksmith shop, and a justice of the peace. Peak population (1876) was about 800. Several privately-owned stone buildings, in fair-to-good condition, ruins of numerous others, and one inhabitant, remained in 1955.

JESSUP, Churchill Co., 40 m. S.W. Lovelock. Back in 1908 this place gave promise of becoming quite a town, but only one resident was holding the fort in 1954.

JOHNNIE, Nye Co., 60 m. N.W. Las Vegas. The Johnnie and Congress mines, mainstays of the camp, were discovered about 1890. The Congress was worked profitably until 1895 when trouble developed, 2 men were killed, a 10-stamp mill and the cookhouse burned, and the mine office dynamited. The Johnnie continued in production until 1913, with spasmodic operation since by leasers. Numerous old wooden buildings were still standing in 1954.

JOY, White Pine Co., 35 m. N.E. Eureka. After ore discoveries in 1869, the town of Joy grew up at the S. end of the Ruby range, in the pass between Bald Mtn., and S. Bald Mtn.

KAWICH, Nye Co., E. side of Kawich range, 60 m. S.E. Tonopah. Following locations made in 1904, several hundred men collected and, by 1905, a small business district had taken form.

KENNEDY, Pershing Co., 45 m. E.N.E.

Lovelock (58 m. by road). Rumors of a rich gold discovery on Cinnabar creek brought an influx of prospectors in 1893. The Imperial mine was located by Chas. E. Kennedy and, within two years, the town named for him embraced 3 stamp mills, general store, P.O., several saloons, and a "restricted" district. Marking the spot in 1955 were 9 big ore leaching tanks (stone and cement); mill foundations, mine shafts and dumps, the old P.O., several wooden cabins, and crumbling ruins of stone and adobe buildings.

KINGSTON, Lander Co., E. slope Toiyabe Mtns., 20 m. S. Austin. Mining began here in 1863, and the town was founded the following year. Two water-powered mills of 20 stamps each had been built by 1867; and by '75, 4 amalgamating mills had been erected. Milling costs were high and bulk of the ore failed to pay out. Property of the Kingston mine was once optioned to Geo. Hearst, who became piqued by some action of the owners, dropped the option, and took up the Homestake mine, at Lead, S.D. Remaining in the canyon in 1952 was the shell of one large mill, and foundations and ruins of other buildings.

KLONDIKE, Esmeralda Co., a small, old camp—the few ruins of which are visible about a mile to the W. of U.S. 95, at a point midway between Tonopah and Goldfield. First ore values were found here in 1899, and it was to this place Jim Butler was bound when he made the historic strike that launched Tonopah in May, 1900. Klondike once had a P.O., was a station on the T. & G.R.R., and supported a small business district.

LANDER CITY, Lander Co., on Reese River, at mouth of Big Creek, 12 m. S.W. Austin. As early as 1863 this place had several hundred inhabitants, and David E. Buel had built a telegraph line to give it rapid communication with Austin and the Coast. By 1869, the town was only a fading memory.

LANE CITY, White Pine Co. (See MINERAL CITY)

LA PLATA, Churchill Co., E. slope Stillwater Range, 30 m. E. Fallon. Rich ore discoveries caused many locations to be made here between 1862 and '65, and 3 mills had been built by '66. In 1863, LaPlata succeeded Buckland as seat of Churchill county, but 5 years later, with her ore growing hungrier and her future dimmer, she lost the courthouse, in turn, to Stillwater. Most of her miners and her largest mill joined the stampede to White Pine district, in 1869, and LaPlata folded her wings. Rock ruins.

LEADVILLE, Washoe Co., 38 m. (by road) N. Gerlach, and 1 m. W. Rte. 34. Work started here in 1909 and continued with fair regularity until the 1920s. Mine dumps, mill ruins, and about a dozen wooden buildings, remained in 1954.

LEELAND, Nye Co., 22 m. S.E. Beatty. Formerly a station on the T. & T.R.R., and a small but active camp in the early 1900s.

LEWIS, Lander Co., 12 m. S.E. Battle Mountain. A thriving gold and silver camp as early as 1875, Lewis was supported by the Starr-Grove and Eagle mines and mills, as well as others, and for 8 months (1881-82) was terminus of the Battle Mountain & Lewis R.R. During its peak the town numbered several thousand persons, with P.O., school, dancehall, hotels, jail, stores, saloons, etc. Still visible in 1955 were the jail and "company" house, foundations of the old mills, nearly-vanished ruins of many cabins and stores, and a small cemetery.

LIDA, Esmeralda Co., on Rte. 3, 19 m. W. of U.S. 95, and 34 m. (by road) S.W. Goldfield. Founded in 1872, Lida prospered as well as could be expected of a town 100 miles from its county seat and 187 miles from the nearest R.R. In 1904-5, after nearly 30 years of barely "getting by," Lida's biggest boom got under way, a newspaper, The *Enterprise,* was founded, and the town flourished for about a year. All that remained in 1955 were numerous empty buildings, 4 families, a cemetery, and a pleasant, tree-shaded site. (Plate 28; Map, p. 143; Page 81)

LODI, Nye Co., 45 m. N.N.E. Luning. After ore discoveries in 1874, Lodi grew to embrace a large hotel, store, blacksmith shop, boarding house, saloon and smelting furnace. By 1880 the town was deserted, and all that remained in 1954 was one vacant store building, and stone foundations.

LOGAN CITY, Lincoln Co., 10 m. W. Hiko, and 52 m. (by road) W. Caliente. Founded in the 1860s, Logan retained its P.O. into the present century, but is now a ghost.

LONGSTREET, Nye Co., 40 m. E. Tonopah. A short-lived camp of the early 20th century, never as famous or colorful as its founder, Jack Longstreet, a squaw man with several notches on his gun, and who wore his hair long to conceal a cropped ear bestowed in his youth as penalty for being caught with another man's cattle. Jack died in 1928, and both he and his Indian wife, Fanny, are buried at Belmont.

LORENA, Mineral Co., 16 m. S.W. Rawhide. (Page 234)

LOWER ROCHESTER, Pershing Co., 20 m. N.E. Lovelock. A camp that knew its greatest period of activity early in the current century. Several wooden buildings and stone ruins remained at the site in 1950. (Map, p. 9)

LUDWIG, Lyon Co., 5 m. W. Yerington. An important copper camp during World War I, and formerly terminus of the Nevada Copper Belt R.R., connecting with the main line at Wabuska. Named for John D. Ludwig, early California Indian fighter, who located the main mine. Extensive cement foundations, stone ruins, and shells of several large mills, remained in 1948. (Plate 43)

MANHATTAN, Nye Co., 50 m. (by road) N.N.E. Tonopah. (Map, p. 50)

MARDIS, Elko Co. (See CHARLESTON)

MARIETTA, Mineral Co., 18 m. S.W. Mina. Founded soon after salt-harvesting operations were begun on Teel's Marsh, in 1867, Marietta knew its balmiest days about 1873 when borax was discovered in the marsh and a large plant for processing it was built. During the salt harvesting interlude, the product was shipped from Marietta to the silver mills of the Comstock by camel train, and to the mills at Aurora, by pack mules.

MAZUMA, Pershing Co., 25 m. N.W. Lovelock. Mazuma, in 1908, was a lively town with good payrolls, a bank, hotel, stores, and assorted shops and services—a state of affairs that continued until July 19, 1912, when a cloudburst broke on Seven Troughs mountain and a 20-foot wall of water roared down on the canyon town. At least 8 persons, including the postmistress, were drowned; and with exception of a few small buildings on the upper walls of the canyon, every home and business house in the town

was swept away. The place was never rebuilt.

METALLIC CITY, Mineral Co., 15 m. S. Mina. (Page 116)

METROPOLIS, Elko Co., 10 m. N.W. Wells. (Page 245, Plate 54)

MIDAS (originally GOLD CIRCLE) On S.E. slope Owyhee Bluffs, 42 m. (by road) N.E. Golconda. (Page 124, Plate 36)

MILL CITY, Pershing Co., on U.S. 40, 28 m. (by road) S.W. Winnemucca. Founded in 1863 in anticipation of the projected "Humboldt Canal," and as a milling town for ore from the Buena Vista mining district, Mill City enjoyed 20 years of fair prosperity, and in 1880 embraced a P.O., hotel, water works, stores, saloons, livery stable and blacksmith shop, and an iron foundry. Although still a station on S.P.R.R., its business section and P.O. has ceased to exist. (Map, p. 9)

MILLERS, Esmeralda Co., 15 m. (by road) W.N.W. Tonopah. During the years when it functioned as milling town for Tonopah ore, Millers embraced a P.O. and a small business district. Ruins of several buildings, including the mill, and a large tailings dump, remain.

MILLETT, Nye Co., in Smoky Valley, 0.3 m. E. of Rte. 8-A, 42 m. (by road) S. Austin. An important freighting station in the 1860s, when travel was heavy between Ophir Canyon and Austin, this place later became supply point for nearby mines. Maximum extent of its business district or population is not known, but it had, at least, a P.O., hotel—"The Lakeview" — general store, blacksmithing and wagon shop, etc. Its remaining buildings are now utilized as headquarters of the Frawley cattle ranch. (Ask permission to visit.)

MINERAL CITY (later, LANE CITY) White Pine Co., on U.S. 50, 4 m. N.W. Ely. Founded 1869 as result of silver, lead and copper discoveries, Mineral City soon claimed a population of 1500. Later, it declined until interest was revived by spectacular gold discoveries—ore assaying more than $20,000 to the ton being taken from the Chainman mine, and $13,-000 ore from the Emma! Gold mining continued in the area until 1900, after which time the local product has been chiefly copper. A few residents remain, and numerous old buildings mark the townsite.

MINERAL HILL, Eureka Co., W. slope Sulphur Spgs. range, 45 m. N.W. Eureka. When rich silver ledges were discovered here in 1869, a mad rush ensued and by 1870 the town included numerous dwellings (built mainly of dressed lumber), 2 hotels, 2 lodging houses, 2 stores, 4 saloons, 2 blacksmith shops, meat market, bakery, 2 restaurants, Wells Fargo office, and a brickyard; and the year following found there a 10-stamp mill, a new 3-story hotel, "The Grand," and a large schoolhouse was being built by public subscription. No one seems to remember what happened to this burgeoning metropolis, but it's not there, now!

MONARCH, Nye Co., on the Ralston desert, N.E. of Manhattan. Possibly the flashiest flash-in-the-pan Nye county ever knew, Monarch was the brainchild of the Rev. Benj. Blanchard who, in 1906, platted and sold 2300 town lots, plus numerous "mining claims" and "ranch sites" in the immediate environs. Stores, shops, boarding houses and hotels, sprang from the desert dust, and freight and stage lines, giving connection with Tonopah and the railroad, were established. When it was learned that the camp's daddy had absconded with $75,000 of investor's money, and left $73,000 in debts owed to supply houses and for labor, the new town folded—but quick!

MONTEZUMA, Esmeralda Co., N.W. side Montezuma Peak, 7 m. W. Goldfield. Rumor insists that this district was mined by Mexicans or Spaniards in the early 1800s, but so far as known definitely, the first discoveries of gold and silver ore were made here in 1867. A smelter was built, a 10-stamp mill imported from Yankee Blade, and a settlement embracing P.O., stores, etc., collected. The town has been abandoned for many years, but stone ruins remain.

MOREY, Nye Co., 75 m. N.E. Tonopah. Founded on the strength of silver ore discovered in 1865, Morey, at its peak, embraced a P.O., store, boarding house, express office, and blacksmith shop. Ruins.

MT. AIRY, Lander Co., in the Mt. Airy range, about 15 m. W. of Austin. A stage and mail station of the 1860s. Foundations, and a few old graves, mark the spot.

NATIONAL, Humboldt Co., 60 m. N.N.E. Winnemucca. (Page 219)

NATIONAL CITY, Lincoln Co. (See BRISTOL CITY)

NELSON, Clark Co., at terminus of Rte. 60, 29 m. (by road) S.E. Boulder City (Page 36, Plates 6, 8)

NEWARK, White Pine Co., 12 m. N. of U.S. 50, at a point 15 m. (by road) S.E. Eureka. After Stephen and John Beard discovered silver ore in this district, in 1866, the principal mines were purchased by Centenary Silver Co. A 20-stamp pan amalgamation mill was brought from Kingston district, but after $100,000 had been taken from shallow workings in the course of a few years, the camp died. In 1955, the tall brick mill chimney was still standing at the foot of the hills, surrounded by acres of crumbled foundations and rubbish piles.

NORTHUMBERLAND, Nye Co., E. side Toquima range, 75 m. N.E. Tonopah. Silver discoveries in 1866 brought delayed founding of a town in '79, and by '81 the place was largely deserted. One mill continued to operate on gold ore until 1942 and this, together with several other buildings, were standing in 1953.

OLINGHOUSE (or ORA) Washoe Co., 10 m. W.N.W. Wadsworth. Situated on the E. slope of Pah-Rah range, the Olinghouse area was prospected in 1860 and first locations made in '64. The camp saw its greatest activity 1901-3 when production of local mines (gold and silver) averaged around $100,000 annually. Several old buildings.

OPHIR, Washoe Co., W. side Washoe Lake, 3 m. S. Washoe City (ghosttown) and 22 m. (by road) S. Reno. Coming into being with construction of Ophir Silver Mining Co. mill in 1860, the town of Ophir flourished, and at its peak (1862-64) numbered some 1500 residents, with good stores, hotels, public hall, school, and several doctors and lawyers. Despite an imposing appearance, the Ophir mill was a white elephant, and after operating at a fraction of capacity until 1867, closed permanently. Only foundation stones and a few pieces of heavy milling equipment remained in 1953.

OPHIR CITY, Nye Co., E. slope Toiyabe Mtns., 45 m. S. Austin. Silver values in Ophir Canyon were first reported in 1863, following which the Murphy mine was located in '64, and building of a town and mill got under way. Working 1864-68, and again 1875-90, the mine produced about

$800,000 but paid no dividends. Ophir City, with a population of 400, had a P.O., fair business district, school, and several lodges. Remaining to mark the townsite in 1953 were picturesque stone and log buildings, and ruins of the Murphy mill.

OREANA, Pershing Co., on U.S. 40, 14 m. (by road) N.E. Lovelock. World attention was focussed on Oreana in 1867 when its smelter assertedly became first in the U.S. to ship lead into the commercial market. (Smelters in several western states had produced lead prior to that time, but their entire output, presumably, had been retained for local usage.) As long as nearby mines continued active, Oreana was a busy place, with five furnace chimneys belching smoke, her stores thronged, and her Jockey Club staging races on a local track. As lead mining declined, the town shriveled until 1951 when she lost her P.O., virtually her last symbol of urbanity. (Map, p. 9)

ORIENTAL, Esmeralda Co., 30 m. S.W. Goldfield. (Page 144; Map, p. 143)

ORO CITY, Mineral Co., 9 m. S.E. Hawthorne. Early in 1907 the Oro City Townsite & Water Co. was organized, building lots were advertised for sale, a whirlwind of construction was begun, and an auto stage line opened between that place and Hawthorne. On a map published four years later by U.S. Geological Survey, the name of the town is followed by the notation, "Abandoned."

OSCEOLA, White Pine Co., 30 m. S.E. Ely. (Page 159)

PALISADE, Eureka Co., 10 m. S.W. Carlin. Formerly a wild town at jct. of the S.P.R.R., W.P.R.R., and Eureka & Palisade R.R. Many old buildings, a few inhabitants, a 4th class P.O., and a large cemetery, remain.

PALMETTO, Esmeralda Co. On Rte. 3, 50 m. (by road) S.W. Goldfield. Following discovery of gold and silver ore in the Palmetto Mtns., in 1866, a 12-stamp mill was installed and a town blossomed. The ore was soon exhausted and the town died, only to be revived in 1880, and again in 1900. By 1906, the revived town had a main street a mile long, with P.O., bank, hotel, stores, assay offices, restaurants, saloons, stage and express offices, and a newspaper, *The Herald*. Ruins remaining include the chimney of Palmetto's third mill, roofless walls of the P.O. and stage station, and crumbled foundations of other buildings.

PALMYRA, Lyon Co., 12 m. S.E. Dayton. An early-day camp once numbering about 400 inhabitants. Likely named for the Syrian city built by Solomon.

PARK CANYON, Nye Co., 4 m. (by road) W. Millett, on Rte. 8-A. Early history of this place is somewhat obscure, but by the forepart of 1867, contemporary newspapers reported a "sprightly little town" springing up at the mouth of the Canyon, where the LaPlata Co. was building a large mill. A persistent rumor insists that Queen Liliuokalani, deposed monarch of the Hawaiian Islands, was briefly a resident at Park Canyon, where—according to the story—she owned mining property. Interesting stone ruins of mill and cabins.

PATSVILLE, Elko Co., 2 m. S. Mountain City, and 82 m. (by road) N. Elko. (Page 184)

PEAVINE, Washoe Co. (See POE CITY)

PHILLIPSBURG, Esmeralda Co., at extreme S.W. end of the W. range of Lone Mtn. foothills, 18 m. N.W. Goldfield. When G. H. Phillips, in May, 1906, discovered gold ore running $5000 to the ton, "while its value in silver," it was stated by *Tonopah Bonanza*, "can hardly be approximated," a rush took place, a townsite was surveyed, 150 building lots were sold the first week, and a saloon was the first business house erected. Nothing remains.

PHONOLITE, Nye Co., N. end Paradise range, 45 m. S.W. Austin. Late in 1906, soon after prospectors in the Paradise region had found ore assaying $2500 a ton in gold and silver values, Phonolite Townsite, Water & Light Co. was incorporated at $1,000,000, a townsite was platted, and sale of lots begun. Options were taken by the company on all water sources in the vicinity, and plans were made to install a city water system and build an electric light plant. Unfortunately, Phonolite proved to be a phoney. . .

PICKHANDLE GULCH, Mineral Co. (See METALLIC CITY)

PINEGROVE, Mineral Co., E. flank Smith Valley range, 20 m. S. Yerington. One year after discovery of gold, in 1866, the new town of Pinegrove had 300 inhabitants, 3 ore mills were in operation, and the district was soon shipping $10,000 per week in gold bullion. After experiencing several reincarnations, the old town, in 1948, was deserted. Stone and wooden buildings, and mill ruins, remain.

PIONEER, Nye Co., in Bullfrog Hills, 2 m. S.W. Springdale; 10 m. N.W. Beatty. Discovery of the Pioneer mine was made in 1907 but excitement lagged and the boom did not begin until 1908. The town that developed had the customary line-up of business houses, and briefly supported a newspaper—*The Pioneer Times*. Little of interest remains.

PITTSBURG, Lander Co., a small camp on the N. flank of Mt. Lewis, between Maysville and Dean Canyons, 15 m. S.E. Battle Mountain. Home of the Pittsburg mine, developed in the early 1880s.

POE CITY (or PEAVINE) Washoe Co., E. side Peavine Mtn., 9 m. N.W. Reno. First rail shipment across the Sierra Nevada is said to have been gold-silver ore shipped in 1866 from this district to Sacramento, for reduction. On strength of the discovery, a town was platted by John Poe, building lots enjoyed good sale and the burg, at its peak, numbered 1500 residents, with a fair business district, mill, smelter, and scores of brick and log houses. All that remains to mark the site are several long, gray mine dumps.

PUEBLO, Nye Co., E. base Toiyabe Mtns., W. edge Big Smoky Valley, 45 m. S. Austin. After this district had been mined since 1863, a prospector, in 1905, came upon a man's skeleton with a panful of dirt alongside. Panning the dirt, he found it to be almost pure gold, later discovering its source to be a 3-foot ledge of ore running $5000 to the ton! The townsite of Pueblo was laid out on a tract of land crossed by two running streams, and 500 persons flocked to the district in a few weeks' time. But the vein proved to be wider than it was deep, and Pueblo was short lived.

PYRAMID CITY, Washoe Co., 4½ m. S.W. Pyramid Lake, and 26 m. N.E. Reno. Laid out in 1876, Pyramid soon had 300 citizens, and regular stage connection with Reno. Almost nothing remains.

QUARTZ MOUNTAIN, Nye Co., 15 m. N. Gabbs. Following discovery of gold-silver ore, in the early 1920s, the town of Quartz Mountain was platted, building lots were sold, and business flourished until 1927, when the boom

subsided. Several wooden buildings were standing in 1954.

QUEEN CITY, Humboldt Co., 5 m. N.E. Paradise Valley. Founded in 1874 as milling town for ore mined at nearby Spring City, the Queen prospered until the mill closed, after which most of her subjects departed. By 1880, she had neither stores nor P.O. Scattered ruins.

QUINCY, Nye Co. (See ROYSTON)

RABBITHOLE, Pershing Co., 35 m. E. N.E. Gerlach. Due to insufficiency of water, placer gold discoveries made here by covered-wagon emigrants in the 1850s, were not worked until nearly 40 years later, when gravel was transported to a distant spring for washing. Water, eventually was brought in from Cow Canyon. Some mining is still in progress, but the town is gone. Extensive tailing piles remain.

RAILROAD CITY, Elko Co., 28 m. S.W. Elko. A lusty rival of Bullion City, one mile distant, this was a town laid out in 1870, near the main mines of Railroad mining district. Business houses soon included a hotel, store, butcher shop, and livery stable.

RAMSEY, Lyon Co., 18 m. N.E. Virginia City. When Tom Ramsey, in the winter 1905-6, discovered ore running $800 a ton in gold, a rush ensued. First building lots in the new town were sold in July, 1906. By September, of that year, no land within a radius of 12 blocks was available for purchase except at fantastic prices, and the town had grown to embrace 600 residents, 4 stores, hotel, assay office, 6 saloons, 2 restaurants, real estate and brokerage offices, a feedyard, and a newspaper, *The Record*. Several moderate fortunes were made before the boom subsided and the town died, about 1910. Only mill ruins and a few superficial scars remain.

RAWHIDE, Mineral Co., 40 m. N.N.W. Luning. (Page 222, Plates 33, 40, 41, 42)

REVEILLE, Nye Co., 70 m. E. Tonopah. Discovery of hornsilver in the Reveille range, in 1866, sparked a mild rush, and the town of Reveille (named for Austin's indestructible newspaper, the *Reese River Reveille*) was born. After 1000s of tons of ore had been freighted 140 miles to Austin, for reduction, a 10-stamp mill was built at the nearest water source, 12 m. W. of Reveille, in 1869, and between $3,000,000 and $4,-

000,000 worth of ore was ox-freighted from the mines to the mill. Operations ceased in the 1870s, and only rock ruins and a cemetery remained in 1952.

RHODES, Mineral Co., on U.S. 95, 8 m. S. Mina. Originally a borax-mining town and later a station on the Carson & Colorado R.R. Even the "X" that marks the spot has almost faded from view.

RHYOLITE, Nye Co., 5 m. W. Beatty. (Page 204, Plates 38, 39)

RIEPETOWN, White Pine Co., 4 m. S.W. Ely. "Blow-off" town for employees of the company-owned centers of Ruth and Kimberly, where "sporting" women and spiritous potations were not tolerated. With coming of automobile transportation and good roads to the nearby City of Ely, Riepetown died on the vine.

RIO TINTO, Elko Co., 2 m. S.W. Mountain City, (Page 184)

ROCHESTER, Pershing Co., 20 m. (by road) N.E. Lovelock. First ore values were discovered here in 1860 and desultory mining continued until 1911, when a silver ledge assaying $350 to the ton was discovered. With this development the camp boomed and by 1913 had a population of 1500, a small business district, and a newspaper, The *Rochester Weekly*. Prosperity smiled for a number of years, and before the town's abandonment, its mines had produced close to $10,-000,000. (Map, p. 9)

ROCKLAND, Mineral Co., 20 m. S.E. Yerington. Following discovery of the Rockland mine, in 1868, a 10-stamp mill was erected in 1870, and a town founded. Before closing, the mine had yielded around $1,000,000 in gold and the bistros of Rockland had produced numerous hangovers and black eyes, and several defunct citizens.

ROSEBUD, Pershing Co., 45 m. N.N.W. Lovelock. A short-lived boom was inspired by discovery of silver ore here in 1906. Rosebud Development Co. platted a townsite, opened sale of lots, and erected a hotel and bank. By spring, 1907, the camp had 800 inhabitants and telephone and stage connections with Humboldt House, on the S.P.R.R.

ROYSTON (or QUINCY), Nye Co., at S. tip Cedar Range, 39 m. N. Tonopah. This place won copious publicity in 1921 when $20,000 in silver was mined in 6 weeks, from a shaft 24 feet deep. By 1923, the camp had around 300 residents and a small business section, and application for a P.O. had been made. By the time the postal inspector arrived to establish the office, the camp had died so completely that not one patron remained to welcome him!

RUBY HILL, Eureka Co., 2 m. W. Eureka. Throughout the 1870s and '80s, Ruby Hill supported the usual palaces of pleasure, a Methodist Sunday School, a theater characterized as the "coziest" opera house in the state, a weekly newspaper—*The Mining News*—city waterworks, boot and shoemaking shop, and a brewery. In 1953, only extensive ruins and rubble marked the former site of the town.

RYE PATCH, Pershing Co., 24 m. (by road) N.E. Lovelock. Rye Patch mine was located in 1864 and a 10-stamp mill built in '70. The town that grew up around the two operations was never large, but embraced a P.O. and small business district. After producing more than $1,000,000, the mine closed, and Rye Patch wilted.

ST. THOMAS, Clark Co., 45 m. N.E. Las Vegas. Settled in 1864 as part of the "Mormon Corridor" to the Coast, St. Thomas became an attractive, farm supported village, with school, P.O., stores, and shops. Before the town was two years old, it had been selected as second seat of Pah-Ute county, Arizona Territory—as this portion of the state was then designated — and by 1867 the town was credited officially with 500 inhabitants. St. Thomas, however, was considered expendable to the general welfare, and on June 11, 1938, its site was flooded by the rising waters impounded behind Hoover Dam.

SALT WELLS, Churchill Co., 15 m. (by road) S.E. Fallon. With construction here of a salt refinery at a cost of $175,000, salt production, which had begun in 1863, reached 150 tons per month in '66, and 250 tons monthly in '67. With bulk of the output being absorbed by silver mills of the Comstock area, discovery of the nearer supply point of Eagle salt marsh, in 1870, left Salt Wells holding the bag. For a few more years, the marsh produced about 20 tons of borax, monthly, but with suspension of even this small activity, the town died. Only the salt marsh remains.

SAN ANTONIO, Nye Co., in Big Smoky Valley, between N. end of San Antonio Mtns. and S. end of the Toiyabes, 28 m. N.N.W. of Tonopah. With ore discoveries in this district in 1863, a two-story brick stage station and P.O. was established at San Antonio, and a 25-stamp mill built. The mill was not especially successful, the stage line was abandoned with coming of the railroads, and the P.O. was discontinued in 1906. Only the fire-gutted shell of the old brick station, and partly-fallen walls of several smaller buildings, were standing in 1955.

SANDY, Clark Co., 30 m. W. Las Vegas. A camp that grew up around the Keystone mine and mill and was active until about 1910. In the 1890s the town embraced a P.O., school, store and saloon.

SANTA FE, Lander Co. (See GUADALAJARA)

S C H E L L B O U R N E (or SCHELL CREEK) White Pine Co., 42 m. (by road) N.E. Ely. (Page 27, Plate 9; Map, p. 29)

SCOSSA, Pershing Co., 50 m. N.W. Lovelock. When the brothers, Charles and Jim Scossa discovered "jewelry gold" ore in this district, in 1907, a townsite was laid out and a small camp soon flowered. Several wooden cabins and the Scossa drug store were still standing in 1950, but no inhabitants remained.

SEVEN TROUGHS, Pershing Co., 28 m. (by road) N.W. Lovelock. Following discovery of gold in this area, in 1905, A. L. Friedman brought the district to attention of Salt Lake capitalists in 1906. By the following spring a boom was under way, a daily stage line to Lovelock had been inaugurated, and buildings were being erected as rapidly as the boards could be cut and fitted. During its opulence the town had 3 ore mills and supported a good business district and a newspaper, *The Miner.* Some mining is still in progress here, but no town remains. (Plate 51)

SHERMANTOWN, White Pine Co., 35 m. W.S.W. Ely. (Page 100) Shermantown boomed mightily during 1869 and the '70s, when lots on main street were selling at $2000 each, 5 mills were in operation, and the town was supporting a good business district and two newspapers, The *White Pine*

Telegram, and the *Reporter.* With her fortunes bound inescapably to those of her contemporaries, Hamilton and Treasure City, Shermantown died as they died. Mill ruins and roofless walls remain.

SILVER BOW, Nye Co., W. flank Kawich range, 53 m. E. Tonopah. Ore was rich in the Silver Bow district in 1904-5 and a plague of claim jumping developed. While discussing one such case over a convivial drink in a local bistro, Edward Johnson and his best friend, Hugh Fulton, entered into an argument, hot words followed, and the men ended by "shooting it out" on the main street of town. Fulton was killed and Johnson acquitted on grounds of self defense. Silver Bow's other chief bid for fame came in 1906 when her newspaper, *The Standard,* printed the front page of one entire edition in ink mixed with gold dust assaying $80,000 to the ton!

SILVERGLANCE, Nye Co., 1 m. from Hannapah, and 17 m. E.N.E. Tonopah. Advance sale of lots in the new townsite of Silverglance had been "phenomenal," said *Tonopah Bonanza* in Feb. 1906. Sale of even one lot there, today, would be phenomenal.

SILVER PEAK, Esmeralda Co., 30 m. S.W. Tonopah. Mining has been carried on in this vicinity from 1864 until the present time, and the town was once one of the leading camps in Nevada, with a diversified business district and a newspaper, *The Post.* Time brought assorted griefs, culminating in a fire that swept the business district in 1948, and leveled most of the buildings then standing. Some mining is still in progress, and the camp still supports a fourth class P.O. and a couple of small business houses.

SIMON, Mineral Co., 20 m. N.E. Mina. A small silver-lead camp at the N. end of the Cedar Range. Named for P.A. "Pop" Simon, owner of the main mine, which became an important ore producer after World War I. Stock in this development created a financial sensation by sky-rocketing from 10c a share to $29.50. Pop, who owned thousands of the shares, held out for $30 and took the beating of his life when the stock plummeted to a level below its original quotation. Ruins.

SODAVILLE, Mineral Co., 3 m. S. Mina. Today little more than a scar on the desert's face, Sodaville was once the most important town between Tonopah and Reno. In the wild, boom days following the original discoveries at Tonopah and Goldfield, most of the freight destined for these seething camps left the railroad at this point, to be transported to its destination in wagons drawn by 16 and 20 horses each. In 1903, an automobile stage line was inaugurated between the two points, each 32 h.p. coach carrying 16 passengers and making the 60-mile trip in 6 hours. Mill ruins.

SPRING CITY, Humboldt Co., E. slope Santa Rosa range, 8 m. N.W. Paradise Valley; 48 m. N.N.E. Winnemucca. Discovered in 1868, mines of this area enjoyed their main activity between 1871 and '91, during which period Spring City flourished. In 1881 the town was described as "a lively place" with P.O., daily mail, 2 hotels, 2 general stores, restaurant, brewery, 7 saloons, and a book store.

SPRUCE (or SPRUCEMONT) Elko Co., 40 m. S. Wells. A lively camp in the late 1860s, when local mines were yielding large amounts of rich ore and the costly smelter of the Ingot Co. was converting that ore into bullion. In 1872, for some unknown reason, the smelter closed—although the ore veins assertedly gave no evidence of being worked out. Other companies erected furnaces, but without success, and by 1880 the town had deteriorated until it embraced only 2 hotels, 2 saloons, a butcher shop, livery stable, blacksmith shop, 6 families, and 50 miners. Ruins.

STAR CITY, Pershing Co., 3 m. W. Rte. 50 at a point 10 m. S. Mill City. (Page 16)

STEPTOE CITY, White Pine Co., W. flank Schell Ck. Range, 20 m. N. Ely. Founded in the 1890s Steptoe continued active, with intermittent lapses, until time of World War I, and at its peak was a tough town with saloons, dancehalls, and "restricted" district, as well as stores, cafes, school, and P.O. (Map, p. 29)

STILLWATER, Churchill Co., 15 m. (by paved road) E.N.E. Fallon. Founded in 1862 as a station on the Overland Mail line, Stillwater, in '68 became third seat of Churchill Co. By 1880 the town embraced a P.O., courthouse jail, school, stores, hotel, saloon, restaurant, blacksmith shop, and stage station. In 1955, the P.O. was functioning in the last remaining

store, and a few of the original buildings remained.

SUTRO, Lyon Co. Visible from U.S. 50 at a point 5 m. E. Dayton. Situated at the mouth of Sutro tunnel (built by Adolph Sutro to drain the hot-water-flooded mines of the Comstock) this was an important town throughout the protracted construction of that mighty engineering project. Sutro's newspaper, The *Independent*, was published for 5 years beginning 1875. The shell of one large mill, an immense pile of mill tailings, the barred mouth of the tunnel, and other mementoes of the early days remained here in 1954.

SWANSEA, White Pine Co., ¾s of a mile N. Shermantown; 35 m. W. Ely. Named for the famous smelting center in Wales, Swansea served for several years as milling town for ores of Hamilton and Treasure City. (Page 100)

SYLVANIA, Esmeralda Co., 4 m. (by road) S.W. of Rte. 3, at a point 50 m. (by road) S.W. of Goldfield. After Silver-lead discoveries in 1870, this small town developed and remained active for several years. According to local legend it was once site of a general store operated by Chris Zabriskie of borax fame, and had several other business buildings. Ruins of old mills, and a 30-ton lead smelting furnace built in 1875, as well as picturesque stone and log cabins, are strung along the canyon for a distance of two miles.

TAYLOR, White Pine Co., in Schell Creek range, 18 m. S. Ely. Founded 1873, Taylor soon became a town of 1500 persons supported largely by the Monitor and Argus silver mines. By 1951 nothing remained but a few ruins and the old cemetery, one of whose graves presumably marks the resting place of "Buzz" Craven, famous early-day fiddler of the Rocky Mountain region, who was found frozen to death at Taylor in the 1880s.

TENABO, Eureka Co., 25 m. S.E. Battle Mountain. Many mines were in operation here in 1908-10, at which time a daily stage ran between this place and Beowawe, on the S.P.R.R.

TREASURE CITY, White Pine Co., near summit Treasure Hill, 30 m. W. Ely. (Page 104, Plate 22)

TROY, Nye Co., W. side Grant range, near its S. end, (30 m. S. Currant, on U.S. 6.) After discoveries of gold and silver ore in 1867, the town of Troy was founded in '69 and by 1870 had a P.O., 2 stores, boarding house, express office, blacksmith shop, and other adjuncts. Soon after their discovery the principal mines were purchased by an English company and a 20-stamp mill was erected and worked until 1872. The camp was deserted soon afterward, and only a few stone ruins remain.

TUSCARORA, Elko Co., 40 m. N.W. Elko. (Page 119, Plates 3, 37)

TYBO, Nye Co., in Tybo canyon, E. slope Hot Creek range, 60 m. N.E. Tonopah. (Page 135) After 70-odd years of decadence and periodic revivals, Tybo was completely uninhabited in 1955. Business buildings, homes, mill and smelter ruins, and a cemetery, mark its site.

UNION, Nye Co., in Union Canyon, W. slope Shoshone Mtns., 8 m. (by road) S.E. Ione. (Page 85)

UNIONVILLE, Pershing Co., Buena Vista canyon, E. side Humboldt range, 40 m. (by road) N.E. Lovelock. (Page 8; Map, p. 9)

VERNON, Pershing Co., 25 m. N.W. Lovelock. A short-lived camp of the early 1900s. Ruins of stone jail, other buildings.

WAHMONIE, Nye Co., 50 m. E. Beatty. Near Frenchman's Flat, where Uncle Sam's fractured atoms would later go Boom, the town of Wahmonie boomed briefly in 1928. When word got around that high-grade silver-gold ore had been discovered by McRae and Lefler, automobile-borne miners began pouring out of Tonopah toward the new bonanza, and in April, two months after the original strike, the town had a population of 1500, the Gilbert brothers had installed an electric light plant, and numerous stores and cabins had been built. Almost before it was possible to say, "Wahmonie, Nevada," the boom collapsed. (Plate 53)

WARD, White Pine Co., E. slope Egan range, 16 m. S. Ely. After important ore discoveries here in 1872, the Martin White Co. built 2 smelting furnaces and a 20-stamp mill, and the town of Ward was founded in '76. Before close of the following year the place had a population of 1500, 2 newspapers, The *Reflex,* and The *Miner,* 2 breweries, stores of all sorts, and several lodges and societies. Except for headstones in the old cemetery, and 6 beehive-type charcoal kilns, (2 miles S. of town) there are few tangible reminders of this once-busy place. (Plate 7)

WASHINGTON, Nye Co., W. slope Toiyabe Mtns., 28 m. S. Austin. An active silver mining camp for several years after organization of the district in 1863. By 1864-65 the town embraced several stores, saloons, and the first billiard parlor in Nye county.

WASHOE CITY, Washoe Co., on U.S. 395, 18 m. (by road) S. Reno. (Page, 88)

WEEPAH, Esmeralda Co., 18 m. S.W. Tonopah. Beginning in March, 1927, all roads led to Weepah, where ore assaying $78,000 a ton assertedly had been found. One of the first to arrive on the scene was a newsreel cameraman; dancehall girls came from Tonopah in evening gowns and high-heeled dancing slippers, and staked claims by moonlight; stock promoters arrived by plane. Within 5 weeks, 1500 persons had congregated, 15 syndicates were preparing to work claims, and many business houses had risen. But Weepah was born to wither and weep, and within a year her site was practically deserted.

WHISKEY SPRING, Mineral Co., 22 m. W. Mina. In the 1870s a stage stop, mail and telegraph station, and a lodging and eating point for travelers on the Bodie-Candelaria road.

WHITE PINE CITY, White Pine Co., S. side Treasure Hill, between Treasure City and Menken, 35 m. W. Ely. A short-lived camp of the 1870s.

WHITE PLAINS, Churchill Co., 30 m. S.W. Lovelock, 28 m. N. Fallon. Site of the Desert Crystal Salt Co. plant, this town also embraced a P.O., telegraph office, etc., and on March 31, 1888, gave birth to a newspaper, The *Churchill News,* which claimed the largest circulation of any journal then published in the county.

WILLIAMSBURG, (later LIMA) Pershing Co., in Sacramento mining district, 18 m. N.E. Lovelock. Founded in the early 1860s, this town was going strong by 1865, with a large general store, public hall, meat market, saloon, grocery, restaurant, and telegraph office.

WONDER, Churchill Co., 12 m. N. of U.S. 40, at a point 40 m. E. Fallon. Founded in 1906, soon after a strike produced assays up to $1300 per ton. Wm. Seymour, one of the original locators, sold his claim for $300,000, a rush got under way, and by 1908 the town embraced a good business district, including a newspaper, The *Min-*

ing News. Between 1907 and '21 the camp produced bullion to a reported value of $5,838,765—most of this from the Nevada Wonder mine. Only a few wooden cabins, cement foundations and cellars, and a row of dead locust trees which had bordered main street, remained in 1950.

YANKEE BLADE, Lander Co., 4 m. N. Austin. Founded soon after discovery here of silver-bearing lodes, in 1863, Yankee Blade enjoyed fair prosperity, even though her mines operated spasmodically in what Austin's *Reese River Reveille* termed " a kind of open-and-shut game . . . worked one month and closed three." The *Reveille* further likened Yankee Blade's activity to a Missouri sawmill, in which the saw went up one day and came down the next, and laid off on Sundays. A few stone ruins remain.

UTAH

AJAX, Tooele Co., E. side Rte. 36, at a point 24 m. (by road) S.S.W. Tooele. (Page 168)

ALTA, Salt Lake Co., 20 m. S.W. Salt Lake City. Development of three great silver mines, the Emma, Prince of Wales, and South Hecla, brought seething activity to this canyon camp between the years 1865 and '73, when the place attained a peak population of 5000, with more than 100 business buildings, many of them 2 and 3 stories in height. The presence here of 6 breweries and 26 saloons may account, in part, for the fact that the town's boothill assertedly holds the remains of 110 men killed in brawls, or murdered, while another 140 lives were lost as result of disastrous snowslides. Now a popular ski resort, almost nothing of historical interest remains.

CAINESVILLE, Wayne Co., on Rte. 24, 24 m. (by road) E.N.E. Fruita, in Capitol Reef Nat'l Monument. An agricultural town, settled by colonists of the Church of Jesus Christ of Latter Day Saints, (Mormons) in 1880, this place once knew the importance of a P.O., store, school and church. In 1953, only one family remained, but numerous cabins and the old schoolhouse were still standing.

CALLAO, Juab Co., 60 m. S.S.E. Wendover (Page 129, Plate 13)

CLIFTON, Tooele Co., 45 m. S. Wendover (Page 186; Plate 20; Map, p. 187)

CONNELLSVILLE, Emery Co., head of Huntington Canyon, on Rte. 21, about 12 m. (by road) E. of Fairview. Named for the famous coking center in Pennsylvania, Connellsville was founded about 1875 by Fairview Coal Mining and Coke Co., composed of NYC, Salt Lake, and Fairview men, who built a number of coke ovens at the mouth of Coal Canyon and attempted to set up a Western center for manufacture of coking coal. When the effort was abandoned, 3 years later, the town died.

DIAMOND CITY, Juab Co., 6 m. S.E. Eureka. Fame and fate of Diamond rested on the Shoebridge silver mine, discovered by Wm. McIntosh soon after founding of the town, about 1870. Soon a lusty settlement of some 900 residents, Diamond prospered for a few years and then went the way of all flesh and most mining camps. Her last house was moved away in 1923, and all that remains to mark the spot are a few old mine dumps, caving cellars, and the tattered remnants of a cemetery.

DIVIDEND, Juab Co., 1 m. S. of U.S. 6, at a point 5 m. E. Eureka. A model mining town built by Tintic Standard Mining Co., Dividend had modern stores, an ice plant, recreational facilities, and during 1924-5 a newspaper, the *Standard.* By 1951, only a few buildings and a watchman remained.

FAIRFIELD, Utah Co., 18 m. S.W. American Fork, (or 23 m. by road via Rtes. 73 and 191.) Settled in 1855, Fairfield began booming in 1858-9 when Johnston's Army was stationed at Old Camp Floyd, nearby. By 1860 the town had a population of 7000 persons, mainly soldiers, teamsters, gamblers, loose women, and other camp followers (the settlement during this period being known slurringly as Frogtown.) Around 2500 troops were stationed here until outbreak of the Civil War, after which Fairfield gradually declined. Today finds it a peaceful, pretty, and extremely proper, farming community.

FRISCO, Beaver Co., 46 m. (by road) N.E. Beaver. (Page 154, Plate 32)

GILES, Wayne Co., in Blue Valley, 35 m. E. Fruita. Settled by Mormon colonists in the middle 1880s, an irrigation system capable of serving 200 families was developed, a school and church built, and the townsite of Giles dedicated. By 1900 the colony had attained self sufficiency with more than 3000 acres under irrigation and planted to crops and orchards. Later, as a result of recurrent flooding by the Fremont (Dirty Devil) river, fields were eroded and under cut, and 3 large irrigation dams were destroyed in a single year. The erstwhile prosperous settlement never recovered from this blow, and by 1919 the town was deserted.

GOLD HILL, Tooele Co., 40 m. (by road) S. Wendover. (Page 186, Plate 21; Map, p. 187)

GRAFTON, Washington Co., S. bank Virgen river, 2 m. W. Rockville. Settled by Mormon colonists in 1859 (the original settlement being about a mile down-river from site of later town) Grafton knew eventually the dignity of a P.O., school, church, and numerous homes. Years of losing battles against floods and silt-choked irrigation ditches gradually wore down determination of the settlers, and after the town was virtually abandoned, a Hollywood concern bought its site and remaining buildings for use as a moving picture set.

HARRISBURG, Washington Co., along U.S. 91, 15 m. N.E. St. George. Founded in 1861 by Mormon colonists, this soon was a pretty village of 200 residents, all housed in substantial rock dwellings surrounded by prosperous fields, young orchards and vineyards. Scarcity of water soon became a major problem, and in 1869 the discouraged settlers began a general exodus. By '92 the town had shriveled to 6 families, and eventually to none. Extensive stone ruins, miles of stone fences, and an old cemetery, remain.

HATTON, Millard Co., 3 m. N.W. Kanosh (5 m. by road.) Settled in 1854, Hatton soon became an important station on the daily stage line linking Salt Lake City and Pioche, Nev., and embraced a P.O., store, school, LDS church, and numerous homes. After Brigham Young, in 1867, advised its settlers to move farther up Corn Creek to conserve water, avoid early frost, and enjoy more fertile soil, Hatton was virtually deserted. Nine persons still resided there in 1950.

HEBRON, Washington Co., on Shoal Creek, 5 m. W. Enterprise, and 48 m. N.N.W. St. George. Settled by Mormon colonists in 1862, this became a prominent town, with stone and brick buildings, stores, school, church, etc. Stock raising flourished in the area, and as long as mines and mills in Southern Utah and Eastern Nevada were operating, Hebron prospered; with decline of mining, Hebron followed suit. Scarcity of water further forced abandonment of the colony, and soon after 1900 the last of Hebron's settlers moved to Enterprise. Caving cellars, foundations, a few old apple trees, and cemetery, mark the site.

HOMANSVILLE, Utah Co., 1 m. E. Eureka. Settled in 1872, Homansville was important as a water source and pumping station, and later became site of a mill operated by the Eureka Silver Mining Co. Peak population of the town (in the middle '70s) was about 300. A few ruins remain.

IBEX , Juab Co. A small, rough mining camp of the 19th century, with 2 saloons, store, restaurant, and the tents and shacks of 200 miners. During its 14 years of life, Ibex shipped but $46,000 worth of ore, and with its death left scarcely a scar on the desert's face.

IOSEPA, Tooele Co., 15 m. (by road) S. of Timpie, on U.S. 40-50. (Page 200, Plate 18)

IRON CITY, Iron Co., 25 m. (by road) S.W. Cedar City. (Page 77)

IRONTON, Juab Co., 5 m. S.W. Eureka. Settled in 1871, Ironton came into prominence in '78 when the Utah Southern Extension R.R. was built west from Lehi Jct., by way of Fairfield, to this Juab county point, which thereupon became R.R. terminus for the rich Tintic mines and enjoyed several years of rousing prosperity.

KNIGHTSVILLE, Juab Co., 2 m. S. Eureka. Founded in 1897 by Jesse Knight, owner of the Humbug, Uncle Sam, May Day, and Yankee mines. When rich silver-lead ore was encountered in the Beck tunnel, in 1907, Knightsville boomed and in a short while its former population of 300 had grown to more than 1000. A smelter, built in 1908, operated for only a few years; and by 1940, the concrete foundation of the schoolhouse was all that remained of what had been called "The Mining Camp Without a Saloon."

LA PLATA, Cache Co., 58 m. (by road) N.N.E. Ogden. As a result of rich galena ore taken from the Sunset mine, a stampede to this region had its beginning in the early 1890s and town of La Plata soon boasted a P.O., bank, newspaper, stores, saloons, gambling halls, and other sensual attractions. When the vein played out, the inhabitants departed and La Plata is now only a memory. Ruins.

LEWISTON, Tooele Co., (see MERCUR)

MANNING, Utah Co., 3 m. E. of Mercur. Formerly site of the Manning mill. Ruins.

McCORNICK, Millard Co., about 22 m. N. Fillmore. Settled in 1919, when Sevier River Land and Water Co. built an irrigation canal which tapped the Sevier river 7 m. above Leamington, McCornick later became a station on the Delta-Fillmore branch of the Los Angeles & Salt Lake R.R., and at its peak embraced a P.O., school, church, store, cemetery, and 40 homes. In 1929, due to protracted drought conditions, the school was closed and its building moved to Flowell; and by 1930, the town was deserted.

MERCUR, Tooele Co., 28 m. W. American Fork. After its founding as LEWISTON, in 1869, about $1,000,-000 in silver was taken from nearby mines before the camp folded, in 1880, and everyone left. In 1893, after being revived as a gold camp under the name of Mercur, the town experienced its greatest boom, a substantial business district took form, and a newspaper, The *Mercur Mercury,* was established. Since that time the town has boomed and died periodically, and in 1953 all that remained were shells of rock buildings, mammoth ore dumps and tailing piles, a few cabins and 2 inhabitants—Mr. and Mrs. Helmer Grane.

MOSIDA, near Tooele-Juab county line, a few miles W. Eureka. Founded in 1910 as a farm colony, Mosida soon knew the elegance of a $15,000 hotel and $3000 schoolhouse, and water was being piped from Utah lake to irrigate an 8000-acre tract. By 1912, 50,000 fruit trees had been planted in the town's environs, and that year saw harvested 50,000 bushels of wheat. By 1915, however, the Reclamation Co. was hopelessly in debt, and with the settlers demanding larger canals, more water, and improved pumping facilities, the sponsors were forced into receivership. Scarcely an "X" remains to mark the spot.

NEWHOUSE, Beaver Co., 2 m. E. of

Rte. 21, at a point 30 m. N.E. Milford. Many unprofitable attempts to work the Cactus mine had been made between the time of its discovery, about 1870, and 1900, when the property was acquired by Samuel Newhouse. Founding the camp which was to bear his name, the Salt Lake City financier began work on the property in 1905, and for the next 5 years Newhouse was a model mining community with comfortable dwellings, well-managed clubs and cafes, and a commendable amount of law and order. Before the ore body ran out in 1910, the Cactus had produced around $3,500,000. Stone and wooden ruins, and mine dumps. (Plate 24)

OPHIR, Tooele Co., 20 m. (by road) S.S.E. Tooele. (Page 23)

PARIA, Kane Co., on the Paria river, 40 m. N.E. Kanab. Settled by Mormon colonists as a farming community, in 1868, Paria grew rapidly at first but soon became plagued by recurrent floods. High waters, in 1912, nearly annihilated the town, and the place was abandoned soon afterward. Later, a gold mining company erected buildings and installed sluiceways and made an attempt to realize riches from placer mining. In 1953, the site was completely deserted, but still harbored remainders of both its "cultures"—old log cabins, assay office, splintered sluice boxes, rusty plows, and a small cemetery.

PARK VALLEY, Box Elder Co., on Rte. 70, 38 m. W.S.W. Snowville. Settled by cattle ranchers, in 1869, Park Valley knew a brief period of excitement near the end of the century when a gold vein was struck, hundreds of "boomers" streamed into the area, and a 5-stamp mill began turning out $500 a day in gold. After this flurry had passed, a group of Russians attempted to colonize the valley in 1914, but drought forced abandonment of their project, 6 years later. Since that time the valley has been used chiefly for sheep and cattle grazing.

PINE VALLEY, Washington Co., 20 m. N.N.E. St. George. (Page 57, Plates 10, 12)

SHOEBRIDGE, Juab Co. (See TINTIC)

SILVER CITY, Juab Co., 4 m. (by road) S. Eureka. The first important camp in the Tintic district, Silver City was settled in 1870 and soon expanded into quite a town. When the mines reached water level and pumping costs became prohibitive, the camp's population fell from a lusty 800 to almost 0.

SILVER REEF, Washington Co., 18 m. N.E. St. George. (Page 162, Plate 15)

SULPHURDALE, Beaver Co., 1 m. E. of U.S. 91, at a point 26 m. N. Beaver. A small town that grew up around a sulphur mine. Discovered in the late 1880s and worked by the open pit method, most of the mine's yield was used in the manufacture of gunpowder, and in refining sugar.

TINTIC MILLS, Juab Co., near Eureka. Known as Shoebridge at the time of its founding in 1870, this place attracted numerous settlers and by '71 an ore mill had been built and a town of considerable extent had developed. Nothing remains.

TOPAZ, Millard Co., in the Sevier Desert, 15 m. N.W. Delta. Settled in 1942 as a wartime relocation camp, Topaz quickly became the 5th largest city in Utah with a population of 8778 —practically all Japanese, or persons of Japanese descent. Its 19,800-acre townsite was divided into 34 blocks, each with 12 barracks buildings, dining hall, laundry, and administrative office; while the camp, as a whole, was served by a P.O., stores, fire department, 128-bed hospital, 5 churches, and 3 schools. At close of the war (1945) Topaz was vacated, material and equipment was sold; and soon all that remained were cement foundations and the tall stack of one laundry boiler.

WIDTSOE, Garfield Co. After being settled by ranchers in 1876, land on the E. fork of the Sevier river near the mouth of Sweetwater creek, was surveyed in 1910 and the townsite of Winder was platted. Five years later this name was changed to Widtsoe, and by 1920 the town embraced 1100 residents, with P.O., school, LDS church, 2 hotels, 4 stores, and a social hall. Surrounding farms eventually began failing, due to long sustained drought, and settlers moved away until only 17 families remained in 1935, and by 1949 this number had been reduced to four. Except for a cemetery of about 100 graves, and a few wooden buildings, little of historical interest remains.

CALIFORNIA

BALLARAT, Inyo Co., 21 m. N.N.E. Trona, and 3.6 m. (by road) E. Trona-Death Valley highway. Founded in early 1890s on strength of gold discoveries on W. side Panamint Range, Ballarat also served as general supply point for mines throughout adjacent area. After boom collapsed, the otherwise deserted town was for many years the home of Frank "Shorty" Harris, dean of desert prospectors, who died in 1934 and is buried in Death Valley. About a dozen adobe buildings, and ruins of others, were standing in 1953.

BODIE, Mono Co., 15 m. E.S.E. Bridgeport. Although its district had been combed by prospectors as early as 1859, Bodie's boom did not get under way until the middle 1870s, after which the camp developed quickly to the status of a frontier city, where 30 mines and mills were operating actively, and 10,000 citizens were supporting 60 gin mills and gambling halls, 3 breweries, 3 local newspapers, and many mercantile establishments. After producing an estimated $70,-000,000 in bullion, Bodie called it quits, and in 1953, only one inhabitant remained. Presence of many old buildings and ruins, including stores, homes, mills, firehouse, school, church, and two cemeteries, make this one of the most fascinating ghosttowns in the West. (Plate 5)

CARTAGO, Inyo Co., 3 m. N. Olancha. With its several towns supported by milling, mining, freighting, shipping, woodcutting, charcoal burning, and ranching, the Owens Lake region formerly was a busy and prosperous place. Between Cartago, at the lake's S. end, and Swansea, on its E. shore, plied the 85-foot steamers, Bessie Brady and Mollie Stevens—eastbound trips seeing their decks stacked high with cordwood cut in the foothills and consigned to desert smelters, while return voyages found them laden with Cerro Gordo ore to be landed at Cartago and thence freighted more than 200 miles to Wilmington. As long as mining and shipping continued, Cartago was a rough and rousing port.

CERRO GORDO (Sp. fat hill) Inyo Co., 20 m. N.E. Olancha. After discovery here of rich outcroppings of silver-lead ore in the 1860s, Cerro Gordo grew quickly to a peak population of

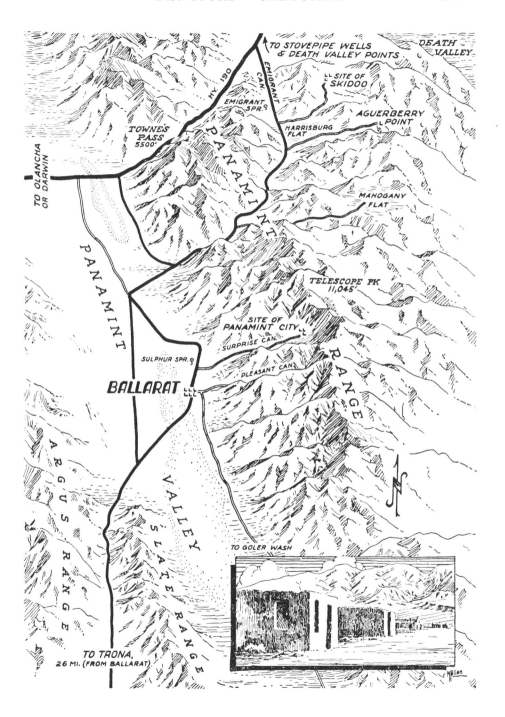

2000 and remained active through the 1870s. Operating 56 fast teams of 12 and 14 mules each, Remi Nadeau's freight line carried out of the camp daily some 400 bars of silver-lead bullion, transporting the treasure to Swansea, on Owens Lake. Later, ore was sent down the mountain to Keeler on an aerial tramway built in 1911 at a reported cost of $250,000. Still visible are the high cables and swinging ore cars of the tram, as well as numerous old buildings; but the entire population of Cerro Gordo, in 1953, consisted of one watchman and his family.

DOGTOWN, Mono Co., 8 m. S. Bridgeport. What is probably the earliest mining settlement in this region enjoyed a short life, its population being lured to Monoville in 1859. A few remnants of stores and houses remain.

FURNACE, Inyo Co., near head of Copper Canyon, 3.2 m. (by road) off Furnace Creek-Shoshone road, at a point 2.8 m. S.E. Dante's View Jct. Following discovery of ore yielding 20 per cent copper, Furnace zoomed into spectacular existence in 1905. Guggenheim Brothers interested themselves in the development, and "Bet a Million" John T. Gates ran the stock up to $6 a share on the New York stock exchange. By 1907, the boom was over, the town deserted, and the only mementos remaining in 1954 were a few crumbled foundations and many heaps of rusted tin cans.

GREENWATER, Inyo Co., E. slope Black Mtns., 23 m. S.E. Furnace Creek Hotel, and 14 m. S.W. Death Valley Junction. (Inquire at either place, or at Shoshone.) With discovery of copper ore, in 1905, Greenwater leaped into prominence as "The World's Biggest Copper Deposit." Such moguls of mining finance as Charles M. Schwab, August Heinze, Tasker L. Oddie, "Borax" Smith, and Senator W. A. Clark, flocked to the new camp or sent their agents, stocks skyrocketed, 2500 claims were sold for $4,125,000, and the business district of the new town soon embraced many business houses, including a bank, hotels, two newspapers, and a "district" controlled by Diamond Tooth Lil. When veins failed to hold up to original expectations, the camp died as rapidly as it had lived, and only foundations and rubble mark its site.

LEADFIELD, Death Valley National Monument. In narrow Titus Canyon (restricted to one-way travel—east to west only) Leadfield's P.O. opened Aug. 25, 1926, with mail for 200 persons, and closed Jan. 15, 1927, with mail for one last survivor. During the few months separating those dates, C. C. Julian, of oil fame, had promoted here a fantastic mine swindle in which he and other fast talkers took millions of dollars from gullible investors. A few wooden cabins, cement foundations, and rubble, remained in 1952.

LEE, Inyo Co., between Daylight Pass and Death Valley Junction, about 1 m. W. of Nevada state line. Named for Dick Lee, Shoshone halfbreed, who early in the current century discovered here a ledge of rich gold quartz. The town briefly attracted a population of 300, but virtually nothing remains to show where it stood.

LUNDY, Mono Co., 5 m. W. of U.S. 395, and partially submerged by Lundy Lake, lies all that remains of this early day mining town, from which ore was packed out on burros. (Inquire at Mono Inn, on Mono Lake.)

MASONIC, Mono Co., 12 m. N.E. Bridgeport, near California-Nevada line. A mining camp of the 1860s, Masonic still embraces a number of rather picturesque ruins, including old stone and log cabins, the shell of a large mill, and the high, swaying cables of an overhead tram used formerly to carry ore from mine to mill. No human inhabitants remained in 1953.

MONO MILLS, Mono Co. At S.E. end Mono lake, 12 m. E. of U.S. 395, and about 5 m. E. of Mono craters, is site of the former logging and sawmill camp of Mono Mills, active around 80-90 years ago.

MONOVILLE, Mono Co. After placer gold was located in this area in 1857, the town of Monoville developed, and by 1860 contained some 900 inhabitants—most of whom flocked to Aurora upon discovery of the rich silver lodes at that place. As even homes and business houses of Monoville were moved to scene of the new strike, there is little to identify the town's one-time location.

PANAMINT CITY, Inyo Co., at head of Surprise canyon, W. side Panamint range, 50 m. N.E. Inyokern; 60 m. S.E. Lone Pine. Although prospectors had been searching over this region since the 1860s, the copper-silver strike that sparked Panamint's boom was not made until 1872. When Comstock Financiers John P. Jones and Wm. M. Stewart gave the new camp their blessing and backing, its future seemed assured, and by 1874 the mountain town contained 5000 persons served by scores of business houses set beside a mile-long main street—its upper end some 1000 feet higher than its lower end. Lawlessness flourished, 20 saloons did a lusty business, and boothill grew fat. After a cloudburst roared down Surprise Canyon, destroying the town and drowning 15 of its citizens in the summer of 1876, Panamint never rebuilt. Still marking its site are a tall, brick smelter chimney and other ruins, accessible only afoot, or by jeep or truck.

RYAN, Death Valley Nat'l Monument, 1½ m. E. of the paved road between Furnace Creek Inn and Dante's View. Here, nearly 50 years ago, was centered the extensive mining activities of Pacific Coast Borax Co., and after 1907, the Western terminus of Death Valley R.R., whose borax-laden trains connected with the Tonopah & Tidewater R.R. at Beatty, Nev. The little line gained passing notoriety in 1915 when the *Technical World* alluded to it as "the world's most remarkable railroad" — its 16-miles of narrow gauge track laid on a maximum grade of 1.5 per cent having been built in 10 months at a cost of $300,000, with 400 men and 200 mules employed on the job. (Note: The camp known as "Old Ryan," which preceded the town described, was situated at the Lila C. borax mine, 7 m. W.S.W. of Death

Valley Junction, where little remains but broken bottles, foundations, and a few dugouts. Everything usable was moved from the Lila C. mine to the Biddy McCarthy, at New Ryan, about 1913. Buildings, etc., remain at the latter site.

SKIDOO, Inyo Co., in Death Valley Nat'l Monument, 8 m. E. of Emigrant Pass road. En route to the new strike at Harrisburg, in Jan. 1906, One-Eye Thompson and Harry Ramsey got lost in a fog and discovered a rich gold ledge, subsequently purchased by Bob Montgomery, Nevada mining tycoon, for $600,000. News of the discovery sparked a mild stampede, and resulted in founding the boomcamp of Skidoo, which, at its peak, had 500 inhabitants, a bank, real estate offices, 2 stores, a printing plant and newspaper — *The News*, 5 saloons, 2 barber shops, assay office, restaurant, rooming house, clubhouse, poolhall, etc. Water sold at 10 cents a gallon, and mesquite wood, freighted from Death Valley, at $55 a cord. Output of the Skidoo mill averaged around $15,000 monthly until 1916, when it was closed by litigation. Remaining in 1953 were the company boarding house, several wood cabins, and a small cemetery—every inmate of which is said to have died a violent death. (Plate 31)

SWANSEA, Inyo Co., on E. shore Owens Lake, about 3 m. N. Keeler. Named for the famous smelting center in Wales, this was a busy shipping port in the days when shallow-draught steamers plied Owens Lake. (See CARTAGO.) Former site of the town has been virtually swallowed by shifting sand dunes.

M

Macdonald, Malcolm, 214
Mackay School of Mines, 185
Maher, M. A. & Co., 148
Mahogany peak, 83
Mammoth City, Nev., 100
Manhattan, Nev., 51-56, 255, 263, 264
Manhattan gulch, 51, 54, 55
Manning, Utah, 273
Marchand, Edward, 101
Mardis. See Charleston.
Mardis, Geo. W. "Allegheny," 176-177
Marietta, Nev., 263- 109, 115, 116
Mariger, Marietta, (quoted) 163, 164, 165
Marijilda, the Mexican, 96-97, 93
Marriott home & store, 160
Marsh, Billy, 93
Martin, Leonard, 81-82
Masonic, Calif., 276
Masonic Order, 12, 42, 121, 142, 164, 196
Mason Valley, Nev. See Greenville.
Masterson, Jim, 64
Matthews, Allan F., (quoted) 192
Mazuma, Nev., 263
McCauley, Tom, 229
McCornick, Utah, 273
McCullough, C. W., (quoted) 183-184
McDermitt, Nev., 221
McDowell, "Three-Fingered Jack," 64
McFarlane, John, 165
McGarry, Len, 207
McGee, J. B., 135
McGillis, Johnny, Plate 23
McIntosh, Wm., 271
McIntyre, Charlie, 46
McKey, Alex, 137
McKissick's saloon, 117-118
McLaughlin, Tom, 116
McRae & Lefler, 270
McWilliamstown, Nev., 205, 206
Meadows, Charles, Plate 23
Menken, Nev., 270, 100
Mercur, Utah, 273, 30, 168
Meretvich, Tom, 136
Metcalf, June, (quoted) 185
Metallic City, Nev., 116-118, 109, 263
Metropolis, Nev., 246-250, 124, 263, Plate 54
Midas, Nev., 124-127, 263, Plate 36
Milford, Utah, 157, 273
Millard, Leatha, 188-190
Mill City, Nev., 263, 12, 257, 258, 269
Miller, B. F. (quoted) 182
Miller, G. W., (quoted) 198
Millers, Nev., 263
Millett, Nev., 263, 265
Mina, Nev., 234, 235, 255, 256, 258, 263, 267, 268, 270
Mineral City, Nev., 263
Mineral Hill, Nev., 264

Mineral Resources of Nye County, Kral, (quoted) 54

Mines: Alvarado, 190, 192; Anaconda, 24; Argus, 269; Arizona, 8, 12, 18, 19, 20; Beck, 272; Betty O'Neal, 256; Biddy McCarthy, 277; Black Mammoth, 259; Bluster, 239, Bonanza, 155; Buckeye, 165; Buckskin, 256; Bullfrog, 205; Cactus, 273; Cane Springs, 190, 192; Chainman, 263; Congress, 261; Copper King, 184; Copper Queen, 190; Copperopolis, 190; Dark Secret, 97; Dean, 258; Dexter, 119, 122; Duck Creek, 259; Dusty Bob, 144; Eagle, 262; Eberhardt, 105-106, 258; Elko Prince, 126-127; Emma (Nev) 190, 263; Emma (Utah) 24, 271; Emperor, 116; Escallon, 240, Exchange, 159; Flaxie, 239; Getchell, 124; Gettysburg, 36; Gold Hill, 190, 192; Good Templar, 144; Grand Prize, 119; Hidden Treasure, 101, 105; Hidden Treasure Consolidated, 101; Highbridge, 43; Homestake, 262; Horn Silver, 155-158; Humbug, 272; Imperial, 262; Jackrabbit, 199; Johnnie, 261; Juniata, 70; Kearsage, 25; Keystone, 268; Lila C., 277; Lost Breyfogle, 147, 204; Lost Gunsight, 204; Lost Sheepherder, 239; Lucy L., 190; Magnolia, 170; May Day, 272; Metallic, 116; Midas, 132; Miner's Delight, 24; Monitor, 269; Montezuma, 255; Mount Diablo, 110, 111, 116; Murphy, 264; National, 220-221; Navajo, 119; Nevada Hills, 259; Nevada Queen, 119; Nevada Wonder, 271; North Belle Isle, 119; Northern Belle, 111, 114, 115; Nova Zembla, 144; Ophir Hill, 24; Oriental, 144; Osceola, 159; Pilot, 159; Pioneer, 266; Pittsburg, 266; Pocatello, 24; Prince of Wales, 271; Queen City, 37; Reaper No. 3, 191; Rio Tinto, 184; Rockland, 267; Rube, 192-193; Rye Patch, 267; St. Louis, 23; Shoebridge, 271; Silver Bend, 44-45; Slavonian Chief, 136; South Hecla, 271; Star Hill, 178; Starlight, 239; Starr-Grove, 262; Stateline, 142; Success, 239; Sunset, 272; Techatticup, 36, 38, Plates 6, 8; Tintic, 272; Two G, 135, 136; Tybo Consolidated, 135; Uncle Sam, 272; Velocipede, 24; Western Slope, 159, Wild Delirium, 24; White Caps, 53; Yankee, 272; Zella, 24

Mining and Scientific Press, (quoted) 69

Mining Districts: Buena Vista, 263; Bullfrog, 213, 214; Colorado, 36; Gold Circle, 126; Harrisburg, 163, 164; Kingston, 264; Oneota, 260; Railroad, 266; Sacramento, 270; Tintic, 190, 273; Union, 83; White Pine, 100-108, 262

Mining Districts and Mineral Resources

Other Books from Nevada Publications

NEVADA GHOST TOWNS & MINING CAMPS, by Stanley W. Paher. Here is Nevada's all-time best selling history book, with more than 66,500 copies sold. Large 8-1/2 x 11 format, 500 pp. Here is the largest ghost town book of all time. In all, 668 ghost towns are described with travel directions. Contains more pictures and describes more localities than any other Nevada book. Nearly every page brings new information and unpublished photos of the towns, the mines, the people and early Nevada life. This book won the national "Award of Merit" for history. Clothbound with color dust jacket, glossary, desert travel hints, reading list. 710 illus., maps, index.

NEVADA GHOST TOWNS & DESERT ATLAS. by Stanley W. Paher. Of interest for both the casual desert visitor and the serious off-road explorer. Color covers, 8¹/²" x 11", 552 photographs show places of historic interest. Here is a guide to more than 2,220 desert destinations in the Nevada-Death Valley backcountry. There are 725 ghost towns and stage stations keyed to the popular book above. Prominent mining areas, emigrant trails, Pony Express and the Old Spanish trail. Abandoned railroads, desert cemeteries, unusual desert features, 115 placer gold mining sites, 180 gemstone sites, campgrounds, hot springs, caves, recreation areas, state parks, scenic byways.
• **VOLUME ONE** - Northern Nevada, Reno - Ely, and points north. 104 pp., 37 maps. • **VOLUME TWO** – Southern Nevada – Death Valley – 104 pp., 34 maps.
• **COMBINED EDITION** – All material presented in the two above books are in one paperback edition. 71 maps, 208 pp. *A limited hardback binding has a color dust jacket, and combines with the popular ghost town book above to make a two-volume set.*

MY ADVENTURES WITH YOUR MONEY, by George Graham Rice. 334 pp., 110 illus., maps and line drawings. Here are the memoirs of get-rich-quick financing of central Nevada and Death Valley mines, with interesting anecdotal material on the author's advertising agency and mining and stock promotions. Rice capitalized the stocks of Goldfield, Greenwater and Rawhide mines, listed them on national exchanges, and reaped profits until he was convicted of mail fraud in 1911. Hardback with dust jacket.

GOLD IN THEM HILLS, by C.B. Glasscock. 330 pp., illus., map. The author saw the reversals of fortune, had a part in the mining frenzies, and experienced the hardships. He tells the development of early Tonopah and Goldfield's freighting, high-grading, the big mines, society, and the fast-talking promoters of Greenwater and Rawhide. Here is a book that will be cherished by all those who love old Nevada. Color cover.

WESTERN ARIZONA GHOST TOWNS, by Stanley W. Paher. 64 pp., 9 x 12, illus., color cover. Within a day's drive of Las Vegas, Kingman, Parker, and Yuma are more than five dozen ghost towns, each described in a lively text with historic photographs. Includes Oatman, Eldorado Canyon, Searchlight, Chloride, Gila City, Laguna, LaPaz, Ehrenburg, and more. Also information about steamboats. A stunning 1862 color map showing the mines along the Colorado River occupies the back cover.

NEVADA PUBLICATIONS
4135 Badger Circle • Reno, Nevada 89519
(775) 747-0800
www.spaher@sbcglobal.net

NEVADA ROAD & RECREATION ATLAS, by Benchmark Maps. This over-sized atlas captures Nevada's great and varied outdoor potential. Thorough field checking and local research assure users of the best outdoor experience possible, whether hunting, fishing, or just traveling backroads in search of scenic country, historic trails, mining camps, etc. This atlas faithfully discriminates between paved routes and maintained gravel roads, and even 4x4 roads. 96 large pages.

CALIFORNIA ROAD & RECREA-TION ATLAS from Benchmark Maps, 144 pp., oversized format. This accurate reference features hunting and fishing and desert exploration locations. In addition, similar quality atlases are available for Arizona., Utah, New Mexico, Wash., Idaho, Oregon, Colorado.

Books on
Aurora and Bodie

MINING CAMP DAYS, by Emil W. Billeb. 229 pp., illus. The author provides insights into Nevada and eastern California mining camps after 1905. Dozens of unpublished photographs were taken by this observer-participant, augmenting a good text.

BODIE BONANZA, by Warren Loose. 246 pp., illus. A Bodie native chronicles the social picture of the camp during its heyday (1878-1880), lacing the text with news stories of the fortunes, failures, the rowdiness, businesses, the "red lights," and entertainments.

BODIE...BOOM TOWN, GOLD TOWN! The Last of California's Old-Time Mining Camps, by Douglas McDonald. 48 pp., illus., color cover, 7 x 10. Though Bodie was discovered in 1859, no significant mining started until rich strikes in 1877 brought about a furious mining rush two years later. Photos show mines and miners, street scenes, buildings, the mill, and the crowds which made up Bodie.

AURORA, NEVADA'S GHOST CITY OF THE DAWN, by Robert E. Stewart. 144 pp., 7 x 10, illus., maps. 2nd edition. The town of Aurora, (8 miles east of Bodie), was among Nevada's largest 19th century gold mining camps. Here is the story of its mines and mills and everyday mining camp life during he turbulent Civil War. Accompanied by many unpublished photographs.

BODIE'S GOLD, by Marguerite Sprague. 264 pp. Author interviewed many former Bodie residents to produce her lively history of California's official Gold Rush ghost town. Numerous historic photographs included.

BODIE BONANZA, by Warren Loose. 246 pp., illus. A Bodie native chronicles the social picture of the camp during its heyday (1878-1880), lacing the text with news stories of the fortunes, failures, the rowdiness, businesses, the "red lights," and entertainments.

BODIE'S BOSS LAWMAN, The Odyssey of Constable John F. Kirgan, by Bill Merrell, with David Carle. 176 pages, 75 illus., 16 in color, maps, notes, index. Fate brought John Kirgan to Bodie in 1877, where he served as constable, jailer and deputy sheriff during the boom years. Included are lively essays on Commerce, Gambling and Saloons, Mining and Speculation, Bodie's 'High' School, the Jail, Fire, at Home in Bodie, Trans-portation, and Law and Disorder.

BODIE: THE MINES ARE LOOKING WELL, by Michael Piatt. 288 pp., 8-1/2 x 11, illus. "The mines are looking well" reassured speculators during the Bodie boom of 1877-1881. Here, in one location, the author has written the largest single history of any mining camp, complete with 145 photographs (several unpublished 1879-1880 street scenes and views of the mines), and numerous untold stories embodied in the text and historical sidebars. Color cover with dust jacket.

Books on Virginia City & Lake Tahoe

THE COMSTOCK LODE, by Douglas McDonald. 128 pp. Large 9 x 12 format, 75 illus., index. The discovery and development of the West's largest silver lode is recounted in extensive text and both line drawings and photographs. There are essays on familiar Comstock figures such as the Big Four, Adolph Sutro and the discoverers, and also information on stock manipulations, the unions, and various institutions. Camels, the V&T Railroad, Mark Twain, law and order, square-set mine timbering, are all featured. Old and new maps help tell the story.

THE HISTORY OF THE COMSTOCK LODE, by Grant H. Smith. 325 pp., illus., index. In addtion to invaluable mining information which updates Virginia City through the mid-20th century, this book includes the personal histories of the Comstock's colorful men—"Old Virginny," John Mackay, Mark Twain, Dan De Quille, Charles Shinn, and others.

DESTINATION LAKE TAHOE: The Story Behind the Scenery, S.W. Paher. 64 pp., illus., map. Interspersed amid a flowing text of the history of Lake Tahoe and Virginia City, are 70 stunning color photographs of the Tahoe Basin: historic sites, ski resorts, animal and plant life.

ELEGANCE ON C STREET, Virginia City's International Hotel, by Richard C. Datin. 49 pp., illus. The author recreates the history, the people, and the splendor of Virginia City. The hotel typified it all: kings, financiers, president U.S. Grant, and queens of the footlights.

MY MEMORIES OF THE COMSTOCK by Harry M. Gorham, 208 pp. Author lived in Virginia City, 1877-1903, reminiscing about various people. His writing provides a contrast with earlier written Comstock books which describe the glories of 1859-1878.

JULIA BULETTE AND THE RED LIGHT LADIES OF NEVADA, by Douglas McDonald. 32 pp., illus., map. Here is the best written historical sketch to date of Virginia City's famed prostitute, who was murdered in 1867. An overview of Nevada's "red lights" occupies the last part of the book, augmented by interesting photographs. Color cover.

SKETCHES OF VIRGINIA CITY, N.T., by J Ross Browne. 48 pages, illus. In 1860, agent J. Ross Browne visited the newly discovered Comstock and commented extensively on the miners and their madness over minerals, the Chinese, the Indians, stagecoach drivers, proprietors, barroom brawlers, etc. Charming, humorous cartoons of these appear throughout the book. It was originally entitled *A Peep at Washoe*.

MARK TWAIN IN VIRGINIA CITY, by Mark Twain. 192 pp. Twain portrays the life in Virginia City: mining litigation, horse breaking, fighting a tarantula, a funeral, and the "Washoe zephyr" winds. He mined for silver, labored in a silver mill and was a reporter for Virginia City's *Territorial Enterprise*. Includes numerous line drawings which depict scenes of everyday life. Cloth, paper.

THE BIG BONANZA, by Dan DeQuille (William Wright). 433 pp., illus., with intro. by Oscar Lewis. Indexed. Subtitled "An authentic account of the discovery, history, and working of the Comstock Lode," the Big Bonanza covers every phase of the epic rise of Virginia City, especially the special technology required to work the deep silver mines. Color cover.

NEVADA PUBLICATIONS

4135 Badger Circle • Reno, Nevada 89519

(775) 747-0800

www.spaher@sbcglobal.net

NEVADA LOST MINES AND BURIED TREASURE, by Douglas McDonald. 128 pp., 6 x 9, illus. Legends of lost mines in Nevada date from the Gold Rush of 1849 when westbound emigrants discovered silver in the desolate Black Rock Desert. The author recounts 74 of these stories which also include tales of buried coins, bullion bars, stolen bank money, etc. Two-color maps show general treasure locations. Color cover.

NEVADA TOWNS AND TALES, S.W. Paher, ed. 2 vols., 224 pp. each., 8-1/2 x 11. Chapters focus on economic, social and geographic factors. Other major sections discuss state emblems, gambling, politics, mining, business, and casino entertainment. There is much material on ghost towns, prospecting, legends, early day women, ranching, native animals, industries, banking and commerce, railroads, atomic testing, transportation, etc. Indexed. Color cover. Vol. 1, North, Vol. 2, South.

DEVILS WILL REIGN, by Sally Zanjani. 222 pp., illus, index. Here is a record of Gold Canyon, significant because at its northern end the great silver discovery was made at Virginia City in 1859. The author describes the fluctuations of population and general activity in Gold Canyon throughout the decade of 1850. Includes new information about Johntown and the pioneer Grosh brothers. Since the community of Dayton (two miles away from the southern end of Gold Canyon) has misappropriated the history of Gold Canyon as its own, the author's findings of discontinuity of placer mining, social and political activity renders moot Dayton's claim of Nevada's oldest settlement.

GOLDFIELD THE LAST GOLD RUSH ON THE WESTERN FRONTIER, by Sally Zanjani. 338 pp., illus, map. Author captures the spirit of Goldfield's boom years of 1905-1907 and the crowds, the prospectors, miners, stock promoters, bankers, gamblers, merchants, restaurateurs, red lights and lawmen. $24.95.

JACK LONGSTREET, LAST OF THE DESERT FRONTIERSMAN, by Sally Zanjani. 172 pp., illus. Early in the 20th century Longstreet roamed the southern Nevada deserts, working in ranching, prospecting, saloon-keeping, and as a hired gun.

Books on Southwestern Gold Prospecting and Gem Hunting

GOLD FEVER AND THE ART OF PANNING AND SLUICING, by Lois DeLorenzo. 80 pp., illus. A how-to-book for the beginning gold panner. $6.95.

GOLD PROSPECTOR'S HANDBOOK, by Jack Black. 176 pp., illus. How to pan gold, prospect streams, geology, lode gold, sluices, portable dredges, etc.

WHERE TO FIND GOLD AND GEMS IN NEVADA, by James Klein. 112 pp., illus., county maps. Placer gold and precious gem sites described.

WHERE TO FIND GOLD IN THE DESERT, by James Klein. 132 pp., illus. Explains where to look, and what to look for, throughout the Southwest, especially California, Arizona, and southern Nevada.

PLACER GOLD DEPOSITS OF NEV ADA, by Maureen Johnson. USGS Bull. 1356. 118 pp., index. Valuable catalog of locations, geology, production; 115 placer sites all located on a two-color map. Also available: **PLACER GOLD DEPOSITS OF ARIZONA; NEW MEXICO.**

PLACER GOLD DEPOSITS OF THE SIERRA NEVADA, Paul Morrison, ed. A survey of California Sierra gold placer, hydraulic, and drift mines; also covers dredging areas of the American, Feather, and Yuba rivers. Maps locate gold districts and old mines from Kern County northward to Plumas County. 192 pp., maps, appendices.

RECREATIONAL GOLD PROSPECT-ING FOR FUN AND PROFIT by Gail Butler. 206 pp., illus. This book reviews basic techniques of gold prospecting for both the beginner and veteran. Recovering gold with a common pan and a sluice box, as well as how to stake a claim, are described. Included are full descriptions of publications and organizations to assist you. Here are straightforward answers to questions about what to take when entering gold-bearing localities. Color cover.

THE ROCKHOUNDER'S HANDBOOK, by James Mitchell. 184 pp., illus. Covers what to look for in the field, tools for the job, gem and mineral identification, and trip preparation. New edition.

PLACER MINING IN NEVADA, by William O. Vanderburg. 178 pp., map, illus. Here is a county-by-county summary of rock gravel gold sites, describing mining methods and equipment. $14.95. Also available: **ARIZONA GOLD PLACERS AND PLACER-ING**.

GEM TRAILS OF NEVADA, by James Mitchell. 192 pp., illus. More than 75 locations for gemstone collecting are described and located on new maps giving highway and off-road directions to the sites to the 1/10 mile. About 30 Nevada minerals are covered. Also available: **GEM TRAILS OF ARIZONA, UTAH, NEW MEXICO**.

GEM TRAILS OF NORTHERN CALIFORNIA, by James R. Mitchell. 160 pp., illus., some in color. Maps show roads to gem collecting sites with 1/10 mile accuracy; the text concentrates on gem fields north of Bishop and Fresno, but also includes some areas of western Nevada.

GEM TRAILS OF SOUTHERN CALI-FORNIA, by James R. Mitchell. 176 pp., illus., maps. Contains detailed maps and travel directions to 71 collecting sites, with 1/10 mile accuracy. The Mojave Desert and the areas south and west of Death Valley are well covered. There is a color photo section for gem identification. Newly updated.

CALIFORNIA GHOST TOWN TRAILS, by Russ Leadebrand. 112 pp. Same format as above book.

Colorful Nevada Tour Books

GEOLOGIC TOURS IN THE LAS VEGAS AREA, by Joseph Tingley. Expanded edition with GPS coordinates. Five trips out of Las Vegas take the explorer to mining sites, petroglyphs, as well as information on animal and plant life.

GEOLOGIC AND NATURAL HISTORY TOURS IN THE RENO AREA, by Joseph Tingley. 184 pp., maps, illus. Four trips out of Reno takes the explorer to area historic sites and mining camps, especially Virginia City. Includes color plates of animal and plant life.

TRAVELING AMERICA'S LONELIEST ROAD, A Geologic and Natural History Tour Through Nevada Along U.S. Highway 50, by Joseph Tingley. 132 pp., maps. Includes ghost towns and historic sites, color plates of plant life, animals, birds. mining camps, etc.

A GEOLOGIC AND NATURAL HISTORY TOUR THROUGH NEVADA... ALONG U. S. HIGHWAY 93, by Joseph Tingley. Emigrant and mining history also included, with coverage in Las Vegas, Pioche, Ely and Wells areas. Many color plates and maps aid the explorer.

---

320 DESERT WATERING PLACES IN SOUTHEASTERN CALIFORNIA AND SOUTHWESTERN NEVADA, by W.C. Mendenhall. 104 pp., illus., index. This water supply paper covers numerous springs between Death Valley and the Salton Sea, all keyed to a 14 x 20 color map.

MINES OF THE GOLDFIELD, BULLFROG AND OTHER SOUTHERN NEVADA DISTRICTS, by F. L. Ransome. 144 pp., maps, index. Also covers Searchlight, Eldorado, Crescent and Gold Mountain. Two popular illustrated magazine articles, written in 1907, capture the flavor and excitement of the mining era. #60-1. Color map laid in.

Books on Death Valley

50 YEARS IN DEATH VALLEY, Memoirs Of a Borax Man, by Harry Gower. 148 pp. Anecdotes of DV area, 1909-1960 by an observer-participant. Included are rare, often humorous insights.

DEATH VALLEY'S SCOTTY'S CASTLE, by S.W. Paher. 48 pp., large 9 x 12 format, heavily illustrated in color. Built with funds supplied by a Chicago insurance executive benefactor, the Castle ultimately took its name from a local prospector who publicized it and jealously guarded its development — Walter "Death Valley" Scott. Besides a history of Scott, there are about fifty intricate color pictures of the Castle.

DEATH VALLEY GHOST TOWNS, VOL. I, by S.W. Paher. 32 pp., 9 x 12, map, 50 old-time photographs. Though Death Valley is known for its colorful eras of borax mining, there were gold and silver rushes also. The first one included Panamint and Calico, while the early 20th century boom produced Rhyolite, Greenwater, and others. About 35 mining camps are included.

DEATH VALLEY GHOST TOWNS, VOL. II, by S.W. Paher. 32 pp., 9 x 12, 50 old-time photos. Mining camps such as Skidoo, Panamint City, and Old Stovepipe Wells — are joined by those immediately to the west, including Cerro Gordo, Darwin and Cartago. There are essays on the prospector, the Tonopah & Tidewater Railroad. Color cover.

GOODBYE, DEATH VALLEY! The Tragic 1849 Jayhawker Trek, by L. Burr Belden. 60 pp. Emigrants battled hunger and thirst, elements, Indians. Much on trail route, variants.

THE LOST DEATH VALLEY 49ER JOURNAL OF LOUIS NUSBAUMER, by George Koenig. 80 pp., illus., map. The Jayhawkers, and other emigrants are detailed with day to day activities.

SCOTTY'S CASTLE, DEATH VALLEY,

by S. W. Paher. Large 9 x 12 format, 48 pp, heavily illustrated in color. Besides a history of Death Valley Scotty, there are many intricate pictures of the castle itself, with large captions to explain them. paperback, with color cover.

THE CAMELS OF NEVADA, by

Douglas McDonald. 32 pp, illus. In Nevada camel pack trains hauled salt, wood and even freight, also aiding early surveyors. But the beasts also brought problems. Modern camel races in Virginia City are recounted.

THE BIG BONANZA, by Dan DeQuille

(William Wright). 488 pages, illustrated, with intro. by Oscar Lewis. Indexed. Subtitled "An authentic account of the discovery, history, and working of the Comstock Lode," the Big Bonanza by DeQuille covers every phase of the epic rise of Virginia City, especially the special technology required to work the deep silver mines.

GHOSTS OF THE GLORY TRAIL, by

Nell Murbarger. 316 pages, illus. Indexed. Subtitled "Intimate glimpses into the past and present of 275 western ghosttowns," Ghosts of the Glory Trail is a fast-moving chronicle depicting the early-day mining stampedes. All Nevada counties are represented either in the 39 chapters on specific towns (such as Aurora, Rhyolite, Candelaria, Tuscarora, Delamar, etc.) or in the valuable ghost town directory containing 225 additional listings, some in eastern Calif. and western Utah.

THE HISTORY OF NEVADA, by Sam

P. Davis. 2 volumes. 1279 pages, illus. Reprint of the rare 1913 first edition. There are chapters on every phase of Nevada history including Indians, topography, the emigrants, mining, politics, journalism, education, religion, railroads, medicine, banking, agriculture, fraternal societies, drama, reclamation, divorce law, and a chapter on every Nevada county.

NEVADA POST OFFICES, AN ILLUSTRATED HISTORY, by James Gamett

and S. W. Paher. 160 pp, 7 x 10, illus. About 760 Nevada towns had post offices and here is a detailed list of them. There are chapters of the Pony Express, Wells-Fargo, and how to collect postal materials. 110 postal illustrations are in this research tool. Hardcover with color dust jacket.

NEVADA GHOST TOWN TRAILS, by Mickey Broman. 80 pp, illus., maps. Quick reference and guide to 120 ghost towns. Also available in same format is **CALIFORNIA GHOST TOWN TRAILS.**

GEM TRAILS IN CALIFORNIA, by Mickey Broman, 84 pp, illus., maps. Good maps lead traveler to numerous gem stone collecting areas.

GOLD FEVER AND THE ART OF PANNING AND SLUICING, by Lois DeLorenzo. 80 pp, illus. A how-to book for the amateur.

WHERE TO FIND GOLD AND GEMS IN NEVADA, by James Klein. 112 pp, maps, illus. Gold and gem sites in every county are included.

THE WEEKEND GOLD MINER, by A. H. Ryan. 64 pp. A simple, easy-to-follow handbook.

YOSEMITE TRAILS, by Lew and Ginny Clark. 144 pp, illus., maps, index. Complete guide to this National park.

HIGH MOUNTAINS AND DEEP VALLEYS, by Lew and Ginny Clark. 191 pp, b&w and color illus., maps, index. Coverage is from Virginia City southward to all of eastern California (including Death Valley), and Tonopah-Goldfield-Beatty, Nevada.

JOHN MUIR TRAIL COUNTRY, by Lew and Ginny Clark. 176 pp, illus., maps, index. A knowledgeable guide of the authors' beloved Sierra.

COMSTOCK MINING AND MINERS, by Eliot Lord. 578 pp, illus., maps. Reprint of valuable 1883 mining report.

RAILROADS OF NEVADA AND EASTERN CALIFORNIA, [Vol. 1, Northern Nevada; Vol. 2, Southern Nevada and Death Valley], by David F. Myrick. 469 and 492 pp, illus., maps, index. Valuable economic and railroad history with much politics and mining included.

LOST LEGENDS OF THE SILVER STATE, by Gerald Higgs. Short stories on various Nevada topics.

A NATURALIST'S DEATH VALLEY, by Edmund Jaeger. 70 pp, illus. Mammals, birds, insects, trees, wild flowers, fossils, all described. A chapter on Indians rounds out the text.

DEATH VALLEY CABINS, by Death Valley '49'ers, Inc. 64 pp., color throughout. Twenty stone and wood cabins are described, along with the desert men who built them. Here are tales of a lost gold mine, a noted gambler and Death Valley's most successful prospector, John Lemoigne. Death Valley Scotty, the namesake of the popular Scotty's Castle, actually lived in a nearby cabin which is now infrequently visited.

DEATH VALLEY TAILINGS, Rarely Told Tales… by George Koenig. 124 pp., illus. Earliest explorers, surveyors, emigrants and their inscriptions, mineral discoveries, Manly rescue.

DEATH VALLEY TALES, by various authors. 72 pp. John Rogers, Christmas in Death Valley in 1849, Death Valley Scotty, John Lemoigne, freighting, mining, Greenwater, other mining camps.

DEATH VALLEY IN 1849, the Luck of the Gold Rush Emigrants, by John Southworth. 132 pp., illus. The epic Manly-Rogers-Bennett-Arcane 1849 rescue is told at length.

For other books on the '49ers to California, mining, geology, Virginia City, Bodie, Goldfield and other ghost towns and mining camps, write for a complete catalog:

NEVADA PUBLICATIONS

4135 Badger Circle, Reno, Nevada 89519

spaher@sbcglobal.net • 775-747-0800